W9-AVK-171

Evidence-Based Treatment of Stuttering

Empirical Bases and Clinical Applications

Evidence-Based Treatment of Stuttering

Empirical Bases and Clinical Applications

Edited by

Anne K. Bothe
The University of Georgia

LEA

LAWRENCE ERLBAUM ASSOCIATES, PUBLISHERS

2004   Mahwah, New Jersey   London

Lawrence Erlbaum Associates, Inc., Publishers
10 Industrial Avenue
Mahwah, New Jersey 07430

Cover design by Sean Trane Sciarrone

Library of Congress Cataloging-in-Publication Data

Evidence-based treatment of stuttering : empirical bases and clinical
applications / edited by Anne K. Bothe.

    p. cm.

Includes bibliographical references and index.
ISBN 0-8058-4632-8 (cloth : alk. paper)
ISBN 0-8058-4633-6 (pbk. : alk. paper)
1. Stuttering—Treatment. 2. Evidence-based medicine.   I. Bothe, Anne
    K.   [DNLM: 1. Stuttering—therapy. 2. Evidence-Based Medicine.
    WM 475 E93 2003]
RC424.E83   2003
616.85′5406—dc21
                                         2003049222
                                             CIP

Books published by Lawrence Erlbaum Associates are printed on acid-
free paper, and their bindings are chosen for strength and durability.

Printed in the United States of America
10   9   8   7   6   5   4   3   2   1

Contents

List of Contributors

Joseph Attanasio, PhD
Department of Communication Sciences and Disorders
Montclair State University

Anne K. Bothe, PhD
Department of Communication Sciences and Disorders
The University of Georgia

Bradley T. Crowe, MS
Department of Communication Sciences and Disorders
The University of Georgia

Jason H. Davidow, MA
Department of Communication Sciences and Disorders
The University of Georgia

Patrick Finn, PhD
Department of Speech & Hearing Sciences
University of Arizona

Paul Hagler, PhD
Institute for Stuttering Treatment and Research
University of Alberta

Anna Huber, PhD
Australian Stuttering Research Centre
The University of Sydney

Roger J. Ingham, PhD
Department of Speech and Hearing Sciences
University of California, Santa Barbara
and Research Imaging Center,
University of Texas Health Science Center at San Antonio

Marilyn Langevin, MS
Institute for Stuttering Treatment and Research
University of Alberta

Marilyn A. Nippold, PhD
Communication Disorders and Sciences Program,
Speech and Hearing Sciences
University of Oregon

Sue O'Brian, PhD
Australian Stuttering Research Centre
The University of Sydney

Mark Onslow, PhD
Australian Stuttering Research Centre
The University of Sydney

Rosalee C. Shenker, PhD
The Montreal Fluency Centre and
McGill University

William G. Webster, PhD
School of Communication Sciences and Disorders
University of Western Ontario

Preface

This book is the result of a 2002 University of Georgia "State of the Art Conference" about the evidence-based treatment of stuttering. Administered by the office of the Senior Vice President for Academic Affairs and Provost, the State of the Art Conferences program allows University of Georgia faculty to organize specialized meetings of persons with international expertise in a specific area. The prescribed format requires all participants to present relatively long original works, with substantial time allowed for the group's thoughtful discussion after each presentation. In accordance with these guidelines, the authors of these chapters were originally invited to present and discuss current data and issues related to the data-based treatment of stuttering. This topic was defined as including evidence about stuttering, evidence about stuttering treatment, and discussions of how that evidence should guide our continuing research and guide our practice, with specific presentation topics determined by the presenters on the basis of their own current work or interests. Thus, these chapters are intended to provide one of the many possible samples of "state of the art" information to researchers, clinicians, and students who are interested in developing, identifying, or using the best possible evidence-based treatments for stuttering.

It is interesting to note, however, that the phrase *evidence-based practice*, which has come into use recently as an extension of *evidence-based medicine* (see chap. 1, this volume), was not an explicit part of the original invitations to the conference presenters. Terminology from evidence-based medicine is becoming very popular and is also becoming rather predictably controversial; the terms have been interpreted as euphemisms for such negative

ideas as health care rationing, the devaluation of worthwhile clinical experience and intuition, and the triumph of simplistic computer-driven meta-
analyses over complex human clinical reasoning and decision making (see
Trinder, 2000). At their best, however, evidence-based medicine and evidence-based practice refer to an old, extremely simple, and very positive
idea: All procedures we use with our clients should be those that we have
been convinced, after thoughtful consideration of all the available evidence, are the most likely to result in the achievement and maintenance of
mutually agreed upon goals. The same idea was expressed for a previous
related State of the Art Conference in terms of seeking the empirical bases
of stuttering treatment (Cordes & Ingham, 1998). It is also the sense in
which many researchers, clinicians, and consumers assumed for decades
(see Thorne, 1947; Ventry & Schiavetti, 1980), long before Sackett and colleagues (see Sackett, Richardson, Rosenberg, & Haynes, 1997) formalized
the ideas for medicine, that of course clinical decisions should be based on
the best possible evidence. Indeed, with some allowance for what the word
evidence can mean, it would seem difficult to develop any reasonable oppo-
sition to the basis of evidence-based practice: To disagree with the fundamental premise of evidence-based practice is to assert that one selects
treatments with complete disregard for the evidence that they do or do not
work, a patently absurd position.

    In reality, of course, some of these issues quickly become more complex
than they first appear. One of the first problems involves the definition of
evidence, which is described by such authors as Sackett et al. (1997) as meaning primarily research evidence. Does the weight of tradition, common
practice, or clinical experience count as evidence, however, or is tradition-
based practice the antithesis of evidence-based practice? Such arguments
are at the heart of many critiques of evidence-based medicine (see Trinder,
2000). Even the most introductory clinical textbooks address another part
of the problem (e.g., Silverman, 1998): For the case in which no good research is yet available, should we assume that a treatment works until it is
shown not to work, or should we assume that it does not work until it is
shown to work? If *evidence* is interpreted to mean published research, and if
the quality of the available research is mixed, then how much weight
should we place on better, worse, more popular, more familiar, more scientifically stringent, or more politely worded sources? In the case of stuttering
treatment in particular, how can the well meaning but chronically over-
worked graduate student or clinician possibly distill the decades of contradictory research, opinion, and recommendations into a reasonable sense of
which treatment approaches are well supported by good evidence that they
will result in the achievement of which goals for which clients?

    The chapters collected here are intended to provide one small part of a
possible solution to these questions. Part I contains just one chapter, which
addresses the notion of evidence-based practice and considers its implica-

tions for stuttering treatment. Part II then combines six loosely related chapters that all address the intersection of at least three issues: the nature of stuttering; our theories of stuttering; and the implications of nature, theory, and other knowledge for stuttering treatment decisions. The two chapters in Part III address two of the many measurement issues facing stuttering treatment. As the authors in this section make clear, the development and use of defensible, evidence-based treatments for stuttering require the existence of psychometrically sound instruments for measuring the outcomes of those treatments. Part IV includes three chapters devoted to the quality of treatment research evidence, for specific treatments and in terms of some more general methodological and professional issues. Part V again consists of just one chapter, a summary of the clinical recommendations made throughout the book and a discussion of evidence-based, outcomes-focused clinical decisions for stuttering.

As is clear from this breadth of topics, it was the goal of the chapter authors, and it is the goal of this volume, to review some of the evidence that was available about stuttering and stuttering treatment as of approximately 2002 in a fashion that respects the complexities surrounding that evidence and its use. The chapters included here certainly do not exhaust the topics that might be of interest; they do, however, provide ample food for thought. Overall, we hope that this volume can capture the most important components of evidence-based practice: The evidence produced by treatment researchers must be as internally valid and as externally relevant as possible; the currently available research evidence must be identified, evaluated, analyzed, and synthesized, not only to aid current clinical practice but also to guide future research; and the implications of the currently available research evidence must be carefully applied on a case-by-case basis in thoughtful discussion between one clinician and one client. As many other "champions" (Trinder, 2000) of evidence-based practice have concluded, such an approach can provide some very real and very positive benefits, both for a discipline as a whole and for individual clinicians and clients. Those benefits include a solid basis and structure for defensible practice, the reassurance that one is doing everything possible to help not only current clients and families but also future clients and families, and the means to be "an efficient and competent health professional for the rest of your clinical career" (Dawes, 1999, p. 245).

REFERENCES

Cordes, A. K., & Ingham, R. J. (Eds.). (1998). *Treatment efficacy for stuttering: A search for empirical bases.* San Diego, CA: Singular.
Dawes, M. (1999). Defeating unknowingness. In M. Dawes, P. Davies, A. Gray, J. Mant, K. Seers, & R. Snowball (Eds.), *Evidence-based practice: A primer for health care professionals* (pp. 243–245). London: Churchill Livingstone.

Sackett, D. L., Richardson, W. S., Rosenberg, W. M. C., & Haynes, R. B. (1997). *Evidence based medicine: How to practice and teach EBM.* New York: Churchill Livingstone.

Silverman, F. H. (1998). *Research design and evaluation in speech-language pathology and audiology* (4th ed.). Boston: Allyn & Bacon.

Thorne, F. C. (1947). The clinical method in science. *American Psychologist, 2,* 161–166.

Trinder, L. (2000). A critical appraisal of evidence-based practice. In L. Trinder & S. Reynolds (Eds.), *Evidence-based practice: A critical appraisal* (pp. 212–243). Oxford: Blackwell Science.

Ventry, I., & Schiavetti, N. (1980). *Evaluating research in speech-language pathology and audiology.* Reading, MA: Addison-Wesley.

Acknowledgments

I am pleased to extend my sincerest thanks for substantial financial support to The University of Georgia's "State of the Art Conferences" program, administered at the time of the conference through the office of Dr. Karen Holbrook, Senior Vice President for Academic Affairs and Provost of The University of Georgia. Thanks also to Dr. Louis Castenell, Dean of the College of Education, Dr. Cheri Hoy, Director of the School of Professional Studies, Dr. Anne van Kleeck, Head of the Department of Communication Sciences and Disorders, and Dr. Rex Forehand, Director of the Institute for Behavioral Research, for their financial, institutional, and personal support of the conference that led to this book. Thanks to the many workers at the Georgia Center for Continuing Education, our outstanding on-campus hotel and conference facility. Thanks to several members of the award-winning University of Georgia chapter of the National Student Speech Language Hearing Association, especially Robyn Davis, Lori Guimond, and Jessica Myers, for their help at several stages. Thanks to Cathleen Petree, Bonita D'Amil, Marianna Vertullo, and others at Lawrence Erlbaum Associates, who have been the models of supportive professionalism and efficiency as we have prepared this book; thanks to Jenna Levy and Kay Taylor for their assistance with manuscript preparation; and thanks to David and Rachel, who took care of each other and took care of me so I could enjoy the conference and enjoy the process of putting together this book.

Finally, my thanks to the conference participants and their co-authors who prepared the chapters that I have had the privilege to gather here. It is perhaps also worth nothing that the authors represented in this volume make no claim to be the only ones capable of addressing these issues; many others are producing important work of direct relevance to the evidence-based treatment of stuttering. To all who are working toward a common goal of effective, efficient, evidence-based and outcomes-focused treatments for stuttering, my thanks.

—Anne K. Bothe

I

INTRODUCTION

1

Evidence-Based Practice in Stuttering Treatment: An Introduction

Anne K. Bothe
The University of Georgia

EVIDENCE-BASED PRACTICE: EXPLORING THE DEFINITIONS

Phrases like *evidence-based practice* are used by different authors to mean several distinctly different things. Some equate *evidence-based* with *research-based*, using the phrase to mean that assessment and treatment choices in health-related disciplines should be based on the evidence available in published research. Others broaden the idea to include personal and clinical experience as relevant evidence, thus diminishing the emphasis on published research. Similarly, some authors include reference to the implementation or evaluation phases of treatment, emphasizing that evidence-based treatment can mean gathering evidence during treatment that a client is improving (or not improving, in which case the treatment is changed). Still others appear to use the term *evidence* to refer to such potentially questionable sources as "textbooks (often 3 years obsolete at the time of printing) ... any fact attached to a 'reference' or merely the strong opinion of a respected authority in the field" (Gross, 2001, p. vi).

The health-care approach that has come to be known as *evidence-based medicine* (EBM) or, more inclusively, *evidence-based practice* (EBP), however, has a much more specific and much more complex meaning. EBP, in this sense, is generally credited to ideas presented by Cochrane (1972) and to specific techniques developed (e.g., Haynes et al., 1986a; Oxman, Sackett, & Guyatt, 1993) and then formalized by Sackett and colleagues (Sackett, Haynes, Guyatt, & Tugwell, 1991; Sackett, Richardson, Rosenberg, & Haynes, 1997; Sackett, Rosenberg, Gray, Haynes, & Richardson, 1996). Cochrane has been credited with nothing short of introducing randomized controlled trials (RCTs) to medicine, introducing systematic and critical review of the research literature to medicine, and introducing meta-analyses to medicine (Reynolds, 2000; Silverman, 1998). Whether such changes can literally be attributed to any one person or not, Cochrane's contributions were clearly substantial; they have been recognized in the name of the Cochrane Collaboration (http://www.cochrane.co.uk), established several years after his death and currently a leading mechanism for providing relevant clinical evidence to health-care providers in Great Britain. Sackett and colleagues, similarly, are credited with nothing short of introducing the notion to medical education, and to practicing physicians, that individual practitioners can routinely evaluate the quality of clinical research publications and then use the most worthwhile results to guide their practice. Their specific recommendations for the use of on-line library databases (e.g., Haynes et al., 1986c; Sackett et al., 1997) may also fairly be said to have brought clinical medicine (and, by extension, allied health and several related fields) into the age of information technology.

The aspect that sets EBP apart from other approaches to clinical work, and from more general descriptions of evidence-based clinical work, is its emphasis on the individual clinician's identification, evaluation, and thoughtful application of published clinical research. Perhaps the most quoted explanation of EBP comes from an editorial by Sackett et al. (1996):

> Evidence based medicine is the conscientious, explicit, and judicious use of current best evidence in making decisions about the care of individual patients. The practice of evidence based medicine means integrating individual clinical expertise with the best available external clinical evidence from systematic research.... Good doctors use both. (p. 71)

Similarly, Dawes (1999) defined EBP as "the acknowledgment of uncertainty followed by the seeking, appraising and implementation of new knowledge. It enables clinicians to openly accept that there may be different, and possibly more effective, methods of care than those they are currently employing" (p. ix).

Based largely on the work of Sackett and colleagues, EBP has therefore developed into a set of specific techniques, or a series of specific activities, that clinicians are advised to use to identify the best tests, procedures, or treatments for individual patients. Thus, as described by Sackett et al.

(1997) and in several subsequent textbooks, EBP is "partly a philosophy, partly a skill and partly the knowledge about, and application of, a set of tools" (Dawes, 1999, p. ix). Those tools are usually summarized in relation to the following steps (see, e.g., Law, 2002a; Reynolds, 2000):

Step 1. The clinician formulates a specific question about the approach to be used in caring for a particular client (e.g., which diagnostic test will be most sensitive for this case, or which treatment will be most effective and efficient with this client).

Step 2. The clinician finds the available published evidence on point.

Step 3. The clinician evaluates the quality of the evidence obtained at Step 2.

Step 4. The clinician makes a reasonable decision about the approach to be used in caring for this client, based in large part on the high-quality evidence identified at Step 3.

Step 5. The clinician evaluates the impacts and outcomes of the care provided to the client.

It is especially important to note that EBP includes, by definition, all of these steps. First, practitioners must recognize the need to ask a pointed question: Would my default, favorite, or standard treatment be the best choice for this client, or is there an approach that has a better chance of meeting this client's goals more easily, more completely, more inexpensively, more quickly, or more permanently? Such a question is unnerving; it requires the "humble attitude" (Law, 2002b, p. 5) that one's default, favorite, or standard treatment might not be the best choice for one's clients. Practitioners must then take the large and equally unnerving step of acknowledging that they do not have all the information necessary to answer such a question, followed by the larger and possibly even more unnerving step of turning to the research literature for possible information. Equally, practitioners must approach that research literature with a healthy skepticism. They must have the skills and take the time to evaluate not only whether each potentially relevant study or review was done well, and therefore has drawn a valid conclusion as to the impact of the treatment for the study's participants, but also whether any of the potentially relevant studies or reviews do in fact have any relevance for a particular clinical case. At this point, practitioners must take the time to combine the new knowledge they have gained from well conducted and validly interpreted research studies with their own expertise and with a particular client's idiosyncratic beliefs and desires, in order to make and implement a well-reasoned clinical decision; some critics omit this step from their straw-person versions of EBP (Trinder, 2000), but it is crucial and it exists by definition. Finally, EBP explicitly includes a phase of evaluating the results of the decision and of the selected procedure; there is clinical evidence to be gained from each client, too.

EBP has been widely accepted by many scholars and many practitioners, and descriptions of its strengths and its advantages abound. Among the most important of these is, clearly, that evaluating the available research literature, and then basing treatment decisions on relevant, high-quality studies, should allow practitioners to provide each client with the best possible individualized and research-based treatment. This client-focused aspect of EBP cannot be underestimated: Regardless of the extent or the quality of research support for any particular treatment, the goal of EBP is not to impose that treatment on all practitioners or any individual client. Indeed, despite substantial overlap in many of the issues, EBP is very different from attempts to designate certain treatment approaches as empirically supported (Chambless & Hollon, 1998) in an abstract sense unrelated to a specific client; EBP emphasizes a manner of practice, not an academic classification exercise. Thus, EBP specifies that practitioners should actively formulate questions about the needs and desires of each client, seek high-quality empirical evidence that bears on those questions, and use that evidence to serve that client in the best possible manner. If these procedures are followed, then the widespread adoption of the principles of EBP will lead to the widespread adoption of well-researched and empirically supported treatments—this adoption will occur, however, not because those treatments have been imposed or so labeled, but because those treatments have been supported in the research literature and are then purposefully selected by individual clinicians who have an individual client's best interests in mind.

CRITICS AND CONTROVERSIES

As might be expected, of course, EBP also has its critics. Cochrane's (1972) original analysis of issues facing health care providers, for example, has repeatedly been characterized as a call for rationing health care, a controversial issue that serves as a relatively predictable flashpoint for arguments (Gray, 1997). Cochrane's point was not that health care should be rationed, however; his point was that, given that all resources are by definition limited, then perhaps the best use of those resources will be within treatments that have been shown to be effective (Deyo, 2000; Trinder, 2000). Many of the other arguments against EBP are similar in that they capture an important point but border on being inaccurate (see Law, 2002b).

A frequent criticism of EBP, one with special relevance if we begin to consider applying these principles to stuttering treatment, is that EBP has limited itself and its applicability by requiring high-quality research evidence to be large, well-conducted, random-assignment experimental studies with control groups, or RCTs. This criticism is accurate, as far as it goes, but it also reflects a limited view of EBP. Most EBP authors and textbooks do describe RCTs as the "gold standard," or the best evidence that a single study can provide of a treatment's effects; some even suggest that busy practitioners can cull less relevant or less important articles from the never-ending stream of new publications by focusing primarily on RCTs or on systematic reviews or meta-analyses of RCTs (e.g., Haynes et al., 1986a, 1986b). Based on such a recommendation, EBP leaves itself open to the standard clinical criticism that group averages represent no single client, or that no individual client is well served by conclusions drawn only from groups (see, e.g., Barlow & Hersen, 1984). More importantly, the EBP process fails if the research literature does not include sufficient relevant RCTs for the practitioner to evaluate and potentially apply with an individual client; if there is no evidence to assess and apply, then how does one assess and apply the evidence?

The solution here, as most EBP authors recognize, is multifaceted. First, at the level of research policy, RCTs should be encouraged, supported, conducted, and published (i.e., an absence of RCTs is not a stopping point, it is a starting point). In the meantime, at the level of individual practice, the larger principles of EBP suggest that a scarcity of RCTs is not necessarily a problem. In this case, and it is the case for stuttering treatment, clinicians can and should evaluate the published research that does exist, integrating results to develop a treatment plan for each client that is based as soundly as possible in the best designed and best conducted studies to be found (see, e.g., Snowball, 1999).

This notion, that individual clinical decisions should be based on the research literature, as evaluated and interpreted by individual practitioners, represented a radical step for the practice and teaching of medicine. Until approximately the beginning of the 20th century (and even continuing today, according to some commentators; Paauw, 1999), medicine was a skill, a trade, or a body of quasi-religious knowledge that was taught by great teachers and perpetuated essentially unchanged in the next generation by chosen students (see Silverman, 1998). Some 17th- to 20th-century authors recognized that many common prescriptions or remedies did little good (see Thomas, 1983), but it is probably fair to claim that most practitioners, and most members of most communities, generally accepted the available remedies and accepted that the reason they were used was that they had previously been used or were part of a recognized tradition. This trust was most likely encouraged by what a behavioral psychologist would call the power of intermittent reinforcement and a logician would call the fallacy of confirming evidence: Just often enough, someone who had been bled or been given an infusion of completely inert herbs would, in fact, recover, and that recovery could easily be taken as evidence that the treatment had, in fact, been helpful. Other factors are proposed by many authors as part of a general tendency to accept both the traditions and the limitations of medical practice throughout most of human history: the human need for the doctor to "do something" (Silverman, 1998, p. 90), the human need to believe that caregivers provide good care, the tendency of the human body to fight and sometimes cure its own ills, the power of placebo treatments, and, conversely, a general acceptance that many variations on the human condition are simply beyond human control regardless of the physician's specific choices or prescriptions (Trinder, 2000). All of these factors, in other words, have combined throughout history to produce a general belief, among practitioners as well as in the wider community, that tradition-based practice is as effective as any form of practice can possibly be. This belief may or may not be supported by present or future objective research evidence; the implications if it is not supported are an important contributor to the current tensions between tradition-based practitioners and evidence-based practitioners in all areas of medicine and allied health (see, e.g., Geyman, Deyo, & Ramsey, 2000; Trinder, 2000).

APPLICATIONS TO STUTTERING TREATMENT

Speech-language pathology, and stuttering treatment in particular, represent special cases with respect to several of these issues. First, the notion that individual practitioners can and should evaluate the research literature, and should use those evaluations as the basis for their practice, is not new to speech-language pathology and does not need to be borrowed from medicine (see, e.g., Ventry & Schiavetti, 1980). Indeed, it would not be entirely unwarranted for many practitioners in speech-language pathology, psychology, and other allied health fields to feel a certain amount of smug superiority to those in medicine who have only recently discovered a research based, continually improving, and objectively evaluated approach to clinical practice; clinical psychology, for example, was founded in the 1890s on the notion of a research-based scientist practitioner (see Hayes, Barlow, & Nelson-Gray, 1999).

For stuttering treatment in particular, however, a research-based or evidence-based orientation is only one of the currently prevailing orientations. Indeed, stuttering might accurately be described as ahead of its time not because of a widespread acceptance of EBP but because of a widespread tension between research-based practice and tradition-based practice. Authors in EBP have discussed the recent development of such tensions (e.g., Geyman et al., 2000; Trinder, 2000), yet tension has been the norm for stuttering since at least the 1950s, when behavioral psychologists began investigating stuttering from a position and in a manner that were completely separate from the traditions that had by then already developed in the mainstream research and practice of speech-language pathology in the United States (see, e.g., Attanasio, Onslow, & Menzies, 1996; Martin & Siegel, 1966; Van Riper, 1973). The initial "behavioral" studies about reducing stuttering in children and adults (e.g., Goldiamond, 1965; Martin &

Berndt, 1970; Martin, Kuhl, & Haroldson, 1972), and the very large literature that developed subsequently (see Ingham, 1984), continue to function more as a source of intradisciplinary tension than as an evidence base for practice, for many reasons (see Ingham & Cordes, 1999). Among many other issues, it appears that clinicians and authors who were trained in, or who feel more comfortable with, the traditional approaches to stuttering treatment either are not aware of this evidence (Onslow, 1999) or simply do not believe that these empirical demonstrations, and the decades of resulting research, have any relevance to what they see as the methods and the goals of stuttering treatment (Starkweather, 1999). Such a belief is not incomprehensible, in the sense that most of the research programs in the world clearly have no relevance to an individual clinician's practice with clients who stutter; as a general rule, it does seem reasonable to focus on what one was taught or what one has always done, if the alternative is to spend an enormous amount of time reading research about completely unrelated topics only to decide that that research was irrelevant to stuttering treatment. This belief may also be reciprocated: Many stuttering clinicians who work from an evidence-based point of view may not believe that traditions and nonexperimental clinical descriptions are relevant to their methods and goals for stuttering treatment. The questions that must be resolved, however, regardless of one's initial stance on the political and philosophical issues facing stuttering treatment, are very basic: Why do individual clinicians select a certain treatment (or combination of treatments) for an individual client who stutters, what do they expect to achieve through its use, what is their basis for that expectation, and do they achieve their goals? Although there are clearly many ways to answer these questions, EBP suggests that among the best is to select a treatment that the research literature suggests will eliminate the disorder.

The historical idea that it is not within the abilities of any caregiver to cure many diseases, however, and an associated acceptance that traditional practice does not and can not cure or eliminate some problems, is also clear in the stuttering literature. Cooper (1987), for example, designated some stuttering as a "chronic perseverative syndrome"; similarly, many authors argue that stuttering treatments should assist the speaker in living with the problem instead of targeting fluent speech, "a goal they may not be capable of achieving consistently" (Yaruss & Quesal, 2001, p. 14). In summary, the underlying differences between the *Iowa tradition* and the *behavioral tradition*, to use two oversimplified but standard labels for the ends of the complex continuum in question, have led to a steady stream of commentary and controversy through the decades, focusing on such elements as the goal of stuttering treatment, the relevance of speech data, and whether the lack of published research support for some treatment approaches should be seen as a problem or not (e.g., Yaruss, 1998; Yaruss & Quesal, 2002). In fact, views currently being presented by those opposed to EBM (see Trinder, 2000) are echoed almost perfectly in some opinions expressed in defense of tradition-based stuttering treatment:

> We use our clinical skill and intuition—the *art* of clinical practice—to develop a unique treatment approach that is tailored to the client's needs. Does this mean we are unethical for not employing strictly evidence based treatment approaches? No, for we *are* drawing upon well-established and widely used procedures in developing our individualized treatments. (Yaruss & Quesal, 2002, p. 23)

The implications that well-established, widely used, and individualized treatments are necessarily good, and that evidence-based treatments are either not well established, not widely used, not individualized, or otherwise not desirable, are precisely the implications that EBP, and the chapters in the remainder of this book, attempt to refute.[1] It is also important to note, however, that none of the chapters in this book is the report of a randomized controlled trial, and only one (see Davidow, Crowe, & Bothe, chap. 10) approaches being a true systematic review. In fact, none of these chapters was written explicitly from the perspective of EBP, as that term has been defined in this chapter. Nevertheless, all are research-based and data-based, and all start from a position that is the direct opposite of that expressed by Yaruss and Quesal (2002); that is, the authors represented here believe that all clinical decisions should be based, in large part, on the best available relevant research evidence, and that appeals to tradition can be correctly categorized as a potential logical fallacy (see, e.g., Halpern, 1989). Thus, the hope is that this book might serve practitioners who work with persons who stutter by serving as a source of information (see Step 2, as previously discussed) and as an evaluation of information (see Step 3, as previously discussed). At the same time, these chapters also clearly identify many remaining research needs. Even before all possible knowledge has been gathered, however, EBP means that speech-language pathologists will begin with the information that is available, combine it with their own clinical experience and their own clinical data, and use the entire package to the benefit of every client. At the risk of alienating those who already believe in the central importance of empirical evidence, and in hopes of convincing those who do not, Sackett et al.'s (1996) point about research evidence and individual clinical experience bears repeating: Good clinicians use both.

REFERENCES

Attanasio, J. S., Onslow, M., & Menzies, R. (1996). Australian and United States perspectives on stuttering in preschool children. *Australian Journal of Human Communication Disorders, 24,* 55–61.

---

[1]Bothe (2003) also wrote, while this chapter was in press, that the art of clinical practice is not simply "clinical skill and intuition" but might actually be best exemplified by all the complexities of EBP. Ingham (2003), in the same series, provided an excellent introduction to the notion of EBP in stuttering treatment.

Barlow, D. H., & Hersen, M. (1984). *Single-case experimental designs: Strategies for studying behavior change* (2nd ed.). New York: Pergamon.

Bothe, A. K. (2003). Evidence-based treatment of stuttering: V. The art of clinical practice and the future of clinical research. *Journal of Fluency Disorders, 28*, 247–258.

Chambless, D. L., & Hollon, S. D. (1998). Defining empirically supported therapies. *Journal of Consulting and Clinical Psychology, 66*, 7–18.

Cochrane, A. L. (1972). *Effectiveness and efficiency: Random reflections on health services.* London: Nuffield Provincial Hospitals Trust.

Cooper, E. B. (1987). The chronic perseverative stuttering syndrome—incurable stuttering. *Journal of Fluency Disorders, 12*, 381–388.

Dawes, M. (1999). Preface. In M. Dawes, P. Davies, A. Gray, J. Mant, K. Seers, & R. Snowball (Eds.), *Evidence-based practice: A primer for health care professionals* (pp. ix–x). London: Churchill Livingstone.

Deyo, R. A. (2000). Cost-effectiveness of primary care. In J. P. Geyman, R. A. Deyo, & S. D. Ramsey (Eds.), *Evidence-based clinical practice: Concepts and approaches* (pp. 111–118). Boston: Butterworth Heinemann.

Geyman, J. P., Deyo, R. A., & Ramsey, S. D. (2000). *Evidence-based clinical practice: Concepts and approaches.* Boston: Butterworth Heinemann.

Goldiamond, I. (1965). Stuttering and fluency as manipulatable operant response classes. In L. Krasner & L. P. Ullman (Eds.), *Research in behavior modification* (pp. 106–152). New York: Holt, Rinehart, & Winston.

Gray, J. A. (1997). *Evidence-based health care.* London: Churchill Livingstone.

Gross, R. (2001). *Decisions and evidence in medical practice: Applying evidence-based medicine to clinical decision making.* St. Louis, MO: Mosby.

Halpern, D. F. (1989). *Thought and knowledge: An introduction to critical thinking.* Hillsdale, NJ: Lawrence Erlbaum Associates.

Hayes, S. C., Barlow, D. H., & Nelson-Gray, R. O. (1999). *The scientist practitioner: Research and accountability in the age of managed care* (2nd ed.). Boston: Allyn & Bacon.

Haynes, R. B., McKibbon, K. A., Fitzgerald, D., Guyatt, G. H., Walker, C. J., & Sackett, D. L. (1986a). How to keep up with the medical literature: I. Why try to keep up and how to get started. *Annuals of Internal Medicine, 105*, 149–153.

Haynes, R. B., McKibbon, K. A., Fitzgerald, D., Guyatt, G. H., Walker, C. J., & Sackett, D. L. (1986b). How to keep up with the medical literature: II. Deciding which journals to read regularly. *Annuals of Internal Medicine, 105*, 309–312.

Haynes, R. B., McKibbon, K. A., Fitzgerald, D., Guyatt, G. H., Walker, C. J., Sackett, D. L. (1986c). How to keep up with the medical literature: V. Access by personal computer to the medical literature. *Annuals of Internal Medicine, 105*, 810–816.

Ingham, J. C. (2003). Evidence-based treatment of stuttering: I. Definitions and application. *Journal of Fluency Disorders, 28*, 197–208.

Ingham, R. J. (1984). *Stuttering and behavior therapy: Current status and experimental foundations.* San Diego: College-Hill.

Ingham, R. J., & Cordes, A. K. (1999). On watching a discipline shoot itself in the foot: Some observations on current trends in stuttering treatment research. In N. B. Ratner & E. C. Healey (Eds.), *Stuttering research and practice: Bridging the gap* (pp. 211–230). Mahwah, NJ: Lawrence Erlbaum Associates.

Law, M. (Ed.). (2002a). *Evidence-based rehabilitation: A guide to practice.* Thorofare, NJ: Stack Inc.

Law, M. (2002b). Introduction to evidence-based practice. In M. Law (Ed.), *Evidence-based rehabilitation: A guide to practice* (pp. 3–12). Thorofare, NJ: Stack Inc.

Martin, R. R., & Berndt, L. A. (1970). The effects of time-out on stuttering in a 12 year old boy. *Exceptional Children, 36,* 303–304.

Martin, R. R., Kuhl, P., & Haroldson, S. K. (1972). An experimental treatment with two preschool stuttering children. *Journal of Speech and Hearing Research, 15,* 743–752.

Martin, R. R., & Siegel, G. M. (1966). The effects of response contingent shock on stuttering. *Journal of Speech and Hearing Research, 9,* 340–352.

Onslow, M. (1999). Stuttering: An integrated approach to its nature and treatment, 2nd edition [book review]. *Journal of Fluency Disorders, 24,* 319–332.

Oxman, A. D., Sackett, D. L., & Guyatt, G. H. (1993). Users' guide to the medical literature. I. How to get started. The Evidence-Based Medicine Working Group. *Journal of the American Medical Association, 270,* 2093–2095.

Paauw, D. S. (1999). Did we learn evidence-based medicine in medical school? Some common medical mythology. *Journal of American Board of Family Practice, 12,* 143–149.

Reynolds, S. (2000). The anatomy of evidence-based practice: Principles and methods. In L. Trinder (Ed.), *Evidence-based practice: A critical appraisal* (pp. 17–34). Oxford: Blackwell Science.

Sackett, D. L., Haynes, R. B., Guyatt, G. H., & Tugwell, P. (1991). *Clinical epidemiology: A basic science for clinical medicine* (2nd ed.). Boston, MA: Little Brown.

Sackett, D. L., Richardson, W. S., Rosenberg, W. M. C., & Haynes, R. B. (1997). *Evidence based medicine: How to practice and teach EBM.* New York: Churchill Livingstone.

Sackett, D. L., Rosenberg, W. M. C., Gray, J. A. M., Haynes, R. B., & Richardson, W. S. (1996). Evidence based medicine: What it is and what it isn't. *British Medical Journal, 312,* 71–72.

Silverman, W. A. (1998). *Where's the evidence? Debates in modern medicine.* Oxford: Oxford University Press.

Snowball, R. (1999). Finding the evidence: An information skills approach. In M. Dawes, P. Davies, A. Gray, J. Mant, K. Seers, & R. Snowball (Eds.), *Evidence-based practice: A primer for health care professionals* (pp. 15–46). London: Churchill Livingstone.

Starkweather, C. W. (1999). The effectiveness of stuttering therapy: An issue for science? In N. B. Ratner & E. C. Healey (Eds.), *Stuttering research and practice: Bridging the gap* (pp. 231–244). Mahwah, NJ: Lawrence Erlbaum Associates.

Thomas, L. (1983). *The youngest science.* New York: Viking.

Trinder, L. (2000). A critical appraisal of evidence-based practice. In L. Trinder & S. Reynolds (Eds.), *Evidence-based practice: A critical appraisal* (pp. 212–243). Oxford: Blackwell Science.

Van Riper, C. (1973). *The treatment of stuttering.* Englewood Cliffs, NJ: Prentice-Hall.

Ventry, I. M., & Schiavetti, N. (1980). *Evaluating research in speech pathology and audiology.* Reading, MA: Addison-Wesley.

Yaruss, J. S. (1998). Treatment outcomes in stuttering: Finding value in clinical data. In A. K. Cordes & R. J. Ingham (Eds.), *Treatment efficacy for stuttering: A search for empirical bases* (pp. 213–242). San Diego, CA: Singular.

Yaruss, J. S., & Quesal, R. W. (2001). The many faces of stuttering: Identifying appropriate treatment goals. *The ASHA Leader, 6*(21), 4–5, 14.

Yaruss, J. S., & Quesal, R. W. (2002). Research-based stuttering therapy revisited. *Perspectives on Fluency and Fluency Disorders* [Newsletter of Special Interest Division 4, American Speech-Language Hearing Association], *12*(2), 22–24.

II

THE NATURE AND THEORY OF STUTTERING: IMPLICATIONS FOR EVIDENCE-BASED TREATMENT

2

From Hand to Mouth: Contributions of Theory to Evidenced-Based Treatment

William G. Webster
Brock University

When I was first contacted about contributing this chapter, I faced something of a dilemma about an appropriate focus. The theme of the book is, of course, "evidence-based treatment in stuttering." I am not a speech-language pathologist, and I have done no research on evaluating the effectiveness of treatment or even on the effectiveness of the clinical manual (Webster & Poulos, 1989) that I co-authored some years ago with the objective of facilitating transfer and maintenance of fluency in adult stuttering treatment programs. That said, it seemed to me that I might still make a useful contribution because one aspect of evidenced-based treatment relates to linkages between theory and treatment. Accordingly, the chapter is organized around the theoretical perspective that has emerged from my experimental research on unimanual and bimanual movement control in people who stutter, and on what that theoretical perspective may tell us about approaches to stuttering treatment. The "hand" in the chapter title relates to the origin of the theoretical perspective, and the "mouth" relates to the implications of that perspective for speech.

The motivation underlying my research program is derived from a personal interest in understanding variability of stuttering severity. This characteristic of stuttering is what makes the disorder so frustrating for those of us who stutter, but also it is what makes stuttering such an interesting phenomenon from a scientific perspective. It was trying to understand the variability in my own fluency that raised questions for me, as both a person who stutters and an experimental neuropsychologist, about what is different about the brains of people who stutter and what changes in the brain with changes in fluency.

The focus of my research has been on understanding transient changes in fluency in persistent stuttering, in other words those changes that occur from moment to moment and situation to situation, but I would like to think that understanding transient change may tell us something about the underlying mechanisms of more permanent change associated with recovery (or relapse). I do not study speech mechanisms per se. Instead, I have relied on the theory and methods of experimental neuropsychology to make inferences about brain organization based on differences between stutterers and nonstutterers with respect to unimanual and bimanual motor performance. Based on the evidence that the mechanisms for the control of manual movement overlap those that control speech (Kimura, 1982; Mateer, 1983; Ojeeman, 1983), our basic assumption is that as we come to understand anomalies in manual movement control in people who stutter, we can come to understand something of the anomalies in speech movement control.

The kinds of experiments carried out have been described elsewhere (e.g., Webster, 1997, 1998), and so I will comment on them only briefly here. Some of the studies have involved sequential finger tapping whereby subjects tap telegraph keys repeatedly in certain specified sequences. The rationale for this methodology comes from the evidence that each hand is controlled by the opposite hemisphere, and so by studying finger tapping rates of the two hands one can infer something about how the mechanisms for the control of sequential movement are lateralized in the two hemispheres. We found that both stutterers and nonstutterers show a right-hand advantage in sequential finger tapping speed and accuracy (Webster, 1985) suggesting that the mechanisms of sequential movement control in people who stutter are lateralized in the left hemisphere just as they are in those who do not stutter.

Other work has involved what is called *Sequence Reproduction Performance*. This task differs from Sequential Finger Tapping in that on each trial a new sequence is demonstrated on a display panel and the subject reproduces the sequence with finger tapping as quickly but as accurately as possible as soon as a tone sounds. This kind of task tells us something about the efficiency with which stutterers and nonstutterers can plan and initiate new sequences of movements, which would seem to be a critical component of speech production. On this task stutterers are slower and make more errors than nonstutterers in reproducing the sequences under both speeded (Webster, 1986b, 1989a) and nonspeeded (Webster, 1989b) conditions.

Still other research has involved subjects doing two different things with the two hands at the same time so we can study interference effects. On both sequential finger tapping and sequence reproduction performance, stutterers were found to show more response decrement than nonstutterers when the task was performed concurrently with one that involved turning a knob back and forth in response to a tone (Webster, 1986a, 1989a). Similarly, on a bimanual handwriting task stutterers performed slower and less accurately than nonstutterers in writing initial letters of words simultaneously with the two hands (Webster, 1988). On tasks of this sort, everyone shows interference. The critical point is that stutterers show more interference than nonstutterers. The significance of this finding is that because each hand is controlled by the opposite hemisphere, hand interference really reflects how the hemispheres communicate and interact with one another. It is useful to consider stuttering to be an interference phenomenon, analogous to static on a radio. It is there sometimes; it is absent at other times. It is variable. This analogy implies that some part of the system is susceptible to interference and some other part of the system is a source of interference. The results from my experiments on bimanual control imply that one source of interference on the left hemisphere speech motor mechanisms may come from the right hemisphere.

SPEECH-MOTOR CONTROL LATERALIZATION AND STUTTERING

In order to develop further these ideas on interference, here are four propositions that are later tied together with a schematic or conceptual model and linked to clinical practice.

Proposition 1. Stutterers have normal left-hemisphere lateralization of the neural mechanisms for the control of speech and other forms of sequential motor movement. This proposition is based on the right-hand advantage for sequential finger tapping we have found in stutterers (Webster, 1985). It is also consistent with results using intracarotid sodium amytal injections to assess hemispheric representation of speech and language mechanisms. In right-handed nonstutterer patients, injection of sodium amytal into the right carotid artery temporarily suppresses right-hemisphere activity resulting in a contralateral hemiparesis. Injection into the left carotid artery results not only in a right-hemiparesis but also in transient aphasia, which reflects the left-hemisphere representation of speech and language. This same pattern of results has been reported for neurologically normal stutterers (Luessenhop, Boggs, Laborwit, & Walle, 1973; Quinn, 1976).

Proposition 2. Although the neural mechanisms for speech are lateralized normally as they are in fluent speakers, the left-hemisphere mechanisms of stutterers are "fragile" and susceptible to interference from other on-going neural activities, particularly those in the right hemisphere. This proposition reflects our consistent findings that stutterers show more intermanual task interference than do nonstutterers (Webster, 1986a, 1988, 1989a). What is unclear is whether the inference in these paradigms reflects a greater than normal left-hemisphere vulnerability to interference or a heightened right-hemisphere activation.

Proposition 3. In right-handed fluent speakers, there is an inherent bias toward left-hemisphere activation; in left-handers, there is a more equal distribution of activation. This proposition is based on a body of literature in experimental neuropsychology (Peters, 1987, 1990) that indicates that in most people the left hemisphere is in a greater state of readiness to respond or to process information than the right, and this in turn leads to an attentional bias to right hemi-space. This asymmetry in information processing readiness is what is meant by *activation bias.* There is a left-hemisphere activation bias in most people because the bias seems to be found in right-handers but not in left-handers (Peters, 1987). This idea then leads to a fourth proposition, which is based on experiments we have done (Forster & Webster, 1991; Webster, 1990).

Proposition 4. Stutterers (right- and left-handed) do not show a left hemisphere activation bias but are similar to fluent left-handers. As argued by Forster and Webster (1991), stutterers show a similar pattern of activation between the hemispheres and, as a consequence, greater than normal lability of right-hemisphere activation. In other words, the right hemisphere of stutterers tends to be more readily activated than in nonstutterers, and this has been observed in electroencephalographic studies involving recordings from the right and left hemispheres of stutterers (Boberg, Yeudall, Schopflocher, & Bo-Lassen, 1983; Moore & Haynes, 1980).

A CONCEPTUAL MODEL OF STUTTERING

These four propositions form the basis of a conceptual model that was developed to illustrate what we believe may be going on in the brains of people who stutter (Webster, 1997, 1998). It has three major elements that relate directly to the propositions:

1. Speech motor control mechanisms of stutterers are localized in the left hemisphere just as they are in nonstutterers;
2. The left hemisphere speech motor control mechanisms in people who stutter are vulnerable to interference from other on-going brain activity. Although the focus of our research has been on interhemispheric sources of interference, there is evidence of intrahemispheric sources as well (Forster & Webster, 1991; Webster, 1987). In this model, variation in stuttering severity reflects variation in interference; and
3. There is a lack of left-hemisphere activation bias in people who stutter.

With respect to the left-hemisphere mechanisms, the critical area being considered is the supplementary motor area (SMA), which has received substantial research attention during this past 20 years (Goldberg, 1985; Marsden et al., 1996). Its organization and functions have been studied using a number of methodologies including brain imaging (Lotze et al., 1999; Roland, 1984), neuropsychological analysis of brain lesions (Brinkman, 1984; Jonas, 1981), neurophysiology in both human and nonhuman species (Simonetta, Clanet, & Rascol, 1991; Tanji, 1994; Tanji, Shima, & Mushiake, 1996), and the study of neuroanatomical connections (Goldman-Rakic, 1995). Four sets of consistent research findings have emerged from this research to suggest the function of the SMA in the normal organization of behavior.

1. First, as evidenced in single-cell recording studies of nonhuman primates as well as in brain imaging studies of humans, activity in the SMA is associated with the planning of complex sequential movements of either the limbs or the speech musculature. The critical words are *planning* and *complex* or *sequential*, words used earlier in the context of the finger tapping studies.

2. Second, there are rich intrahemispheric and interhemispheric connections involving the SMA. In fact most interhemispheric connections between the motor areas go through the SMA.

3. In light of the interhemispheric connections, it is not surprising that the area has been implicated as being crucial in bimanual coordination (and probably more generally in bilateral coordination). Damage to the SMA interferes with the ability to coordinate hand movements and to do two different things with the hands at the same time. Along a similar vein, single-cell recordings from awake nonhuman primates indicate increased activity associated with bilateral movements.

4. And the fourth point is that the there is evidence that the SMA is particularly crucial for the planning of *self-initiated* and *internally guided* movements rather than ones that are externally signaled and externally guided. The distinction between externally guided and internally guided is the difference between, for example, visually guided movement and kinesthetically guided movement.

The reasons for the attraction to the SMA as a critical locus for stuttering are probably quite apparent earlier in the chapter, but let us focus for just a moment on the last point, the idea of internal versus external guidance of movement. My former doctoral student, David Forster, carried out a study (Forster & Webster, 2001) that included having subjects turn two cranks simultaneously to move a cursor through a track on a computer screen, as in an Etch-A-Sketch® toy. In one testing condition, the cursor went out of view half way up the track and the task was to continue to turn the cranks at the same rates to keep the cursor in the track, which also could no longer be seen. This involved guidance of the movements by kinesthetic cues rather than visual cues. Consequently once the task began it was transformed from one involving external guidance to one requiring internal guidance. The adult stutterers were found to be impaired relative to nonstutterers under both guidance conditions (not surprising considering this is a bimanual coordination task), but they were far more impaired when they had to rely on the kinesthetic cues alone.

The findings are not dissimilar to those of involving kinesthetic versus visual control of tongue movements in people who stutter (Archibald & De Nil, 1999), and they are important because they say something fairly specific about the nature of the underlying speech-motor control impairment in stutterers: It may be kinesthetically based.

The second factor in the model is the lack of left-hemispheric activation bias which, as suggested earlier, may lead to a relative overactivation of the right hemisphere. This is not a new idea but one that has attracted considerable attention over the years (Moore, 1984; Moore & Haynes, 1980). One of a number of possible reasons for how this right hemisphere over activation contributes to stuttering may relate to the neuropsychology of emotion.

A substantial body of evidence (Davidson, 1995; Davidson & Fox, 1981) suggests that when positive emotions are experienced that motivate us to approach a situation, the left hemisphere becomes increasingly active. In contrast, and this is the critical part, when negative emotions are experienced that motivate us to withdraw from a situation, the right hemisphere becomes increasingly active. This leads to the suggestion that (a) the fear and anxiety and apprehension associated with stuttering is associated with right-hemisphere activation, (b) the right hemisphere is readily activated in people who stutter, (c) this activation in turn interferes with the left hemisphere SMA, (d) the interference results in stuttering, and (e) the stuttering then reinforces the fear and apprehension of being in a speech situation. In other words, we envisage a positive feedback system through which the neurology of stuttering and the psychology of stuttering intersect.

EMPIRICAL AND CLINICAL IMPLICATIONS

This chapter is concluded by commenting on linkages between, on the one hand, this basic research and the theoretical ideas that have emerged from it and, on the other hand, clinical practices. This is done in regard to two realms: recovery from stuttering in children and adult stuttering treatment programs.

David Forster's (Forster & Webster, 2001) doctoral thesis research, alluded to earlier in the context of bimanual crank turning, was in fact concerned primarily with brain mechanisms in adults who had recovered from stuttering. Very briefly, the experiment involved adults who stutter, those who reported having once stuttered as children but no longer do so, that those who reported having never stuttered. The participants were tested on four tasks, two designed to assess the integrity of the supplementary motor area and two designed to assess hemispheric activation. On the two motor control tasks, thought to be sensitive to SMA function, recovered or exstutterers were the same as nonstutterers, and these groups performed better than the persistent stutterers. However, on the two tests thought to be sensitive to hemispheric activation, the recovered stutterers and the persistent stutterers both showed evidence of a lack of left-hemispheric activation bias, whereas the nonstutterers showed evidence of the normal left-hemispheric activation bias. In other words, people who once stuttered as children but no longer do show evidence of normal left-hemisphere motor speech mechanisms but show the lack of left-hemisphere activation bias found with persistent stuttering.

One implication of this, which is really a hypothesis to be tested, is that recovery from stuttering in children is associated with maturation of the supplementary motor area, and interventions that are effective in facilitating recovery may do so through facilitating such maturation.

With respect to stuttering treatment in adults, the type of positive feedback system suggested earlier involving the interplay between the hemispheres and between emotions and speech implies that successful therapy or management of stuttering must have at least two components. The first is to counteract the fragility of the left hemisphere system. This is done when speech is modified through the use of fluency shaping skills, or through the use of stuttering modification skills. The deliberate use of gentle onsets, linking phonation or respiration control, for example, focuses attention on motor skills and brings speech within the capability of an inefficient and fragile speech motor system. Our recent work (Forster & Webster, 2001) showing the deficits in kinesthetically controlled movement suggests an important place for feeling speech targets or movements in speech motor control by stutterers. If kinesthetic cues are either not fully available to the person who stutters or are not being attended to, a focus on feeling movements and being deliberate in making movements may be ways to compensate for that deficit.

The second component of successful treatment or management of stuttering is to remove sources of interference with speech. A major source of interference is right-hemisphere activity. One implication is that therapy include dealing with avoidance, withdrawal, and apprehension. As these tendencies are overcome, the right-hemisphere activation associated with them decreases and then the interference with the left-hemisphere SMA decreases.

Most adult treatment programs today include both factors, at least implicitly, and the theory suggests that both are critical. Moving directly to the theme of this book, the linkage between the theory that emerges out of research, on the one hand, and clinical practice, on the other hand, provides evidence to support that treatment approach.

REFERENCES

Archibald, L., & De Nil, L. F. (1999). The relationship between stuttering severity and kinesthetic acuity for jaw movements in adults who stutter. *Journal of Fluency Disorders, 24,* 25–42.

Boberg, E., Yeudall, L. T., Schopflocher, D., & Bo-Lassen, P. (1983). The effect of an intensive behavioral program on the distribution of EEG alpha power in stutterers during the processing of verbal and visuospatial information. *Journal of Fluency Disorders, 8,* 245–263.

Brinkman, C. (1984). Supplementary motor area of the monkey's cerebral cortex. Short- and long-term deficits after unilateral ablation and the effects of subsequent callosal section. *Journal of Neuroscience, 4,* 918–929.

Davidson, R. J. (1995). Cerebral asymmetry, emotion, and affective style. In R. J. Davidson & K. Hugdahl (Eds.), *Brain asymmetry* (pp. 361–387). Cambridge, MA: MIT Press.

Davidson, R. J., & Fox, N. A. (1981). Asymmetrical brain activity discriminations between positive and negative affective stimuli in human infants. *Science, 218,* 1235–1237.

Forster, D. C., & Webster, W. G. (1991). Concurrent task interference in stutterers: Dissociating hemispheric specialization and activation. *Canadian Journal of Psychology, 45,* 321–335.

Forster, D. C., & Webster, W. G. (2001). Speech-motor control and interhemispheric relations in recovered and persistent stuttering. *Developmental Neuropsychology, 19,* 125–145.

Goldberg, G. (1985). Supplementary motor area structure and function: Review and hypotheses. *Behavioral & Brain Sciences, 8,* 567–616.

Goldman-Rakic, P. S. (1995). Anatomical and functional circuits in prefrontal cortex of nonhuman primates: Relevance to epilepsy. In H. H. Jasper (Ed.), *Epilepsy and the functional anatomy of the frontal lobe. Advances in neurology* (Vol. 66: pp. 51–65). New York: Raven Press.

Jonas, S. (1981). The supplementary motor region and speech emission. *Journal of Communication Disorders, 14,* 349–373.

Kimura, D. (1982). Left-hemisphere control of oral and bachial movements and their relation to communication. *Philosophical transactions of the Royal Society of London, B298,* 135–149.

Lotze, M., Montoya, P., Erb, M., Huelsmann, E., Flor, H., Klose, U., Birbaumer, N., & Grodd, W. (1999). Activation of cortical and cerebellar motor areas during executed and imagined hand movements: An fMRI study. *Journal of Cognitive Neuroscience, 11,* 491–501.

Luessenhop, A. J., Boggs, J. S., Laborwit, L. J., & Walle, E. L. (1973). Cerebral dominance in stutterers determined by Wada testing. *Neurology, 23,* 1190–1192.

Marsden, C. D., Deecke, L., Freund, H. J., Hallet, M., Passingham, R. E., Shibasaki, H., Tanji, J., & Wiesendanger, M. (1996). The functions of the supplementary motor area. *Advances in Neurology, 70,* 477–487.

Mateer, C. (1983). Motor and perceptual functions of the left hemisphere and their interaction. In S. J. Segalowitz (Ed.), *Language functions and brain organization* (pp. 145–170). New York: Academic Press.

Moore, W. H. (1984). Central nervous system characteristics of stutterers. In R. F. Curlee & W. H. Perkins (Eds.), *Nature and treatment of stuttering: New directions* (pp. 49–71). San Diego, CA: College-Hill.

Moore, W. H. J., & Haynes, W. O. (1980). Alpha hemispheric asymmetry and stuttering: Some support for a segmentation dysfunction hypothesis. *Journal of Speech & Hearing Research, 23,* 229–247.

Ojeeman, G. A. (1983). Brain organization for language from the perspective of electrical stimulation mapping. *The behavioural and brain sciences, 2,* 189–230.

Peters, M. (1987). A nontrivial motor performance difference between right-handers and left-handers: Attention as intervening variable in the expression of handedness. *Canadian Journal of Psychology, 41,* 91–99.

Peters, M. (1990). Interaction of vocal and manual movements. In G. R. Hammond (Ed.), *Cerebral control of speech and limb movements* (pp. 535–574). Amsterdam: North Holland.

Quinn, P. T. (1976). Cortical localization of speech in normals and stutterers. *Australian Journal of Human Communication Disorders, 4,* 118–121.

Roland, P. E. (1984). Organization of motor control by the normal human brain. *Human Neurobiology, 2,* 205–216.

Simonetta, M., Clanet, M., & Rascol, O. (1991). Bereitschaftspotential in a simple movement or in a motor sequence starting with the same simple movement. *Electroencephalography & Clinical Neurophysiology: Electromyography & Motor Control, 81,* 129–134.

Tanji, J. (1994). The supplementary motor area in the cerebral cortex. *Neuroscience Research, 19*(3), 251–268.

Tanji, J., Shima, K., & Mushiake, H. (1996). Multiple cortical motor areas and temporal sequencing of movements. *Cognitive Brain Research, 6,* 117–122.

Webster, W. G. (1985). Neuropsychological models of stuttering: I. Representation of sequential response mechanisms. *Neuropsychologia, 23,* 263–267.

Webster, W. G. (1986a). Neuropsychological models of stuttering: II. Interhemispheric interference. *Neuropsychologia, 24,* 737–741.

Webster, W. G. (1986b). Response sequence organization and reproduction by stutterers. *Neuropsychologia, 24,* 813–821.

Webster, W. G. (1987). Rapid letter transcription performance by stutterers. *Neuropsychologia, 25,* 845–847.

Webster, W. G. (1988). Neural mechanisms underlying stuttering: Evidence from bimanual handwriting performance. *Brain & Language, 33,* 226–244.

Webster, W. G. (1989a). Sequence initiation performance by stutterers under conditions of response competition. *Brain & Language, 36,* 286–300.

Webster, W. G. (1989b). Sequence reproduction deficits in stutterers tested under nonspeeded response conditions. *Journal of Fluency Disorders, 14,* 79–86.

Webster, W. G. (1990). Evidence in bimanual finger-tapping of an attentional component to stuttering. *Behavioural Brain Research, 37,* 93–100.

Webster, W. G. (1997). Principles of human brain organization related to lateralization of language and speech motor functions in normal speakers and stutterers. In W. Hulstijn, H. F. M. Peters, & P. H. H. M. van Lieshout (Eds.), *Speech production: Motor control, brain research and fluency disorders* (pp. 119–139). Amsterdam: Elsevier.

Webster, W. G. (1998). Brain models and the clinical management of stuttering. *Journal of Speech-Language Pathology & Audiology, 22,* 220–230.

Webster, W. G., & Poulos, M. (1989). *Facilitating fluency: Transfer strategies for adult stuttering treatment programs.* Tucson, AZ: Communication Skill Builders.

AUTHOR'S NOTE

This chapter is based on a paper first presented at the 2002 University of Georgia State of the Art Conference on evidence-based treatment of stuttering. The research described in this chapter was supported by grants from the Natural Sciences and Engineering Research Council of Canada. The author is now at the School of Communication Sciences and Disorders, University of Western Ontario, London, Ontario.

3

Emerging Controversies, Findings, and Directions in Neuroimaging and Developmental Stuttering: On Avoiding Petard Hoisting in Athens, Georgia

Roger J. Ingham
University of California, Santa Barbara,
University of Texas Health Science Center at San Antonio

The subtitle of this paper probably needs explaining—even for the local cognoscenti. Those who attended the 1997 Athens conference might recall that this author's paper also addressed the (then) emerging impact of neuroimaging on stuttering research, but it included a potential "petard hoister." It was argued (Ingham, 1998) that functional brain imaging could be an exciting development for stuttering research, provided it avoids falling into the same clinically barren wasteland that speech-motor (SM) research on stuttering has fallen into. The paper contended that the massive investment in SM research during the previous decade or more had contributed remarkably little towards either understanding or treating stuttering.[1] One reason, it was argued, was a preoccupation with descriptive rather than experimental research that failed to seek variables that can change stuttering. But therein resides a first-rate "petard hoister": it is far from clear that brain-imaging research has done much better. Consequently, this chapter updates the 1998 chapter and also tries to determine if imaging research might have started to fall into the very same wasteland. It will do so by overviewing the current direction of this research and its possibilities for identifying neural changes that might be critical or beneficial to therapy.

METHODOLOGICAL CONCERNS

A recurring issue in brain-imaging research is whether the methodology routinely used to find functional neural regions can actually identify neural regions that functionally control a problem behavior. Of equal importance, though, is whether it is possible to take advantage of the knowledge generated by this research methodology to remediate stuttering. The former issue is addressed initially and then an attempt is made to answer the latter.

The subtraction design has been the favored strategy that brain-imaging researchers have used, at least until recently, to identify neural regions that differentiate between the presence and absence of the behavior. It can be summarized as follows:

$$\text{If } A = x \text{ and } A + B = y, \text{ then } B = y - x$$

Where A and B are performance conditions and y and x are neural regions associated with those conditions. It is then inferred that those differentiating regions $(y - x)$ are functionally related to the behavior of interest. But, there is an inherent problem with this design: It is notoriously difficult to prove that when comparisons are made between conditions with and without the variable of interest (i.e., A vs. $A + B$) that the findings are not vulnerable to the *fallacy of pure insertion*. In other words, the design assumes that A functions in exactly the same way with or without the presence of B, thus making it possible to argue that B is a *pure insertion* (or perhaps *pure excision*) within the subtraction design. In imaging research, for instance, it is often assumed that the neural processes that occur during an A condition are no different to those that occur when B is added to (or removed from) that A condition. Ever since Boring (1950) labeled this threat to experimental validity it has been the well recognized and often ignored Achilles' heel within the subtraction design. Incidentally, the subtraction design is often surreptitiously embedded within

---

[1]There are some well-known SM variables that can control or treat stuttering such as modified phonation or even altered speech rate. They were known well before publication of Zimmermann's (1980) paper that, it was argued (Ingham, 1998), was largely responsible for initiating the SM research program. But none have been added as a result of the SM research that followed.

many areas of neurology. For example, it is recognizable within neurological investigations that draw inferences of functionality from lesion studies; the lesioned area in patients with a cerebral insult or lesion is often inferred to be the area that is responsible for the behavior that is either changed or added to the patient's repertoire. One interesting and relevant example would stem from Dronker's (1996) recent finding that lesions were consistently found in L. anterior insula in adult patients with dyspraxia, but not in those without dyspraxia—leading to the widespread inference that L. anterior insula is functionally related to dyspraxia.[2]

There is no simple solution to the validity problems within the subtraction design. However, one that has been gaining favor in positron emission tomography (PET) and functional magnetic resonance imaging (fMRI) research is to integrate the subtraction model with *performance correlation* (Silbersweig et al., 1995; Stern et al., 2000). In other words, the analysis is not simply confined to comparisons between the presence and absence of a condition; it is extended to take advantage of the target behavior's variability. This composite model gains inferential strength by arguing that if variations in the target behavior produce correlated cerebral blood flow (CBF) changes in critical neural regions, then there is a somewhat stronger probability that the identified regional activations are functionally related to the behavior of interest.

SOME EMERGING THEORETIC CHALLENGES

Relevant to this topic are theories that appear to reflect or reject a neuroscience perspective. Undoubtedly the ghost of Cerebral Dominance Theory (Orton, 1928; Travis, 1931, 1978) still haunts neurologic perspectives on stuttering theories. However, the ghosts are now being replaced by far more palpable or neurologically specific concepts. For instance, Webster's (1993; 1998) Interhemispheric Interference Theory has postulated that the source of anomalous neural activity probably resides in supplementary

---

[2]Much the same argument was made recently by Devinsky (2000) in critiquing an event-related PET study that reported finding neural regions that correlated with the frequency of tics in patients with Tourette's Syndrome (Stern et al., 2000) Devinsky reproduced an apt metaphor [from Walsh (1947)] for misunderstanding brain function:

that of an automobile transmission with a gear tooth knocked off, causing a "clunk" when the drive shaft turns slowly and a vibration at faster speeds. One might conclude (using functional imaging logic) that the gear tooth prevents clunks and vibrations, which is supported by the fact that those clunks and vibrations are removed when that tooth is replaced. The gear teeth, however, transmit power from the drive to the shaft. (p. 753)

Of course, whenever brain imaging studies find regions that appear to be abnormal, then the logic behind those claims might either vulnerable or suspect. But it is a problem that may have less serious clinical implications. For instance, and to use the same analogy, if the broken gear tooth was replaced (or if an alternative drive system was found), then the result might be a trivial matter as far as the health of the car is concerned.

motor area (SMA), a region considered pivotal for sequencing and initiating coordinated movements (Goldberg, 1985; Marsden et al., 1996). Webster's hemispheric laterality concept is that stuttering is characterized by an overflow of excessive activity from the right to the left hemisphere that causes interference in SMA. Caruso (1991) also partially used this idea by theorizing that the impaired neuromotor mechanisms underlying developmental stuttering reside in SMA or the basal ganglia. More recently nascent theoretic models proposed by Salmelin et al. (2000) and Sandak and Fiez (2000) postulated an aberrant sequencing of neural processing for speech production in the left hemisphere—even during a stuttering speaker's fluent speech. To say the least, plenty of neural regions are given prominence among these theories.

Other current theorists are much less enthusiastic about attributing stuttering to anomalous neural activity. Perkins, Kent, and Curlee's (1991) multi-component Neuropsycholinguistic Theory argues that aberrant neural processing is merely one part of a constellation of converging factors that need to be considered. Indeed, Perkins recently took the position (Perkins, 2002) that the cause of stuttering will not be a specific neuroanatomic abnormality. This "neural agnostic" position is maintained rather more stridently by Smith (1990, 1999) with her "dynamic, multi-factorial theory" of stuttering. Indeed, this theory states quite categorically (Smith & Kelly, 1997, p. 210) that the search for a specific neural source of developmental stuttering is probably futile. Why? Because, to quote Smith (1999):

> The multiple factors that underlie the emergence of stuttering behaviors ... are not located in a single site in the brain. Indeed, it may prove that group differences in brain function for individuals who stutter will be elusive and unreliable across investigations and imaging methods, as the behaviors that produce the diagnosis of stuttering may arise from the interactions of component neural systems that are essentially normal. (pp. 36–37)

In an interesting way, therefore, dynamic, multifactorial theory has emerged as a direct challenge to a purely neurologic theory or model of stuttering by claiming that specific abnormal neural regions or systems are unlikely to be found to be functionally related to stuttering. It is a challenge that certainly cannot be easily rejected at present.

NEUROIMAGING AND NORMAL SPEECH PRODUCTION: WHAT HAVE WE LEARNED?

This challenge is best addressed by taking a slight detour and reviewing just what has been learned from imaging research about the neural regions or systems that are implicated in *normal speech production*. Petersen, Fox, Posner and Raichle's (1988) classic PET study achieved that status by being the first imaging study to demonstrate CBF differences among the regions that are activated when words are read and when verbs are generated from those same words. Subsequently, imaging researchers have gradually identified the regions that appear to constitute the active "eloquent brain." For instance, Fiez and Petersen (1998) surveyed nine imaging studies on speech production and concluded that during oral reading the following areas were usually active: "left-lateralized regions in occipital and occipitotemporal cortex, the left frontal operculum, bilateral regions within the cerebellum, primary motor cortex ... the superior and middle temporal cortex, and medial regions in the supplementary motor area and anterior cingulate" (p. 914).

However, this was at best an inconsistent finding across these studies. Indeed, this inconsistency caused some to doubt their validity (Poeppel, 1996; but see Démonet, Fiez, Paulesu, Petersen, & Zatorre, 1996), which in turn has spawned vigorous efforts to rectify these inconsistencies (Hickock, 2001). One basis for a resolution was offered recently by Grabowski and Damasio (2000) in a review of imaging and language research. They contended that these inconsistencies are most likely the result of substantive and important differences among the methodologies and data analysis techniques. They identified at least four likely sources:

1. *The problem of paradigm design:* The uncertain stability of a cognitive state across the experimental and control conditions within subtraction designs (the "pure insertion" problem),
2. *The obstacles to fine-grained anatomical interpretation of results:* The variability between individual anatomy and its transformation into "Talairach space" (Talairach & Tournoux, 1988) anatomy, including variability across studies in mapping Talairach coordinates to regions (see Brett, Johnsrude, & Owen, 2002),
3. *The problem of implicit assumptions about the signal in which one is interested:* Differences among the various smoothing filters that are used to improve the signal to noise ratio and which may affect the spatial and temporal shape of responses (see White et al., 2001),
4. *The problem of negative results:* By using conservative statistical thresholds to avoid false positive activations, imaging may demonstrate systems that participate in task performance, but they do not necessarily fully identify the sufficient systems.

Researchers can surely only hope to offset these potential sources of error by seeking replicated findings across studies using reasonably similar methods. That goal may have been partly achieved within Indefrey and Levelt's (2000) much-cited meta-analysis of 58 imaging studies of speech production. They too found large across-study differences in the regions that were reported to be activated during word production—probably because of equally large differences among the speaking tasks. But there were some striking consistencies in regions activated during oral reading and these are shown in Table 3.1.

Unfortunately, Indefrey and Levelts' (2000) review did not include studies involving either connected speech or continuous oral reading—probably because there are so few. Consequently Table 3.1 was augmented by the findings from four recent studies that have reported regions activated during continuous speaking tasks. The addition of these studies suggests, not surprisingly, considerable overlap between regions activated by word repetition and by connected speech. In summary, the principal regions include (for right-sided speakers) a strong, although not exclusive, pattern of activations in the left hemisphere. These occur most prominently in the frontal lobe motor areas [SMA, precentral gyrus (M1), and inferior frontal gyrus (including BA 44/45)], the left- and right-superior temporal gyrus (with some middle-temporal gyrus involvement), and the medial and lateral regions of cerebellum. In addition activations should be expected in L. anterior insula, anterior cingulate, postcentral parietal lobe, as well as in the basal ganglia and thalamus. This is a rather unremarkable conclusion, but it is equally clear that the degree of involvement of these regions during speech is very task-dependent.

Meanwhile, it is now generally accepted that the process of speech production requires the prior retrieval of phonologic codes (see Indefrey & Levelt, 2000). This process appears to originate in the temporal lobe or Wernicke's region, and then implicates a discrete region of the left insula and, in varying degrees, the inferior frontal cortex or Broca's area (see Grabowski & Damasio, 2000). For instance, in an interesting magnetoencephalography (MEG) study Dhond et al. (2001), using a word stem task, determined that activation occurred at primary visual cortex approximately 100 ms after the stimulus word appeared, then proceeded to Wernicke's area (by approximately 210 ms) and then on to the insulo-opercular regions, arriving at Broca's area by approximately 370 ms. Concurrently, posteroventral and posterosuperior temporal regions were activated (by about 200–245 ms), but they were followed by *deactivations* in the prefrontal and anterior (not posterior) temporal regions at 365–500 ms. In short, normal speech production obviously involves a complex and task-dependent sequence of activations and deactivations in the motor and auditory regions.

Neuroimaging and Neural Plasticity

This digression continues a little more so as to consider briefly the role of neuroimaging in studying plasticity within the eloquent brain. This research carries immense implications for understanding the development of and recovery from stuttering.

TABLE 3.1.
Summary of the Neural Regions Identified by Indefrey and Levelt (2000)
as Activated by Single Word Oral Reading

Lobe	Gyrus/Structure	SIDE/BA or Area	Indefry & Levelt (2000)	Added by Continuous Speech*
Frontal	Medial frontal	L. BA 6 (SMA)	X	X
		R. BA 6 (SMA)	X	
	Precentral	L. BA 4	X	X
		R. BA 4	X	X
	Posterior inferior frontal	L. BA 44/45	X	X
		R. BA 44/45		X
		L. BA 46		X
		L. BA 46/9		X
		L. BA 47		X
Limbic	Cingulate	L. anterior	X	
		R. anterior		X
		L. posterior		X
Parietal	Postcentral	L. BA 3,1,2	X	
	Anterior	L. BA 40		X
	Posterior	L. BA 39/40		X
Occipital	Lingual	L. medial	X	
		R. medial	X	
	Occipital	L. lateral	X	
Temporal	Anterior superior temporal	L. BA 22		X
	Mid superior temporal	L. BA 22/42	X	
		R. BA 22/42	X	X
	Posterior superior temporal	L. BA 22	X	
		R. BA 22		X
	Posterior middle temporal	L. BA 21/37/39	X	
	Fusiform	L. BA 37	X	X
Sublobar	Insula	L. anterior	X	X
		R. anterior		X
	Basal ganglia	L.	X	
	Thalamus	L.	X	
		R.	X	

(continued on next page)

TABLE 3.1 (continued)

Lobe	Gyrus/Structure	SIDE/ BA or Area	Indefry & Levelt (2000)	Added by Continuous Speech*
Subcortical	Cerebellum	L. medial		X
		R. medial	X	
		L. lateral		X
		R. lateral		X

*The right column shows the regions that were activated and deactivated during continuous speech in at least one of four imaging studies (Kircher et al., 2000; 2001; Müller et al., 1997; Riecker et al., 2000).

It is well known that full recovery of speech and language function often occurs in children who suffer a stroke—but it is generally accompanied by substantial neural reorganization in the contralateral homologous regions and in ipsilateral adjacent spared areas (Chugani, Müller, & Chugani, 1996). Neural reorganization is also well documented in adult stroke cases (Mimura et al., 1998; Vallar et al., 1988), but of course recovery tends to be less successful. Evidence of an interaction between age and neural reorganization in recovery from communication disorders has been mainly documented in studies of focal brain injury (Müller et al., 1997), but there are signs of this difference in other sensory disorders.[3] This "age effect" is also consistent with findings that neural glucose uptake tends to peak between 4 and 10 years and then declines thereafter (see Chugani, 1998), presumably producing "synaptic pruning" that limits the possibilities for successful recovery or useful plasticity. This all seems to fit with conventional wisdom, but this wisdom is now being thoroughly disturbed by the findings on the effects of Constraint Therapy (Liepert et al., 2000; Taub & Morris, 2001) with stroke patients—many of whom suffered their stroke at least a decade earlier. The effects of restraining the patient's use of spared or able limbs for lengthy periods (2 hours per day for 2 weeks) are still in a preliminary stage. Nevertheless the findings are remarkably positive and seem to be accompanied by such extensive neural reorganization, that they suggest that the limits on neural plasticity in adults are far from established (Taub, Uswatte, & Elbert, 2002). In short, the age-dependent limits on recovery

---

[3]For instance, individuals who became blind in early childhood may maintain much higher levels of glucose metabolism in visual cortex when compared with individuals who became blind after 13 years of age (Wanet-Defalque et al., 1988). Similar effects have been reported in the A1 and A2 areas of persons deafened prior to 2 years of age when compared with adult onset of deafness (Catalán-Ahumeda et al., 1993).

may be more speculative than real—and may depend on finding similar techniques for inducing neural plasticity.

NEUROIMAGING STUDIES
OF DEVELOPMENTAL STUTTERING

Over the past decade there has been increasing acceptance that developmental stuttering is associated with neurophysiologic and, more recently, neuroanatomic abnormalcy. But the grounds for identifying particular neural regions as related to stuttering are extremely shaky. There certainly appear to have been some exciting findings from neuroimaging studies of stuttering, but there is surprisingly little across-study consistency among their findings.

The Search for a Neuroanatomic Abnormality
in Developmental Stuttering

It has long been suspected that developmental stuttering may be related to abnormal neuroanatomy (Strub, Black, & Naeser, 1987), but that suspicion was dramatically fortified in a recent morphometric study by Foundas et al. (2001). This study used 3-D MRIs and reported some seemingly important neuroanatomic differences between 16 adult persistent stutterers and 16 controls (matched for age, sex, hand preference, and education), particularly within the perisylvian fissure. The most prominent being "a second diagonal sulcus and extra gyri along the superior bank of the sylvian fossa" (Foundas et al., 2001, p. 207) that was unique to the stutterers. It was also reported that the stutterers' planum temporale was enlarged and showed reduced interhemispheric asymmetry. However, there is at least one important concern about these findings—and maybe another. The first qualifier is that the morphometric analysis was restricted to very few regions. Given the evidence from imaging studies, a number of other regions, notably anterior insula, SMA, M1 (mouth), basal ganglia and cerebellum, might have been reasonable places to look for anomalous neuranatomic features. Nonetheless, this is an immensely important study because this anatomic abnormality may form a critical link between the current neurological findings and the genetic basis of developmental stuttering (Yairi, Ambrose, & Cox, 1996). A second qualifier is that this study urgently awaits replication. Partial replication is provided in the findings of a study by Sommer, Koch, Paulus, Weiller, and Büchel (2002) who used diffusion tensor imaging and found differences between neural white and gray matter volume in adult persistent stutterers and controls. The regional differences were reported to be close to those identified by Foundas et al. (2001), however Sommer et al. failed to confirm that the volumetric differences were confined solely to the reported region of interest. The concern over the significance of these findings is fortified by the results of a preliminary attempted replication of the Foundas et al. study in San Antonio. The author and colleagues studied the 3-D MRIs of 5 persistent stutterers, 5 recovered stutterers and 5 controls— participants in PET studies—and the result was not encouraging. Extra gyri were found on the perisylvian fissure for 4 out of 5 (not 5 out of 5) of the persistent stutterers, but extra gyri were also found within the perisylvian fissures of 3 out of 5 recovered stutterers and 3 out of 5 controls.

The Search for a Neurophysiological Abnormality in Developmental Stuttering

As mentioned earlier, numerous nonimaging studies have suggested that developmental stutterers display unusual neural processing during speech or speech related tasks (see Bloodstein, 1995). Signs that this might definitely be the case appeared in an early nontomographic CBF study by Woods, Stump, McKeehan, Sheldon, and Proctor (1980) and a single photon emission computed tomographic (SPECT) study by Pool, Devous, Freeman, Watson, and Finitzo (1991), but these studies contained major methodological problems.[4] More substantial evidence emerged in a series of PET imaging studies of stuttering that have been interpreted (see Curlee & Siegel, 1999; Webster, 1998) to mean that stuttering is functionally related to aberrant neural processing of speech in regions associated with the speech-motor and auditory system. Most of these studies used subtraction designs with different speaking tasks in order to compare the regional activations and deactivations during stuttered and nonstuttered speech. The tasks have required adult stutterers (mainly dextral adult males) to read orally paragraphs, generate sentences or produce single words at intervals (Braun et al., 1997; De Nil, Kroll, Kapur, & Houle, 2000; Fox et al., 1996) and then compare the resulting brain images with images obtained during induced stutter-free speech (Braun et al., 1997; Fox et al., 1996) or with the speech of controls (De Nil et al., 2000). In addition to the PET studies, there have been two magnetoencephalography (MEG) studies that have also found that adult stutterers display unusual auditory activations during speech and an unusual sequence of neural processing of the speech signal (Salmelin et al., 1998; Salmelin, Schnitzler, Schmitz, & Freund, 2000). In both MEG studies, however, only stutter-free utterances were analyzed.

In the midst of the promising findings of these neuroimaging studies at least two important issues appear to have been generally overlooked (but see Lebrun, 1998). Firstly, there are very few consistent findings across

---

[4]The Wood et al. imaging system was nontomographic and had limited scanning capability. Pool et al's (1991) SPECT analysis, which used only a single brain slice during nonspeaking conditions, has obvious spatial problems. In addition, Pool et al.'s findings are complicated by their report that their stutterers' whole-brain blood flow levels were 20% below those found in their controls—equivalent to levels reported in the later stages of Alzheimers (see Fox, Lancaster, & Ingham, 1993).

these studies. With the possible exception of unusual right-hemisphere activations in the premotor area and deactivations in the auditory area, it appears that the differences among the PET study findings grossly outweigh their similarities. Secondly, none of these studies has attempted to isolate the neural activations and deactivations that occur in conjunction with moments of stuttering during speech. One obvious reason is that PET does not lend itself to imaging specific utterances, which is especially problematic if (like stuttering) they occur with unpredictable frequency. That is less of a problem with MEG, but so far stuttering behavior has not been recorded via MEG.[5] A major drawback, though, with MEG is that it has very poor spatial resolution (especially compared with PET; see Posner & Raichle, 1994).

Comparisons Across PET Studies of Stuttering

At this point it is worth trying to deduce what has actually been learned from the PET studies of stuttering. Five studies have been published, and each used a subtraction design to locate neural regions that are functionally related to stuttering (Braun et al., 1997; De Nil et al., 2000; Fox et al., 1996; Ingham, Fox, Ingham, & Zamarripa, 2000; Wu et al., 1995). Those studies have been supplemented by two performance correlation studies using data derived from the condition contrasts (Braun et al., 1997; Fox et al., 2000). All five studies have used different speaking tasks and (except for Fox et al. and Ingham et al.) different analysis techniques. Nevertheless, if the regions that are functionally associated with stuttering are common across developmental stutterers, then it seems reasonable to expect that they should be common across these studies.

Unfortunately, as Table 3.2 shows, this is far from the case. Table 3.2 lists the regions that each study reported as significantly associated with stuttering and not present among controls during the same speaking task. The Ingham et al. (2000) study is not included in this table because some of that study's data were drawn from Fox et al. (1996). It is necessary to be aware of some important differences among these studies when comparing their findings. In the Wu et al. (1995) study, for instance, no rest-state scans were obtained making it difficult to isolate CBF activity that is unrelated to speech. That study also used F-18 fluoro-deoxyglucose (FDG) rather than ^{15}O as a tracer and failed to scan in the SMA region. In addition, only two studies (Braun et al., 1997; Fox et al.,1996) reported regional activations and deactivations—De Nil et al. (2000) did not derive deactivation data. Nonetheless,

---

[5]On the other hand, even if MEG were used to this end, then its spatial resolution problem makes it difficult to directly relate MEG-identified locations to regions obtained with PET or fMRI. There are frequent calls for hybridized MEG-fMRI studies (e.g., Dale et al., 2000), but there continue to be some fundamental reasons why this marriage of convenience may not be harmonious. For instance, as Nunez and Silberstein (2000) point out, very different cell types generate MEG and fMRI signals which means these methods are "generally sensitive to a different kind of source activity and to different spatial and temporal states" (p. 79).

TABLE 3.2a
Positive Activations

LOBE	GYRUS/Structure	SIDE/BA	Subtraction Design Studies					P-C Studies	
			W	F1	B	D	# Agree	F2	I
								Male	Female
Frontal	Medial frontal	L. BA 6 (SMA)				X		X	X
		R. BA 6 (SMA)		X				X	
	Lateral frontal	L. BA 6				X			
		R. BA 6		X	X		2		X
	Precentral	L. BA 4							X
		R. BA4						X	X
	Prefrontal	L. BA 8,9,10			X				
		R. BA 8,9,10			X				
		L. BA 11			X				
		R. BA 11			X				
	Posterior MFG	R. BA 46/9				X			
		L. BA 47			X				
Limbic	Cingulate	R. anterior			X				
		L. mid				X			X
Parietal		R. BA 40				X			
Occipital	Lingual	L. medial				X		X	X
		R. medial						X	X
	L. lateral						X		
	Fusiform	L. BA 19/37							X
Temporal	Mid STG	R. BA 22/42				X			
Sublobar	Insula	L. anterior	X						X
		R. anterior	X					X	X
		R. posterior				X			
	Claustrum	L	X						
	Caudate	R.			X				X
	Lentiform	L		X					X
		R							
	Thalamus	L		X		X	2		
		R.				X			

38

LOBE	GYRUS/ Structure	SIDE/ BA	Subtraction Design Studies					P-C Studies	
			W	F1	B	D	# Agree	F2	I
								Male	Female
Subcortical	Cerebellum	L. medial		X	X	X	3	X	X
		R. medial		X	X	X	3	X	X
		L. lateral		X				X	
		R. lateral		X					
	Periaque-ductal	L				X			
		R				X			

TABLE 3.2b
Negative Activations (Deactivations)

LOBE	GYRUS/ Structure	SIDE/BA	Subtraction Design Studies					P-C Studies	
			W	F1	B	D	# Agree	F2	I
								Male	Female
Frontal	Prefrontal	L. BA 8,9,10	X					X	
		R. BA 8,9,10	X					X	X
		L. BA 11	X						
		L. BA 6 (lat)							X
	Anterior IFG	L. BA 44-46	X					X	X
		R. BA 44-46							X
		L. BA 47		X		X	2		
Limbic	Cingulate	L. anterior							X
		R. anterior						X	X
		R. mid							X
		L. posterior	X			X	2		
		R. posterior	X					X	
		L. parahippoc						X	
		R. parahippoc							X
Parietal	Anterior	L. BA 40						X	
		R. BA 40	X						X
	Posterior	L. BA 7							
		R. BA 7						X	X
	Postcentral	L. BA 3,1,2							
		R. BA 3,1,2							X

(continued on next page)

TABLE 3.2b (continued)

LOBE	GYRUS/ Structure	SIDE/BA	W	F1	B	D	# Agree	F2 Male	I Female
Occipital	Mid OG	L. lateral				X			X
		R. lateral				X			X
Temporal	STG	L. BA 22			X			X	X
		R. BA 22		X				X	X
	MTG	L. BA 21							X
		R. BA 21						X	X
		L. BA 39						X	X
		R. BA 39						X	X
	Fusiform	L. BA 37/20						X	
		R. BA 37/20							X
	TG	L. BA 41/42				X			
		R. BA 41/42						X	
Sublobar	Caudate	L.	X						X
		R.							X
	Thalamus	L.							X
		R.							X
	Midbrain	L	X						
		R	X						
Sub-cortical	Cerebellum	R. medial	X						

Note. Tables show 47 regions in which stuttering-related positive activations or negative (deactivations) were identified in at least one of the Subtraction Design Studies (W = Wu et al., 1995; F1 = Fox et al., 1996; B = Braun et al., 1997; D = De Nil et al., 2000). Note that only 6 regions were similar for at least 2 of the studies and in only one of these six regions did three of the four studies agree (L and R medial cerebellum). The Performance-Correlation Studies (P-C studies: F2 = Fox et al., 2000; I = Ingham et al., in press) reported 17 regions that were related to stuttering in either gender. There were seven regions where both genders showed positive correlations with stuttering frequency in the same region.

Wu et al. and De Nil et al. did report stutterers' regional activations that were higher or lower than those found in their controls, thereby providing a crude approximation to the deactivation findings in other studies.

A perusal of Table 3.2 shows that across the four PET studies a total of 45 different regions were identified as significantly activated or deactivated during stuttered speech. However, not one region was common to all four studies. In fact, only one region was common to three studies and only seven regions were common to two studies. If this summary is restricted to the three $H_2^{15}O$ PET studies, then the picture is essentially the same. In fact across those three studies only one region, right cerebellum, was common to all 3 out of 36 identified regions. Furthermore, because right cerebellum is a large region composed, at the very least, of medial and lateral areas, there may have been essentially no agreement among these studies.[6]

Such differences among brain imaging study findings should not be too surprising given the variability among imaging studies of language function. Indeed, as Grabowski and Damasio (2000) rather glibly concluded from their review of these studies, "When two functional imaging studies attempt to isolate a specific language-processing component using different tasks, the results usually differ" (p. 445). It should not be too surprising, therefore, that attempts to derive common neural regions related to stuttering are very likely to be bedeviled by the effects of task differences. And that might be even more the case when the stuttering event is not actually isolated for investigation in these studies.

At the risk of appearing to be self-serving, it would seem that the situation is not quite so dismal if some recent studies in San Antonio are added to the picture. These studies do show strong signs of across-study consistency in their findings when the imaging task is consistent—and even when the tasks and imaging methodologies differ. In Table 3.2 the two right columns provide the regional comparisons between the findings from the performance correlation analyses on male stuttering speakers (from Fox et al., 2000) and on female stuttering speakers (Ingham et al., in press) who completed the same chorus reading protocol. The two studies produced a total of 17 regions in which voxel clusters were positively correlated with stuttering frequency—and in 7 out of 17 regions the sexes had activations in identical regions. This comparative study was actually designed to identify gender differences. These differences are quite distinctive in normally fluent subjects (Gur et al., 2000; Shaywitz et al., 1995), and so gender differences were anticipated in regions activated during stuttering. In fact, the number of common regions between the sexes with respect to stuttering-related regions was greater than has been found across the stuttering studies—and those commonalities were even greater for syllable rate correlations. Not shown in the Table 3.2 are the across-gender voxel clusters that were positively correlated with syllable rate; among the stutterers there were 12

---

[6]In the De Nil et al. study the coordinates given for the right cerebellum activation ($x = 10$, $y = -100$, $z = -20$; see Table 3, p. 1045) refer to a location that is 13 mm beyond (on the Y-axis) cerebellum in the Talairach atlas—quite literally outside of the brain. Consequently, it is possible that across all three $H_2^{15}O$ PET studies not one region was found to be consistently associated with stuttering.

out of 24 matched regions and for the controls there were 12 out of 21 matched regions. This is not perfect agreement, but it is certainly much better than the across-study regional agreements.

CONVERGING EVIDENCE FOR NECESSARY AND SUFFICIENT NEURAL CONDITIONS ASSOCIATED WITH STUTTERING: THE SAN ANTONIO STUDIES

PET Studies

Somewhat ignored in the Fox et al. (2000) performance correlation (P-C) study on male stutterers is that many of the regions that were significantly correlated with stuttering frequency (actually, the frequency of stuttered and nonstuttered 4 s intervals) were also correlated with syllable rate. And that raises an interesting issue. From one perspective it could be argued that because these regions correlated with syllable rate and stutter rate, then they cannot be distinctive to stuttering. But it can also be argued that the regional activations associated with syllable production and stuttering are necessary for producing stuttering, whereas those that are only stuttering related are likely to be essential or sufficient for stuttering to occur. To that end the author and colleagues have recently reanalyzed the performance-correlation findings that were reported by Fox et al. (2000) and then related the results to those obtained when we replicated the study on which it was based (Fox et al., 1996) with female stutterers and their controls.

Surprisingly, there have been only two studies on female stuttering speakers—and none at all on their neurophysiology. Comparisons of male and female stutterers yield no differences on bimanual handwriting (Webster, 1988) or central auditory processing (Nuck et al., 1987) tests—but these findings may not be relevant to neural processing of speech. This paucity of research on stuttering in females is intriguing because it is obvious that adult female stuttering speakers differ in some important ways from their male counterparts: they are fewer in number and tend to recover in childhood more frequently than males (Yairi & Ambrose, 1999). Added to that is evidence that normal adult females and males display neuroanatomic differences (Harasty et al., 1997) and, as aforementioned, females show less regional laterality than males during speech production (Jaeger et al., 1998; Shaywitz et al., 1995). For this reason there should be some important similarities and differences in regions associated with stuttering in adult male and female stuttering speakers

The results of the comparison of performance correlation findings from both sexes during the chorus reading PET study are shown in Table 3.3.

Specifically, the table shows the local maxima coordinates for the voxel clusters (≥ 15) that are significantly correlated ($r \geq + 0.30$ or $\leq - 0.30$). In the left side of the table are the positive and negatively correlated regions for

TABLE 3.3
Local Maxima Voxel Cluster Coordinates for Females' and Males' Positive and Negative Correlations With Stutter Rate

| | Females | | | | | | | | Males | | | | | | | |
| | Left Hemisphere | | | | Right Hemisphere | | | | Left Hemisphere | | | | Right Hemisphere | | | |
Region	r	x	y	z	r	x	y	z	r	x	y	z	r	x	y	z
Positive Correlations																
Frontal Lobe																
SMA (6)	0.39	-2	-6	54	–	–	–	–	0.36	-6	-8	56	0.42	12	0	58
M1-Mouth (4)	0.41	-44	-16	30	0.35	52	-16	34	–	–	–	–	0.35	50	-16	28
SLPrM (6)	–	–	–	–	0.32	44	-8	35	–	–	–	–	–	–	–	–
Limbic Lobe																
Mid Cingulate (24)	0.32	-4	10	36	–	–	–	–	–	–	–	–	–	–	–	–
Occipital Lobe																
Medial (18)	0.41	-6	-89	-8	0.38	4	-86	10	0.40	-14	-93	14	0.43	2	-88	2
Lateral (18)	–	–	–	–	–	–	–	–	0.39	-30	-88	-4	–	–	–	–
Fusiform (18)	0.32	-20	-84	-21	–	–	–	–	–	–	–	–	–	–	–	–
Sublobar																
Anterior Insula (13)	0.31	-31	18	4	0.35	44	20	1	–	–	–	–	0.37	36	8	-2
Basal Ganglia	0.32	-14	-5	-1	0.34	16	19	10	–	–	–	–	–	–	–	–
Cerebellum																
Medial	0.35	-10	-78	-16	0.33	0	-72	-22	0.34	-8	-72	-8	0.51	10	-70	-16
Lateral	–	–	–	–	–	–	–	–	0.42	-36	-66	-28	–	–	–	–

(continued on next page)

TABLE 3.3 (continued)

Region	Females								Males							
	Left Hemisphere				Right Hemisphere				Left Hemisphere				Right Hemisphere			
	r	x	y	z	r	x	y	z	r	x	y	z	r	x	y	z
Negative Correlations																
Frontal Lobe																
Prefrontal (8,9)	-0.34	–	–	–	-0.36	20	32	33	-0.34	-25	16	47	-0.31	39	10	40
Inferior Frontal (44/45)	-0.33	-34	34	5	-0.41	43	14	25	-0.33	-29	2	28	–	–	–	–
SLPrM (6)	-0.33	-30	-4	31	–	–	–	–								
Limbic Lobe																
Anterior Cingulate (32)	-0.33	-18	38	9	-0.32	18	36	20	–	–	–	–	-0.37	12	39	-3
Mid Cingulate (24)	–	–	–	–	-0.33	20	-4	33	–	–	–	–	–	–	–	–
Posterior Cingulate (31)	–	–	–	–	-0.32	6	-54	26	–	–	–	–	-0.31	5	-60	24
Parahippocampal (36)	–	–	–	–	-0.35	39	-23	-17	-0.31	-16	-16	-20	–	–	–	–
Parietal Lobe																
Anterior (40)	–	–	–	–	-0.31	61	-34	30	-0.34	-49	-41	38	–	–	–	–
Posterior (7)	–	–	–	–	-0.34	4	-62	44	–	–	–	–	-0.39	6	-54	36
Postcentral gyrus (5)	–	–	–	–	-0.31	36	-28	38	–	–	–	–	–	–	–	–

Region	Females								Males							
	Left Hemisphere				Right Hemisphere				Left Hemisphere				Right Hemisphere			
	r	x	y	z	r	x	y	z	r	x	y	z	r	x	y	z
Occipital Lobe																
Lateral (19)	-0.38	-37	-69	13	-0.32	32	-75	30	–	–	–	–	–	–	–	–
Temporal Lobe																
Superior temporal gyr (22)	-0.31	-53	-41	-1	-0.31	64	-32	8	-0.31	-48	-56	26	-0.35	54	-54	20
Middle temporal gyus (21)	-0.34	-44	-30	-2	-0.30	60	-34	-8	–	–	–	–	–	–	–	–
Middle (39)	-0.35	-34	-70	28	-0.31	52	-56	22	-0.31	-43	-67	22	-0.33	51	-64	14
Fusiform gyrus (37, 20)	–	–	–	–	-0.32	36	-38	-10	-0.33	-46	-26	-16	–	–	–	–
Transverse gyrus (41)	–	–	–	–	–	–	–	–	–	–	–	–	-0.35	53	-18	11
Sublobar																
Basal Ganglia	-0.33	-20	-6	22	-0.36	36	-20	-8	–	–	–	–	–	–	–	–
Thalamus	-0.31	-26	-28	10	-0.31	26	-28	9	–	–	–	–	–	–	–	–

*Where multiple foci were identified in a given area, the one with the highest correlation is shown here.

45

the female stutterers and in the right half are those for the males. In general, there were fewer positively correlated regions than negatively correlated regions. The principal positively correlated regions are in the frontal, limbic, and occipital lobes, anterior insula, basal ganglia, and cerebellum. Most obvious, though, is that there were no positively correlated voxels in the temporal lobe. Negatively correlated regions appear in almost every lobe and are more widely distributed in the females than in the males. It is also clear that both sexes displayed negatively correlated voxels in the temporal lobe—and mainly in the right hemisphere. As mentioned earlier, it was hypothesized that these regions are probably necessary for stuttering, but they also include a sub set of regions that only correlate with stuttering. And it is that subset of regional activations and deactivations that it is now hypothesized provide the sufficient conditions for stuttering to occur.

Table 3.4 shows the local maxima voxel for that subset of regions. They were derived from the Table 3.3 data using boolean logic on images to derive voxel clusters (> 3) that were isolated, correlated with stuttering frequency, but did not correlate with syllable rate. The most obvious finding was that the genders do show considerable differences, but there are some important overlaps. The commonalities or overlaps are highlighted in bold type. They show that in the positively correlated regions both genders strongly activated R. anterior insula, whereas in the negatively correlated regions both genders showed strong deactivations in Broca's area (L. BA 44/45) and in the right auditory association area (R. BA 21/22). There are some obvious gender differences. Females show strong activations in L. anterior insula and in basal ganglia (L. globus pallidus, R. caudate), whereas males show strong L. medial occipital lobe and R. medial cerebellum activation.

The negatively correlated regions continue to be more extensive in the females, especially in the right hemisphere (prefrontal, homologous Broca's, cingulate, parahippocampus, posterior parietal, and fusiform gyrus). They also showed bilateral BA 22 and L. lateral occipital lobe deactivations. In the males the only additional distinctive deactivation was in R. A1 (BA 41). An interesting feature of Table 3.4 is that among the regions that are common to the genders, the females show bilateral effects while the males do not (females L/R anterior insula, L/R. BA 44/45, L/R. BA 22; males R anterior insula, L. BA 44/45, R. BA 21). This is consistent with evidence mentioned earlier of more decisive lateralization in males that females during language related tasks.

Imagining Stuttering Study

The implications of this finding may be better understood by a brief account of three other studies from the San Antonio group. The first (Ingham, Fox, Ingham, & Zamarripa, 2000) was a PET study conducted with four stutterers and four matched controls, all participants in the original Fox et

TABLE 3.4

Region	Females								Males							
	Left Hemisphere				Right Hemisphere				Left Hemisphere				Right Hemisphere			
	r	x	y	z	r	x	y	z	r	x	y	z	r	x	y	z
Positive Correlations																
Occipital Lobe																
Lateral (18)	0.31	-31	18	4	—	—	—	—	0.40	-14	-93	14	—	—	—	—
Sub-lobar																
Anterior Insula (13)	—	—	—	—	0.35	44	20	1*	—	—	—	—	0.37	36	8	-2
Basal Ganglia (caudate nucleus)	—	—	—	—	0.34	16	19	10	—	—	—	—	—	—	—	—
Basal Ganglia (globus pallidus)	0.32	-14	-5	-1	—	—	—	—	—	—	—	—	—	—	—	—
Cerebellum																
Medial	—	—	—	—	—	—	—	—	—	—	—	—	0.51	10	-70	-16*
Negative Correlations																
Frontal Lobe																
Prefrontal (8,9)	—	—	—	—	-0.36	20	32	33	—	—	—	—	—	—	—	—
Inferior Frontal (44/45)	-0.34	-34	34	5*	-0.41	43	14	25*	-0.33	-29	2	28	—	—	—	—
Limbic Lobe																
Mid Cingulate (24)	—	—	—	—	-0.33	20	-4	33	—	—	—	—	—	—	—	—
Parahippocampal (36)	—	—	—	—	-0.36	37	-19	-9*	—	—	—	—	—	—	—	—
Parietal Lobe																
Posterior (7)	—	Œ	—	—	-0.34	4	-62	44	—	—	—	—	—	—	—	—

(continued on next page)

TABLE 3.4 *(continued)*

Region	Females								Males							
	Left Hemisphere				Right Hemisphere				Left Hemisphere				Right Hemisphere			
	r	x	y	z	r	x	y	z	r	x	y	z	r	x	y	z
Occipital Lobe																
Lateral (19)	-0.38	-37	-69	13	–	–	–	–	–	–	–	Œ	–	–	–	–
Temporal Lobe																
Superior temporal gyr (22)	-0.31	-53	-41	-1	-0.31	64	-32	8	–	–	–	–	–	–	–	–
Middle temporal gyrus (21)	–	–	–	–	-0.32	36	-38	-10	–	–	–	–	0.39	55	0	-13*
Fusiform gyrus (37, 20)	–	–	–	–	–	–	–	–	–	–	–	–	–	–	–	–
Transverse gyrus (41)	–	–	–	–	–	–	–	–	–	–	–	–	-0.35	53	-18	11*

Note. Regional coordinates* for females' and males' positive and negative correlations with stutter rate that are correlated significantly with stutter rate and are NOT correlated significantly with syllable rate. The local maxima coordinates are shown for voxel clusters 3 or larger and isolated from syllable rate voxels by a 5 cube voxel kernel.
*Multiple foci were identified in this area—highest correlation is shown here.

al. (1996) PET study. These individuals completed exactly the same protocol as was used in the Fox et al. study but with one exception: They were told to *imagine they were stuttering* during the SOLO reading condition and *imagine they were not stuttering* during the CHORUS reading condition. The most important finding was that many of the activations that occurred during overt stuttering also occurred when stuttering was imagined. For instance, prominent right-sided activations in SMA, and BA 46, plus activations in L. thalamus, L/R anterior insula and L/R cerebellum were found during overt stuttered speech, and they also appeared when the same stutterers imagined they were stuttering. Furthermore, the deactivations in the A2 region that occurred during overt stuttering also occurred when stuttering was imagined. An equally fascinating finding was that most of the stutter-related activations and deactivations were normalized when the stutterers imagined they were reading fluently. In short, overt stuttering during oral reading was not a prerequisite for the stutter-related activations and deactivations. Of course this was a subtraction design study that did not incorporate performance-correlation, so it is difficult to compare its results to those obtained by Fox et al. (2000) and Ingham et al. (in press). Nevertheless, the findings did replicate the activations in R. anterior insula, the absence of Broca's activation and the deactivations in R A2.

ERP Investigation

The second study was an Event Related Potential (ERP) investigation using nonspeech and nonstuttering tasks to investigate the temporal lobe deactivations in stutterers (Liotti et al., 2001). The origin of this study resides in findings from some MEG studies that suggested that neural responses to auditory stimuli, including speech, are usually somewhat suppressed in normal speakers (e.g., Numminen, Salmelin, & Harris, 1999). For instance, Curio, Neuloh, Numminen, Jousmaki, & Hari, (2000) used ERP and demonstrated inhibitory gating of auditory responses to the production of vowels in normal adults. This led Ludlow (2000) to question whether the temporal lobe deactivations during stuttered speech were necessarily abnormal. The resulting ERP study designed to address this issue (Liotti et al., 2001), actually replicated Curio et al.'s procedure. Scalp electrical activity was recorded (64-channels) in eight adult dextral male stutterers and eight age-matched male controls while they repeatedly produced the vowel /a/ for 1 s at 3 s intervals, and then later listened to a recording of their utterances that were digitized and replayed at the same intensity level (~70 dB) as the vowel utterance. All participants passed a hearing screening.

The results, summarized in Fig. 3.1, show that the stutterers displayed significantly suppressed early auditory processing (N100) in right temporal lobe (relative to the controls) for both spoken and listened speech

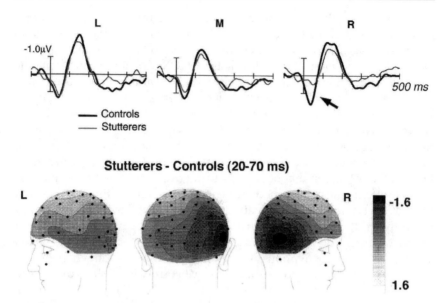

FIG. 3.1   Summarized results from Liotti et al.'s (2001) ERP study.

sounds. This finding is quite consistent with the findings of deactivation in the right temporal lobe reported in earlier PET studies. In addition, just prior to uttering /a/, the stutterers exhibited an abnormal motor potential over regions that overlap Broca's area.

Event-Related fMRI Investigation

The third study is still in progress, but the emerging results appear to be quite cogent. For some time now there has been some concern that all of the reported brain imaging investigations of stuttering (including the San Antonio studies) have only approximated the analysis of stuttered speech or stuttered events. In a typical ^{15}O PET study the analyses are based on CBF measures made during a series of 40 s intervals that may contain widely different amounts of stuttered and nonstuttered speech. The solution seemed to be to use fMRI with its time resolution advantages, but only if there was a way to overcome the movement artifact problems produced during overt speech, the confounding effects of variations in the time course of the haemodynamic [blood oxygenation level dependent (BOLD)] response to stimuli, and the problem of recording in the presence of the immense levels of coil noise. Of course, fMRI is also appealing because it does not use radioactive tracers to plot blood flow, thereby making it possible to scan repeatedly—and even scan children.

Many of these impediments of fMRI began to dissipate with the development of Event-Related fMRI (Buckner et al., 1996). During event-related fMRI each stimulus event, such as an utterance (as long as its duration is no more than ~2 s) is presented at widely separated intervals (approximately 20 s) in order to allow for the variations in the lag time of the regional BOLD responses to recover their baserate levels. This solved the problem of associating the BOLD response with a particular stimulus event. In addition, algorithms for identifying and correcting modest movement artifacts (Barch et al., 1999) have been developed that successfully correct for the speech movement problem. Those algorithms have been improved on in San Antonio and now make it possible to image reasonably severe stuttered utterances. And finally a suitable directional microphone located beneath the lip and used in conjunction with a carefully positioned camera make it possible to record speech in the scanner with satisfactory fidelity. Hence, it is now possible, in principle, to image the neural processes that occur in conjunction with a stuttered utterance and compare them with processes that occur during a matched nonstuttered utterance or another control stimulus condition such as a simulated stuttered utterance. This final section, therefore, is a preliminary report on an ER-fMRI study that is attempting to make such comparisons.

Studying stuttering with ER-fMRI raises a number of interesting methodological problems. Firstly, it is necessary to ensure that stuttering will occur on single words while the subject wears earplugs to reduce the coil noise. This became a relatively simple empirical issue that was solved by using prescanning trials that matched the scanning task. During these trials each stutterer read aloud an individually selected corpus of words, each word separated by a 20 s interval, until the individual produced a minimum of 20 words that were stuttered consistently and 40 that were not stuttered on three consecutive occasions. Secondly, it was also necessary to ensure that the recovered stutterers and controls could produce simulated stuttering events that were perceptually indistinguishable from real stuttering events. This was achieved by using a combination of video samples and feedback training until the each participant's simulated stuttering events and real stuttering events were indistinguishable to an independent observer.

The specific aim of this ER-fMRI study was twofold: (a) to test whether the neural systems that accompany stuttered words differ from those that accompany fluent nonstuttered words, and (b) to determine if the neural systems associated with stuttered words differ from systems associated with simulated stuttered words produced by late recovered stutterers and controls. An additional aim was to test whether the aberrant regional activations and deactivations reported in earlier studies (Fox et al., 1996, 2000) were reproduced using a very different task (single words vs. connected reading) and methodology.

The inclusion of late recovered stutterers in this study relates to a growing interest in information that might be gleaned from this population with respect to recovery. It is hypothesized, in general terms, that individuals who have recovered from stuttering, preferably without formal intervention, have probably achieved a "successful" neural reorganization. Indeed, their reorganized neural system may contain features that are essential to successful recovery.

To date results are only available from six dextral adult males: 2 persistent stutterers, 2 controls and 2-late self-recovered stutterers. Admittedly this is a very small sample to use to draw any strong conclusions. However, the image analyses have only focused on those activated and deactivated regions that occurred in both subjects within a subgroup and where the across-condition (stuttered or simulated stuttered vs. nonstuttered utterances) voxel numbers showed identical trend changes for both individuals within a subgroup.

In considering these initial results it is important to recall that the PET studies conducted in San Antonio have indicated that stuttering in both sexes is likely related to abnormal neural activity in three regions: excessive right anterior insula activation and unusual deactivations in Broca's area and right BA 21/22. The results are summarized in Fig. 3.2, which shows the total number of significantly activated and deactivated voxels in the left and right hemisphere regions of interest for the three groups.[7]

The figure shows that Broca's area was deactivated during real stuttering—as it was in the PET P-C studies. But, it was also deactivated in the controls and recovered stutterers during simulated stuttering, which obviously diminishes the significance of this regional deactivation to stuttering. It is also noteworthy that Salmelin et al's (2000) finding of unusual inactivity in Broca's area during the fluent utterances by stutterers was not replicated.

The temporal lobe findings are complicated by the fact that ER-fMRI occurs in a very noisy environment and so temporal lobe activations were expected. This probably accounts for the activations in the A2 regions (BA 21/22) in all groups. However, the most surprising finding was that in the stutterers the A1 regions, both left and right, became completely inactive during the production of stuttered words—after being very active when the stutterers produced nonstuttered words. Literally the reverse was the case for the controls and the recovered stutterers, who showed little or no A1 activity during their fluent words but large activity during their simulated stuttering.

---

[7]An ER-fMRI report by Palmer et al. (2001) on the effects of a word-stem task showed activations and deactivations in their non-patient subjects that closely resembled those reported in the present investigations with two control subjects.

Event-related fMRI study

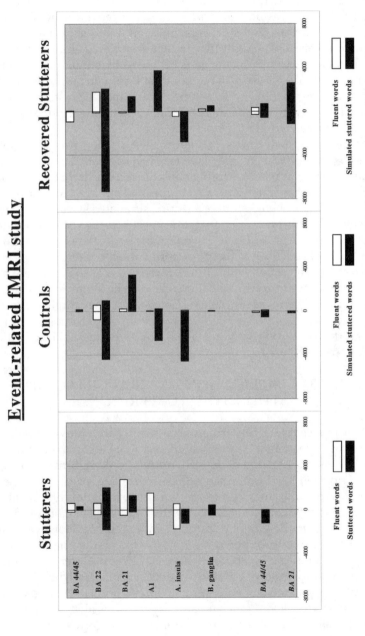

FIG. 3.2. Preliminary results from an ER-fMRI study conducted at the University of Texas Health Sciences Center at San Antonio: Activated and deactivated voxels in left and right hemisphere regions of interest, for six dextral adult males.

Left and right anterior insula were very active during stuttered and non-stuttered words by stutterers. By contrast, the nonstuttered words produced by the controls showed no left or right anterior insula activations, but the left anterior insula was dramatically activated during simulated stuttering. In the recovered stutterers, only left anterior insula was activated—and it was activated during simulated stuttered and nonstuttered words. The fact that anterior insula is activated by simulated stuttering may tend to diminish its claim to be a central player in real stuttering—but its activity during fluent words by stutterers and recovered stutterers suggests that it remains an area of interest. It may well be one region that is not completely normalized in recovered stutterers.

Perhaps the most distinctive stutter-related finding was that globus pallidus within the basal ganglia was excessively activated on the left during stuttering but was inactive during nonstuttered words. In the controls it was only slightly activated on the right during simulated stuttering, but was active in the recovered stutterers during simulated stuttered and nonstuttered words. It is interesting that unusual subcortical activations have also been reported in Tourette's Syndrome (TS) patients (Dermikol et al.,1999; Stern et al., 2000). A recent performance correlation study on TS (motor tics were correlated with CBF) by Stern et al. (2000) is of interest because they also found strong correlations between tic frequency and activations in the lentiform and in insula. Cerebellum activations were also prominent. However, the parallels are not complete: TS subjects (unlike stutterers) showed strong activations in Broca's area and no deactivations in the temporal lobe area.

CLINICAL IMPLICATIONS OF BRAIN IMAGING STUDIES OF STUTTERING

Given that this chapter was written for a conference on evidence-based treatment research, then it may appear that imaging research has little immediate relevance to treatment. Indeed, readers could rightfully ask; "just what contribution has brain imaging research made, or could make, to treatment?" Arguably, imaging research will have minimal clinical value if it simply used to identify abnormal stuttering-related regions and then map the changes in those regions during or after therapy. However, it will make an immense contribution if it can be used to predict therapy effects. Thus imaging studies with children (none have yet been reported) might make it possible, for example, to recognize consistent neural differences between children who recover with minimal intervention and those who require therapy to recover. A much greater payoff seems likely, however, if it becomes possible to identify an individual stuttering speaker's aberrant neural system and then tailor the speaker's treatment to modify that individual's aberrant system or systems.

Some Recent Endeavors

One attempt to integrate neuroimaging and stuttering treatment was recently reported by De Nil, Kroll, and Houle (2001). They used ^{15}O PET to monitor changes in cerebellar activation during oral reading and verb generation tasks given before, during and a year after treatment by the Precision Fluency Shaping Program (Webster, 1980). Compared with controls they reported increased cerebellar activation during reading immediately after treatment and then a decrease to near normal levels at the 1-year follow-up scan. The verb generation task showed a consistent decrease in cerebellar activation over the three scans. They concluded that the findings "suggest that automaticity in motor and cognitive processes during speech production may need to be considered as an important factor in future investigations of stuttering" (De Nil et al., 2001, p. 77). However, it is not at all clear how they could have reached that conclusion by imaging only cerebellum—or, indeed, what is to be learned about treatment from this study. The changes in cerebellar activation in this study were not linked to measures of automaticity of speech production—in fact, automaticity was not measured.

The importance of establishing the clinical significance of neural regions identified within the imaging studies is underscored by the findings from our lab. As the preceding review shows, the prominence of SMA in the Fox et al. (1996) condition contrast PET data has subsequently been found to be neither a robust nor consistent finding. This is a sobering reminder (as if that were needed) of the importance of replication studies. Why? It was the apparent prominence of SMA in the Fox et al. (1996) study that prompted a series of transcranial magnetic stimulation (TMS) studies that were designed to reduce SMA activations and, thereby, stuttering. That endeavor ultimately proved to be fruitless, although not entirely useless (see Ingham et al., 2000). However, a part of the problem in trying to locate regions that might be treatment targets is uncertainty about the parameters or characteristics of the neural systems that must be present to support both normal and abnormal speech, such as stuttering. Consider, for instance, the idea of a treatment that is directed towards correcting for the lesioned anterior insula in dyspraxia based on Dronkers's (1996) findings. If a nonlesioned anterior insula is required for normal speech production, then it could be reasonably presumed that excising the anterior insula region would produce speech deficiencies. Not necessarily, according to a report by Duffau, Bauchet, Lehericy, and Capelte (2001). They recently described surgically removing the entire dominant insula in a patient with mild dysphasia and a left insular glioma. The patient was reported to show no postoperative speech disability, and even recovered from the preoperative dysphasia. This case illustrates the brain's ability to maintain normal language without the left insula. It also suggests that neural reorganization may occur and produce systems that will preserve normal speech—and these may need to become the target of treatment activation, rather the site displaying obvious abnormalcy.

Future Directions

If the fully recovered stutterers' data in the previously described ER-fMRI study in San Antonio provides valid information about the neural regions that are and are not normalized with recovery, then what has been learned? It appears that anterior insula is not completely normalized, but the temporal lobe deactivations do seem to return to normal. It may not be too simplistic to suggest, therefore, that the abnormal temporal lobe deactivations in stutterers need to return to normalcy if recovery is to be sustained. Perhaps it is not too far fetched to suggest that procedures that require heightened self-monitoring of speech production might be favored over those that do not. Many stuttering treatments advocate the use of self-monitoring procedures, but so far no method exists for determining if that self-monitoring is occurring at a neurophysiological level. This is one area where ER-fMRI could play a useful role.

Another avenue, although less adventuresome, is to use neuroimaging to monitor therapy effects and therapy changes. One of the most exciting developments in TMS work is the combination of TMS and fMRI to identify regional connections during different speech and language tasks (e.g., Rijntjes & Weiller, 2002). The accurate aiming of the TMS "paddle" has been a problem that has taken much longer than expected to solve. However, colleagues in San Antonio have finally achieved a link between a robotic system and MRI for aiming the stimulator at precise neural locations. In principle this should make it possible to determine if therapy changes have altered neural pathways or whether they continue unchanged.

Is TMS treatment for stuttering feasible? At present the jury is out. There is some evidence that TMS can produce clinically beneficial changes in regional activations associated with depression and other disorders (Burt, Lisanby, & Sackeim, 2002; George & Belmaker, 2000). But it is not at all clear that it can be used successfully in regions associated with the temporal lobe. The ungarnished truth (as this author will attest) is that it can be extremely painful to receive TM stimulation in the superior and middle temporal lobe regions. Thus, even if rTMS was temporarily successful, it questionable as to whether patients would be able to tolerate extensive periods of stimulation in these regions.

There is one important issue within the brain imaging studies that does have relevance for evidence-based treatment research—the choice of dependent variables in studies that have been used to identify the contribution of neural systems to stuttering. A recurring argument by some theorists (Smith, 1999) and clinical researchers (Manning, 1996; Yaruss, 2001) is that measuring occurrences of stuttering behavior is not a valid indication of the status of the disorder. Undoubtedly stuttering is often accompanied by affective and even cognitive problems (Bloodstein, 1995) that, in turn, could be interpreted as reasons for the previously described variability among the imaging study findings. However, there is a also a growing pattern of consistency among the PET, MEG and ER-fMRI findings with respect to the motor and auditory regions that are appear to be functionally related to stuttering—a growing pattern that does not align with the claims that affective, behavioral and cognitive variables are essentially equivalent contributors to stuttering. The fact is that virtually all of the main imaging findings have emerged from studies in which observable stuttering has been manipulated and the resulting changes in stuttering frequency have even been shown to occur without confounding by speech rate or speech naturalness (Ingham, 2000). In fairness, the affective and cognitive variables associated with chronic stuttering have yet to be manipulated during imaging studies; conceivably they could be responsible for reports of neural differences between the "fluent" speech of stutterers and controls (Braun et al., 1997; Fox et al., 1996). However, there has been almost no dispute about the significance of the imaging findings to our understanding of the disorder, although the findings rest on measures of occurrences of stuttering. Indeed, any clinical investigation of the neurology of stuttering is destined to have little or no clinical importance unless it is clear that the changes in the neural system are associated with changes in overt stuttering behavior. In this respect, therefore, any contribution of neural imaging to stuttering treatment will, for the foreseeable future, be inextricably associated with evidence-based treatment.

Perhaps for the immediate future the most profitable treatment research avenue will be to try to bring together the best of behavioral procedures with the best of neuroscience systems. That is now being done to advantage in many areas of rehabilitation and will obviously continue (see Taub, Uswatte, & Elbert, 2002). Another exciting possibility is to find a way for CBF levels in certain regions to be fedback to the stuttering speaker so as to find ways by which the speaker can directly modify those regions. This is not an overly inspiring conclusion, but then this is only an interim report on an unfolding story—one that may yet avoid any petard hoisting.

REFERENCES

Barch, D. M., Sabb, F. W., Carter, C. S., Braver, T. S., Noll, D. C., & Cohen, J. D. (1999). Overt verbal responding during fMRI scanning: empirical investigations of problems and potential solutions. *Neuroimage, 10*, 642–657.

Bloodstein, O. (1995). *A handbook on stuttering*. San Diego: Singular Publishing Group.

Boring, E. G. (1950). *A history of experimental psychology*. New York: Appleton.

Braun, A. R., Varga, M., Stager, S., Schulz, G., Selbie, S., Maisog, J. M., Carson, R. E., & Ludlow, C. L. (1997). Altered patterns of cerebral activity during speech and language production in developmental stuttering. An $H_2^{15}O$ positron emission tomography study. *Brain, 120,* 761–784.

Brett, M., Johnsrude, I. S., & Owen, A. M. (2002). The problem of functional localization in the human brain. *Nature Reviews Neuroscience, 3,* 243–249.

Buckner, R. L., Bandettini, P. A., O'Craven, K. M., Savoy, R. L., Petersen, S. E., Raichle, M. E., & Rosen, B. R. (1996). Detection of cortical activation during averaged single trials of a cognitive task using functional magnetic resonance imaging. *Proceedings of the National Academy of Science USA, 93,* 14302–14303.

Burt, T., Lisanby, S. H., & Sackeim, H. A. (2002). Neuropsychiatric applications of transcranial magnetic stimulation: a meta analysis. *International Journal of Neuropsychopharmacology, 5,* 73–103.

Caruso, A. J. (1991). Neuromotor processes underlying stuttering. In H. F. M. Peters, W. Hulstijn, & C. W. Starkweather (Eds.) *Speech motor control and stuttering* (pp 101–116). Amsterdam: Excerpta Medica.

Catalán-Ahumada, M., Deggouj, N., De Volder, A., Melin, J., Michel, C., & Veraart, C. (1993). High metabolic activity demonstrated by positron emission tomography in human auditory cortex in case of deafness of early onset. *Brain Research, 623,* 287–292.

Chugani, H. T. (1998). A critical period of brain development: studies of cerebral glucose utilization with PET. *Preventive Medicine, 27,* 184

Chugani, H. T., Muller, R. A., & Chugani, D. C. (1996). Functional brain reorganization in children. *Brain Development, 18,* 347–356.

Curio, G., Neuloh, G., Numminen, J., Jousmaki, V., & Hari, R. (2000). Speaking modifies voice-evoked activity in the human auditory cortex. *Human Brain Mapping, 9,* 183–191.

Curlee, R. F., & Siegel, G. M. (Eds.). (1999). *Nature and treatment of stuttering.* Boston: Allyn & Bacon.

Dale, A. M., Liu, A. K., Fischl, B. R., Buckner, R. L., Belliveau, J. W., Lewine, J. D., & Halgren, E. (2000). Dynamic statistical parametric mapping: Combining fMRI and MEG for high-resolution imaging of cortical activity. *Neuron, 26,* 55–67.

De Nil, L. F., Kroll, R. M., & Houle, S. (2001). Functional neuroimaging of cerebellar activation during single word reading and verb generation in stuttering and nonstuttering adults. *Neuroscience Letters, 302,* 77–80.

De Nil, L. F., Kroll, R. M., Kapur, S., & Houle, S. (2000). A positron emission tomography study of silent and oral single word reading in stuttering and nonstuttering adults. *Journal of Speech, Language, and Hearing Research, 43,* 1038–1053.

Demirkol, A., Erdem, H., Inan, L., Yigit, A., & Guney, M. (1999). Bilateral globus pallidus lesions in a patient with Tourette syndrome and related disorders. *Biological Psychiatry, 46,* 863–867.

Démonet, J. F., Fiez, J. A., Paulesu, E., Petersen, S. E., & Zatorre, R. J. (1996). PET studies of phonological processing: A critical reply to Poeppel. *Brain and Language, 55,* 352–379.

Devinsky, O. (2000). A mind that tics. *Archives of General Psychiatry, 57,* 753.

Dhond, R. P., Buckner, R. L., Dale, A. M., Marinkovic, K., & Halgren, E. (2001). Spatiotemporal maps of brain activity underlying word generation and their modification during repetition priming. *Journal of Neuroscience, 21,* 3564–3571.

Duffau, H., Bauchet, L., Lehericy, S., & Capelle, L. (2001). Functional compensation of the left dominant insula for language. *Neuroreport, 12,* 2159

Fiez, J. A., & Petersen, S. E. (1998). Neuroimaging studies of word reading. *Proceedings of the National Academy Sciences, USA, 95,* 914–921.

Foundas, A. L., Bollich, A. M., Corey, D. M., Hurley, M., & Heilman, K. M. (2001). Anomalous anatomy of speech-language areas in adults with persistent developmental stuttering. *Neurology, 57,* 207–215.

Fox, P. T., Ingham, R. J., Ingham, J. C., Hirsch, T., Downs, J. H., Martin, C., Jerabek, P., Glass, T., & Lancaster, J. L. (1996). A PET study of the neural systems of stuttering. *Nature, 382,* 158–162.

Fox, P. T., Ingham, R. J., Ingham, J. C., Zamarripa, F., Xiong, J.-H., & Lancaster, J. (2000). Brain correlates of stuttering and syllable production: A PET performance-correlation analysis. *Brain, 123,* 1985–2004.

Fox, P. T., Lancaster, J. L., & Ingham, R. J. (1993). On stuttering and global ischemia: Interpretation and validity of findings reported by Pool et al. (1991). *Archives of Neurology, 50,* 1287–1288.

George, M. S., & Belmaker, R. H. (2000). *Transcranial magnetic stimulation (TMS) in neuropsychiatry.* New York: American Psychiatric Press.

Goldberg, G. (1985). Supplementary motor area structure and function: Review and hypotheses. *Behavioral and Brain Sciences, 8,* 567–615.

Grabowski, T. J., & Damasio, A. R. (2000). Investigating language with functional neuroimaging. In A. W. Toga & J. C. Mazziotta (Eds.), *Brain mapping: The systems* (pp. 425–461). San Diego CA: Academic Press.

Gur, R. C., Alsop, D., Glahn, D., Petty, R., Swanson, C. L., Maldjian, J. A., Turetsky, B. I., Detre, J. A., Gee, J., & Gur, R. E. (2000). An fMRI study of sex differences in regional activation to a verbal and a spatial task. *Brain and Language, 74,* 157–170.

Harasty, J., Double, K. L., Halliday, G. M., Kril, J. J., & McRitchie, D. A. (1997). Language-associated cortical regions are proportionally larger in the female brain. *Archives of Neurology, 54,* 171–176.

Hickock, G. (2001). Functional anatomy of speech perception and speech production: psycholinguistic implications. *Journal of Psycholinguist Research, 30,* 225–235.

Indefrey, P., & Levelt, W. J. M. (2000). The neural correlates of language production. In M. S. Gazzaniga (Ed.), *The new cognitive neurosciences* (2nd ed., pp. 845–866). Cambridge, MA: The MIT Press.

Ingham, R. J. (1998). On learning from speech-motor control research on stuttering. In A. K. Cordes & R. J. Ingham (Eds.), *Treatment efficacy for stuttering: A search for empirical bases* (pp. 67–101). San Diego, CA: Singular Publishing Group.

Ingham, R. J. (2001). Brain imaging studies of developmental stuttering. *Journal of Communication Disorders, 34,* 493

Ingham, R. J., Fox, P. T., Ingham, J. C., Collins, J., Pridgen, S. (2000). TMS in developmental stuttering and Tourette's Syndrome. In M. S. George and R. H. Belamker (Eds.), *Trancranial magnetic stimulation (TMS) in neuropsychiatry* (pp. 223–236). New York: American Psychiatric Press.

Ingham, R. J., Fox, P. T., Ingham, J. C., & Zamarripa, F. (2000). Is overt stuttered speech a prerequisite for the neural activations associated with chronic developmental stuttering? *Brain and Language, 75,* 163–194.

Ingham, R. J., Fox, P. T., Ingham, J. C., Zamarripa, F., Xiong, J.-H., Hardies, L. J., & Lancaster, J. L. (in press). Brain correlates of stuttering and syllable production: A gender replication. *Journal of Speech, Language and Hearing Research.*

Jaeger, J. J., Lockwood, A. H., Van Valin, R. D., Jr., Kemmerer, D. L., Murphy, B. W., & Wack, D. S. (1998). Sex difference in brain regions activated by grammatical and reading tasks. *Neuroreport, 9,* 2803.

Kircher, T. T., Brammer, M., Tous Andreu, N., Williams, S. C., & McGuire, P. K. (2001). Engagement of right temporal cortex during processing of linguistic context. *Neuropsychologia, 39,* 798–809.

Kircher, T. T., Brammer, M., Williams, S. C., & McGuire, P. K. (2000). Lexical retrieval during fluent speech production: an fMRI study. *Neuroreport, 11,* 4093–4096.

Lebrun, Y. (1998). Clinical observations and experimental research in the study of stuttering. *Journal of Fluency Disorders, 23,* 119–122.

Liepert, J., Bauder, H., Wolfgang, H. R., Miltner, W. H., Taub, E., & Weiller, C. (2000). Treatment-induced cortical reorganization after stroke in humans. *Stroke, 31,* 1210–1216.

Liotti, M., Ingham, R. J., Ingham, J. C., Kothmann, D., Perez, R., & Fox, P. T. (2001). Abnormal event-related potentials to spoken and replayed vowels in stuttering. *Neuroimage, 13,* (Part 2 Suppl.), S560.

Ludlow, C. L. (2000). Stuttering: Dysfunction in a complex and dynamic system. *Brain, 123,* 1983–1984.

Manning, W. H. (1996). *Clinical decision making in the diagnosis and treatment of fluency disorders.* Albany, NY: Delmar.

Marsden, C. D., Deecke, L., Freund, H.-J., Hallett, M., Passingham, R. E., Shibasaki, H., Tanji, J., & Wiesendanger, M. (1996). The functions of the supplementary motor area. *Advances in Neurology, 70,* 477–487.

Mimura, M., Kato, M., Kato, M., Sano, Y., Kojima, T., Naeser, M., & Kashima, H. (1998). Prospective and retrospective studies of recovery in aphasia. Changes in cerebral blood flow and language functions. *Brain, 121,* 2083–2094.

Müller, R. A., Rothermel, R. D., Behen, M. E., Muzik, O., Mangner, T. J., Chakraborty, P. K., & Chugani, H. T. (1997). Plasticity of motor organization in children and adults. *Neuroreport, 8,* 3103–3108.

Nuck, M. E., Blood, G. W., & Blood, I. M. (1987). Fluent and disfluent normal speakers' responses on a synthetic sentence identification (SSI) task. *Journal of Communication Disorders, 20,* 161.

Numminen, J., Salmelin, R., & Hari, R. (1999). Subject's own speech reduces reactivity of the human auditory cortex. *Neuroscience Letters, 265,* 119–122.

Nunez, P. L., & Silberstein, R. B. (2000). On the relationship of synaptic activity to macroscopic measurements: Does co-registration of EEG with fMRI make sense? *Brain Topography, 13,* 79–96.

Orton, S. T. (1928). A physiological theory of reading disability and stuttering in children. *New England Journal of Medicine, 199,* 1045–1052.

Palmer, E. D., Rosen, H. J., Ojemann, J. G., Buckner, R. L., Kelley, W. M., Petersen, S. E. (2001). An event-related fMRI study of overt and covert word stem completion. *Neuroimage, 14,* 182–193.

Perkins, W. H. (2002). Anomalous anatomy of speech-language areas in adults with persistent developmental stuttering. *Neurology, 58,* 332–334.

Perkins, W. H., Kent, R. D., & Curlee, R. F. (1991). A theory of neuropsycholinguistic function in stuttering. *Journal of Speech and Hearing Research, 34*, 734–752.

Petersen, S. E., Fox, P. T., Posner, M. I., & Raichle, M. E. (1988). Positron emission tomographic studies of the cortical anatomy of single word processing. *Nature, 311*, 585–589.

Poeppel, D. (1996). A critical review of PET studies of phonological processing. *Brain and Language, 55*, 317–351.

Pool, K. D., Devous, M. D., Freeman, F. J., Watson, B. C., & Finitzo, T. (1991). Regional CBF in developmental stutterers. *Archives of Neurology, 48*, 509–512.

Posner, M. I., & Raichle, M. E. (1994). *Images of mind.* New York: Scientific American Library.

Price, C. J., Warburton, E. A., Moore, C. J., Frackowiak, R. S., & Friston, K. J. (2001). Dynamic diaschisis: anatomically remote and context-sensitive human brain lesions. *Journal of Cognitive Neuroscience 13*, 419–429.

Ramsey, N. F., Sommer, I. E., Rutten, G. J., & Kahn, R. S. (2001). Combined analysis of language tasks in fMRI improves assessment of hemispheric dominance for language functions in individual subjects. *Neuroimage, 13*, 719–733.

Riecker, A., Ackermann, H., Wildgruber, D., Dogil, G., & Grodd, W. (2000). Opposite hemispheric lateralization effects during speaking and singing at motor cortex, insula and cerebellum. *Neuroreport, 11*, 1997–2000.

Rijntjes, M., & Weiller, C. (2002). Recovery of motor and language abilities after stroke: the contribution of functional imaging. *Progress in Neurobiology, 66*, 109–122.

Rosenfield, D. B., & Jerger, J. (1984). Stuttering and auditory function. In R. F. Curlee & W. H. Perkins (Eds.), *Nature and treatment of stuttering: New directions* (pp. 73–87). San Diego, CA: College-Hill Press.

Salmelin, R., Schnitzler, A., Schmitz, F., & Freund, H.-J. (2000). Single word reading in developmental stutterers and fluent speakers. *Brain, 123*, 1184–1202.

Salmelin, R., Schnitzler, A., Schmitz, F., Jäncke, L., Witte, O. W., & Freund, H.-J. (1998). Functional organization of the auditory cortex is different in stutterers and fluent speakers. *Neuroreport, 9*, 2225–2229.

Sandak, R., & Fiez, J. L. (2000). Stuttering: A view from neuroimaging. *The Lancet, 356*, 445.

Shaywitz, B. A., Shaywitz, S. E., Pugh, K. R., Constable, R. T., Skudlarski, P., Fulbright, R. K., Bronen, R. A., Fletcher, J. M., Shankweller, D. P., Katz, L., & Gore, J. C. (1995). Sex differences in the functional organization of the brain for language. *Nature, 373*, 607–609.

Silbersweig, D. A., Stern, E., Frith, C., Cahill, C., Holmes, A., Grootoonk, S., Seaward, J., McKenna, P., Chua, S. E., Schnorr, L., Jones, T., & Frackowiak, R. S. J. (1995). A functional neuroanatomy of hallucinations in schizophrenia. *Nature, 378*, 176–179.

Smith, A. (1990). Toward a comprehensive theory of stuttering: A commentary. *Journal of Speech and Hearing Disorders, 55*, 398–401.

Smith, A. (1999). Stuttering: A unified approach to a multifactorial, dynamic disorder. In N. Ratner & E. C. Healey (Eds). *Stuttering research and practice: Bridging the gap.* (pp 27–44). Mahwah, NJ: Lawrence Erlbaum Associates.

Smith, A., & Kelly, E. (1997). Stuttering: A dynamic, multifactorial model. In R. F. Curlee & G. M. Siegel (Eds.), *Nature and treatment of stuttering* (pp. 204–217). Boston: Allyn & Bacon.

Sommer, M., Koch, M. A., Paulus, W., Weiller, C., & Büchel, C. (2002). Disconnection of speech-relevant brain areas in persistent developmental stuttering. *Lancet, 360*, 380–383.

Stern, E., Silbersweig, D. A., Chee, K. Y., Holmes, A., Robertson, M. M., Trimble, M., Frith, C. D., Frackowiak, R. S., & Dolan, R. J. (2000). A functional neuroanatomy of tics in Tourette syndrome. *Archives of General Psychiatry, 57*, 741–748.

Strub, R. L., Black, F. W., & Naeser, M. A. (1987). Anomolous dominance in sibling stutterers: Evidence from CT scan asymmetries, dichotic listening, neuropsychological testing, and handedness. *Brain and Language, 30*, 338–350.

Talairach, J., & Tournoux, P. (1988). *Co-planar stereotaxic atlas of the human brain.* Verlag: Thieme Medical Publishers.

Taub, E., & Morris, D. M. (2001). Constraint-induced movement therapy to enhance recovery after stroke. *Current Atherosclerosis Reports, 3*, 279–286.

Taub, E., Uswatte, G., & Elbert, T. (2002). New treatments in neurorehabilitation founded on basic research, *Neuroscience Reviews, 3*, 228–236.

Travis, L. E. (1931). *Speech pathology.* New York: D. Appleton.

Travis, L. E. (1978). The cerebral dominance theory of stuttering: 1931–1978. *Journal of Speech and Hearing Disorders, 43*, 278–281.

Vallar, G., Perani, D., Cappa, S. F., Messa, C., Lenzi, G. L., & Fazio, F. (1988). Recovery from aphasia and neglect after subcortical stroke: Neuropsychological and cerebral perfusion study. *Journal of Neurology, Neurosurgery and Psychiatry, 51*, 1269–1276.

Walsh, F. M. R. (1947). On the role of the pyramidal system in willed movement. *Brain, 70*, 329

Wanet-Defalque, M. C., Veraart, C., De Volder, A., Metz, R., Michel, C., Dooms, G., & Goffinet, A. (1988). High metabolic activity in the visual cortex of early blind human subjects. *Brain Research, 446*, 369–373.

Webster, R. L. (1980). *The precision fluency shaping program: Speech reconstruction for stutters* (Clinician's program guide). Roanoke, VA: Communication Development Corporation.

Webster, W. G. (1988). Neural mechanisms underlying stuttering: Evidence from bimanual handwriting performance. *Brain and Language, 33*, 226.

Webster, W. G. (1993). Hurried hands and tangled tongues. In E. Boberg (Ed.), *Neuropsychology of stuttering* (pp. 73–127). Edmonton, Canada: The University of Alberta Press.

Webster, W. G. (1998). Brain models and the clinical management of stuttering. *Journal of Speech-Language Pathology and Audiology, 22*, 220–230.

Weiller, C., & Rijntjes, M. (1999). Learning, plasticity, and recovery in the central nervous system. *Experimental Brain Research, 128*, 134–138.

White, T., O'Leary, D., Magnotta, V., Arndt, S., Flaum, M., & Andreasen, N. C. (2001). Anatomic and functional variability: the effects of filter size in group fMRI data analysis. *Neuroimage, 13*, 577–588.

Wood, F., Stump, D., McKeehan, A., Sheldon, S., & Proctor, J. (1980). Patterns of regional cerebral blood flow during attempted reading aloud by stutterers both on and off haloperidol medication: Evidence for inadequate left frontal activation during stuttering. *Brain and Language, 9*, 141–144.

Wu, J. C., Maguire, G., Riley, G., Fallon, J., LaCase, L., Chin, S., Klein, E., Tang, C., Cadwell, S., & Lottenberg, S. (1995). A positron emission tomography (F-18) de-oxyglucose study of developmental stuttering. *Neuroreport, 6,* 501–505.

Yairi, E., & Ambrose, N. (1999) Early childhood stuttering I: Persistence and recovery rates. *Journal of Speech, Language, and Hearing Research, 42,* 1097.

Yairi, E., Ambrose, N., & Cox, N. (1996). Genetics of stuttering—a critical review. *Journal of Speech and Hearing Research, 39,* 771–784.

Yaruss, J. S. (2001). Evaluating treatment outcomes for adults who stutter. *Journal of Communication Disorders, 34,* 163.

Zimmermann, G. (1980). Stuttering: A disorder of movement. *Journal of Speech and Hearing Research, 23,* 122–136.

AUTHOR'S NOTE

This chapter is based on a paper first presented at the 2002 University of Georgia State of the Art Conference on evidence-based treatment of stuttering.

4

The Demands and Capacities Model: Implications for Evidence-Based Practice in the Treatment of Early Stuttering

Ann Packman
Mark Onslow
The University of Sydney

Joseph Attanasio
Montclair State University

There is little doubt that theories have played a significant role in the development of treatments for stuttering (see Siegel & Ingham, 1987). Because the cause of stuttering is unknown, a theoretical explanation suggests how it might be managed. To give an extreme example, a surgical procedure in which part of the tongue was removed was adopted in the nineteenth century because it was believed that stuttering was caused by spasm of the tongue muscles (see Van Riper, 1973). Thankfully—and perhaps this is an early example of the triumph of evidence over theory—this procedure was short lived. Other causal theories of stuttering have suggested quite different forms of clinical intervention, such as changing parental behavior. The diagnosogenic theory (Johnson & Associates, 1959), for example, proposed that stuttering is caused by parents labeling normal disfluencies as stuttering. For decades afterwards, the belief that drawing attention to a child's speech was harmful was the cornerstone of the management of stuttering in early childhood. Again, the popularity of this treatment approach finally waned, largely in response to the decline in support for Johnson's diagnosogenic theory but also because evidence for the success of the intervention prompted by it was not forthcoming (see Bloodstein, 1993).

Currently, the influence of theory on treatment for adults who stutter appears to be minimal (Siegel, 1998). However, the literature suggests that the management of stuttering in young children is still predominantly theory driven (Logan & Caruso, 1997). Specifically, the theoretical perspective that drives much current treatment for young children is that stuttering is a multifactorial disorder.

Multifactorial models describe stuttering as the result of a combination of a number of innate and environmental factors. In their strongest form, multifactorial models maintain that any combination of a range of innate and environmental factors may cause stuttering and that the combination of causal factors is different in each person. Further, according to these models, it is not necessary for any of the factors, of themselves, to be pathological or abnormal (e.g., see Smith & Kelly, 1987). The factors simply interact in unique ways to cause stuttering. In short, proponents of this type of multifactorial model maintain that the innate and environmental factors are together necessary—but neither is sufficient—for a child to begin stuttering (Conture, 1990), and no one factor in either domain is either necessary or sufficient for the condition to occur (Zebrowski & Cilek, 1997).

Multifactorial models of stuttering have risen to prominence over the past decade or more, to the extent that there is even a view among some current writers that this view of stuttering is indisputable (e.g., see Cook & Rustin, 1997; Smith & Kelly, 1997; Zebrowski & Cilek, 1997). It has been argued that dissatisfaction with previous theories and models of stuttering was instrumental in this rise to prominence because they looked for purely physical or purely environmental factors to account for stuttering (Adams, 1990) and failed to account for the variability and unpredictability of stuttering (Smith & Kelly, 1997). However, we have argued elsewhere that all this does not necessarily mean that stuttering has many causes and that these causes must be different in each person (Attanasio, 1999, 2000; Attanasio, Onslow, & Packman, 1998).

Of course, there is no doubt that stuttering is multidimensional and that a number of factors impact on its appearance and severity. Perhaps this is what protagonists of multifactorial models find so appealing about them. However, there is nothing revolutionary about viewing stuttering as multidimensional, and indeed it has been characterized in this way for some time (e.g., see Homzie & Lindsay, 1984; Van Riper, 1971). However, it is not necessary to invoke multiple and varied causes to explain the fact that stuttering varies in severity across individuals and across situations and that its topography is different in each affected person. This is returned to later in the discussion of the Demands and Capacities model, which is a prominent example of multifactorial models of early stuttering.

THE DEMANDS AND CAPACITIES MODEL

The Demands and Capacities (DC) model has been developed over a number of years (see Adams, 1990; Gottwald & Starkweather, 1995; Starkweather, 1987, 1997; Starkweather & Givens-Ackerman, 1997; Starkweather & Gottwald, 1990; Starkweather, Gottwald, & Halfond, 1990) and is reported to have evolved in response to various writings on interactions between genetics and the environment (see Starkweather & Gottwald, 2000). The DC model is intended to explain stuttering in young children, stating that children stutter when their capacity for fluent speech is insufficient to meet demands to produce it.

According to early reports of the DC model, a child's capacity for fluency depends on developmental levels of speech motor control, language development, social and emotional functioning, and cognitive development. Demands on those capacities may arise within the child or in the external environment, or both, and include time pressure and innate and environmental pressure to use increasingly more complex language, high levels of excitement and anxiety, and parental demands for increased cognitive functioning. As described, according to the DC model these demands and capacities may exist in any configuration, and it is not necessary for the child to have a deficit in capacity or for there to be excessive demands on that capacity (Adams, 1990). For example, Starkweather and Givens-Ackerman (1997) stated that at the time of onset for most children with "garden variety" (p. 55) stuttering: "nothing unusual is happening in the child's environment; the stuttering seems to develop without warning and with no environmental events—stress or excitement—that could account for it" (p. 55).

According to the DC model, then, it is simply the unique combination of factors in each child, whether aberrant or not, that causes that child to stutter.

Starkweather (1997) has said that the DC model is not a causal model but is intended simply as a framework for positioning the knowledge we have about stuttering. However, the model does in fact provide a causal explanation for stuttering (see Ingham & Cordes, 1997). For example, in discussing the unique combination of factors proposed by the DC model, Starkweather and Givens-Ackerman (1997) state, "there is no single etiology, but as many etiologies as there are stories of stuttering development" (p. 24).

A forum devoted the DC model in a recent edition of Journal of Fluency Disorders (see Bernstein Ratner, 2000; Curlee, 2000; Kelly, 2000; Manning, 2000a, 2000b; Siegel, 2000; Starkweather & Gottwald, 2000; Yaruss, 2000) is a testament to the widespread acceptance of the model. The forum was initiated by Siegel, who raised concerns about the logical consistency of the model and the use of the term *capacity for fluency*. This concern was echoed to some extent by almost all the respondents. It was surprising, then, that all respondents still concluded that the model has merit and none formed the opinion that it should be rejected.

However, there have been previous criticisms of the DC model (e.g., see Bernstein Ratner, 1997; Ingham & Cordes, 1997; Karniol, 1995). Again, these criticisms have focused on the internal logic of the model. Ingham and Cordes pointed out, with an illustration, that the reasoning in the model is faulty because it involves the logical fallacy known as *affirming the consequent*. Making a similar point, Karniol argued that the reasoning of the model is circular, and concluded that "any model that suffers from circularity is unlikely to prove scientifically useful in the long run" (p. 111). The reasoning in the DC model then, can be seen as faulty, and as simply a restatement—albeit an elegant one—of the problem. It is self-evident that every time a child stutters, the demands for fluency are greater than the child's capacity to produce it. Otherwise the child would not stutter. The DC model does not provide any understanding of why children actually stutter in response to what are purported to be excessive communicative demands. Why, for example, do such demands result in repeated movements and fixed postures of the speech mechanism, and not some other type of verbal behavior? Adams (1990) appears to have addressed this issue. According to Adams, "fluency more than any other developing skills, is vulnerable to disorganization. Being more vulnerable, fluency is the proverbial weak link in the child's behavioral repertoire" (p. 139) and "the demands are specific to speech and over-ride capacities that are integral to fluent speech production" (p. 139). Again, however, the argument here is circular because it says that children stutter because demands are greater than capacity. Further, saying that fluency is prone to disorganization explains nothing about the mechanisms that might be operating at the moment of stuttering.

These objections to the logic of the DC model are raised here because they have considerable implications for the management of early stuttering. If one accepts that the logic of a model or theory is flawed, then it would seem imprudent, at best, to use it as a basis for treatment. Of course, it is important to be cautious here because a treatment may be effective, despite being based on a faulty model, for reasons that are not apparent. The following sections, outline the treatment for early stuttering driven by the DC model and investigate the extent to which it is supported by evidence.

TREATMENT BASED ON THE DEMANDS AND CAPACITIES MODEL

If one accepts the DC model as an explanation of stuttering, then it is logical to attempt in treatment to decrease demands for fluency or increase capacity for fluency, or both (see Gottwald & Starkweather, 1995, 1999; Starkweather,

1997; Starkweather & Givens-Ackerman, 1997; Starkweather & Gottwald, 1993; Starkweather, Gottwald, & Halfond, 1990). The treatment driven by the DC model is known as the Multiprocess Stuttering Prevention and Early Intervention Program (see Gottwald & Starkweather, 1999). As stated by Starkweather and Givens-Ackerman (1997), the goals of this treatment are to:

> increase the child's capacities in the motor, language, emotional, and cognitive areas, or let nature increase them through development, while at the same time reducing the demands of the child's communicative environment through counseling and training the child's parents, siblings, teachers, day care workers and others who have an influence on the child. (p. 105)

Specific strategies to reduce demands in the child's environment include "changing a number of different parental behaviors, such as rate of speech, number of questions, number of interruptions, and negative verbal and nonverbal reactions to stuttering behaviors" (Starkweather & Gottwald, 1993, p. 55). Treatment directed at the child includes "reduction of negative reactions to disfluency, use of the speech mechanism with reduced muscular tension, slower rate of speaking, simpler language, the use of normal nonfluency behaviors, and more appropriate turn-taking" (Starkweather & Gottwald, 1993, p. 55).

According to Starkweather and Gottwald (1993), the importance of internal and external variables differs in each child. Thus, in order to plan and implement DC-based treatment, clinicians must (a) hypothesize about the extent of each child's capacities and then address any of them that they think contribute to the child's stuttering; and (b) hypothesize about the extent of the demands placed on those capacities and have families and other people in the child's environment change various aspects of their daily life and communicative style. According to Starkweather and Gottwald (1993) hypotheses about environmental variables should be "systematically tested" (p. 55) at the start of treatment. After deciding that a factor may be relevant for a particular child, the clinician investigates whether the child's stuttering varies when that factor varies. If this is not immediately apparent, the clinician introduces a trial period of treatment to see if this has an ameliorative effect. If it doesn't, this presumably indicates that this variable, or this variable in combination with other variables, is not important in that child. Because the DC model states that the combination of variables causing or contributing to stuttering is different in each child, it would seem that the clinician is then placed in the rather unenviable position of having to continue treating the child by addressing other variables, or combinations of variables, until something works.

There are reports that children achieve normal fluency after this treatment (e.g., see Gottwald & Starkweather, 1999; Starkweather et al., 1990;

Starkweather & Gottwald, 1993). However, there are no outcome data to support these reports. Although measures of discontinuous speech time were apparently made before and after the intervention described by Starkweather and Gottwald (1993), only the pretreatment measures were reported.

In any event, the value of having parents change their communicative style, which is a major component of multiprocess treatment, has been seriously questioned recently (see Bernstein Ratner & Silverman, 2000; Miles & Bernstein Ratner, 2001; Wilkenfeld & Curlee, 1997). Bernstein Ratner and Silverman reported that parents of young children who stutter do not appear to have unrealistic perceptions of their children's communicative abilities, and Miles and Bernstein Ratner found that the linguistic input of parents of stuttering children was appropriate to the children's levels of language development. Importantly, the children in these two studies were all within 3 months of onset of stuttering. This is particularly relevant here because the findings provide no support for advising parents of stuttering children to reduce linguistic complexity. Such advice may even be contra-indicated for some children (Miles & Bernstein Ratner) because it results in parents reducing the very communicative behaviors that are known to contribute to linguistic development (Bernstein Ratner & Silverman).

Further, it appears that adults' questioning does not have a deleterious effect on young children's stuttering. Wilkenfield and Curlee (1997) conducted single-subject experiments to compare the effects of parental questioning and parental commenting. They found no differences in stuttering in these two conditions, in three preschool-age stuttering children. This finding provides no support for advising parents of stuttering children to ask fewer questions of them. Wilkenfeld and Curlee concluded that "more research is needed if the efficacy of clinical management tactics now used with many young stuttering children are to meet the standards currently expected of professional service providers" (p. 88).

In referring to the lack of empirical support for DC-based treatment, Manning (2000b) said "we tend to employ these techniques during treatment with children because they tend to work" (p. 379). If this statement is true, it is unfortunately at odds with the commitment within speech-language pathology to evidence-based practice (see Logemann, 2000). The cornerstone of evidence-based practice is that the clinician relies on scientific evidence rather than opinion when attempting to answer questions about clients and treatment (Worrall & Bennett, 2001).

So far, this discussion has covered the weaknesses of the logic of the DC model and the lack of supportive evidence for DC-based treatment. We now turn to evidence that in fact poses a direct threat to the DC model: namely, that a number of experimental and treatment studies have shown that stuttering may in fact reduce in the face of procedures that increase, rather than decrease, demands for fluency. This is discussed in the following.

INCREASING "DEMANDS FOR FLUENCY": EXPERIMENTAL AND TREATMENT DATA

Extensive experimental evidence has shown that stuttering may decrease in both children and adults in response to reinforcement for increases in fluency (for reviews of operant research findings see Ingham, 1984; Prins & Hubbard, 1987). The success of these procedures in reducing stuttering has underpinned the development of a number of operant treatments for stuttering. The important point here, in terms of the current discussion, is that treatments for early stuttering that are based on operant procedures are diametrically opposed to the procedures suggested by the DC model. Three prominent examples are Extended Length of Utterance (ELU, see Costello Ingham, 1999); The Monterey Fluency Program (see Ryan & van Kirk Ryan, 1999), and the Lidcombe Program (see Onslow, Packman, & Harrison, 2003). Being operant in nature, these three treatments convey to the child an expectation that they speak without stuttering. To illustrate this, a brief overview is presented of one with which we have been associated, namely the Lidcombe Program.

The Lidcombe Program

The Lidcombe Program for early stuttering (see Harrison & Onslow, 1999; Onslow & Packman, 1999; Onslow et al., 2003) has been developed over the past 12 years. The program manual is available from the Web site of the Australian Stuttering Research Center.

In the Lidcombe Program parents provide treatment each day in the child's natural environment. Parents learn how to do this during weekly visits with the child to the speech-language pathologist. Treatment consists of parental verbal contingencies for stutter-free speech and for stuttering. Contingencies for stutter-free speech consist of (a) acknowledging that stutter-free speech has occurred, for example, "There were no bumpy words," (b) praising stutter-free speech, for example, "Great, you said that smoothly," and (c) requesting self-evaluation, for example, "Did you hear any stutters?" Contingencies for stuttering consist of (a) acknowledging stuttering, for example, "I heard a stutter that time" and (b) requesting self-correction, for example, "Try that again smoothly." At the start of the program, treatment occurs for a period each day during structured conversations, for example while the parent and child are engaging in an activity that allows the parent to control the conversational exchange. Later in the program the parent gives the verbal contingencies during unstructured conversations at various times during the day. The child is not instructed to change speech production in any way and language output is not addressed. It is true that parent–child conversational exchanges are structured in the early part of the program, but this occurs only so the parent can give the contingencies safely. The treatment is conducted in two stages. Stage 1 is complete when stuttering is at a low level or is no longer present, both inside and outside the clinic. The goal of Stage 2 is to maintain this low level over a year or more.

Research data for the program indicate that stuttering in preschool-age children is eliminated, or almost eliminated, after this treatment (Lincoln & Onslow, 1997; Onslow, Andrews, & Lincoln, 1994; Onslow, Costa, & Rue, 1990). A recent clinical report presents data on 250 children who participated successfully in the program in Australia (Jones, Onslow, Harrison, & Packman, 2000). These clinic data have been replicated in clinics the United Kingdom (Hayhow, Kingston, & Ledzion, 1998: Kingston, Huber, Onslow, Jones, & Packman, 2003) and Canada (Shenker, see chap. 5, this volume). The efficacy of the Lidcombe Program is yet to be established, however, there is growing evidence that the reductions in stuttering that occur with the program are due primarily to the treatment rather than to other factors, such as natural recovery (see Harris, Onslow, Packman, Harrison, & Menzies, 2002; Onslow & Packman, 2001).

DISCUSSION

The problem to be solved here is that the most widely used theoretical model of children's stuttering does not seem able to explain a substantial body of experimental and clinical evidence with children who stutter. This evidence indicates that stuttering can decrease in the face of procedures that demand more fluency than the child is currently producing.

The Lidcombe Program, for example, clearly imposes demands on the child to speak without stuttering. Indeed, that is the essence of the treatment. The parent draws the child's attention to stuttering in everyday speaking situations, conveys to the child that he or she should try to speak without stuttering, and reinforces stutter-free speech when the child produces it. This approach is diametrically opposed to that of DC-based treatment, which advocates reducing demands for fluency rather than increasing them. Further, children stop stuttering in the face of these increased demands without any apparent increase, in the terminology of the DC model, in capacity for fluency. The program does not incorporate any of the procedures that Starkweather and colleagues suggested increase capacity, and preliminary research indicates that there is no reason to think that children achieve stutter-free speech by adopting an unusual way of talking (Lincoln, Onslow, & Reed, 1997; Onslow, Stocker, Packman, & McCleod, 2002) or because the children and their parents change the way they use language (Bonelli, Dixon, Bernstein Ratner, & Onslow, 2000). Also, capacity for fluency presumably does not increase through maturation, as children take only a median of 11 weekly clinic sessions to complete Stage 1 of the program (Jones et al., 2000). Yet, the DC model predicts that capacity must be greater than demands after treatment because the children are not stuttering. According to the DC model, children stutter when demands are greater than capacity and the logical converse of this is that if a child does not stutter, or no longer stutters, then capacity is greater than—or equal to—demands.

Thus, in trying to interpret the Lidcombe Program evidence in terms of the DC model we are left with a conundrum: The program does not employ any of the procedures that are supposed to increase capacity, yet, in the terminology of the DC model, capacity must increase during the program to accommodate the increased demands for fluency that are inherent in it. If capacity had not increased, given that demands clearly increase, then, according to the DC model the Lidcombe Program would cause children to stutter more, not less.

This conundrum calls for resolution, and the resolution lies in the elusive definition of capacity for fluency. In the recent forum on the DC model Siegel (2000) argued that the term is vacuous, as capacity for a behavior can only be identified with reference to the performance of that behavior. According to Siegel:

> If capacity is nothing more than an inference drawn from observed speech behavior, nothing new is learned by including capacities in the model and the clinician is caught up in circular reasoning, using speech behavior to infer capacity, and then using capacity to explain the behavior. (p. 323)

In their response to Siegel (2000), Starkweather and Gottwald (2000) asserted that capacity for fluency is not identified in relation to the fluency of a child's speech. For example, they said that the slower reaction times observed in stutterers are an indication of reduced capacity for fluency. They also argued that capacity for fluency includes "adequate speech motor control to coarticulate smoothly, rapidly, and with minimal effort" (p. 370). Consequently, "it is not circular to measure a child's speech rate, and to infer, if it is unusually slow, that he may lack one or more of the speech motor skills that underlie fluency" (p. 371).

Further, in relation to impaired word finding:

> Nor is it circular ... to conclude that the extra time taken up by the child during this process makes it a little more likely that he might, through reacting to time pressure, begin to struggle in speaking. The same could be said of any of the assessments of capacity. If the literature shows that a certain skill is associated with fluent speech production, clinicians are well advised on empirical as well as logical grounds, to assess that skill and to see if therapy can be planned in such a way as to increase it. (p. 371)

The reasoning here seems to suggest that in order to increase a stuttering child's capacity for fluency, therapy should seek to increase skills that are prerequisites for fluent speech. However, this argument is flawed, as stuttering is not the converse—or counterpart—of fluent speech (Finn & Ingham, 1989). Examples are needed to illustrate this point. A child with dysarthric speech resulting from cerebral palsy obviously has a deficit in speech motor control, and will speak slowly but will not necessarily stutter. As far as we know, the child will not be more at risk of stuttering, despite the considerable demands, such as time pressure, that are likely to be placed upon the child's communication. According to Starkweather and Gottwald's (2000) definition of *capacity* this child has reduced capacity for fluent speech. However, although the child's speech is dysfluent, it is not dysfluent in the way that stuttered speech is dysfluent. Nor will a child who has impaired word finding necessarily stutter, or be at increased risk of stuttering. Watkins, Yairi, and Ambrose (1999) found that 84 children who stuttered scored near or above developmental expectations for expressive language when compared with normative data. If word finding difficulties increase the likelihood of stuttering, then Watkins et al. should have found a higher incidence of expressive language problems in children who stutter. To illustrate the argument again, according to Starkweather and Gottwald a child with word finding problems has reduced capacity for fluency. However, again, although this child's speech is dysfluent, it is not dysfluent in the way that stuttered speech is dysfluent. Many factors, including language proficiency and an intact motor system, underpin fluent speech. Impairment of any of those factors will contribute to dysfluent speech, but not necessarily to stuttering. In other words, it is not logical to argue that an impairment in any of the processes known to underpin fluent speech causes—or is even related to—stuttering. In truth, it is simply not known what causes stuttering. It is also not logical to argue that stuttering therapy should necessarily aim to improve a process simply because it underpins fluent speech.

Interestingly, at the conclusion of their response to Siegel's criticism of the DC model, Starkweather and Gottwald (2000) explained that the inclusion of "skills" in their conceptualization of "capacity for fluency" is a recent development "capacities" does indeed suggest something inherent, and perhaps static, and in the beginning we were thinking of inherent traits, and so came to use the term "capacity." Later, as we expanded the model, we came to see capacities more as skills that could be learned or modified" (p. 374).

We can conclude from this, then, that capacity for fluency may now be a static trait, or it may be a skill that can be learned or modified, or both. The addition of skills to the concept of capacity, however, only serves to compound the problems encountered in attempting to define it. Capacity for fluency can not be defined in a way that renders it measurable because it can apparently mean many things and, in any event, it is purported to be different in each child. In the absence of an operational definition, then, capacity for fluency is simply a mentalistic construct.

The fact that capacity for fluency can not be defined operationally means that the DC model can accommodate any findings that appear at first blush to contradict it. This means that the model can never be shown to be false. As far as treatment goes, for example, it can be argued from the perspective of the DC model that the Lidcombe data are not in fact a challenge because capacity for fluency increases during the program as children learn the skills needed for fluent speech. Although this is a beguiling and apparently common sense explanation, the logic is still circular: It simply says that children no longer stutter because they have learned the skills they need to speak without stuttering. And of course, this is what we would expect from a treatment that is based on the principles of behavior therapy.

In fact, it seems that any treatment that reduces stuttering can be seen as supporting the DC model. It can be said of any treatment that works that it reduces demands, or increases capacities, including the skills required to speak without stuttering, or both. Given Starkweather and Gottwald's (2000) most recent pronouncement on what is meant by capacity for fluency, it is impossible to think of a treatment, or an observation, or indeed even an experiment, that could prove the DC model wrong. Any theory or model that can never be wrong is scientifically untenable. There are countless theories and models of stuttering in the literature that, similarly, can not be proved wrong, and they can not all be right (see Packman, Menzies, & Onslow, 2000).

The fact that there are weaknesses in the logic of the DC model does not necessarily mean that DC-based treatment is not, or could never be, effective. Considering the apparently widespread use of this treatment, evidence of its effectiveness would be most welcome, although it is difficult to see how efficacy could be investigated scientifically, given that treatment is different for each child and so is not replicable. But perhaps such evidence may never even be sought, given that the developer of the DC model has argued strongly that the effectiveness of stuttering therapy is not a matter that can be addressed by science (Starkweather, 1999).

However, it is entirely possible to measure treatment outcomes scientifically. Of course, establishing efficacy is difficult and time-consuming and clinical trials are probably most appropriately conducted by research teams that have access to the requisite resources. Nonetheless, as Wilkenfeld and Curlee (1997) pointed out, more scientific studies are needed if a solid evidence base to support our interventions in speech-language pathology is to be built. Unsubstantiated reports of efficacy and statements that a particular treatment tends to work (Manning, 2002b) are not sufficient justification for implementing a treatment.

The task of collecting evidence in support of treatments for early stuttering has only just begun. While waiting for the results of clinical trials, however, a commitment to evidence-based practice means that the speech-language pathologist will seek out all the available evidence for a particular treatment, before implementing it. This can be a laborious process (see Worrall & Bennett, 2001) but ultimately will be a profitable one for our profession.

REFERENCES

Adams, M. (1990). The demands and capacities model I: Theoretical elaborations. *Journal of Fluency Disorders, 15*, 135–141.

Attanasio, J. (1999). Treatment of early stuttering: Some reflections. In M. Onslow & A. Packman (Eds.), *The handbook of early stuttering intervention* (pp. 189–203). San Diego, CA: Singular Publishing Group.

Attanasio, J. (2000). Where is the gap? A diverse view of stuttering and stuttering research. In R. J. Sternberg (Ed.), *APA review of books* (pp. 53–55). Washington, DC: American Psychological Association.

Attanasio, J., Onslow, M., & Packman, A. (1998). Representativeness reasoning and the search for the origins of stuttering: A return to basic observations. *Journal of Fluency Disorders, 23*, 265–277.

Bernstein Ratner, N. (1997). Linguistic behaviors at the onset of stuttering. In W. Hulstijn, H. F. M. Peters, & P. H. H. M. van Lieshout (Eds.), *Speech production: Motor control, brain research, and fluency disorders* (pp. 585–593). Amsterdam: Elsevier Science.

Bernstein Ratner, N. (2000). Performance or capacity, the model still requires definitions and boundaries it doesn't have. *Journal of Fluency Disorders, 25*, 337–348.

Bernstein Ratner, N., & Silverman, S. (2000). Parental perceptions of childrens' communicative development at stuttering onset. *Journal of Speech, Language, and Hearing Research, 43*, 1252–1263.

Bloodstein, O. (1993). *Stuttering: The search for a cause and a cure*. Needham Heights, MA: Allyn & Bacon.

Bonelli, P., Dixon, M., Bernstein Ratner, N., & Onslow, M. (2000). Child and parent speech and language and the Lidcombe Program of early stuttering intervention. *Clinical Linguistics and Phonetics, 14*, 427–446.

Conture, E. G. (1990). *Stuttering* (2nd ed.). Englewood Cliffs, NJ: Prentice Hall.

Cook, F., & Rustin, L. (1997). Commentary on the Lidcombe Programme of early stuttering intervention. *European Journal of Communication Disorders, 32*, 250–258.

Costello Ingham, J. (1999). Behavioral treatment of young children who stutter: An extended length of utterance method. In R. F. Curlee (Ed.), *Stuttering and related disorders of fluency* (2nd ed., pp. 80–109). New York: Thieme.

Curlee, R. F. (2000). Demands and capacities versus demands and performance. *Journal of Fluency Disorders, 25*, 329–336.

Finn, P., & Ingham, R. J. (1989). The selection of "fluent" samples in research on stuttering: Conceptual and methodological considerations. *Journal of Speech and Hearing Research, 32*, 401–418.

Gottwald, S. R., & Starkweather, C. W. (1995). Fluency intervention for preschoolers and their families in the public schools. *Language, Speech, and Hearing Services in Schools, 26*, 117–126.

Gottwald, S., & Starkweather, C. W. (1999). Stuttering prevention and early intervention: A multiprocess approach. In M. Onslow & A. Packman (Eds.), *Handbook of early stuttering intervention* (pp. 53–82). San Diego, CA: Singular Publishing Group.

Harris, V., Onslow, O., Packman, A., Harrison, E., & Menzies, R. (2002). An experimental investigation of the impact of the Lidcombe Program on early stuttering. *Journal of Fluency Disorders, 27,* 203–214.

Harrison, E., & Onslow, M. (1999). Early intervention for stuttering: The Lidcombe Program. In R. F. Curlee (Ed.), *Stuttering and related disorders of fluency* (2nd ed., pp. 65–79). New York: Thieme.

Hayhow, R., Kingston, M., & Ledzion, R. (1998). The use of clinical measures in the Lidcombe Programme for children who stutter. *International Journal of Language and Communication Disorders, 33,* 364–369.

Homzie, M. J., & Lindsay, J. S. (1984). Language and the young stutterer: A new look at old theories and findings. *Brain and Language, 22,* 232–252.

Ingham, R. J. (1984). *Stuttering and behavior therapy: Current status and experimental foundations.* San Diego, CA: College-Hill.

Ingham, R. J., & Cordes, A. K. (1997). Self-measurement and evaluating stuttering treatment efficacy. In R. F. Curlee & G. M. Siegel (Eds.), *Nature and treatment of stuttering: New directions* (2nd ed., pp. 413–437). San Diego, CA: Singular Publishing Group.

Johnson, W., & Associates. (1959). *The onset of stuttering.* Minneapolis, MN: University of Minnesota Press.

Jones, M., Onslow, M., Harrison, E., & Packman, A. (2000). Treating stuttering in young children: Predicting treatment time with the Lidcombe Program. *Journal of Speech, Language and Hearing Research, 43,* 1440–1450.

Karniol, R. (1995). Stuttering, language, and cognition: A review and a model of stuttering as suprasegmental sentence plan alignment (SPA). *Psychological Bulletin, 117,* 104–124.

Kelly, E. M. (2000). Modeling stuttering etiology: Clarifying levels of description and measurement. *Journal of Fluency Disorders, 25,* 359–368.

Kingston, M., Huber, A., Onslow, M., Jones, M., & Packman, A. (2003). Predicting treatment time with the Lidcombe Program: Replication and meta-analysis. *International Journal of Language and Communication Disorders, 30,* 165–177.

Lincoln, M., & Onslow, M. (1997). Long-term outcome of an early intervention for stuttering: The Lidcombe Program. *American Journal of Speech-Language Pathology, 6,* 51–58.

Lincoln, M. A., Onslow, M., & Reed, V. (1997). Social validity of the treatment outcomes of an early intervention program for stuttering. *American Journal of Speech-Language Pathology, 6,* 77–84.

Logan, K., & Caruso, A. J. (1997). Parents as partners in the treatment of childhood stuttering. *Seminars in Speech and Language, 18,* 309–327.

Logemann, J. A., (2000, March 14). What is evidence-based practice and why should we care? *ASHA Leader, 3.*

Manning, W. H. (2000a). The demands and capacities model. *Journal of Fluency Disorders, 25,* 317–319.

Manning, W. H. (2000b). Appeal of the demands and capacities model: Conclusions. *Journal of Fluency Disorders, 25,* 377–383.

Miles, S., & Bernstein Ratner, N. (2001). Parental language input to children at stuttering onset. *Journal of Speech, Language, and Hearing Research, 44,* 1116–1130.

Onslow, M. (2003). Verbal response-contingent stimulation. In M. Onslow, A. Packman, & E. Harrison (Eds.), *The Lidcombe Program of early stuttering intervention: A
clinician's guide* (pp. 71–79). Austin, TX: Pro-Ed.

Onslow, M., Andrews, C., & Lincoln, M. (1994). A control/experimental trial of an
operant treatment for early stuttering. *Journal of Speech and Hearing Research, 37,*
1244–1259.

Onslow, M., Costa, L., & Rue, S. (1990). Direct early intervention with stuttering:
Some preliminary data. *Journal of Speech and Hearing Disorders, 55,* 405–416.

Onslow, M., & Packman, A. (1999). The Lidcombe Program of early stuttering intervention. In N. Bernstein Ratner & E. C. Healy (Eds.), *Treatment and research:
Bridging the gap* (pp. 193–209). Mahwah, NJ: Lawrence Erlbaum Associates.

Onslow, M., & Packman, A. (2001). The Lidcombe Program of early stuttering intervention: Awaiting the results of a randomised controlled trial. *Asia Pacific Journal
of Speech, Language, and Hearing, 6,* 85–89.

Onslow, M., Packman, A., & Harrison, E. (2003). *The Lidcombe Program for early stuttering intervention: A clinicians' guide.* Austin, TX: Pro-Ed.

Onslow, M., Stocker, S., Packman, A., & McLeod, S. (2002). Speech timing in children
after the Lidcombe Program of early stuttering intervention. *Clinical Linguistics
and Phonetics, 16,* 21–33.

Packman, A., Menzies, R. G., & Onslow, M. (2000). Anxiety and the anticipatory
struggle hypothesis. *American Journal of Speech-Language Pathology, 9,* 88–89.

Prins, D., & Hubbard, C. P. (1988). Response contingent stimuli and stuttering: Issues and implications. *Journal of Speech and Hearing Research, 31,* 696–709.

Ryan, B., & van Kirk Ryan, B. (1999). The Monterey Fluency Program. In M. Onslow
& A. Packman (Eds.), *Handbook of early stuttering intervention* (pp. 170–188). San
Diego, CA: Singular Publishing Group.

Siegel, G. M. (1998). Stuttering: Theory, research and therapy. In A. K. Cordes & R. J.
Ingham (Eds.), *Treatment efficacy for stuttering: A search for empirical bases* (pp.
103–114). San Diego, CA: Singular Publishing Group.

Siegel, G. M. (2000). Demands and capacities or demands and performance? *Journal
of Fluency Disorders, 25,* 321–327.

Siegel, G., & Ingham, R. J. (1987). Theory and science in communication disorders.
Journal of Speech and Hearing Disorders, 52, 99–104.

Smith, A., & Kelly, E. (1997). Stuttering: A dynamic, multifactorial model. In R. F.
Curlee & G. M. Siegel (Eds.), *Nature and treatment of stuttering: New directions* (2nd
ed., pp. 204–217). Boston: Allyn & Bacon.

Starkweather, C. W. (1987). *Fluency and stuttering.* Englewood Cliffs, NJ:
Prentice-Hall.

Starkweather, C. W. (1997). Therapy for younger children. In R. F. Curlee & G. M.
Siegel (Eds.), *Nature and treatment of stuttering: New directions* (2nd ed., pp.
257–279). Boston: Allyn & Bacon.

Starkweather, C. W. (1999). The effectiveness of stuttering therapy: An issue for science? In N. Bernstein Ratner & E. C. Healey (Eds.), *Stuttering research and practice:
Bridging the gap* (pp. 231–244). Mahwah, NJ: Lawrence Erlbaum Associates.

Starkweather, C. W., & Givens-Ackerman, J. (1997). *Stuttering.* Austin, TX: Pro-Ed.

Starkweather, C. W., & Gottwald, S. R. (1990). The demands and capacities model ll:
Clinical applications. *Journal of Fluency Disorders, 15,* 143–157.

Starkweather, C. W., & Gottwald, S. R. (1993). A pilot study of relations among specific measures obtained at intake and discharge in a program of prevention and early intervention for stuttering. *American Journal of Speech-Language Pathology, 2,* 51–58.

Starkweather, C. W., & Gottwald, S. R. (2000). The demands and capacities model: Response to Siegel. *Journal of Fluency Disorders, 25,* 369–375.

Starkweather, C. W., Gottwald, S. R., & Halfond, M. M. (1990). *Stuttering prevention: A clinical method.* Englewood Cliffs, NJ: Prentice Hall.

Van Riper, C. (1971). *The nature of stuttering.* Englewood Cliffs, NJ: Prentice-Hall.

Van Riper, C. (1973). *The treatment of stuttering.* Englewood Cliffs, NJ: Prentice-Hall.

Watkins, R. V., Yairi, E., & Ambrose, N. G. (1999). Early childhood stuttering III: Initial status of expressive language abilities. *Journal of Speech, Language, and Hearing Research, 42,* 1125–1135.

Wilkenfeld, J. R., & Curlee, R. F. (1997). The relative effects of questions and comments on children's stuttering. *American Journal of Speech-Language Pathology, 6,* 79–89.

Worrall, L. E., & Bennett, S. (2001). Evidence-based practice: Barriers and facilitators for speech-language pathologists. *Journal of Medical Speech-Language Pathology, 9,* xi–xvi.

Yaruss, J. S. (2000). The role of performance in the demands and capacities model. *Journal of Fluency Disorders, 25,* 347–358.

Zebrowski, P., & Cilek, T. D. (1997). Stuttering therapy in the elementary school setting: Guidelines for clinician-teacher collaboration. *Seminars in Speech and Language, 18,* 329–341.

AUTHOR'S NOTE

This chapter is based on a paper first presented at the 2002 University of Georgia State of the Art Conference on evidence-based treatment of stuttering.

5

Bilingualism in Early Stuttering: Empirical Issues and Clinical Implications

Rosalee C. Shenker
The Montreal Fluency Centre and McGill University

In a recent review of stuttering and bilingualism, Van Borsel, Maes, and Foulon (2001) cited the early studies of Travis, Johnson, and Shover (1937), and Stern (1948), who calculated the prevalence of stuttering in bilingual school children in Chicago and South Africa. The findings of these studies, which were based on clinical judgments made from a single assessment, suggested that stuttering was more prevalent among bilinguals. A recent study by Au-Jeung, Howell, Davis, Charles, and Sackin (2000), however, suggests that the percentage of bilingual speakers self-reporting stuttering is almost identical to the prevalence in monolingual speakers. Whether stuttering is equally likely or more likely in bilingual or multilingual speakers than in monolingual speakers, it is clear that most speech-language pathologists have a good chance of seeing bilingual children who stutter. The relation between bilingualism and stuttering is not well understood, however, and most clinicians do not have adequate guidelines for responding to the commonly posed questions of parents and educators (see Finn & Cordes, 1997).

The diverse multilinguistic and multicultural nature of the Canadian population makes Canada an ideal setting in which to explore questions related to bilingualism and stuttering. It is common practice in Canada to evaluate children who are exposed from early childhood to two or more languages at home, in school and in daily life. The richness of this linguistic–cultural diversity has resulted in valuable opportunities for the assessment and treatment of early stuttering in bilingual children, as well as for the study of related issues in early language development that may affect the fluency of bilingual children. In Montreal, accessibility to the scientists at the McConnell Brain Imaging Centre at the Montreal Neurological Institute, and the academics in the interdisciplinary program in Language Acquisition at McGill University, allows a broad-based multidisciplinary collaboration for the study of these issues. Within the past several years we have begun to explore the clinical relation between stuttering and bilingualism within our own clinical practice.

This chapter discusses some of the contributions to the literature that are relevant to the assessment and treatment of early stuttering in bilingual children. Emphasis is placed on description of evidence-based work that has clinical significance. Thus, the objectives of this chapter are to (a) define some relevant terminology, (b) identify some of the important empirical and clinical issues, (c) summarize studies that are relevant to the treatment of stuttering in young bilingual children, and (d) describe the work currently underway at the Montreal Fluency Centre. It is hoped that this discussion and our experiences will contribute to a better understanding of early stuttering in bilinguals.

DEFINING BILINGUALISM

One methodological problem in identifying the prevalence of bilingualism among children, or in drawing conclusions from research in this area, is that the same terminology may also be used to denote different phenomena. *Bilingualism* can be defined as "the total, simultaneous and alternating mastery of two languages;" however, it is also used to denote "some degree of knowledge of a second language in addition to the spontaneous skills which any individual poses in his first language" (Siguan & Mackay, 1987, pp. 8–12). The fact that multiculturalism is also a factor in consecutive bilingualism, or second language learning, has additional implications for accurate identification of stuttering and for providing treatment. Another dilemma faced by clinicians is that dysfluencies may reflect a child's limited proficiency in English rather than be an expression of stuttering (Van Borsel et al., 2001). Therefore, describing the heterogeneity in bilingualism is also important; identification of subgroups may be an essential first step making diagnostic decisions about stuttering in bilingual children. Therefore, in our practice the following definitions of bilingualism in children are used:

Early bilingualism (spontaneous) refers to those children who speak or have been spoken to in two or more languages in the home since birth and who continue to be spoken to in one or both of those two languages at school or daycare.

Second language (consecutive) bilingualism refers to those children who speak or have been spoken to in only one language in the home since birth, who are then exposed to a second language, beginning after the age of 3.

Bilingual + third language bilingualism (consecutive) refers to children who speak or have been spoken to in two or more languages in the home since birth, who are then exposed to another language, beginning after the age of 3.

Monolingual refers to children who speak or have been spoken to in one language in the home since birth. In Montreal all children who are classified monolingual may have been introduced informally to a second language through popular media, in informal playgroups, and such, and some point during early linguistic development.

IDENTIFYING THE ISSUES

Van Borsal et al. (2001) identified several issues that are important to consider in the treatment of bilingual stutterers. These include:

1. The difficulties in making reliable and valid judgments about the presence of stuttering and its severity in a language that is not one's own.
2. The advisability of asking parents of a child who stutters to stop exposing the child to two languages until he or she has acquired good control over one language in order to decrease stuttering.
3. The need for evaluation of treatment outcomes in bilingual stutterers compared to monolingual stutterers.

Few studies have responded to these issues, leaving the speech-language pathologist with little credible evidence on which to formulate clinical practice. The remainder of this chapter highlights the issues earlier posed.

TREATMENT OF STUTTERING
IN YOUNG BILINGUAL STUTTERERS

Making Reliable Judgments About Stuttering

One barrier in treating bilingual stutterers concerns clinicians' inability to make accurate judgments about frequency and severity of stuttering in a language that is not their own (Finn & Cordes, 1997). No empirical evidence exists that would indicate how well clinicians are able to perform this task. Finn and Cordes raised further questions related to the difficulty in establishing the presence or absence of stuttering in young children and distinguishing between stuttering and normal speech disfluency. Although it is commonly agreed that these judgments are integral to treatment of stuttering in young children, judgments are often restricted to pre and post treatment assessment.

Finn and Cordes (1997) also recommended that a comparison be made between the clinician's or client's judgments and judgments made by a speaker familiar with the language that is unfamiliar to the clinician, such as an interpreter or translator. Although interpreters or translators often assist in identification of stuttered moments, a potential problem with the use of translators is the low level of interjudge agreement and intrajudge stability for stuttering judgments in English-language studies (Cordes & Ingham, 1994). This suggests that it would be difficult to arrive at a reliable consensus between untrained interpreters and clinicians in an unfamiliar language. One way of achieving more reliable judgments about the presence of stuttering may be through consensus agreement between parent and clinician (Cordes, 2000). This can be particularly helpful in making reliable judgments about the presence of stuttering in unfamiliar languages and could be used to verify the presence of stutter-free speech throughout treatment.

Parent Participation

At the Montreal Fluency Centre, the Lidcombe Program of Early Intervention for Stuttering (Onslow, Packman, & Harrison, 2003) is used as the clinical model for best practice. This model adapts well for use with multicultural and multilingual families (Shenker et al., 2001). In the Lidcombe Program parents are taught to accurately identify moments of unambiguous stuttering in order to give feedback about stutter-free speech, request correction of unambiguous stutters, and provide perceptual judgments of severity. In parent training those moments of stuttering that are ambiguous are ignored. It is possible through observation of videotaped speaking samples, and ultimately online, to arrive at consensus between parents and clinicians concerning agreement of unambiguous moments of stuttering. When children are bilingual, agreement of unambiguous stutters by consensus between the clinician and parent helps to identify stutters in a language that may be unfamiliar to the clinician. Normal speech disfluencies or ambiguous moments of stuttering are not counted. In the Lidcombe Program, it is the parent who provides the therapy in the home language, in beyond-clinic settings. The results of treatment using the Lidcombe Program with bilingual children in our settings indicate that stutterfree speech is attained within the same time frame as with monolingual children. This suggests that parent–clinician consensus agreement of unambiguous stuttering can be attained when the clinician is not familiar with the home language of the child (Shenker et al., 2001).

Parent participation in therapy with multicultural and multilingual children can also lead to improved treatment outcomes. In a study done at Toronto's Hospital for Sick Children, Waheed-Khan (1998) adapted a traditional fluency-shaping model to involve mandatory participation of a family member after it was noted that the bilingual children were not improving at the same rate of change as the monolingual children. In her study parents attended treatment sessions, reviewed lessons with the child, modeled target-assisted speech at home, provided the clinician with culturally appropriate stimulus materials and assisted the clinician in developing a home program. As a result, the bilingual children became more successful in achieving fluency and improved in self-correction of stutters. This study provides some guidelines for clinicians faced with identification of stuttering and treatment of young stutterers when a common language does not exist.

Treating Bilingual Children: One Language or Two?

There is little clinical documentation to provide guidelines for assessment and treatment of stuttering in bilingual children (Agius, 1995; Druce, Debney, & Byrt, 1997; Humphrey, 1999; Shenker, Conte, Gingras, Courcy, & Polomeno, 1998; Waheed-Khan, 1998; Watson & Kayser, 1994; Weliky & Douglass, 1994). Additionally, there is a paucity of studies comparing intervention with monolingual and bilingual children in order to evaluate treatment outcomes.

The contemporary cultural belief that currently shapes our clinical practice is the persistent recommendation that it is better to expose children who stutter to a second language only after they acquire good control of their first language. It is frequently suggested that parents reduce the number of languages input to the child temporarily, when stuttering onset coincides with the addition of a second language (Karniol, 1999; Rustin, Botterill, & Kellman, 1996). This advice appears to be mediated by the model of Demands and Capacities (Adams, 1990), which would propose that introducing a second language might increase the demands on a developing system and result in increased dysfluencies. Therefore, when stuttering develops in bilingual children, speaking two languages is believed to place demands on them that may exceed their capacities to be fluent. This recommendation may not always be practical, especially when the home language of the child may be different than the language of treatment.

The theoretical rationale for this common clinical practice might be the speculation that early bilinguals are more vulnerable to stuttering because the same brain structures are utilized for learning both languages, and stuttering reflects a functional overload of these structures. This link between stuttering and bilingualism has been attributed to syntactic overload, and the input of linguistically mixed utterances that might trigger stuttering onset in bilingual children who are predisposed to stuttering. However, if stuttering onset coincides with the introduction of a second language, as some authors have suggested (Karniol, 1992; Pichon & Borel-Maisonny, 1964), then it is important to note the other factors, such as age of acquisition, proficiency in the language, and genetic and cultural vulnerability to disfluency, that may have contributed to the onset of stuttering.

An alternative to the limiting demands and capacities viewpoint can be found in the work of researchers in Quebec (Genesee, 2002; Paradis & Crago, 2000). They suggested that early exposure to two languages might be beneficial, and that children should receive substantial exposure to both languages at all times, avoiding any radical changes to the language environment which may be disruptive to language development. Paradis and Crago (2000), for example, described the development of bilingualism in children with Specific Language Impairment (SLI) with no mention of stuttering as a consequence of early simultaneous exposure to two languages in these children.

Before advising parents to reduce languages of input we also need to know if speech fluency and bilingual proficiency are related and if stuttering frequency and bilingual proficiency are related (Roberts, 2002). In young bilingual children stuttering may be more frequent in one language, as it is often the case in early bilingualism that the two languages do not develop equally (Shenker et al., 1998; Van Borsel et al., 2001). This may necessitate a bilingual assessment of fluency in order to consider each developing language separately before making treatment decisions that advise parents to reduce the number of languages input to the child. Overall, it seems that several individual factors related to language development need to be carefully considered before making recommendations for the treatment of young bilingual stutterers, but there is no strong evidence to support the hypothesized need to prohibit families from using one of their languages.

Treatment Studies

Although the demands and capacities model would propose a theoretical link between stuttering in bilingual children and increased demands on a limited capacity, little clinical evidence has been provided to support the commonly given advice to parents to set aside one language. In fact, current data exist that call this advice into question. Only one study has documented the removal of a second language in order to reduce stuttering. In Karniol's (1992) clinical case study, stuttering onset was noted in a male child at 25 months that appeared to coincide with the addition of a second language. One month after onset of stuttering, its severity increased. The second language was removed at that time, followed by a notable decrease in stuttering. Karniol presents this case study as support for the rationale that bilingualism causes a cognitive overload, thereby requiring additional processing time and increasing the delay between language potential and speech production, leading to possible fluency failure. However, because the onset of stuttering was less than 3 months prior to removal of the second language, it is possible that stuttering in this case was temporary and removal of the second language premature. The reduction of stuttering so soon after its stated onset could also have been related to natural recovery.

In a second single case study, Shenker et al. (1998) evaluated the effect on the second language of treating stuttering in the first language. In this study a bilingual preschool age child was treated in only one language while both languages continued to be spoken at home. The purpose of the study was to evaluate whether fluency can be increased in bilingual children by treating in one language only. The study compared gains in fluency in the treated language to gains in fluency in the untreated language to note whether stutter-free speech would extend to the nontreated language. Stuttering was initially treated in the linguistically more complex language, English, as determined from pretreatment analysis of a spontaneous language sample. The less complex language (French) was monitored for changes in stuttering and linguistic complexity during the course of treatment. The subject was a female who was initially assessed at age 2 years 8 months, 3 months post onset of stuttering. Treatment was initiated at 6 months post stuttering onset, and was provided in English. Bilingualism at home was not discouraged although the parents were encouraged to speak in one language at a time, trying to avoid code-mixed utterances upon input. Video-taped samples of spontaneous speech in both English and French were collected at the initial assessment, 1 week pre treatment, and at Clinic Session 30. All samples were transcribed and coded according to The Child Language Data Exchange System (CHILDES; Bernstein-Ratner, Rooney, & MacWhinney, 1996).

For the first 16 weeks, treatment was based on the multifactorial model (Starkweather & Gottwald, 1991). The goals included (a) turn taking to reduce interruptions, (b) reduction of linguistic complexity on input, and (c) rate reduction through frequent pausing. The father modeled these goals in English while the mother observed all sessions. After 16 weeks of treatment the percent of stuttered syllables (%SS) had decreased somewhat from pretreatment assessment, but not significantly enough to consider initiating a maintenance program (see Table 5.1). At Week 16 the Lidcombe Program was introduced. Treatment was continued in English only until stuttering decreased to less than 3%SS for 3 consecutive weeks. At that point (Week 23) stuttering had begun to reduce in French, and bilingual sessions were initiated so that both parents could participate in the treatment. Stuttering continued to decrease in both languages according to measures of %SS taken within the clinic. The outside of clinic measures provided by parents

TABLE 5.1

Single Case Study of a Bilingual Child Treated in English

	Assessment 12 weeks pretreatment	1 week pretreatment	Multifactorial model introduced	Lidcombe Program introduced				
			Clinic Session 16 [English]	Clinic Session 21 [English]	Clinic Session 23 [Bilingual]	Clinic Session 26	Clinic Session 30	
%SS English	13.51	6.63	10.5	4.5	2.5	3.7	2.8	
%SS French	9.89	6.32		12.5	6.0	6.0	4.4	
Parent Rating	None	None	7.0	3.3	2.1	2.6	3.5	

also confirmed that fluency noted in clinic sessions was generalizing to the naturalistic environment. Thus, this single case study suggested that stuttering could be successfully treated in the presence of a bilingual language environment.

In a similar study with a female adult who spoke English and Spanish from birth, Humphrey (1999) also found that fluency could be generalized to a second language following treatment in English only. Although the subject withdrew from the study before completion, she achieved a 70% reduction in percentage of stuttered syllables for the treated language (English), and a 40% reduction of stuttered syllables for the untreated language (Spanish).

Code Mixing and Early Stuttering

Another phenomenon that warrants discussion with respect to the treatment of stuttering in bilingual children is that of code mixing. Code mixing is noted in early bilingualism when vocabulary exists in one language but not the other: The child borrows words from one language to express ideas in a sentence that is primarily constructed in another language. Children who are developing two languages simultaneously may incorporate the lexicon of either language in order to increase the complexity of an utterance. This can also help the child to increase the complexity of the weaker language. Examples of code mixed utterances might include the following:

> **On mettre** this **petit** thing and **on mettre** this one over here
> [we put this little thing and we put this one over here]
>
> **on met** all this one **en premier**
> [we put all this one first]

The possibility that the input of linguistically mixed utterances by the speaker might also trigger the development of stuttering in bilingual children who are predisposed to stuttering has been raised in relation to the code switching noted during critical periods for language learning (Lebrun & Paradis, 1984). Rustin et al. (1991) suggested that when it is not possible to reduce languages to monolingual input, each person with whom the child communicates should use a consistent language on input, avoiding code mixing during critical periods for language. Attention to the "one person, one language" concept would also reduce the potential amount of linguistically mixed utterances that children would receive on input.

Karniol (1992) suggested that bilingual stuttering children may use code mixing as a coping strategy for dealing with disfluencies, but our own experience with the child described earlier (Shenker et al., 1998) did not suggest that increased stuttering occurred on code mixed utterances. In fact, only 7 out of 35 disfluencies noted in the language transcripts included code mixed utterances, and code-mixed utterances appeared to be inserted where word-finding difficulties were noted; code mixing might have been used in place of a normal speech disfluency. The frequency of code mixed utterances should also decrease with increase in linguistic ability, if code mixing is related to linguistic proficiency as suggested by Redlinger and Park (1980). Although several instances of code mixing were noted in the language samples of one 3 year old (Shenker et al., 1998), our preliminary analysis of the conversational and narrative samples of bilingual and monolingual 5-year-old children with average language development found no evidence of code mixed utterances in a conversational or speech narrative samples in English and French as linguistic complexity increased (Shenker, Ohashi, & Ouelette, 2002). Rather, the frequency of normal speech disfluencies increased, ranging between 8% and 10% for both a bilingual and a monolingual stutterer as well as for a bilingual nonstutterer (see Table 5.2). This preliminary finding concurs with suggestions that increased language complexity results in decreased code mixing, with code mixing replaced by normal speech disfluencies. An interesting question for future research to consider would be if the presence of code mixing continues in bilingual stutterers who have delayed language.

Treatment Outcomes: Monolingual and Bilingual Children

As previously stated, there are few studies comparing treatment outcomes of bilingual and monolingual children. This provides little credible evidence to either support or refute the common practice of recommending

TABLE 5.2
Comparison of Narrative Samples and Spontaneous Conversation:
Normal Speech Disfluency and Stuttering

	Eng. St.	Bil St	Bil NS
Narrative sample English			
%SS	0.4%	0.4%	0.3%
%NSD	6.0%	6.7%	6.8%
Narrative sample French			
%SS	N/A	1.1%	0.8%
%NSD		8.3%	5.5%
Spontaneous language sample			
%SS	0.8% (English)	1.1% (English)	0.4% (French)
%NSD	10.8%	4.8%	7.9%

that parents of bilingual stutterers reduce linguistic input to one language only in order to reduce stuttering. Druce et al. (1997) suggested that outcomes of bilingual stutterers are neither worse nor better than those of monolingual speakers. In their investigation of the short- and long-term effects of an intensive, behaviorally oriented treatment program for 6- to 8-year-old children who stuttered, 6 of the 15 participants were described as bilingual. No significant difference between the two linguistic groups and no significant association between bilingualism and outcomes of treatment in this program was noted.

In a preliminary attempt to examine this issue we compared treatment times necessary to reach Stage II (maintenance) for a group of monolingual and bilingual children who had been followed with the Lidcombe Program. The objectives of this study were (a) to determine whether Canadian children exhibit time-to-Stage II values similar to those reported by an Australian study (Jones, Onslow, Harrison, & Packman, 2000), and (b) to determine whether there was a difference between median clinical treatment hours to Stage II exhibited by a group of bilingual children and a group of monolingual children. The group consisted of 17 bilingual children and 39 monolingual children for a total of 56. Monolingual children were defined as those children speaking any one language and having been exposed to or spoken to in that one language in the home since birth. This group was compared to a sample of bilingual children, defined as speaking any two languages (or more) and having been exposed to or spoken to in those two languages in the home since birth. The children ranged in age from 3 years and 3 months (3;3) to 10;3. Severity of pretreatment stuttering ranged from mild to severe (1.5%SS–33%SS). The time from onset of stuttering to first treatment session ranged from 7 to 96 months. A history of stuttering was noted for 34% of the bilingual families and 58% of the monolingual families. There was a presence of other speech or language concerns noted in 23% of the bilingual children and 35% of the monolingual children. These ranged from mild phonological concerns to expressive language difficulties and some concerns for language comprehension. The descriptive data comparing the two groups of children is summarized in Table 5.3.

The outcome measure used was time-to-Stage II, defined as the number of therapy sessions required to attain stuttering of 1%SS or less within the clinic and 1.5%SS or less beyond the clinic for a period of no less than 3 consecutive weeks. Results found that the mean time-to-State II was 11.82 clinic visits for the monolingual group, and 9.9 clinic visits for the bilingual group (Table 5.4). This compared favorably to the mean value of 12.5 clinic visits reported by Jones et al. (2000) and as well for a subsequent study conducted in Great Britain (Kingston, Huber, Onslow, Jones, & Packman, 2003). For this group no significant difference in treatment time was noted between the monolingual and bilingual Canadian children.

TABLE 5.3
Treatment Time for Bilingual and Monolingual Children:
Description of the Subjects

Description	Bilingual Children	Unilingual Children
Age of treatment onset	3;3–10;3	3;0–8;3
Range of session	3-23	4-29
Mean # of sessions to Stage II	9.9	11.82
Median # of sessions to Stage II	9.0	10.0
%SS [pretreatment]	2.8–33.0	1.5–24
Time from onset of stuttering to 1st session	7–96 months	5–55 months
History of stuttering	5/17 (34%)	23/39 (58%)
Presence of other speech and language concerns	4/17 (23%)	14/39 (35%)

TABLE 5.4
Summary Values for Treatment Sessions to Stage 2 With the Lidcombe
Program: Monolingual and Bilingual Children

	Monolingual Group $n = 39$	Bilingual Group $n = 17$	Australian Group $n = 250$
Range	4.0–29.0	3.0–23.0	1.0–85.0
Mean	11.8	9.9	12.5
Median	10.0	9	11
Standard Deviation	5.9	5.2	9.1
Standard Error	0.94	1.25	0.58

$p = 0.245$; where p is the probability of the relative means of the monolingual and bilingual groups assuming no difference.

Another study is in progress to add the treatment outcomes for two sub-groups of children: children who are introduced to a second language at age 4 and a group of multilingual children. This multilingual group includes those children with multicultural diversity who spoke neither English nor French as their first language. It is hypothesized that treatment time to Stage II may be slightly longer for this group.

CLINICAL APPLICATIONS

Our clinical experience and our research have helped us to develop a response to the issue of bilingualism and stuttering that increases our confidence in advising parents of bilingual children who stutter. In summary, our clinical best practice now includes the following.

1.   We advise parents to continue to communicate in their home language. This is based on the results of our clinical work that is described in earlier sections as well as confirmation by Humphrey's (1999) findings that when fluency is established in one language it generalizes to a second language.

2.   Although we consider code mixing by the child part of the process of bilingual language development and even recognize that code mixing may play a role in fluency development in bilinguals, we caution parents to refrain from using code-mixed utterances on input to the child, in accordance with the recommendations of Redlinger and Park (1980), Genesee (2002), and others.

3.   Only in the most severe cases where stuttering exists with a profound phonological or language disorder would we ask parents to temporarily reduce the number of languages to which the child may be exposed on a daily basis. This is supported by the work of Paradis and Crago (2000) treating bilingual children with specific language impairment and our ongoing clinical experience.

4.   When each parent speaks a different language, treatment is given in the language of the parent who accompanies the child to the clinic. When both parents are present, the sessions are bilingual with 50% in each language. It is not uncommon for the child to respond in a different language to each parent. This has been described in the treatment section that discusses our work with bilingual children. We are confident that treatment of stuttering in consecutive bilinguals does not result in longer treatment times, but more is to be done investigating treatment times with multilingual children whose home language is neither French nor English.

5.   Severity ratings are global ratings and reflect the child's overall fluency. We have not found it necessary to document severity in each language spoken in order to monitor increases in stutter-free speech.

6.   Percentage of stuttered syllables (%SS) measures are taken in each of the languages that the child speaks. Using the concepts of the Lidcombe Program we have been able to achieve reliable consensus agreement with parents on unambiguous moments of stuttering in languages with which we may not be familiar.

In conclusion, it has been our experience that early stuttering in bilingual children can be successfully treated without reducing the number of languages spoken on input. Children who have been exposed from birth to two languages can achieve fluency within the same time frame as monolingual children without reducing the number of languages input to the child.

It also appears that the Lidcombe Program is a successful clinical model for treatment of early stuttering in bilingual children. Identification of unambiguous moments of stuttering and stutter-free speech through consensus agreement between parents trained in the Lidcombe Program is a useful model for assessment and treatment of stuttering in a language that the clinician may be unfamiliar with, although the need for continued evaluation of treatment procedures and outcomes in children from bilingual and multicultural backgrounds is great. It is hoped that this work provides some insight for clinical practice with bilingual children. Perhaps it is a preliminary step in a long-term plan to collect a variety of information about the linguistic and fluency variables that are important in the assessment, treatment and long-term maintenance of bilingual children who stutter. Although a better understanding of the relation between brain mechanisms, language development, bilingualism, and stuttering will help us to understand the manifestations of genetic characteristics or develop more precision in future treatment, it is directly relevant to current clinical practice that these studies suggest that bilingualism is probably not a negative factor or a barrier in the treatment of early stuttering.

REFERENCES

Adams, M. R. (1990). The demands and capacities model I: Theoretical elaborations. *Journal of Fluency Disorders, 15*, 135–141.

Agius, J. (1995). Language analysis of a bilingual maltese-English stuttering child. In C. W. Starkweather & H. F. M. Peters (Eds.), *Proceedings of the First World Congress on Fluency Disorders* (pp. 175–178). Nijmegen, Netherlands: International Fluency Association.

Au-Yeung, J., Howell, P., Davis, S., Charles, N., & Sackin, S. (2000, August 7–11). UCL survey on bilingualism and stuttering. Paper presented at the 3rd World Congress on Fluency Disorders, Nyborg, Denmark.

Bernstein-Ratner, N., Rooney, B., & MacWhinney, B. (1996). Analysis of stuttering using CHILDES and CLAN. *Clinical Linguistics and Phonetics, 10*(5), 169–188.

Cordes, A. K. (2000). Individual and consensus judgments of disfluency types in the speech of persons who stutter. *Journal of Speech and Hearing Research, 43*(4), 951–64.

Cordes, A. K., & Ingham, R. J. (1994). The reliability of observational data: II. Issues in the identification and measurement of stuttering events. *Journal of Speech and Hearing Research, 37*, 279–294.

Druce, T., Debney. S., & Byrt, T. (1997). Evaluation of an intensive treatment program for stuttering in young children. *Journal of Fluency Disorders, 22*, 169–186.

Finn, P., & Cordes, A. K. (1997). Multicultural identification and treatment of stuttering: A continuing need for research. *Journal of Fluency Disorders, 22*, 219–236.

Genesee, F. (2001). Portrait of the bilingual child. In V. Cook (Ed.), *Portraits of the second language user.* Clevedon, England: Multilingual Matters.

Humphrey, B. D. (1999, November). *Bilingual stuttering: Can treatment one language improve fluency in both?* Poster session presented at the annual convention of the American Speech-Language-Hearing Association, San Antonio, TX.

Jones, M., Onslow, M., Harrison, E., & Packman, A. (2000). Treating stuttering in children: Predicting treatment time in the Lidcombe Program. *Journal of Speech, Language and Hearing Research, 43*, 1440–1450.

Karniol, R. (1992). Stuttering out of bilingualism. *First Language, 12*, 255–283.

Kingston, M., Huber, A., Onslow, M., Jones, M., & Packman, A., (2003). Predicting treatment time with the Lidcombe Program: Replication and meta-analysis. *International Journal of Language and Communication Disorders, 38*, 165–177.

Lebrun, Y., & Paradis, M. (1984). To be or not to be an early bilingual? In Y. Lebrun & M. Paradis (Eds.), *Early bilingualism and child development.* (pp. 99–118) Amsterdam: Swets & Zeitlinger.

Onslow, M., Packman, A., & Harrison, E. (2003). *The Lidcombe Program of early stuttering intervention: A clinician's guide.* Austin, TX: Pro-Ed.

Paradis, J., & Crago, M. (2000). Tense and temporality: Commonalities and differences in French-speaking children with specific language impairment and French second language speakers. *Journal of Speech Language and Hearing Research, 43*(4), 834–848.

Pichon, E., & Borel-Maisonny, S. (1964). *Le bégaiement. Sa nature et son traitement.* Paris: Masson.

Redlinger, W., & Park, T. (1980). Language mixing in young bilinguals. *Journal of child language, 7*, 337–352.

Roberts, P. (2002). Disfluency patterns in four bilingual adults who stutter. *Journal of Speech-Language Pathology and Audiology, 26*(1), 5–18.

Rustin, L., Botterill, W., & Kellman, E. (1996). *Assessment and therapy for young dysfluent children: Family interaction.* London: Whurr Publishers.

Shenker, R. C., Casey, D., Ouelette, I., Ohashi, K., Butler-Hinz, S., Coucy, A., Lacombe, D., & Wilding, J. (2001, August). *Comparison preliminaire des enfants unilingues et bilingues: Treatment time to stage II (Maintenance) with the Lidcombe Program for Stuttering Intervention.* Poster session presented at the IALP Congress, Montreal QC.

Shenker, R. C., Conte, A., Gringras, A., Courcy, A., & Polomeno, L. (1998, August 18–22). The impact of bilingualism on developing fluency in a preschool child. In E. C. Healy & H. F. Peters, (Eds.), *Second World Congress on Fluency Disorders Proceedings, San Francisco* (pp. 200–204). Nijmegen, The Netherlands: Nijmegen University Press.

Shenker, R. C., Ohashi, K., & Ouelette, I. (2002). *Comparison of linguistic and fluency characteristics in bilingual and unilingual children.* Unpublished manuscript.

Siguan, M., & Mackay, W. F. (1987). *Education and bilingualism.* London: Kagan Page, Ltd.

Stern, E. (1948). A preliminary study of bilingualism and stuttering in four Johannesburg schools. *Journal of Logopaedics, 1*, 15–25.

Starkweather, C. W., Gottwald, S. R., & Halfond, M. H. (1990). *Stuttering presentation: A clinical method.* Englewood Cliffs, NJ: Prentice Hall.

Travis, L. E., Johnson, W., & Shover, J. (1937). The relation of bilingualism to stuttering. *Journal of Speech Disorders, 2*, 185–189.

Van Borsel, J., Maes, E., & Foulon, S. (2001). Stuttering and bilingualism: a review. *Journal of Fluency Disorders, 26*, 179–205.

Waheed-Khan, N., (1998, August 18–22). Fluency therapy with multlingual clients. In E. C. Healey, & F. M. Peters (Eds.), *Second World Congress on Fluency Disorders*

Proceedings, San Francisco (pp. 195–199). Nijmegen, the Netherlands: Nijmegen University Press.

Watson, J. B., & Kayser, H. (1994). Assessment of bilingual/bicultural children and adults who stutter. *Seminars in Speech and Language, 15,* 149–163.

Weliky, B., & Douglass, R. (1994). *Comparative study of speech characteristics of bilingual/monolingual stuttering children.* Paper presented at the annual convention of the American Speech-Language-Speech Association, New Orleans, LA.

AUTHOR'S NOTE

This chapter is based on a paper first presented at the 2002 University of Georgia State of the Art Conference on evidence-based treatment of stuttering.

6

The Child Stutters and Has a Phonological Disorder: How Should Treatment Proceed?

Marilyn A. Nippold
University of Oregon

Clarice, a speech-language pathologist (SLP), has just evaluated Ryan, a 4-year-old boy who stutters and has a co-occurring phonological disorder that significantly hinders his intelligibility. Once an outgoing toddler, Ryan is now a reticent preschooler, clasping his hand over his mouth whenever he speaks to his teacher or classmates. Older children in his neighborhood have begun calling Ryan names such as "Porky Pig" and "Daffy Duck," causing him to withdraw into solitary play. Clarice must decide how to handle Ryan's speech problems and is unsure whether to address them sequentially or simultaneously, or to treat only one disorder, hoping the other will spontaneously remit. Upon examining the clinical literature dealing with stuttering and concomitant phonological disorders, Clarice has become even more confused and is now fearful of making Ryan's speech worse through her intervention efforts.

This chapter has been written for Clarice and the many SLPs around the world who encounter children such as Ryan. It begins with a historical discussion of how the two disorders have been treated individually. It then evaluates the theoretical and empirical underpinnings of contemporary methods of treatment that are often recommended when the disorders co-occur. Various options for managing concomitant disorders are presented, emphasizing the importance of conducting evidence-based treatment. The chapter concludes with a discussion of how SLPs and clinical investigators can work together to improve the services these children receive and what can be done to facilitate fluency and intelligibility in children with concomitant disorders.

TREATMENT OF INDIVIDUAL DISORDERS: HISTORICAL PERSPECTIVES

Treatment of Stuttering

The profession of speech-language pathology has a long history of recommending *indirect* methods of treatment for preschool children (ages 3–5 years) who stutter. For example, in the 1950s, leading authorities in the field such as Charles Van Riper (1954), Mildred Berry, and Jon Eisenson (Berry & Eisenson, 1956) emphasized that the primary goal of therapy was to prevent children's awareness of their own disfluencies, arguing that this awareness would cause heightened anxiety about speaking, resulting in increased stuttering.

Hence, in the 1950s, it was widely recommended that parents rather than children work directly with the speech-language pathologist (SLP). During these counseling sessions, parents were taught to respond more positively to their child's speaking attempts, to refrain from showing surprise or embarrassment in reaction to the child's stuttering, and to improve the emotional tenor of the home environment. According to Van Riper (1954), parents of children beginning to stutter must remove all communicative pressures such as interrupting the child or requiring the child to talk in a different way (e.g., faster, slower, by taking a deep breath). Indeed, any direct attempts by parents or the SLP to modify the child's speech patterns were strictly prohibited for fear of turning the early disfluencies into severe and chronic stuttering.

Interestingly, this advice originated with the diagnosogenic theory of stuttering put forth by Wendell Johnson, a well-known professor of speech pathology who also stuttered. Johnson (1942) argued that parents caused their children to stutter by calling attention to the young child's normal disfluencies and labeling these repetitions and hesitations *stuttering*. According to Johnson, the child—upon hearing this label and internalizing the accompanying negative attitudes—begins to struggle valiantly to avoid disfluencies, leading to increasingly severe disruptions in the flow of speech. Johnson's diagnosogenic theory was firmly embraced after his *Open Letter to the Mother of a Stuttering Child* was published in a major professional journal (Johnson, 1949). In this letter, he described his view of the negative impact of parental behaviors on children's fluency, arguing that "practically any child" (p. 6) can be made to stutter. He also offered recommendations that have become classic advice for parents whose children are disfluent, including the need to avoid the label *stuttering* in relation to the child's speech.

In recent years, reports have indicated that many SLPs still believe that parent counseling should be the focus of treatment when young children stutter and that direct intervention with the child should be avoided (Cooper & Cooper, 1996). During counseling, SLPs attempt to modify parents' speech behaviors when interacting with their child. Typically, parents are trained to talk more slowly, to pause longer between utterances, to reduce their question asking and interrupting, and to refrain from commenting on the child's speech (Adams, 1992; ASHA, 1990; Conture, 1989, 2001; Kelly & Conture, 1991; Peters & Guitar, 1991; Rustin, 1987; Starkweather, Gottwald, & Halfond, 1990; Wall & Myers, 1995; Zebrowski, 1997; Zebrowski & Schum, 1993).

SLPs should know, however, that there is no scientific evidence to demonstrate that this indirect approach to treatment, although widely recommended, is effective with children who stutter. Nippold and Rudzinski (1995) critically reviewed studies published from the 1970s through the mid-1990s concerning parents' speech behaviors and children's stuttering, concluding that factors such as speech rate, interruptions, and question asking had little impact on stuttering, and that attempts to modify parental speech behaviors were unsuccessful in improving children's fluency. Their review also indicated that speech behaviors of parents whose children stuttered did not differ from those of parents whose children were fluent. Subsequent studies (e.g., Wilkenfeld & Curlee, 1997) have also been unsuccessful in showing a relation between adult conversational behaviors (e.g., questions vs. comments) and the frequency of children's stuttering. Moreover, a recent re-examination of Johnson's data that he used to support the diagnosogenic theory indicated serious design flaws in his research and an absence of empirical evidence that would lend credence to his theory (Ambrose & Yairi, 2002).

This is not to say that it is necessarily harmful for parents to alter their speech patterns when talking with their children who stutter, but simply that there is no evidence to show that it has a positive impact on children's fluency. In contrast, studies published since the 1990s have demonstrated that early and direct intervention for stuttering where parents are trained to reward their children for speaking fluently can be highly effective (e.g., Lincoln & Onslow, 1997; Lincoln, Onslow, & Reed, 1997; Onslow, Andrews, & Lincoln, 1994; Onslow, Costa, & Rue, 1990). Indeed, when a young child stutters, valuable time can be lost when an indirect approach is employed rather than a potentially more effective direct approach to treatment (Onslow, 1992).

Treatment of Phonological Disorders

Standing in stark contrast to stuttering is the treatment of phonological disorders: When preschool children exhibit difficulties with phonology, the profession has a long history of recommending direct intervention. For example, during the 1950s, SLPs routinely worked with young children individually or in small groups, attempting to increase their auditory and kinesthetic awareness of the targeted sounds (e.g., /s/, /r/, /l/) before teaching them to produce those sounds through modeling, imitation, and corrective feedback (Van Riper, 1954). Children were encouraged to monitor their speech by listening to tape recordings of themselves, and were rewarded for producing the sounds correctly in words, phrases, sentences, and finally in conversation (Berry & Eisenson, 1956). Individual sounds generally were trained to perfection before moving on to others (Hodson, 1997), and treatment often employed exercises believed to increase the speed, flexibility, and precision of the articulators (Berry & Eisenson, 1956).

Currently, when preschool children receive treatment for phonological disorders, many of these techniques are employed although less emphasis now is placed on exercising the articulators apart from speech production activities (e.g., Bernthal & Bankson, 1998; Gierut, 1998; Hodson & Paden, 1991; Stoel-Gammon & Dunn, 1985). Another change since the early years is the *phonological processes* approach where multiple sounds sharing certain phonetic features are targeted concurrently when they show similar error patterns (e.g., the child produces the velar consonants /k/ and /g/ as the alveolar consonants /t/ and /d/, a process known as *fronting*; (Hodson, 1997). Additionally, activities to enhance phonological awareness, in preparation for literacy, are often incorporated into treatment for phonological disorders (Stackhouse, 1997). Research has shown that the use of direct techniques where children are shown how to produce their targeted sounds, reinforced for using those sounds, and corrected when they make errors is highly effective (e.g., Gierut, 1998; Kwiatkowski & Shriberg, 1993; Shriberg & Kwiatkowski, 1982, 1987, 1990; Shriberg, Kwiatkowski, & Snyder, 1989, 1990).

A Comment on Direct Versus Indirect Treatment

Notably, the direct approach to the treatment of phonological disorders contrasts markedly with the indirect manner in which stuttering traditionally has been managed. With stuttering, parents have been the primary focus of treatment and children have received little direct attention from the SLP. With phonology, however, the SLP has taught children directly to modify their speech behaviors, with parents playing only a minor role (e.g., reviewing word lists or praising correct speech sound productions at home). Additionally, a major goal with stuttering has been to minimize children's awareness of their speech, whereas with phonology, the goal has been to maximize that awareness. Yet many SLPs report their reluctance to perform direct intervention with young children who stutter, preferring instead to work with the child's parents (Cooper & Cooper, 1996). At the same time, these SLPs routinely employ direct techniques in the treatment of phonological disorders in other young children.

These inconsistencies in the management of preschool children with speech disorders are striking. In one situation, professionals fear they may worsen the disorder and cause grave psychological harm by drawing children's attention to their difficulties, yet in the other situation, they do not hesitate to focus children's attention on their errors and to model and request a more appropriate way of speaking. Something is seriously wrong when such vastly different approaches are being employed, particularly when one approach is not supported by science.

STUTTERING AND CONCOMITANT PHONOLOGICAL DISORDERS

During the past decade, the profession has experienced a burgeoning interest in children who stutter and have a concomitant phonological disorder. Reports have indicated that approximately 30% to 40% of children who stutter also have a phonological disorder (e.g., Bernstein Ratner, 1995; Conture, 2001; Conture, Louko, & Edwards, 1993; Louko, 1995; Melnick & Conture, 2000; Wolk, 1998; Wolk, Blomgren, & Smith, 2000), prompting researchers to examine the possibility that the two disorders may impact one another. However, research to date has not provided convincing evidence to demonstrate an interaction between stuttering and phonology (Nippold, 2002). Nevertheless, it is widely believed that a phonological disorder in a young child who stutters can exacerbate the child's disfluencies and further, that attempts to treat the phonological disorder directly can worsen the stuttering (e.g., Arndt & Healey, 2001; Bernstein Ratner, 1995; Conture, 2001; Louko, Conture, & Edwards, 1999).

To avoid this problem, it is widely recommended that young children with concomitant disorders receive indirect treatment for both disorders (Bernstein Ratner, 1995; Conture, 2001; Conture et al., 1993; Louko, 1995; Louko, Edwards, & Conture, 1990; Louko et al., 1999; Wolk, 1998). To express their concerns about the potential dangers of direct intervention for children who stutter and have a phonological disorder, Louko et al. (1999) explained that their goal was "to minimize the chances of winning the battle with the child's phonology, but losing the war by exacerbating and/or worsening the child's stuttering" (p. 135). Similarly, Bernstein Ratner (1995) recommended that the SLP not correct any phonological errors in a child who stutters, claiming that because of "trading relationships" between stuttering and phonology, such efforts "are likely to exacerbate patterns of fluency failure" (p. 182).

In this author's view, the prevailing advice to employ an indirect approach to treatment with young children who stutter and have a concomitant phonological disorder should be rejected. As argued in this chapter, such advice, although well-intentioned, is based on the following beliefs, none of which is well-supported by empirical evidence: (a) stuttering and phonological disorders have a high rate of co-occurrence; (b) "trading relationships" exist between stuttering and phonology; and (c) treatment for phonological disorders causes children to stutter. Following a discussion of these beliefs, various treatment options are presented, and the existing clinical research is examined. Finally, an approach that involves concurrent treatment of the disorders using direct techniques is offered for consideration.

How Frequently do Stuttering and Phonological Disorders Co-Occur?

Reports that 30% to 40% of children who stutter also have a phonological disorder suggest a link between the two disorders, especially when contrasted with reports that 2% to 6% of nonstuttering children have a phonological disorder (Bernstein Ratner, 1995; Conture et al., 1993; Louko, 1995; Melnick & Conture, 2000; Wolk, 1998). Clearly, some children who stutter also have a phonological disorder (Paden & Yairi, 1996; Throneburg, Yairi, & Paden, 1994; Wolk, Edwards, & Conture, 1993), just as some children who do not stutter have a phonological disorder. However, the 30% to 40% figure that is frequently cited should be interpreted cautiously.

Studies that examined the co-occurrence of stuttering and phonological disorders have been analyzed in detail elsewhere (Nippold, 1990, 2001) so will be summarized here briefly. Since the 1920s, at least 15 published studies have addressed this issue (Andrews & Harris, 1964; Arndt & Healey, 2001; Bernstein Ratner, 1998; Berry, 1938; Blood & Seider, 1981; Darley, 1955; Louko et al., 1990; McDowell, 1928; Morley, 1957; Ryan, 1992; Schindler, 1955; Seider, Gladstien, & Kidd, 1982; St. Louis, Murray, & Ashworth, 1991; Williams & Silverman, 1968; Yaruss, LaSalle, & Conture, 1998). Collectively, reports of co-occurrence have varied widely from one study to another, with some investigators reporting no differences between stuttering and nonstuttering children in the frequency of phonological disorders (e.g., Bernstein Ratner, 1998; Ryan, 1992; Seider et al., 1982) and others reporting a substantially higher frequency of phonological disorders in children who stutter (e.g., Andrews & Harris, 1964; Darley, 1955; Louko et al., 1990; Schindler, 1955; Williams & Silverman, 1968).

Unfortunately, many of the studies contained methodological weaknesses that limited the degree to which their findings could be generalized. Examples of these problems include the absence of matched control groups of nonstuttering children (Arndt & Healey, 2001; Blood & Seider, 1981; St. Louis et al., 1991; Yaruss et al., 1998), the use of medical records or parental questionnaires to document phonological disorders instead of direct testing of children's speech (Andrews & Harris, 1964; Berry, 1938; Darley, 1955; Seider et al., 1982), cursory examination of children's phonological skills such as the use of screening tools rather than detailed analyses of conversational speech (Bernstein Ratner, 1998; Morley, 1957; Ryan, 1992; St. Louis et al., 1991), unclear diagnoses of stuttering (Yaruss et al., 1998) or of phonological disorders (Louko et al., 1990), and the use of subjective scoring systems to document a phonological disorder (McDowell, 1928; Schindler, 1955; St. Louis et al., 1991; Williams & Silverman, 1968).

In addition, some of the studies examined clinical samples rather than randomly-selected groups of children (e.g., Arndt & Healey, 2001; Blood & Seider, 1981). It has been reported that many SLPs perceive themselves as more competent to treat phonological disorders than stuttering (Kelly et al., 1997) and that many lack confidence in their ability to treat children who stutter (Cooper & Cooper, 1996). This suggests the possibility that children affected by both disorders may have a greater chance of being treated by the SLP than those whose only speech problem is stuttering. This is an important question for future research. If it is demonstrated through science that children who stutter and have a phonological disorder are more likely to receive treatment, this would emphasize the importance of employing random selection procedures for research projects rather than recruiting children from SLPs' caseloads.

We return now to the question posed earlier: How frequently do stuttering and phonological disorders co-occur? Because of the inconsistencies and weaknesses in the literature described above, it is currently impossible to answer this question. Clearly, additional research is necessary to address the rate of co-occurrence for the two disorders.

Do "Trading Relationships" Exist Between Stuttering and Phonology?

The term *trading relationships* implies that as the frequency of one behavior increases (e.g., stuttering) the other declines (e.g., phonological errors), and that positive changes in one domain (e.g., greater phonological accuracy) come at the expense of the other (e.g., more stuttering). This intriguing hypothesis, which implies that the two behaviors are somehow linked, appears in other aspects of childhood communication as well (e.g., Crystal, 1987; Masterson & Kamhi, 1992; Panagos & Prelock, 1982). For example, Panagos and Prelock investigated syntactic development in 6-year-old children who demonstrated language and phonological disorders. Their findings indicated that, as children attempted to imitate sentences containing words with greater phonological complexity (e.g., CVCVCVC syllable structure), the frequency of syntactic errors increased, particularly when the sentences also contained greater clausal complexity (e.g., center-embedded declaratives). Their findings were interpreted as evidence for the existence of trading relationships between phonology and syntax.

With stuttering, the concept of trading relationships has its roots in the Demands-Capacities (DC) model (see chap. 4, this volume). According to this model, disfluencies occur when communicative demands exceed a child's capacities in one or more areas of development, including linguistic, motoric, emotional, and/or cognitive (Adams, 1990; Starkweather & Gottwald, 1990). This implies, for example, that weaknesses in phonological (linguistic) and/or articulatory (motoric) development could exacerbate stuttering if communicative demands on the child—either self-imposed or environmental—are excessive. In the treatment literature, the DC model has been used to support the argument that, to minimize stuttering, one should refrain from calling attention to any negative aspects of a child's speech, as would occur during direct intervention for a phonological disorder (Bernstein Ratner, 1995; Conture, 2001; Conture et al., 1993; Louko, 1995; Louko et al., 1990, 1999; Wolk, 1998). Notably, this argument harks back to the words of Van Riper (1954), discussed earlier. However, if trading relationships do exist between stuttering and phonology, one might interpret the DC model to argue, alternatively, that a phonological disorder should be treated as quickly as possible to minimize its impact on the child's fluency.

Before drawing any conclusions concerning the DC model, it is emphasized that research has not supported the existence of trading relationships between stuttering and phonology. Detailed analyses of these studies have been described elsewhere (see Nippold, 2002) so are summarized here briefly. One approach has been to calculate correlation coefficients between the number of disfluencies children produce in conversation and the number of phonological errors that occur in their speech (Anderson & Conture, 2000; Louko et al., 1990; Ryan, 1992, 2001; Wolk et al., 2000; Yaruss & Conture, 1996). If trading relationships exist between stuttering and phonology, one might expect to find children with more severe stuttering to have fewer phonological errors and vice versa (i.e., negative correlation coefficients). Alternatively, if phonological errors negatively impact fluency, one might expect to find children with more severe stuttering to have a greater number of phonological errors (i.e., positive correlation coefficients). Out of the six studies that employed this design, none yielded statistically significant correlation coefficients, failing to demonstrate trading relationships.

Another approach to examining possible interactions between stuttering and phonology has been to compare groups of children who stutter in relation to the presence or absence of a phonological disorder (Wolk et al., 1993; Yaruss & Conture, 1996; Yaruss, LaSalle, & Conture, 1998). If trading relationships exist between stuttering and phonology, one might expect to find that children who stutter and have disordered phonology (S + DP) would differ from those who stutter but have normal phonology (S + NP). However, no statistically significant differences have been found between these two groups in the nature or severity of their stuttering.

Investigators have also examined children's stuttering severity in relation to their ability to articulate phonologically complex words such as those containing multiple sounds or syllables, or later developing consonants or clusters (Howell & Au-Yeung, 1995; Logan & Conture, 1997; Melnick & Conture, 2000; Throneburg et al., 1994; Wolk et al., 2000). However, the results of these studies failed to demonstrate statistically significant relationships between stuttering and the production of phonologically complex words, regardless of the severity of children's stuttering or the presence or absence of a phonological disorder.

In summary, then, despite the persistent and varied efforts of researchers to document the presence of trading relationships between stuttering and phonology, none have been successful. Thus, there is no convincing evidence that phonology influences stuttering or vice versa.

Does Treatment for Phonological Disorders Cause Children to Stutter?

Although the answer to this question is often assumed to be *yes* (e.g., Arndt & Healey, 2001; Bernstein Ratner, 1995; Conture, 2001; Louko et al., 1999), in reality, it has yet to be tested through empirical research. Surprisingly, this belief is based on anecdotal clinical reports rather than hard evidence. According to Edwards (1997), interest in the "stuttering-phonology connection" was prompted, in part, by the observation that "young children being seen for their phonological problems sometimes became disfluent during the course of remediation as their phonology improved" (p. 11). Similarly, Conture (2001) expressed "growing suspicion ... that the therapy for correction or modification of the child's speech sound difficulties may have, in some as yet unknown way, contributed to the child's emerging speech disfluency problem" (p. 94). Based on these observations, Conture recommended that children who stutter and have a phonological disorder receive indirect treatment for the two disorders. Given the absence of scientific evidence to support these recommendations, there is no reason to follow them, and it is imperative that these issues be addressed through research.

TREATMENT OPTIONS FOR STUTTERING AND CONCOMITANT PHONOLOGICAL DISORDERS

Ineffective Treatment

There is a lack of scientific evidence to support the three beliefs discussed above. Yet they often serve as the basis for recommending indirect treatment for young children who stutter and have a concomitant phonological disorder. Given that SLPs are left with the responsibility of planning the most appropriate course of action, it is important to consider various options. Among these are the following: (a) treating the disorders concurrently using indirect techniques; (b) treating the disorders sequentially using indirect techniques; (c) treating the disorders concurrently using direct techniques; and (d) treating the disorders sequentially using direct techniques. Bernstein Ratner (1995) expressed a preference for concurrent intervention. In her view, treatment for phonological disorders often extends over a long period of time, and if treatment for stuttering is delayed while phonology is being addressed, the fluency disorder is likely to have an increasingly negative impact on the child's social, emotional, and educational development. By the same token, one could argue that if treatment for the phonological disorder is delayed, the child is left to experience continued frustration resulting from poor intelligibility. For these reasons, it seems appropriate to treat both disorders concurrently. The question then becomes, should treatment employ direct or indirect methods? Bernstein Ratner argued in favor of indirect methods, expressing concern that overt correction of a child's speech sound errors or fluency breakdowns can cause stress, resulting in greater amounts of stuttering. However, as discussed throughout this chapter, there is limited scientific evidence to support this claim.

Surprisingly, of the four treatment options listed above, only the first has been examined through research. Conture et al. (1993) conducted a study that involved eight children who stuttered, four having a concomitant phonological disorder (SP group; mean age = 5:10) and four having normal phonological development (S group; mean age = 5:11). The children participated in weekly group therapy sessions at a university clinic for 1 calendar year, with each session lasting 45 minutes. Children in both the S and SP groups received an indirect approach to the treatment of stuttering where the SLP modeled slow and relaxed speech, and emphasized the use of appropriate turn-taking skills and noninterrupting. Children were encouraged to adopt this speaking pattern and conversational style in the context of games (e.g., Simon Says), and were praised when they did so. Additionally, children in the SP group received indirect treatment for their phonological errors. This consisted of the SLP modeling the targeted sounds in isolation, words, or stories, and engaging children in games where they were rewarded for listening to differences between sounds (e.g., /s/ and /z/) and attempting to produce certain sounds (e.g., /sh/, /th/). At no time were children singled out for instruction or correction in relation to their own phonological errors. Thus, in this investigation, no attempts were made to "explicitly, overtly, or directly try to modify" (p. 76) a child's stuttering or phonological errors.

Another component of treatment in the Conture et al. (1993) study was parent counseling. While the children were receiving group therapy, their parents met with another SLP and were taught to modify their behaviors when interacting with their children, emphasizing slow and relaxed speech and appropriate conversational skills. They also were taught to avoid criticizing or correcting their child's speech or prompting the child to speak fluently (e.g., "Say that again slowly" p. 75). Parents whose children also had a phonological disorder were taught how to model the targeted sounds without correcting the child's errors or giving feedback. In addition, all parents observed their children in group therapy where the desired behaviors were modeled.

Comparisons between the beginning and end of the year indicated that the frequency of stuttering had decreased in both groups of children (mean decrease = 14% for the S group; 11% for the SP group). However, stuttering actually increased for one child in the S group and for two children in the SP group. For the SP group, the use of phonological processes had decreased in all four children (mean decrease = 25%). Unfortunately, it was not reported if any of the children had attained normal fluency (< 1% stuttering) or age-appropriate phonological skills by the end of the year, and no data were reported with respect to changes in parents' speech behaviors as a result of counseling or how this may have impacted the children's speech. The absence of control groups of children matched on factors such as age, gender, fluency, and phonology also makes it difficult to interpret this study. In particular, it is impossible to know if stuttering declined as a result of the intervention program or because of other factors such as natural recovery (e.g., see Jones, Onslow, Harrison, & Packman, 2000; Mansson, 2000; Paden, Yairi, & Ambrose, 1999; Yairi, 1997, Yairi & Ambrose, 1992, 1999). Similar questions pertain to phonology. Given the children's ages (5–8 years), some of the improvements that occurred during the year may have been developmental, as this is a time when many later developing consonants are mastered (e.g., Stoel-Gammon & Dunn, 1985). Again, the absence of control measures makes it impossible to determine the sources of change in this investigation.

Effective Treatment

Given the paucity of scientific evidence concerning the treatment of stuttering and concomitant phonological disorders, it is critical that research be conducted in this area. Despite the profession's strong preference for employing indirect methods of treatment with young children who stutter, studies have demonstrated the effectiveness of direct techniques for children not identified as having a concomitant phonological disorder (e.g., Lincoln & Onslow, 1997; Lincoln et al., 1997; Onslow et al., 1990, 1994). Based on the positive results reported in these studies, support has grown for the view that the treatment of stuttering should begin during the preschool years in order to maximize its effectiveness and efficiency (Onslow, 1996).

Similarly, studies that have employed direct techniques to treat phonolog-ical disorders in children not identified as stuttering have yielded positive ef-fects (Gierut, 1998; Kwiatkowski & Shriberg, 1993; Shriberg & Kwiatkowski, 1982, 1990; Shriberg, Kwiatkowski, & Snyder, 1989, 1990). This suggests that, in designing treatment for young children with concomitant disorders, it is reasonable to draw on the findings from these two areas of clinical research.

With respect to stuttering, Onslow and colleagues (e.g., Harrison & On-slow, 1999; Lincoln & Harrison, 1999; Lincoln & Onslow, 1997; Lincoln et al., 1997; Onslow, 1996; Onslow et al., 1990, 1994) developed an effective evi-dence-based approach called the *Lidcombe Program*. This approach takes ad-vantage of the fact that young children who stutter—including those with severe stuttering—have many instances of fluent speech. Essentially, the SLP trains the child's parents to provide positive reinforcement for fluency in the form of praise (e.g., "Good talking," "No bumpy words that time!") or tangi-ble rewards (e.g., stickers, chips, tokens) that immediately follow the desired behavior—stutter-free speech. Most of the parent's attention focuses on the child's fluent speech rather than the stuttering, especially at the outset of treatment. As the child gradually produces greater amounts of fluent speech, parents begin to correct instances of stuttering by commenting on the child's difficulties in a calm and supportive manner (e.g., "Oops, that was a sticky one," "That was a bumpy word," "I think I heard a stutter"), using a soft tone of voice. Throughout intervention, reinforcement of fluency occurs far more often than correction of stuttering (e.g., 5:1 ratio) because treatment is de-signed to focus children's attention on the adjustments they are making in their speech mechanisms when fluent.

At the outset, the SLP demonstrates for the parents how to reinforce flu-ency and occasionally to correct instances of stuttering. Parents begin to im-plement these techniques in the clinic, under the guidance of the SLP, and later in the home. The SLP carefully monitors the parent–child interactions to ensure that they remain positive and fun for the child and free of frustra-tion. Parents collect data by tape recording these interactions at home and later analyzing them with the SLP. As the amount of fluent speech in-creases, parents raise their expectations and ask the child to repeat a stut-tered word fluently (e.g., "Let's try that word again: baby"). When the child is successful, overcorrections may be encouraged where the child is asked to repeat the word fluently several times, with all of this followed by praise or tangible rewards. As children continue to make progress, instances of positive reinforcement of fluency and correction of stuttering occur less predictably, and eventually, parents encourage their children to produce longer stretches of fluent speech without immediate feedback (e.g., "Let's see if you can talk smoothly the whole time we're at Sally's house"). Over time, children require less feedback from their parents, and are able to mon-itor their speech independently. They also begin to generalize their newly acquired fluency to different situations and conversational partners.

According to Lincoln and Onslow (1997), a follow-up study of children who received the Lidcombe Program when they were of preschool age (2 to 5 years) indicated that many of them had maintained their fluency for up to 7 years. The researchers suggested that this level of success may have occurred for several reasons: (a) children were treated when they were young, before the stuttering had become a firmly entrenched pattern; (b) much of the treatment took place in natural environments selected by the parent rather than in the clinic, helping to promote generalization; (c) children were encouraged to monitor their speech and to correct their stuttering; and (d) many of the parents continued to monitor their children's speech and to correct instances of stuttering long after regular contact with the speech clinic had ended.

Similarly, there is evidence to show that direct intervention for phonological disorders in preschool children can be highly effective in promoting age-appropriate speech sound development. Much of the research in this area was summarized by Gierut (1998), who reported that a wide variety of treatment methods have been shown to be effective and efficient in the treatment of phonological disorders, yielding long term benefits for children's social, emotional, and educational development. In Gierut's review, the following procedures were among those considered to be especially important: (a) emphasis is placed on improving children's awareness of their speech, including their correct and incorrect productions of speech sounds; (b) the SLP models the target sounds, encourages the children to produce those sounds, and provides corrective feedback; (c) children learn to produce the target sounds first in isolation and later, as they show progress, in increasingly difficult phonetic contexts (e.g., words, phrases, sentences, conversation); (d) efficient teaching involves a combination of drill and play activities that are challenging yet interesting and allow the child to be successful; (e) efforts are made to increase children's metalinguistic skills in relation to phonology (e.g., through the use of minimal pairs where a child's production of *thin* as *fin* might be highlighted in a game); and (f) the SLP attempts to build positive interpersonal relationships with the children to secure a high level of motivation and cooperation. When treatment is effective, children generalize their new phonological skills to untrained linguistic contexts and speaking situations beyond the clinic (Kwiatkowski & Shriberg, 1993). Many of these procedures are exemplified in the work of Shriberg and colleagues who have conducted numerous studies with young children (e.g., Shriberg & Kwiatkowski, 1982, 1987, 1990; Shriberg, Kwiatkowski, & Snyder, 1989, 1990). In summary then, there is clear scientific evidence demonstrating that stuttering and phonological disorders in young children can be treated effectively through direct techniques, at least when each disorder occurs in isolation. What remains to be learned is whether or not these techniques are as effective when the two disorders co-occur and how they may need to be modified to achieve maximal improvements in children's fluency and intelligibility.

IMPROVING TREATMENT FOR CHILDREN WITH CONCOMITANT DISORDERS: FUTURE NEEDS

As previously discussed, no published studies have examined the effects of concurrent treatment for stuttering and a concomitant phonological disorder using direct techniques. Given the data supporting the effectiveness of direct intervention when the disorders occur in isolation, it is reasonable to predict that it would be effective when they co-occur. Clearly, this hypothesis must be tested through research where SLPs and clinical investigators work collaboratively, sharing their expertise. In designing such a study, methods successfully employed by Onslow et al. (e.g., 1990, 1994) and Shriberg et al. (e.g., 1989, 1990), respectively, in the treatment of stuttering and phonological disorders in young children could be combined. In addition to providing useful information concerning early intervention, such a study could serve as a robust test of the hypothesis that direct intervention for a phonological disorder in a young child who stutters can make the stuttering worse (e.g., Bernstein Ratner, 1995; Conture, 2001).

Ideally, large numbers of children would participate in this research and each child could serve as his or her own control such that extensive baseline data are collected before treatment begins. Upon starting treatment, each child's progress could be monitored closely in the clinic and at home on a weekly basis. Following the formal completion of treatment, regular follow-up evaluations could be carried out by the SLPs and clinical investigators.

GUIDELINES FOR PRACTICING SPEECH-LANGUAGE PATHOLOGISTS

Meanwhile, in the absence of this vital research, what should an SLP such as Clarice, mentioned earlier, be doing when faced with children such as Ryan who present with concomitant speech disorders? Initially, the SLP could address the child's stuttering in the clinic as the parent is being trained to identify and reward instances of fluent speech. Once the parent is successful in implementing these procedures, the focus in the clinic could shift to phonology using traditional techniques, as described above. Of course, as the child's phonology improves in longer and more complex linguistic units (e.g., words, sentences, conversation), it will be important for the SLP to continue to reinforce fluency and occasionally to correct instances of stuttering and for the parent to continue this at home. Given the concerns that have been raised about the possibility of making the stuttering worse by focusing on the child's phonology (e.g., Conture, 2001), it will be important to monitor children closely for any increases in stuttering in relation to improvements in phonology. However, given the absence of data showing that direct intervention for phonology worsens stuttering, there is no reason to avoid direct techniques.

At the conclusion of treatment, a successful outcome would yield improvements in children's fluency and phonological skills to the point where their speech is indistinguishable from that of their peers with age-appropriate speech development, matched on factors such as age, gender, and linguistic, cultural, and socioeconomic background. Of course, the most important measure of success would be that all of these improvements occur before children are left to suffer the debilitating effects of chronic stuttering and a persistent phonological disorder. The available evidence suggests that SLPs have at their disposal the tools to accomplish just such a goal through the direct treatment of co-occurring stuttering and phonological disorders.

REFERENCES

Adams, M. R. (1990). The demands and capacities model I: Theoretical elaborations. *Journal of Fluency Disorders, 15*, 135–141.

Adams, M. R. (1992). Childhood stuttering under "positive" conditions. *American Journal of Speech-Language Pathology, 1*(3), 5–6.

Ambrose, N. G., & Yairi, E. (2002). The Tudor study: Data and ethics. *American Journal of Speech-Language Pathology, 11*(2), 190–203.

Anderson, J. D., & Conture, E. G. (2000). Language abilities of children who stutter: A preliminary study. *Journal of Fluency Disorders, 25*, 283–304.

Andrews, G., & Harris, M. (1964). *The syndrome of stuttering. Clinics in developmental medicine, 17.* London: Heinemann.

Arndt, J., & Healey, E. C. (2001). Concomitant disorders in school-age children who stutter. *Language, Speech, and Hearing Services in Schools, 32*, 68–78.

ASHA. (1990, June/July). Let's Talk: "I think my child is stuttering. What should I do?" *Asha, 32*, 63.

Bernstein Ratner, N. (1995). Treating the child who stutters with concomitant language or phonological impairment. *Language, Speech, and Hearing Services in Schools, 26*, 180–186.

Bernstein Ratner, N. (1998). Linguistic and perceptual characteristics of children at stuttering onset. In E. C. Healey & H. F. M. Peters (Eds.), *Proceedings from the Second World Congress on Fluency Disorders of the International Fluency Association* (pp. 3–6). Nijmegen, The Netherlands: Nijmegen University Press.

Bernthal, J. E., & Bankson, N. W. (1998). *Articulation and phonological disorders* (4th ed.). Boston: Allyn & Bacon.

Berry, M. (1938). The developmental history of stuttering children. *The Journal of Paediatrics, 12*, 209–217.

Berry, M. F., & Eisenson, J. (1956). *Speech disorders: Principles and practices of therapy.* New York: Appleton-Century-Crofts.

Blood, G. W., & Seider, R. (1981). The concomitant problems of young stutterers. *Journal of Speech and Hearing Disorders, 46*, 31–33.

Conture, E. G. (1989). Why does my child stutter? In E. G. Conture & J. Fraser (Eds.), *Stuttering and your child: Questions and answers* (pp. 13–22). Memphis, TN: Speech Foundation of America.

Conture, E. G. (2001). *Stuttering: Its nature, diagnosis, and treatment.* Boston: Allyn & Bacon.

Conture, E. G., Louko, L. J., & Edwards, M. L. (1993). Simultaneously treating stuttering and disordered phonology in children: Experimental treatment, preliminary findings. *American Journal of Speech-Language Pathology, 2*(3), 72–81.

Cooper, E. B., & Cooper, C. S. (1996). Clinician attitudes towards stuttering: Two decades of change. *Journal of Fluency Disorders, 21*, 119–135.

Crystal, D. (1987). Towards a "bucket" theory of language disability: Taking account of interaction between linguistic levels. *Clinical Linguistics and Phonetics, 1*, 7–22.

Darley, F. L. (1955). The relationship of parental attitudes and adjustments to the development of stuttering. In W. Johnson & R. R. Leutenegger (Eds.), *Stuttering in children and adults* (pp. 74–153). Minneapolis: University of Minnesota Press.

Edwards, M. L. (1997). Historical overview of clinical phonology. In B. W. Hodson & M. L. Edwards (Eds.), *Perspectives in applied phonology* (pp. 1–18). Gaithersburg, MD: Aspen.

Gierut, J. A. (1998). Treatment efficacy: Functional phonological disorders in children. *Journal of Speech, Language, and Hearing Research, 41*, S85–S100.

Harrison, E., & Onslow, M. (1999). Early intervention for stuttering: The Lidcombe Program. In R. F. Curlee (Ed.), *Stuttering and related disorders of fluency* (2nd ed., pp. 65–79). New York: Thieme.

Hodson, B. W. (1997). Disordered phonologies: What have we learned about assessment and treatment? In B. W. Hodson & M. L. Edwards (Eds.), *Perspectives in applied phonology* (pp. 197–224). Gaithersburg, MD: Aspen.

Hodson, B. W., & Paden, E. P. (1991). *Targeting intelligible speech: A phonological approach to remediation* (2nd ed.). Austin, TX: Pro-Ed.

Howell, P., & Au-Yeung, J. (1995). The association between stuttering, Brown's factors, and phonological categories in child stutterers ranging in age between 2 and 12 years. *Journal of Fluency Disorders, 20*, 331–344.

Johnson, W. (1942). A study of the onset and development of stuttering. *Journal of Speech Disorders, 7*, 251–257.

Johnson, W. (1949). An open letter to the mother of a stuttering child. *Journal of Speech and Hearing Disorders, 14*, 3–8.

Jones, M., Onslow, M., Harrison, E., & Packman, A. (2000). Treating stuttering in young children: Predicting treatment time in the Lidcombe Program. *Journal of Speech, Language, and Hearing Research, 43*, 1440–1450.

Kelly, E. M., & Conture, E. G. (1991). Intervention with school-age stutterers: A parent-child fluency group approach. *Seminars in Speech and Language, 12*, 309–322.

Kelly, E. M., Martin, J. S., Baker, K. E., Rivera, N. I., Bishop, J. E., Krizizke, C. B., Stettler, D. S., & Stealy, J. M. (1997). Academic and clinical preparation and practices of school speech-language pathologists with people who stutter. *Language, Speech, and Hearing Services in Schools, 28*, 195–212.

Kwiatkowski, J., & Shriberg, L. D. (1993). Speech normalization in developmental phonological disorders: A retrospective study of capability-focus theory. *Language, Speech, and Hearing Services in Schools, 24*, 10–18.

Lincoln, M., & Harrison, E. (1999). The Lidcombe Program. In M. Onslow & A. Packman (Eds.), *The handbook of early stuttering intervention* (pp. 103–117). San Diego, CA: Singular.

Lincoln, M. A., & Onslow, M. (1997). Long-term outcome of early intervention for stuttering. *American Journal of Speech-Language Pathology, 6*(1), 51–58.

Lincoln, M., Onslow, M., & Reed, V. (1997). Social validity of the treatment outcomes of an early intervention program for stuttering. *American Journal of Speech-Language Pathology, 6*(2), 77–84.

Logan, K. J., & Conture, E. G. (1997). Selected temporal, grammatical, and phonological characteristics of conversational utterances produced by children who stutter. *Journal of Speech, Language, and Hearing Research, 40,* 107–120.

Louko, L. J. (1995). Phonological characteristics of young children who stutter. *Topics in Language Disorders, 15,* 48–59.

Louko, L. J., Conture, E. G., & Edwards, M. L. (1999). Treating children who exhibit co-occurring stuttering and disordered phonology. In R. F. Curlee (Ed.), *Stuttering and related disorders of fluency* (2nd ed., pp. 124–138). New York: Thieme.

Louko, L. J., Edwards, M. L., & Conture, E. G. (1990). Phonological characteristics of young stutterers and their normally fluent peers: Preliminary observations. *Journal of Fluency Disorders, 15,* 191–210.

Mansson, H. (2000). Childhood stuttering: Incidence and development. *Journal of Fluency Disorders, 25,* 47–57.

Masterson, J. J., & Kamhi, A. G. (1992). Linguistic trade-offs in school-age children with and without language disorders. *Journal of Speech and Hearing Research, 35,* 1064–1075.

McDowell, E. D. (1928). *Educational and emotional adjustment of stuttering children.* New York: Columbia University Teachers College.

Melnick, K. S., & Conture, E. G. (2000). Relationship of length and grammatical complexity to the systematic and nonsystematic speech errors and stuttering of children who stutter. *Journal of Fluency Disorders, 25,* 21–45.

Morley, M. E. (1957). *The development and disorders of speech in childhood.* Edinburgh, Scotland: Livingstone.

Nippold, M. A. (1990). Concomitant speech and language disorders in stuttering children: A critique of the literature. *Journal of Speech and Hearing Disorders, 55,* 51–60.

Nippold, M. A. (2001). Phonological disorders and stuttering in children: What is the frequency of co-occurrence? *Clinical Linguistics and Phonetics, 15,* 219–228.

Nippold, M. A. (2002). Stuttering and phonology: Is there an interaction? *American Journal of Speech-Language Pathology, 11*(2), 99–110.

Nippold, M. A., & Rudzinski, M. (1995). Parents' speech and children's stuttering: A critique of the literature. *Journal of Speech and Hearing Research, 38,* 978–989.

Onslow, M. (1992). Choosing a treatment procedure for early stuttering: Issues and future directions. *Journal of Speech and Hearing Research, 35,* 983–993.

Onslow, M. (1996). *Behavioral management of stuttering.* San Diego, CA: Singular.

Onslow, M., Andrews, C., & Lincoln, M. (1994). A control-experimental trial of an operant treatment for early stuttering. *Journal of Speech and Hearing Research, 37,* 1244–1259.

Onslow, M., Costa, L., & Rue, S. (1990). Direct early intervention with stuttering: Some preliminary data. *Journal of Speech and Hearing Disorders, 55,* 405–416.

Paden, E. P., & Yairi, E. (1996). Phonological characteristics of children whose stuttering persisted or recovered. *Journal of Speech and Hearing Research, 39*, 981–990.

Paden, E. P., Yairi, E., & Ambrose, N. G. (1999). Early childhood stuttering II: Initial status of phonological abilities. *Journal of Speech, Language, and Hearing Research, 42*, 1113–1124.

Panagos, J. M., & Prelock, P. A. (1982). Phonological constraints on the sentence productions of language-disordered children. *Journal of Speech and Hearing Research, 25*, 171–177.

Peters, T. J., & Guitar, B. (1991). *Stuttering: An integrated approach to its nature and treatment.* Baltimore, MD: Williams & Wilkins.

Rustin, L. (1987). The treatment of childhood disfluency through active parent involvement. In L. Rustin, H. Purser, & H. Rowley (Eds.), *Progress in the treatment of fluency disorders* (pp. 166–180). London: Taylor and Francis.

Ryan, B. P. (1992). Articulation, language, rate, and fluency characteristics of stuttering and nonstuttering pre-school children. *Journal of Speech and Hearing Research, 35*, 333–342.

Ryan, B. P. (2001). A longitudinal study of articulation, language, rate, and fluency of 22 preschool children who stutter. *Journal of Fluency Disorders, 26*, 107–127.

Schindler, M. A. (1955). A study of educational adjustments of stuttering and nonstuttering children. In W. Johnson & R. Leutenegger (Eds.), *Stuttering in children and adults* (pp. 348–357). Minneapolis: University of Minnesota Press.

Seider, R. A., Gladstien, K. L., & Kidd, K. K. (1982). Language onset and concomitant speech and language problems in subgroups of stutterers and their siblings. *Journal of Speech and Hearing Research, 25*, 482–486.

Shriberg, L. D., & Kwiatkowski, J. (1982). Phonological disorders II: A conceptual framework for management. *Journal of Speech and Hearing Disorders, 47*, 242–256.

Shriberg, L. D., & Kwiatkowski, J. (1987). A retrospective study of spontaneous generalization in speech-delayed children. *Language, Speech, and Hearing Services in Schools, 18*, 144–157.

Shriberg, L. D., & Kwiatkowski, J. (1990). Self-monitoring and generalization in preschool speech-delayed children. *Language, Speech, and Hearing Services in Schools, 21*, 157–170.

Shriberg, L. D., Kwiatkowski, J., & Snyder, T. (1989). Tabletop versus microcomputer-assisted speech management: Stabilization phase. *Journal of Speech and Hearing Disorders, 54*, 233–248.

Shriberg, L. D., Kwiatkowski, J., & Snyder, T. (1990). Tabletop versus microcomputer-assisted speech management: Response evocation phase. *Journal of Speech and Hearing Disorders, 55*, 635–655.

Stackhouse, J. (1997). Phonological awareness: Connecting speech and literacy problems. In B. W. Hodson & M. L. Edwards (Eds.), *Perspectives in applied phonology* (pp. 157–196). Gaithersburg, MD.

Starkweather, C. W., & Gottwald, S. R. (1990). The demands and capacities model II: Clinical applications. *Journal of Fluency Disorders, 15*, 143–157.

Starkweather, C. W., Gottwald, S. R., & Halfond, M. M. (1990). *Stuttering prevention: A clinical method.* Englewood Cliffs, NJ: Prentice Hall.

St. Louis, K. O., Murray, C. D., & Ashworth, M. S. (1991). Coexisting communication disorders in a random sample of school-aged stutterers. *Journal of Fluency Disorders, 16*, 13–23.

Stoel-Gammon, C., & Dunn, C. (1985). *Normal and disordered phonology in children.* Austin, TX: Pro-Ed.

Throneburg, R. N., Yairi, E., & Paden, E. P. (1994). Relation between phonologic difficulty and the occurrence of disfluencies in the early stage of stuttering. *Journal of Speech and Hearing Research, 37,* 504–509.

Van Riper, C. (1954). *Speech correction: Principles and methods* (3rd ed.). Englewood Cliffs, NJ: Prentice-Hall.

Wall, M. J., & Myers, F. L. (1995). *Clinical management of childhood stuttering* (2nd ed.). Austin, TX: Pro-Ed.

Wilkenfeld, J. R., & Curlee, R. F. (1997). The relative effects of questions and comments on children's stuttering. *American Journal of Speech-Language Pathology, 6*(3), 79–89.

Williams, D. E., & Silverman, F. H. (1968). Note concerning articulation of school-age stutterers. *Perceptual and Motor Skills, 27,* 713–714.

Wolk, L. (1998). Intervention strategies for children who exhibit coexisting phonological and fluency disorders: A clinical note. *Child Language Teaching and Therapy, 14,* 69–82.

Wolk, L., Blomgren, M., & Smith, A. B. (2000). The frequency of simultaneous disfluency and phonological errors in children: A preliminary investigation. *Journal of Fluency Disorders, 25,* 269–281.

Wolk, L., Edwards, M. L., & Conture, E. G. (1993). Coexistence of stuttering and disordered phonology in young children. *Journal of Speech and Hearing Research, 36,* 906–917.

Yairi, E. (1997). Disfluency characteristics of childhood stuttering. In R. F. Curlee & G. M. Siegel (Eds.), *Nature and treatment of stuttering: New directions* (pp. 49–78). Boston: Allyn & Bacon.

Yairi, E., & Ambrose, N. (1992). A longitudinal study of stuttering in children: A preliminary report. *Journal of Speech and Hearing Research, 35,* 755–760.

Yairi, E., & Ambrose, N. G. (1999). Early childhood stuttering I: Persistency and recovery rates. *Journal of Speech, Language, and Hearing Research, 42,* 1097–1112.

Yaruss, J. S., & Conture, E. G. (1996). Stuttering and phonological disorders in children: Examination of the covert repair hypothesis. *Journal of Speech and Hearing Research, 39,* 349–364.

Yaruss, J. S., LaSalle, L. R., & Conture, E. G. (1998). Evaluating stuttering in young children: Diagnostic data. *American Journal of Speech-Language Pathology, 7*(4), 62–76.

Zebrowski, P. M. (1997). Assisting young children who stutter and their families: Defining the role of the speech-language pathologist. *American Journal of Speech-Language Pathology, 6*(2), 19–28.

Zebrowski, P. M., & Schum, R. L. (1993). Counseling parents of children who stutter. *American Journal of Speech-Language Pathology, 2*(2), 65–73.

AUTHOR'S NOTE

This chapter is based on a paper first presented at the 2002 University of Georgia State of the Art Conference on evidence-based treatment of stuttering.

7

Self-Change From Stuttering During Adolescence and Adulthood

Patrick Finn
University of Arizona

It is generally accepted that most preschool and early school-age children who stutter will recover without the direct benefit of professional help, usually within the first few years of onset (Yairi & Ambrose, 1999). Recent studies have reported rates of unassisted recovery during early childhood ranging from 50% to 74% (e.g., Brosch, Haege, Kalehne, & Johannsen, 1999; Mansson, 2000; Yairi & Ambrose, 1999). This recovery is often so complete that the children's recovered speech is perceptually indistinguishable from that of normally fluent children (Finn, Ingham, Ambrose, & Yairi, 1997).

It is also widely believed that early childhood stuttering is highly responsive to professional intervention (Curlee, 1999a). Numerous studies have reported on the benefits of treatment for early childhood stuttering, although few are actually supported by scientific evidence (Cordes, 1998). Still, a high percentage of school speech-language pathologists (70%) agree that they are successful in treating preschool children who stutter (Brisk, Healey, & Hux, 1997) and treatment research shows that management of early childhood stuttering often requires minimal treatment time and usually results in satisfactory, long-term outcomes (e.g., Onslow & Packman, 1999).

But what happens to those children who continue to stutter into their elementary school age years and beyond? It is widely believed that the longer they live with the disorder, the more persistent, complex, and chronic it will become (e.g., Guitar, 1998; Van Riper, 1982). Unassisted recovery becomes less and less likely and the need for treatment becomes more and more likely. In fact, by the time stuttering has persisted into adolescence, the disorder is typically viewed as highly resistant to change and difficult to manage (Conture, 1996; Daly, Simon, & Burnett-Stolnack, 1995; Van Riper, 1982). Conture (1996), for example, in a recent review of stuttering treatment efficacy stated "… teenagers' fluency problems make them among the 'toughest clinical cases' a speech-language pathologist must manage" (p. S23). Similarly, Cooper (1987) argued that when stuttering persists for 10 or more years, this is characteristic of a problem that is essentially incurable—it can be alleviated but not eradicated.

Clinician surveys and treatment studies appear to support this view. School speech-language pathologists agree that stuttering treatment is less and less successful as the age level of their stuttering clients advances from elementary to high school levels (Brisk et al., 1997). Treatment research findings documenting long-term stuttering treatment outcome based on adolescents and adults are consistent with this picture. Evidence shows that treatment of persistent stuttering requires considerable professional and economic resources, substantial treatment time, and outcomes that for almost one third will include relapse within 6 to 12 months post-treatment or an improvement that is considered unsatisfactory (Boberg & Kully, 1994; Hancock et al., 1998; Onslow, Costa, Andrews, Harrison, & Packman, 1996).

But in the midst of this rather negative portrayal, there is an often-overlooked body of research suggesting that persistent stuttering is not always as intractable as widely believed. There is evidence suggesting that stuttering is sufficiently changeable that adolescent and adult aged speakers who stutter are capable of improving to a degree that they no longer consider themselves handicapped by stuttering and some even recover to the extent that they are essentially perceived as normally fluent speakers. This improvement in many cases occurs without the benefit of professional help and it appears that most learned to self-manage their disorder. This chapter examines the evidence that supports these statements and focuses on the following questions: Why has the phenomenon been ignored, what are rates of recovery after childhood, what are subjects' perceived reasons for recovery, and what are the implications of these findings for understanding recovery from stuttering?

UNASSISTED RECOVERY FROM STUTTERING AFTER CHILDHOOD: AN OVERLOOKED PHENOMENON

Speech-language pathologists are often surprised to learn that adolescents and adults who stutter have been successfully managing their stuttering for centuries without professional help (St. Louis, 2001). Bormann (1969), for example, provided an account of the 17th-century Colonial American clergyman and author, Cotton Mather, who self-managed his stuttering when he was 18 years old by practicing speaking slowly and deliberately. Similarly, Wingate (1997) described an account from the late 1800s from a speech-related journal, *The Voice*, in which a dentist depicted overcoming his stuttering by practicing reading aloud slowly and deliberately while moving his lips but keeping his teeth touching.

There are also many contemporary accounts of self-managed recovery during adulthood. For example, Heltman (1941) provided a brief account of a male with a severe stuttering disorder who during his high school and college years conquered his problem by developing public speaking skills and actively competing in speaking contests and debates. Freund (1970) detailed a self-improvement regimen that he began when he was 35 years old that included practicing speaking in a smooth, melodic manner in a variety of speaking situations that eventually led to reductions in his avoidance behavior. St. Louis (2001) presented several personal stories from people who stutter who successfully dealt with their disorder during adulthood by changing their speech patterns (see pp. 155–157), reducing their avoidance behavior (see p. 118), or by increasing their self-confidence by engaging in public speaking (see p. 105). More recently, Anderson and Felsenfeld (2003) conducted a thematic analysis of interview material obtained from six individuals who had recovered after childhood—three without the benefit of treatment—and characterized their primary reasons for recovery as a conscious decision to change, an increase in self-confidence, and active changes in speech behavior. Finally, numerous large-scale surveys of recovered speakers have consistently reported similar accounts of self-managed recovery during adolescence and adulthood (e.g., Finn, 1996; Shearer & Williams, 1965; Sheehan & Martyn, 1966).

Several authorities have also independently reviewed the literature on unassisted recovery and they have all arrived at the same conclusion: Many speakers recover from stuttering during adolescence and adulthood and most have managed to do so on their own (see Ingham, 1983, pp. 131–132; Sheehan, 1979, pp. 197–199; Wingate, 1976, pp. 117–118). This consensus is quite remarkable because these same authorities have otherwise held starkly opposing viewpoints on the nature and treatment of stuttering.

It appears then that late recovery from stuttering without treatment is a long-recognized, well-documented phenomenon, yet it is surprisingly overlooked in most contemporary, comprehensive accounts of stuttering. The most widely used textbooks on stuttering (Ratner, 2001), for example, essentially subscribe to the conventional view of recovery from stuttering. That is, unassisted recovery during childhood is usually mentioned but self-managed, late recovery is rarely, if ever, cited.[1]

There are several reasons that may explain why this phenomenon has been ignored. First of all, stuttering has long been viewed from a clinical perspective. In other words, clinicians and researchers are more likely to encounter and study persistent stuttering and thus they are more likely to understand the disorder from this perspective. In contrast, they are far less likely to encounter people who recover without treatment (Blaker, Harbaugh, & Finn, 1996/1997) and thus they are less likely to be aware of the phenomenon or see its relevance to understanding the disorder. Second, the general population regards stuttering as a disorder that can not be effectively changed on the basis of personal effort (i.e., self-control and will-power), unlike other health problems such as obesity or even drug addiction in which they believe personal effort can make a difference (Furnham & McDermott, 1994). Accordingly, professional help is viewed as the only pathway for managing the disorder. Third, there is growing evidence that stuttering is a genetically predisposed, neurophysiologic disorder. This implies that because it is biologically based, it will less readily respond to techniques that are behavior oriented, let alone those that are self-directed (Ingham, 1990). Fourth, research findings on unassisted recovery have often challenged long-held, widely favored views about stuttering. Because of this, some authorities have argued rather convincingly that these contradictory findings have been readily dismissed and even suppressed (Ingham, 1983; Wingate, 1976, 1997). Finally, there are many unresolved methodological and conceptual issues surrounding much of the research on unassisted recovery, such as definitions of recovery and methods for verifying past stuttering behavior. As a result, much doubt has been raised about the meaning and relevance of these findings for understanding recovery from stuttering (Finn, 1998).

The main issue in ignoring the evidence that recovery occurs after childhood is that an incomplete, one-sided view of persistent stuttering is more likely to prevail. Such a curtailed view may have negative implications for both theoretical and clinical perspectives of the disorder. Perhaps then it is time to reconsider a more complete account of persistent stuttering. The re-

---

[1]The author and independent judge (a student in Speech and Hearing Sciences at the University of Arizona) independently examined six textbooks authored or edited by Conture (2001), Curlee (1999b), Curlee & Siegel (1997), Guitar (1998), Manning (2001), and Shapiro (1999). Both the author and independent judge agreed that whereas unassisted recovery during childhood was typically acknowledged, unassisted recovery after childhood typically was not.

mainder of this chapter therefore examines the research literature on unassisted recovery during adolescence and adulthood and considers its implications for understanding recovery from stuttering.

UNASSISTED RECOVERY DURING ADOLESCENCE AND ADULTHOOD: THE EVIDENCE

Rates of Late Recovery

How often is unassisted recovery occurring during adolescence and adulthood? To answer this question, it is necessary for research to meet two criteria: (1) subjects were adolescents or adults at the time of the investigation and (2) they were also able to estimate their age or age range when they believed they had recovered from their stuttering. Five reports that met these criteria are listed in Table 7.1.

As seen in Table 7.1, for these reports the age range of subjects at the time of investigation was 17 to 56 years and, on average, 28.5% (range = 21.5%–36%) were females and 71.4% (range = 64%–78.2%) were males. Subjects were usually obtained from academic settings and most were university students (see Table 7.1). Because investigators did not report estimated age at recovery in terms of childhood or adolescence, data from these reports were reanalyzed using 12 years old as the lower age limit for adolescence based on the following definition: "The exact period of adolescence, which varies from person to person, falls approximately between the ages 12 and 20 ..." (Columbia Encyclopedia, 2001, para. 1). However, for two reports (see Table 7.1) it was necessary to use 11 years old because investigators asked subjects to estimate their age at recovery based on 3-year age ranges with 11 to 14 as one of the required selections. This lower age limit seemed acceptable because 11 years old has also been used to describe adolescents in stuttering treatment research (i.e., Boberg & Kully, 1994).

Table 7.1 shows that on average, 70.7% of the subjects estimated that their age of recovery was during adolescence or adulthood (range = 56.9%–90%).[2] The remaining subjects recovered during their childhood years (M = 29.3%, range = 10%–43.1%).[3] Only two reports provided sufficient information to determine recovery rates for males and females and the results were

---

[2]The reliability of the author's estimates for Table 7.1 was evaluated. An independent judge (see Footnote 1) was provided with copies of the reports from Table 7.1 and the definition of adolescence. The judge was instructed to calculate the percentage of subjects that recovered during adolescence and beyond for each report. Agreement between the author and judge was 80% (4/5 percentages). Disagreement occurred because of an error found in one of the reports. Shearer and Williams (1965) identified 58 recovered subjects, but on page 288 in Table 1 of their report that summarized the subjects' age at recovery, the total was 59 subjects.

[3]Recovery during early childhood is probably underreported in these studies because many respondents would probably not remember their childhood stuttering and, thus, would not nominate themselves as persons who used to stutter.

TABLE 7.1
Subject Characteristics, Age Range, and Rate of Late Recovery From Past Reports

Author(s) (Year)	Age Range at Time of Interview	Sex (F) Females (M) Males	Population Sampled	Age Range of Late Recovery (Years)	Percent Late Recovered (Total Number)	Percent Late Recovered (Sex)
Johnson (1950)	17–39	30.4% (F) 69.6% (M)	University students	12–25	69.6% (16/23)	87.5% (F) 43.8% (M)
Lankford & Cooper (1974)	Not reported	Not reported	High school students	11–18	58.3% (14/24)	Not reported
Sheehan (1979)	17–56	21.8% (F) 78.2% (M)	University students	11–22+	78.8% (78/99)	Not reported
Shearer & Williams (1965)	17–21	25.9% (F) 74.1% (M)	University students	12–17	56.9% (33/58)	Not reported
Wingate (1964)	17–54	36% (F) 64% (M)	University connections	12–40	90.0% (45/50)	83.3% (F) 87.5% (M)
					Total Mean = 70.7%	

Note. Johnson's (1950) report is an unpublished master's thesis and raw data reported in the appendix were used to estimate the values reported in this table. Findings from this thesis were first reported in Wingate (1976). Lankford and Cooper's (1974) findings are based on 24 high school students that parents confirmed used to stutter. Data from Sheehan's (1979) chapter were presented here because this source described the cumulative findings that were originally reported in three separate publications (Martyn & Sheehan, 1968; Sheehan & Martyn, 1966, 1970) and it was the most accurate summation of the data on age at recovery. Estimates based on Wingate (1964) were calculated from individual data displayed in Table 4 from the original report.

decidedly mixed. Both reports agreed that over 80% of the females recovered during adolescence (see Table 7.1); but for males the rate of late recovery from one report (87.5%) was double that of the other (43.8%).

Subjects' Perceived Reasons
for Late Recovery From Stuttering

What do people believe was the basis for their recovery from stuttering especially when it occurred without treatment? Several reports on unassisted recovery have described subjects' perceived reasons for recovery and these results are summarized in Table 7.2. Because most are the same reports described in Table 7.1 it is reasonable to assume that subjects were usually describing their reasons for late recovery from stuttering as well.[4, 5]

For each report, reasons for recovery were assigned to one of four categories and these categories and their definitions were as follows: *Self-change* referred to reasons that indicated speakers managed or modified their own behavior, thoughts, or feelings in order to control or eliminate their stuttering without the benefit of professional help; *Don't Know* referred to speakers who were unable to speculate why a reduction or removal of stuttering symptoms had occurred; *Therapy* referred to improvement that speakers directly attributed to systematic treatment from a trained clinician; and *Other* referred to reasons that did not fit well into the other three categories.

As shown in Table 7.2, self-change was the most frequently reported reason for recovery.[6] These reasons typically consisted of subjects modifying their speech behavior, altering their attitudes towards their speech or themselves, and actively participating in different speaking situations. Subjects usually mentioned more than one reason and oftentimes these reasons co-occurred with each other. Quarrington (1977), for example, stated that virtually all of the subjects:

> ... had adopted new attitudes toward speaking situations, new concepts about themselves as speaking individuals. On the other hand, nearly all had

---

[4]Lankford and Cooper (1974; see Table 7.1) did not report subjects' perceived reasons for recovery. They did, however, ask the subjects' parents if they advised their child on how to overcome stuttering. Seventy-nine percent of the parents said, they made suggestions such as: " 'start over' closely followed in frequency by 'slow down.' Other suggestions frequently offered were reported to include these: 'think before you speak,' 'take your time,' 'wait a minute,' and 'stop and start over' " (p. 178).

[5]Quarrington (1977) did not report age at recovery. However, he did state that these were subjects "who claimed to have stuttered as adolescents or into adulthood [and] ... attained fluency rather late in development without benefit of any professional assistance of any sort" (p. 79).

[6]The reliability of the author's estimates was evaluated. An independent judge (see Footnote 1) was provided with the four categories, their definitions, and copies of the reports from Table 7.2. The judge was instructed to assign the reasons for recovery from each report and calculate the percentage of subjects. Agreement between the author and judge was 95.8%.

TABLE 7.2
Subjects' Perceived Reasons for Late Recovery (Percentage of Total Subjects)
From Past Reports

Author(s) Year	Self-Change	Don't Know	Therapy	Other
Johnson (1950) (N = 23)	Speaking slowly, careful planning, sometimes an increase in maturity and confidence (39.1%) Entering speaking situations, sometimes an increase in maturity and confidence (13.0%) Increase in maturity and confidence only (8.7%)	Undecided (17.4%)	Speech Therapy (21.7%)	N/A
Shearer & Williams (1965) (N = 58)	Speaking more slowly: often combined with other activities listed below (69%) Thinking before speaking (43%) Achieving greater self-confidence (26%) Becoming more aware of problem (22%) Speaking more deliberately (20%) Relaxation (19%)	N/A	N/A	N/A
Wingate (1964) (N = 50)	Change in attitude toward self and/or speech (40%) Practice speaking in different situations (16%) Change in speaking behavior (10%) Relaxation (2%)	Don't know (10%)	Speech Therapy (10%) Psychotherapy (4%)	Environmental Change (8%)
Martyn & Sheehan (1968) (N = 48)	Self-therapy: such as slowing down and change in attitude (62.5%)	Don't know (8.3%)	Speech Therapy (2.1%)	Other (27.1%)
Quarrington (1977) (N = 27)	Change in attitude and speech behavior (74%)	Don't know (26%)	N/A	N/A

Note. Reasons for recovery are, for the most part, paraphrases of the category items or wording used in the original reports. Johnson's (1950, see Appendix, p. 75) raw data were re-analyzed in order to account for 100% of the subjects since multiple reasons for recovery were often reported. Sheehan presented subjects' reasons for recovery in only two of three reports (Martyn & Sheehan, 1968; Sheehan & Martyn, 1966). Martyn and Sheehan's (1968) data were used here because it incorporated data from the 1966 report. Unfortunately, the two studies are not easily compared because the response items for the recovery question were altered across the two reports (see Q. 14: Martyn & Sheehan; Sheehan & Martyn). Wingate (1964) listed primary and secondary factors (see Table 5, p. 316); but for ease of presentation, only the primary factors are listed here and, when appropriate, some of the primary factors were combined.

also made some specific new attack on the speech process itself. The simplicity of these speech changes was striking. Typically the new speech patterns consisted of one principle such as "speaking slowly" or "talking more clearly" or "speaking in a deeper or firmer voice." (p. 79)

Moreover, he added that "[t]heir goal was immediate fluency in a speaking manner that they judged as either natural or at least a completely acceptable way of speaking" (p. 79).

Wingate (1964) also indicated that several subjects identified more than one reason for their recovery. He referred to these as primary and secondary reasons and though he did not specify how these reasons correlated with each other; he illustrated many of them in a later report. For example, *change in attitude toward speech* (see Table 7.2) was described by one subject as "the fact that I admitted openly I stuttered and didn't try to pretend I didn't" (Wingate, 1976, p. 102). Another subject described a *change in attitude toward self* (see Table 7.2) as "an acceptance of myself, an increasing awareness of my capabilities and limitations" (p. 102). Change in attitude also reflected motivation and persistence as suggested by this subject statement: "the knowledge that my father's youngest sister had overcome stuttering and the support my aunt gave me to persevere toward the same end" (p. 102). *Practice speaking in different situations* (see Table 7.2) was represented by subject statements such as "having to speak before groups through debate and public speaking in school, and of having to prepare and practice presentation" or "practice and a lot of speaking to gain self-confidence" (p. 102). Finally, *change in speaking behavior* (see Table 7.2) was illustrated by speech modifications such as "speaking more slowly" or "breath control and learning to relax before speaking or reading out loud" (p. 102).

Johnson (1950) listed subjects' reasons for recovery and, again, more than one reason was sometimes mentioned, as the following examples from four subjects suggests: Case No. 17: "planning thoughts, breathing with diaphram [sic], not thinking about speech," Case No. 15: "socializing with people," Case No. 6 "increased activities," Case No. 3: "maturity and concern over speech," and Case No. 12: "maturity and good rationalization" (pp. 26–32).

Shearer and Williams (1965) also reported that subjects described more than one reason for self-recovery. The most frequently reported reason was "speaking more slowly" which:

> … was usually mentioned in connection with some other activity. Typical responses were: "I tried not to speak until I was ready to slow down," "I began to realize the problem at that age and tried to pronounce things more deliberately," and "Speak more slowly and think first about what you are going to say." (p. 289)

Finally, Martyn and Sheehan (1968) did not report if subjects mentioned more than one reason. But the term, *self-therapy*, that they used to characterize subjects' accounts of recovery clearly included several possible attributions as seen in the following definition they used for this term: "taking some action such as talking more, enrolling in speech courses, slowing down, or otherwise taking the initiative and attacking the problem in some positive way" (p. 304).

As shown in Table 7.2, the second most commonly reported reason for recovery was subjects did not know why they had improved. Quarrington (1977) elaborated that these were "subjects who were not their own therapists, but apparently recovered from stuttering without primary cognitive changes or deliberate attempts to modify their speech" (p. 81). Further, he speculated that there might be a genetic basis for their recovery because most of these subjects also reported a family history of stuttering in concert with noticeable fluctuations in their stuttering severity over time.

The third most frequently mentioned reason was subjects believed that their improvement was the result of professional help, usually speech therapy (see Table 7.2). The successful treatment approach was quite different for each study. Johnson (1950), for example, reported that treatment consisted of speaking drills, reading poems and "dramatic interpretation." In contrast, Wingate (1964) described *symptomatic therapy* which consisted of well-known techniques such as reducing fear and avoidance, building a stronger sense of self, and developing a better understanding of stuttering.

The final reasons cited for recovery in Table 7.2 were described as *Other* (27.1%) or *Environmental change* (8%). Neither Martyn and Sheehan (1968) or Wingate (1964), who reported these reasons respectively, provided examples or specified what they believed subjects meant when these reasons were reported.

Reported Outcomes of Late Recovery

Most of the reports listed in Table 7.2 also indicated the status of the subjects' recovered speech behavior at the time of the investigation as based on investigator judgment or subject self-report. Quarrington (1977), for example, stated that all of the subjects in his study were normally fluent at the time of the interview. Johnson (1950) also judged that 91% of the subjects were normally fluent from a 45-minute face-to-face interview. But, 65% of these subjects reported that they still had a tendency to stutter, including 61% of the subjects who recovered after childhood. Wingate (1964) reported that 50% of the subjects described their speech as normally fluent and 50% reported that:

> [t]hey are usually normally fluent … [but] not entirely free of stuttering tendencies. However, they also indicated that these tendencies present no prob-

lems in communication or adjustment and that they are now accepted as normal speakers. The usual account ... is that some minimal and transitory stuttering might reappear under conditions of particular stress, but that it can be controlled readily. Also, they reported that they are not regarded by their friends and acquaintances as stutterers, and that most people are not aware that they might occasionally "really" stutter. (p. 313)

Similarly, Shearer and Williams (1965) said that although 64% of their subjects reported some occasional stuttering, they were nonetheless considered by themselves and acquaintances as normal speakers. They also reported that many subjects (81%) who recovered after childhood reported a greater tendency to stutter than subjects who recovered during childhood (30%).

Finally, Martyn and Sheehan (1968) did not comment on their subjects' recovered speech behavior. They did, however, find that some subjects (46%) still had some fear of stuttering, but they were significantly fewer than the number of subjects (97%) who still had a persistent stuttering problem.

Late Recovery from Stuttering: Conclusions

Two conclusions are obvious from this re-examination of reports on late recovery from stuttering. First, a high rate of recovery without treatment occurs during adolescence and adulthood. It also appears that females who stutter are more likely to recover than males, a trend also evident during early childhood (Yairi & Ambrose, 1999). Second, at least two thirds of speakers who recover after childhood believe it was because of self-change, their own efforts to reduce or eliminate stuttering without professional help. Furthermore, these self-regulated efforts resulted in speech fluency that was reportedly functional and usually perceived as normal by everyday contacts as well as the investigators who studied them. Occasional stuttering was more likely to occur with late recovery, but this tendency was highly situational and easily managed. Fear of stuttering may still linger for some; but for most it now appears to be absent.

Two methodological concerns, however, moderate the strength of these conclusions. The first and most critical is that most of these reports obtained self-report data to determine if recovered subjects had a recognizable stuttering problem in the past, but only one (see Lankford & Cooper, 1974) crosschecked these reports with people who were familiar with the subjects' past stuttering problem. This absence of collateral evidence can introduce doubts about subjects' claims that they in fact recovered from an actual stuttering problem rather than an over reaction to normal disfluency (Finn, 1998). The second and less critical concern is that some reports (e.g., Johnson, 1950; Martyn & Sheehan, 1968; Wingate, 1964) included subjects who had received some treatment for their stuttering.

This, of course, raises questions about claims that they recovered without professional help. But these concerns are mitigated, first because many subjects claimed that they continued to stutter after treatment (e.g. Sheehan, 1979) and second because some subjects did in fact acknowledge that their recovery was due to treatment (see Table 7.2). Recent research has resolved some of these methodological concerns.

UNASSISTED RECOVERY DURING ADOLESCENCE AND ADULTHOOD: RECENT RESEARCH

Methodological Developments

The use of collateral reports is perhaps the most practical methodological development in recent years for retrospective investigations of unassisted recovery. The validity of recovered speakers' claims that they used to stutter is crosschecked with people who knew them in the past when the stuttering problem was evident. However, a concern with relying on the stuttering judgments of nonprofessionals is that they may mistake normal disfluencies for a stuttering problem. Finn (1996), however, demonstrated that collaterals were able to accurately identify a recognizable stuttering problem and distinguish it from normal fluency. Therefore, collateral evidence can provide a straightforward method for independently confirming recovered subjects' claims that they used to stutter and, thus, insuring that they recovered from a valid stuttering problem. The following report utilized this methodology when investigating late recovery without treatment.

Subjects' Perceived Reasons for Late Recovery

The following results are from an unpublished study on unassisted recovery during adolescence and adulthood. The purpose of this study was to examine subjects' perceived reasons for late recovery without treatment. The participants consisted of 35 adults (23 males, 12 females) who were self-defined as recovered from stuttering without treatment. Their average age at time of the study was 49.9 years ($Mdn = 47$, $SD = 13.8$) with a range of 23 to 85 years. Based on collateral reports, all subjects were judged as speakers who used to stutter. All subjects confirmed that their recovery was independent of any past treatment that they may have received.

All subjects estimated that their recovery occurred during adolescence or adulthood. Mean age of recovery for males was 25.9 years ($Mdn = 23$, $SD = 11.7$, range 13–57 years) and for females was 24.1 years ($Mdn = 19.5$, $SD = 14.7$, range 12–59 years). Thirty-four percent (7 males, 5 females) of the subjects reported a family history of stuttering and five (2 males, 3 females) of them reported that this included a history of recovery.

In either a face-to-face or telephone interview, subjects were asked, "Tell me about your recovery from stuttering." The interviews were audio taped and independently transcribed by a professional typist. A content analysis was used to analyze, categorize, and quantify the interview material. The content analysis protocol consisted of a set of recovery categories and definitions. The categories and definitions were developed on the basis of factors that had been reported in previous research investigating unassisted recovery from stuttering in adults (see Finn, 1996 for details). Five graduate students were trained as judges on (a) the use of the protocol, (b) the category definitions, and (c) the scoring procedures. They were provided with transcripts of the subjects' interviews and instructed to independently score the interview material. The frequency of categories scored by the judges was tabulated for all subjects. Only categories that were agreed upon by at least four of the five judges, in other words 80% agreement, were included as reasons for recovery for the following descriptive analysis.

Table 7.3 displays the reasons that subjects believed played a role in their recovery without treatment. Because the majority of subjects (83%) recounted two or more reasons, the table first shows the number of subjects for each category and then the most frequent coinciding reason. Only three subjects identified a single reason and these were so atypical that they did not fit into the main categories (see *Other* in Table 7.3). *Don't Know* was also a category included in the content analysis (see Finn, 1996), but all subjects provided a reason for recovery so this category was omitted from the table.

As seen in Table 7.3 most subjects (60%) reported that they deliberately changed their speech behavior. Consistent with past research, these changes usually included speaking more slowly, taking a deep breath, and thinking before speaking. Also consistent with past research, many subjects (54.3%) said that motivation—a conscious decision to change—was related to their improvement and, in many cases (68%), this coincided with a change in speech behavior. Less than one half of the subjects (40%) mentioned a change in self-perception—defined as a deliberate re-evaluation of one's self-image as a person who stutters—but, interestingly, this usually co-occurred with a change in speech behavior. Surprisingly few subjects (28.6%) reported speaking more deliberately (i.e., actively speaking in difficult situations associated with stuttering); however, motivation was a clearly related co-factor. There were also very few subjects who reported *environmental change* (20%)—defined as a change in home, community, or occupation—and *relaxation* (20%)—defined as a reduction in physical or mental stress. Although in both of these cases, a change in speech behavior was typically a correlated reason. Similarly, few subjects (20%) said that they changed their attitude toward stuttering, which was defined as deliberate modification in one's evaluation of stuttering and included being more publicly open about stuttering and increased self-awareness of the circumstances and behavior involved in stuttering. Finally, the fewest

TABLE 7.3
Subjects' Perceived Reasons for Late Recovery
From Stuttering Without Treatment

Perceived Reasons for Unassisted Recovery	Percent (N = 35)	Most Frequently Reported Co-Occurring Reason
Change in speech behavior	60.0% (21/35)	Motivation 62% (13/21)
Motivation	54.3% (19/35)	Change in speech behavior 68% (13/19)
Change in self-perception	40.0% (14/35)	Change in speech behavior 57% (8/14)
Speaking more deliberately	28.6% (10/35)	Motivation 90% (9/10)
Other	22.9% (8/35)	Change in self-perception 50% (4/8)
Change in environment	20.0% (7/35)	Change in speech behavior 57% (4/7)
Relaxation	20.0% (7/35)	Change in speech behavior 71% (5/7)
Change in attitude toward stuttering	20.0% (7/35)	Motivation 43% (3/7)
Maturation	11.4% (4/35)	Change in self-perception 75% (3/4)

number of subjects (11.4%) reported maturation as their primary reason for improvement. In this case, *maturation* was defined as an unintentional change that occurred over time as the result of developmental bodily or attitudinal changes. Attitudinal change seems most likely because most of these subjects also reported a change in self-perception as a related reason.

Twenty-three percent of the subjects reported *Other* reasons for improvement that could not be easily categorized and they included factors such as practice speaking using a mirror, practicing yoga, reading about stuttering, and spiritual guidance. But, these subjects also reported co-occurring reasons for improvement such as a change in speech behavior, relaxation, and change in self-perception. Only three subjects related singular reasons for change that have not been reported in past research. Briefly, these reasons included the ingestion of cough syrup, learning to play a wind instrument, and a cranial-sacral adjustment that required the long-term use of a dental molding.

An overall examination of these reasons for recovery indicates that at least 80% (28/35) of the subjects actively changed their behavior, thoughts, or feelings in order to modify their stuttering problem. Consistent with past research, subjects actively engaged their stuttering problem and attempted to modify *both* their speaking behavior and their attitude toward themselves and their speech problem. The remaining subjects (7/35) described reasons for change suggesting that they believed they either grew out of the problem or their recovery was an unintended byproduct of some other change such as learning to play a wind instrument.

During the study, subjects were also asked to describe their current speech. More than one half (62.9%) said that their speech was typically fluent with only occasional stuttering and the remainder (37.1%) said that it was normal or fluent. Some of these subjects ($n = 12$) also participated in a perceptual study to determine if listeners could differentiate the speech of unassisted recovered speakers from normally fluent speakers (see Finn, 1997). The results showed that the speech of subjects who reported an occasional tendency to stutter were perceptually different and more unnatural sounding than normal speakers, but recovered speakers who reported no tendency to stutter were not perceptually different and just as natural sounding as normal speakers. At the same time, all of the unassisted recovered speakers attained more natural sounding speech than most treated recovered adults (see Finn, 1997). This may mean that speech outcomes from unassisted recovery are more functional than speech from treated recovery.

SUMMARY AND IMPLICATIONS

The conventional view of stuttering after childhood is that the disorder becomes resistant to change and difficult to manage. Although treatment outcome research based on adolescents and adults who stutter supports this view to some extent, it is not based on a complete account of all adolescents and adults who have ever stuttered. Contrary to popular perception some adolescents and adults recover from persistent stuttering and, more significantly, this recovery often occurs on the basis of their own self-help efforts and without professional help. Their resulting speech fluency may not always be perceived as completely normal or natural but it is still functional for everyday purposes and although there may be occasional stutters, these are easily self-managed.

It is clear that a more complete view of the course of persistent stuttering after childhood is that there is not one but two pathways: One is persistency and the other is recovery. What are the implications of this view especially when examined relative to early childhood recovery?

First, it is unclear if factors that influence pathways of recovery and persistency after childhood are similar to those reported during early childhood. For example, based on studies of early childhood recovery, epidemiological research suggests genetic factors such as sex and family history may underlie recovery and persistence (Yairi & Ambrose, 1999). Similar to early recovery there does appear to be a sex effect during late recovery because females who stutter are more likely than males to recover later in life, although there is some contradictory evidence (see Table 7.1). Research investigating early childhood recovery also shows that there may be familial patterns of recovery and persistence, where recovered speakers are more likely to have family members who also recovered (Ambrose, Cox, & Yairi, 1997). Unfortunately, researchers investigating late recovery rarely asked subjects if there was a family history of recovery from stuttering. Findings reported in this chapter indicate that it occurs but the amount of evidence is simply insufficient to determine if these patterns are similar in anyway to those reported with early recovery. This is a line of investigation that should be pursued further to find out if there is a family history factor influencing late recovery.

Second, there does appear to be a clear difference between early and late recovery without treatment in terms of mechanisms of change. During early recovery, there is evidence suggesting that environmental factors such as parental admonishments to the young child who stutters to start over or slow down may facilitate recovery without treatment (Ingham, 1983). At the very least, these factors do not make the child's stuttering any worse (Wingate, 1976). During late recovery, on the other hand, self-change from stuttering is the primary mechanism for recovery and the starting point for understanding this is probably related to the fact that it begins during adolescence.

Adolescence is characterized as an escalating period of increased self-awareness, search for self-identity, and a desire to fit in (Hine, 1999). These factors may provide the context that prompts some people who stutter to combat their stuttering on their own, try to be more fluent, reconsider how they think about themselves, and reduce their avoidance of speaking. But, this context alone is probably insufficient to account for self-change because these factors—increased self-awareness, search for self-identity, and a desire to fit in—might just as easily lead to heightened awareness, fear, and avoidance of stuttering.

It is more likely that the primary mechanisms for self-change are speech modification, attitude change, and avoidance reduction (i.e., deliberately speaking in different situations). This review showed that these are the typical approaches people reported for dealing with their stuttering on their own. The reliability of these self-reports is bolstered by the fact that these findings are reported consistently across a wide array of different studies.

However, research is needed to further establish the scientific credibility of self-change from stuttering because the evidence so far is mostly circumstantial. For example, there is the oft-reported and persuasive similarity between these self-change mechanisms and many stuttering treatment procedures (see Ingham, 1983; Sheehan, 1979; Wingate, 1976). But there is as yet no independent evidence that recovered speakers actually engaged in these mechanisms or that people who stutter can successfully self-manage their own behavior. At the same time, there is the rarely cited evidence that recovered speakers are more likely to try and modify their speech behavior and attitudes than nonrecovered speakers (Martyn & Sheehan, 1968). This is an important finding and further comparative as well as longitudinal studies are needed to determine if there are differences in self-regulation strategies employed by persistent and recovered speakers. Carefully designed experimental studies may also help to determine the viability of self-regulation strategies for modifying persistent stuttering.

Finally, there is also a clear difference between early and late recovery without treatment in terms of level of improvement. Early recovery reportedly results in complete removal of stuttered speech (Yairi & Ambrose, 1999) and listeners are unlikely to perceive the result as different from the speech of normally fluent children (Finn et al., 1997). Late recovery, on the other hand, results in improved speech but with occasional stuttering and it may not always be perceived as normally fluent though it is apparently functional and satisfactory for the recovered speaker's everyday purposes. This difference between early and late recovery best captures the signal issue of theoretical and clinical importance for stuttering because it concerns the very nature of recovery from a chronic disorder.

Recovery from stuttering can be examined at multiple levels including speech behavior, subjective experience, and even neurophysiological bases (Finn, 1996). Unfortunately, the complete parameters that might define recovery from persistent stuttering have never been fully established. One parameter that may become increasingly important is that of clinical significance which refers to the meaningfulness or acceptability of change (Kazdin, 1999). The meaningfulness of change, however, depends on whose perspective is most relevant and who has set the standards for recognizing that change: the client, the clinician, or the researcher. In the case of late recovery without treatment, it is the recovered speakers' perspective that is the most relevant and it is their standard of change that is being recognized. Self-defined resolution may also be the most practical for defining improvement since some of the more disabling characteristics of persistent stuttering such as fear and avoidance are subjective experiences. The clinical significance of self-change[7] from stuttering is that recovered speakers engender a change sufficient enough to no longer consider themselves handicapped by the disorder.

There probably will be disagreement in the field of stuttering for a long time to come about standards of recovery from persistent stuttering. One standard that may become more relevant in the near future is the neurophysiological bases of recovery. But so far some fascinating and quite compelling findings from recent reports that were based for the most part on

---

[7]"Self-change" and "stuttering" are terms that aren't usually associated with each other. Although a layperson might infer that people who stutter could stop if only they wanted to that misconception is certainly not intended here.

speakers who had recovered without treatment after childhood have all suggested that these speakers' neurological systems have not completely normalized (Forster & Webster, 2001; Ingham, chap. 3, this volume; Mouradian, Paslawski, & Shuaib, 2000; Webster, chap. 2, this volume). It is still too early to fully understand the implication of these findings. But, it does suggest that normal neurophysiology may not be possible and, therefore, self-defined resolution may continue to be one of the most important and relevant standards of recovery from chronic stuttering.

REFERENCES

Ambrose, N. G., Cox, N. J., & Yairi, E. (1997). The genetic basis of persistence and recovery in stuttering. *Journal of Speech, Language, and Hearing Research, 40*, 567–580.

Anderson, T. K., & Felsenfeld, S. (2003). A thematic analysis of late recovery from stuttering. *American Journal of Speech-Language Pathology, 12*, 243–253.

Blaker, K., Harbaugh, D., & Finn, P. (1996/1997). Clinician attitudes toward stuttering: A survey of New Mexico. *Texas Journal of Audiology and Speech-Language Pathology, 22*, 109–114.

Boberg, E., & Kully, D. (1994). Long-term results of an intensive treatment program for adults and adolescents who stutter. *Journal of Speech and Hearing Research, 37*, 1050–1059.

Bormann, E. G. (1969). Ephphatha, or, some advice to stammerers. *Journal of Speech and Hearing Research, 12*, 453–461.

Brisk, D. J., Healey, E. C., & Hux, K. A. (1997). Clinicians' training and confidence associated with treating school-age children who stutter: A national survey. *Language, Speech, and Hearing Services in Schools, 28*, 164–176.

Brosch, S., Haege, A., Kalehne, P., & Johannsen, H. S. (1999). Stuttering children and the probability of remission-the role of cerebral dominance and speech production. *International Journal of Pediatric Otorhinolaryngology, 47*, 71–76.

Columbia University. (2001). *The Columbia Encyclopedia* (6th ed.). URL retrieved May 2002 from http://www.bartleby.com/65/ad/adolesce.html

Conture, E. (1996). Treatment efficacy: Stuttering. *Journal of Speech and Hearing Research, 39*, S18–S26.

Conture, E. (2001). *Stuttering: Its nature, diagnosis, and treatment*. Needham Heights, MA: Allyn & Bacon.

Cooper, E. B. (1987). The chronic perseverative stuttering syndrome; Incurable stuttering. *Journal of Fluency Disorders, 12*, 381–388.

Cordes, A. K. (1998). Current status of the stuttering treatment literature. In A. K. Cordes & R. J. Ingham (Eds.), *Treatment efficacy for stuttering: A search for empirical bases* (pp. 117–144). San Diego, CA: Singular Publishing.

Curlee, R. F. (1999a). Identification and case selection guidelines for early childhood stuttering. In R. F. Curlee (Ed.), *Stuttering and related disorders of fluency* (2nd ed., pp. 1–21). New York: Thieme.

Curlee, R. F. (1999b). *Stuttering and related disorders of fluency* (2nd ed.). New York: Thieme.

Curlee, R. F., & Siegel, G. M. (1997). *Nature and treatment of stuttering: New directions* (2nd ed.). Needham Heights, MA: Allyn & Bacon.

Daly, D. A., Simon, C. A., & Burnett-Stolnack, M. (1995). Helping adolescents who stutter focus on fluency. *Language, Speech, and Hearing Services in Schools, 26,* 162–168.

Finn, P. (1996). Establishing the validity of recovery from stuttering without treatment. *Journal of Speech and Hearing Research, 39,* 1171–1181.

Finn, P. (1997). Adults recovered from stuttering without formal treatment: Perceptual assessment of speech normalcy. *Journal of Speech, Language and Hearing Research, 40,* 821–831.

Finn, P. (1998). Recovery without treatment: A review of conceptual and methodological considerations across disciplines. In A. K. Cordes & R. J. Ingham (Eds.), *Treatment efficacy for stuttering: A search for empirical bases* (pp. 3–28). San Diego, CA: Singular Publishing.

Finn, P., Ingham, R. J., Ambrose, N., & Yairi, E. (1997). Children recovered from stuttering without formal treatment: Perceptual assessment of speech normalcy. *Journal of Speech, Language, and Hearing Research, 40,* 867–876.

Forster, D. C., & Webster, W. G. (2001). Speech-motor control and interhemispheric relations in recovered and persistent stuttering. *Developmental Psychology, 19,* 125–145.

Freund, H. (1970). Self-improvement after unsuccessful treatments. In M. Fraser (Ed.), *To the stutterer* (pp. 49–53). Memphis, TN: Speech Foundation of America No. 9.

Furnham, A., & McDermott, M. R. (1994). Lay beliefs about the efficacy of self-reliance, seeking help and external control as strategies for overcoming obesity, drug addiction, marital problems, stuttering and insomnia. *Psychology and Health, 9,* 397–406.

Guitar, B. (1998). *Stuttering: An integrated approach to its nature and treatment* (2nd ed.). Baltimore, MD: Williams & Wilkins.

Hancock, K., Craig, A., McCready, C., McCaul, A., Costello, D., Campbell, K., & Gilmore, G. (1998). Two- to six-year controlled-trial stuttering outcomes for children and adolescents. *Journal of Speech, Language, and Hearing Research, 41,* 1242–1252.

Heltman, H. J. (1941). History of recurrent stuttering and recovery in twenty-five year old post graduate college student. *Journal of Speech Disorders, 6,* 49–50.

Hine, T. (1999). *The rise and fall of the American teenager.* New York: Avon Books.

Ingham, R. J. (1983). Spontaneous remission of stuttering: When will the emperor realize he has no clothes on? In D. Prins & R. J. Ingham (Eds.), *Treatment of stuttering in early childhood* (pp. 113–140). San Diego: College-Hill Press.

Ingham, R. J. (1990). Research on stuttering treatment for adults and adolescents: A perspective on how to overcome a malaise. In J. A. Cooper (Ed.), *Research needs in stuttering: Roadblocks and future directions* (pp. 91–95). Rockville, MD: American Speech-Language-Hearing Association.

Johnson, P. A. (1950). *An exploratory study of certain aspects of the speech histories of twenty-three former stutterers.* Unpublished masters thesis, University of Pittsburgh, Pittsburgh, PA.

Kazdin, A. E. (1999). The meanings and measurement of clinical significance. *Journal of Consulting and Clinical Psychology, 67,* 332–339.

Lankford, S. D., & Cooper, E. B. (1974). Recovery from stuttering as viewed by parents of self-diagnosed recovered stutterers. *Journal of Communication Disorders, 7,* 171–180.

Manning, W. H. (2001). *Clinical decision making in fluency disorders* (2nd ed.). San Diego, CA: Singular/Thomson Learning.

Mansson, H. (2000). Childhood stuttering: Incidence and development. *Journal of Fluency Disorders, 25,* 47–57.

Martyn, M. M., & Sheehan, J. G. (1968). Onset of stuttering and recovery. *Behaviour Research and Therapy, 6*, 295–307.

Mouradian, M. S., Paslawski, T., & Shuaib, A. (2000). Return of stuttering after stroke. *Brain and Language, 73*, 120–123.

Onslow, M., Costa, L., Andrews, C., Harrison, E., & Packman, A. (1996). Speech outcomes of a prolonged-speech treatment for stuttering. *Journal of Speech and Hearing Research, 39*, 734–749.

Onslow, M., & Packman, A. (1999). The Lidcombe Programme and natural recovery: Potential choices of initial management strategies for early stuttering. *Advances in Speech-Language Pathology, 1*, 113–121.

Quarrington, B. (1977). How do the various theories of stuttering facilitate our therapeutic approach? *Journal of Communication Disorders, 10*, 77–83.

Ratner, N. B. (2001). The syllabus project. *Special Interest Division 4: Fluency and Fluency Disorders, 11*(4), 16–18.

Shapiro, D. A. (1999). *Stuttering intervention: A collaborative journey to fluency freedom.* Austin, TX: Pro-Ed.

Shearer, W. M., & Williams, J. D. (1965). Self-recovery from stuttering. *Journal of Speech and Hearing Disorders, 30*, 288–290.

Sheehan, J. G. (1979). Current issues on stuttering and recovery. In H. H. Gregory (Ed.), *Controversies about stuttering therapy* (pp. 175–208). Baltimore, MD: University Park.

Sheehan, J. G., & Martyn, M. M. (1966). Spontaneous recovery from stuttering. *Journal of Speech and Hearing Research, 9*, 121–135.

Sheehan, J. G., & Martyn, M. M. (1970). Stuttering and its disappearance. *Journal of Speech and Hearing Research, 13*, 279–289.

St. Louis, K. O. (2001). *Living with stuttering: Stories, basics, resources, and hope.* Morgantown, WV: Populore Publishing Co.

Van Riper, C. (1982). *The nature of stuttering* (2nd ed.) Englewood Cliffs, NJ: Prentice-Hall.

Wingate, M. E. (1964). Recovery from stuttering. *Journal of Speech and Hearing Disorders, 29*, 312–321.

Wingate, M. E. (1976). *Stuttering: Theory and treatment.* New York: Irvington.

Wingate, M. E. (1997). *A short history of a curious disorder.* Westport, CT: Bergin & Garvey .

Yairi, E., & Ambrose, N. G. (1999). Early childhood stuttering I: Persistency and recovery rates. *Journal of Speech, Language, and Hearing Research, 42*, 1097–1112.

AUTHOR'S NOTE

This chapter is based on a paper first presented at the 2002 University of Georgia State of the Art Conference on evidence-based treatment of stuttering. Special thanks to Jesika Benson, Jill Evensen, and Kathy Hamilton for assistance with data collection and reliability.

III

MEASUREMENT ISSUES FOR EVIDENCE-BASED ASSESSMENT AND TREATMENT OF STUTTERING

8

Development of a Scale to Measure Peer Attitudes Toward Children Who Stutter

Marilyn Langevin
Institute for Stuttering Treatment & Research

Paul Hagler
University of Alberta

Although there is a lack of objective data regarding peer attitudes toward children who stutter, there is a broadly accepted clinical need to improve peer attitudes, reduce teasing, and help children who stutter cope in school. Speech language pathologists are encouraged to go into classrooms to make or assist children who stutter in making presentations to educate classmates about stuttering (Langevin, 2000; Manning, 1996; Ramig & Bennett, 1995; Shapiro, 1999; Silverman, 1996). Just as it is incumbent on our profession to evaluate treatment outcome, it is our responsibility to demonstrate that classroom intervention is effective, especially because efforts to educate nonstuttering adults have not necessarily been effective in improving attitudes toward adults who stutter (Snyder, 2001) and, in some respects, have brought about a negative change (Leahy, 1994; McGee, Kalinowski, & Stuart, 1996). There is an urgent need for objective data regarding peer attitudes toward children who stutter. Only after development of a reliable and valid method of assessing children's attitudes can the effectiveness of educational intervention be assessed.

LITERATURE REVIEW

There is evidence that the environment plays at least a mediating role in stuttering (Packman & Onslow, 1999) to the extent that frequency and severity of stuttering varies across listeners, situations, and physical environments (Bloodstein, 1995; Yaruss, 1997). Anecdotal evidence together with Frewer's (1993) report indicate that children who stutter experience increased difficulty in the classroom when they are reading, answering and asking questions, giving presentations, and seeking help from the teacher. Children who stutter also reported that stuttering affects their ability to concentrate in the classroom (Frewer, 1993).

It has been suggested that the quality of peer interactions affects the academic achievement, socialization, and healthy development of children (Johnson, 1981), and the importance of examining the effects of stuttering on peer interactions has long been recognized (Bloch & Goodstein, 1971). Although current research is needed to determine the extent to which children who stutter differ from nonstuttering children in academic and social development, children who stutter were reported to have mild degrees of educational maladjustment, probably as a consequence of stuttering in the school setting (Bloodstein, 1995), with some scoring one-half standard deviation below nonstuttering children on intelligence tests and lagging 6 months behind peers in academic achievement (Andrews et al., 1983). Although Woods (1974) found no differences in social acceptance between boys who stutter and boys who are normally fluent, children who stutter and those with other articulation disorders have generally been found to have lower social positions than nonhandicapped children (Marge, 1966; Perrin, 1954; Woods & Carrow, 1959). Children who stutter also were found to be more introverted than nonstuttering children (O'Kasha, Bishry, Kamel, & Hassan, 1974). In addition, children who stutter appear to be at greater risk for experiencing negative peer interactions as a result of being teased at school more frequently than normally fluent children (Langevin, Bortnick, Hammer, & Wiebe, 1998).

In contrast to our extensive understanding of commonly held negative stereotypes of people who stutter held by adults in various vocations and positions within the community (see references in Appendix A), little is known about peer attitudes toward children who stutter. However, attitudes of 2nd- to 6th-grade students toward children with articulation disorders have been studied. Using variations of semantic differential scales originally created by Osgood, Succi, and Tannenbaum (1957), Gies-Zabrowski and Silverman (1985) found that students held negative attitudes toward an 11-year-old girl with mild dysarthria. Madison and Gerlitz (1991) found negative attitudes toward a 7-year-old girl simulating a frontal lisp and Freeby and Madison (1989) and Crowe Hall (1991) obtained similar results with attitudes toward children with /r/, /s/ and /z/

misarticulations. Given what is known about attitudes toward children with articulation disorders, the existence of negative attitudes toward children who stutter is likely.

To begin development of an attitude scale, one must consider the model of attitude that will be used to guide scale development and the most appropriate ways of establishing validity and reliability. A viable model of attitude is the hierarchical tripartite model of attitude (Ajzen, 1988; Kothandapani, 1971; Ostrom, 1969; Rosenberg & Hovland, 1960; Triandis, 1971), which has been used in measuring peer attitudes toward children with handicaps (Rosenbaum, Armstrong, & King, 1986; Siperstein, 1980; Siperstein, Bak, & O'Keefe, 1988). In this multidimensional model, evaluative attitude is at the highest level of abstraction with cognitive, affective and conative or behavioral responses at an intermediate level. Each component is further made up of verbal and nonverbal responses. The verbal and nonverbal responses toward an attitude object form the measurable indices of attitude.

Content validity has been a major consideration in construction of achievement and proficiency tests, however it is often ignored in the construction of attitude scales (Borhnstedt, 1970). The attitudinal domain must be clearly defined and items constructed must explore various aspects of the domain (Ajzen, 1988). In investigating peer attitudes, potential attitudinal domains include the areas of study, play, and friendships that occur in school, at home, and in public places. Adequate representation of these domains should be considered in generating the initial pool of items and in any processes to reduce the number of items in a scale.

Reliability of a scale is generally measured in terms of stability over time or alternate forms, if such is appropriate, however an estimation of reliability in terms of internal consistency (Mueller, 1986) is a preliminary index of reliability in scale development. Internal consistency, or the correlation between items, is measured using Cronbach's (1951) coefficient alpha. Jackson (1988) indicated that an alpha higher than .70 is good, and Mueller (1986) suggested that a well constructed attitude scale will have coefficients of .80 or .90.

Evidence of construct validity can be obtained using a variety of methods. For example: (a) internal consistency looks for items with high intercorrelations that are "working together to measure the same underlying variable" (Mueller, 1986, p. 71), (b) factor analysis can be used to determine how much a test shares in common with other tests measuring the same construct, and (c) hypotheses can be made and tested to determine if respondents will score in certain ways (Ventry & Schiavetti, 1980). Logical construct validity could thus be evaluated by determining if a scale differentiates between groups of children based on variables, such as gender, age/grade, and amount of contact, that have been associated with attitudes toward children with disabilities and speech disorders.

Gender

Despite contrasting results regarding children's perceptions of lisping (Madison & Gerlitz, 1991) there is strong evidence (Horne, 1985) that females from kindergarten through college demonstrate greater acceptance of handicaps than males (Favazza & Odom, 1996; Ferguson, 1998; Kishi & Meyer, 1994; Voeltz, 1980, 1982). They also have (a) more positive attitudes toward peers with disabilities (Krajewski & Flaherty, 2000; Rosenbaum et al., 1986; Siperstein, Bak, & Gottliebe, 1977; Townsend, Wilton, & Vakilirad, 1993), (b) more positive perceptions of children with articulation disorders (Freeby & Madison, 1989), and (c) more positive perceptions of adult males who stutter (Dietrich, Jensen, & Williams, 2001).

Age/grade

There appears to be a developmental trend wherein beliefs, attitudes, and behavior toward the disabled become increasingly favorable from early childhood until the late teens (Ryan, 1981). Despite some contradictory evidence (Crowe Hall, 1991; Rosenbaum, Armstrong, & King, 1988), younger children have been found to have less positive attitudes toward children with disabilities than children aged 11 to 12 years (Katz & Chamiel, 1989) and children at the intermediate level (Townsend, Wilton, & Vakilirad, 1993). Children in lower elementary grades were also less accepting of children with disabilities than those in higher elementary grades (Voeltz, 1980).

Contact

Children who have had contact with disabled peers tend to be more accepting (Favazza & Odom, 1997; Voeltz, 1980, 1982) and have more positive attitudes (Roberts & Lindsell, 1997; Rosenbaum et al., 1986) toward children with disabilities than children who have not had contact. These differences also have been found in the teen population in terms of (a) attitudes toward children with disabilities (Most, Weisel, & Tur-Kaspa, 1999; Krajewski & Flaherty, 2000), and (b) acceptance of (Kishi & Meyer, 1994) and willingness to interact with peers with disabilities (Carter, Hughes, Copeland, & Breen, 2001). It is interesting to note that adults who had contact with someone who stutters had both less stereotypical (Klassen, 2001) and typically negative (Doody, Kalinowski, Armson, & Stuart, 1993; Turnbaugh, Guitar, & Hoffman, 1979) attitudes toward adults who stutter.

Given the evidence for gender, age/grade, and contact trends in attitudes toward children with disabilities and speech disorders, it could be predicted that more positive attitudes would be found for females, older elementary children, and children who have had contact with someone who stutters.

PURPOSE

The purpose of this study was to begin the process of developing a scale to measure peer attitudes toward children who stutter. To accomplish this, the following research questions were addressed:

1. Which of the items in a field test version of the scale should be retained based on item-total score correlations?
2. Is the peer attitude scale internally consistent?
3. Does the peer attitude scale have logical construct validity in terms of its ability to discriminate between groups of children based on gender, grade, and contact?
4. Does the tripartite model of attitude have construct validity to the extent that validity is evidenced through: (a) measures of internal consistency of subscales purporting to measure each component, and (b) factor analysis of scale scores?

METHOD

This study was carried out in 3 phases, each with distinct activities. Thus, each phase has its own unique organization regarding participants, materials, and findings. The discussion following Phase III is cumulative and relates to the entire project.

Phase I: Scale Construction and Pretesting

Item Generation

To ensure that scale construction proceeded systematically, within well defined boundaries, the tripartite model (Ajzen, 1988; Kothandapani, 1971; Ostrom, 1969; Rosenberg & Hovland, 1960; Triandis, 1971), was adopted to guide item generation and subscale development. Ideas for attitude items were drawn from existing scales that measured attitudes toward children with physical and mental handicaps (Parish & Taylor, 1978; Rosenbaum et al., 1986; Selman, 1980; Siperstein, 1980; Voeltz, 1980; Yuker, Block, & Younng, 1970). Also, ideas were obtained from interviews with children who do and do not stutter (Harter, 1982; Siperstein, 1980).

Interviews were conducted using the protocol described in MacEachern (1991). Four children who stutter, 1 female and 3 males, aged 9 to 12 years, were recruited from the client list at the Institute for Stuttering Treatment and Research in Edmonton, Alberta and were interviewed individually. They responded to questions about their perceptions of peer attitudes toward children who stutter (e.g., How would other kids describe kids who stutter?) and the type of activities in which they engaged. Fourteen children who do not stutter, 8 females and 6 males, aged 8 to 12 years, were recruited from the primary investigator's neighborhood in the greater Edmonton area and were interviewed either individually or in groups of two. Five of the nonstuttering children knew a person who stuttered. The children responded to questions about their beliefs, attitudes, and behavioral intentions toward children who stutter. Children also chose adjectives to describe children who stutter from an adjective checklist that was adapted from Siperstein (1980).

Initial Pool of Items

An initial pool of 116 items was constructed heeding suggestions of Girod (1973), Edwards (1957, cited in Girod, 1973), and Mueller (1986). Efforts also were made to ensure that the content domain and attitudinal components were adequately represented. Age-appropriate vocabulary and simple, clear, direct language were used. Complex or compound sentences were avoided resulting in items that were short, contained only one complete thought and avoided universals such as all, always, none, and never. Positively and negatively worded items were included to disrupt acquiescent responding—a response style in which respondents tend to endorse the same response category for all items. In addition, items were written at the third-grade level as confirmed by the Fry Readability Scale (Fry, 1968) to control for differing reading abilities across grade levels.

Reduction of Items

To reduce the initial pool of 116 items to a subset that would adequately represent the content domain and the tripartite model of attitude, yet be appropriate in length, a three-step process was followed. First, the investigators screened out 42 items that were ambiguous or redundant. Secondly, three experts, one in each of stuttering research, attitude scale construction, and elementary education, reviewed the remaining 72 items to determine face validity, clarity, appropriateness of grammatical structure, complexity, language, and reading level. Based on reviewer comments, 11 items were discarded. Finally, the remaining 61 items were classified into affective (feeling statements), cognitive (belief statements), and conative (behavioral intent statements) by four experienced judges (two psychology graduate students and two professors, one in education and one in speech-language pathology) and four novice judges (college undergraduates in various disciplines). Instructions included component definitions adapted from those devised by Ostrom (1969) with examples. Fifty five items were retained for the pilot scale (see Table 8.1). They consisted of the following: (a) 43 items that had been assigned to one component by all judges; (b) nine items that had been assigned to two or three components (with observed frequencies of 7:1:0 or 6:1:1) but had a significantly different modal component when frequencies were subjected to chi-square tests (Welkowitz, Ewen, & Cohen,

TABLE 8.1
Item-Total Score Correlations for Pilot and Revised Scales, Assignment of Items to Factors, and Assignment of Items to 20-Item Forms A and B

Items[1]	Subscale	Pilot Scale	Revised Scale***	Factor 1	Factor 2	Factor 3	20-Item Scales
1. I would like having a kid who stutters live next door to me.	A+	.63*	.57	.60			B
2. I would avoid a kid who stutters.	B–	.70*	.62	–.59			A
3. I would walk in the hall with a kid who stutters.	B+	.66*	.67	.68			B
4. Kids who stutter do not want to go to parties.	C–	.68*	.31			.67	B
5. Kids who stutter are like normal kids.	C+	.62*	.54			–.53	B
6. I would be ashamed to be seen with a kid who stutters.	A–	.59*	.68			.70	B
7. I would not go bicycle riding with a kid who stutters.	B–	.55*	.69	–.63		.60	B
8. I would enjoy doing a class project with a kid who stutters.	A+	.65*	.64	.70			A
9. Kids who stutter are weird.	C–	.60*	.63			.66	B
10. I would feel foolish if a kid stuttered in front of my parents.	A–	.61*	.71			.60	A
11. I would introduce a kid who stutters to my friends.	B+	.72*	.75	.73			B
12. Kids who stutter are easy to get along with.	C+	.58*	.40	.47			B
13. I would be embarrassed if a kid stuttered in front of a cashier.	A–	.58*	.70	–.60	.57		B
14. I would not play inside my house with a kid who stutters.	B–	.74*	.69	–.61			A
15. I would be happy to have a kid who stutters for a friend.	A+	.73*	.75	.81		.60	A
16. A kid who stutters can be a good friend.[2]	C+	.63*	.55	.60			A
17. I would not go to the store with a kid who stutters.	B–	.86*	.75	.70			A
18. I would walk home with a kid who stutters.	B+	.75*	.75	.72			B
19. I would like to sit beside a kid who stutters.	A+	.82*	.75	.77			A
20. Kids who stutter feel sorry for themselves.	C–	.51*	.28		.62		A
21. I would go to the movies with a kid who stutters.	B+	.70*	.75	.70			A

(continued on next page)

145

TABLE 8.1 (continued)

Items[1]	Subscale	Pilot Scale	Revised Scale***	Factor 1	Factor 2	Factor 3	20-Item Scales
22. I would feel uptight talking with a kid who stutters.	A–	.71*	.53		.59		A
23. Kids who stutter should be allowed to make speeches.	C+	.64*	.52	.51			A
24. I would be frustrated listening to a kid who stutters.	A–	.74*	.57		.67		B
25. I would invite a kid who stutters to my birthday party.	B+	.72*	.78	.80			B
26. I would not do homework with a kid who stutters.	B–	.87*	.68	–.60	.54		A
27. Kids who stutter are friendly.	C+	.57*	.26	.39			B
28. I would like a kid who stutters to talk for my group in class.	A+	.63*		.74	.76		B
29. Listening to a kid who stutters would annoy me.	A–	.70*	.68		.69		A
30. I would let a kid who stutters hang out with us.	B+	.60*	.79	.79			A
31. I would not play with a kid who stutters.	B–	.66*	.75	–.66			B
32. I would enjoy being with a kid who stutters.[2]	A+	.52*	.72	.75			A
33. Kids who stutter expect too much help to do things.	C–	.53*	.41		.62		A
34. I would be best friends with a kid who stutters.	B+	.81*	.70	.71			A
35. I would be embarrassed to be with a kid who stutters.	A–	.80*	.74	–.68			B
36. I would like having a kid who stutters in my class.	A+	.56*	.72	.78			B
37. I would not go to the playground with a kid who stutters.	B–	.80*	.74	–.68			B
38. I would sit on the bus with a kid who stutters[2]	B+	.74*	.77	.76			A
39. Kids who stutter should not play games that involve talking.	C–	.57*	.53		.52		A
40. I would play at recess with a kid who stutters.[2]	B+	.76*	.77	.76			B
I would not know what to say to a kid who stutters.[3]	A–	.49*					B
Kids who stutter are loners.	C–	.48*					
I would be afraid of a kid who stutters.	A–	.44**					

146

Items[1]	Subscale	Pilot Scale	Revised Scale***	Factor 1	Factor 2	Factor 3	20-Item Scales
I would really like to help a kid who stutters.	A+	.44**					
I would stick up for a kid who stutters.	B+	.42**					
I would study with a kid who stutters.	B+	.41**					
I would not invite a kid who stutters to my house.	B–	.38**					
I would be eager to talk to a kid who stutters.	A+	.35**					
Kids who stutter should talk for their group in class.	C+	.33**					
Kids who stutter want lots of attention.	C–	.33**					
Its okay to laugh at kids who stutter.	C–	.31					
I would be nervous around a kid who stutters.	A–	.30					
Kids who stutter are smart.	C+	.26					
I would feel sorry for a kid who stutters.	A+	–.04					
Kids who stutter are nervous.	C–	–.05					

A = affective; C = cognitive; B = behavioral intent; + = positive item; – = negative item. (*$p \leq .01$; **$p \leq .05$; ***$p = .000$); [1]Item numbers are those used in the revised scale; [2]Grammatical corrections were made to these items in the revised scale; [3]Italicized items were not selected for the revised scale.

147

1982) using the null hypothesis of .33. For the observed frequencies of 7:1:0, $\chi^2 = 8.17$, cv $= 7.82$, $p = .02$, and for 6:1:1, $\chi^2 = 6:26$, cv $= 5.99$, $p = .05$; (c) two rejected affective items that were revised; and (d) one unrevised rejected affective item. The rejected affective items were retained to ensure equal representation of the affective component. Minor revisions in terms of directionality of items were made to balance positive and negative items within each subscale.

Scaling and Response Format

Likert (1932) response scaling, which had been used in the measurement of children's attitudes and acceptance of children who are disabled (Rosenbaum et al., 1986; Voeltz, 1980, 1982), was chosen. Two sets of 5 response descriptors were devised for a pretesting procedure with a preliminary behavioral intent scale. For the first half of the preliminary behavioral intent scale, the traditional endpoints of *strongly disagree* and *strongly agree* with *not sure* replacing the usual *undecided* midscale choice were used. For the second half of the scale, the following descriptors, adapted from Harter (1982) were used: *really disagree, sort of disagree, not sure, sort of agree* and *really agree*.

Attitude Referents

Because stimuli used to evoke attitudinal reactions are important and the vagueness of labels may evoke conceptions that are quite different from those of the investigator (Jaffe, 1966), it was important to ensure that all respondents in this study had a standard visual and verbal representation of children who stutter. It was also important to provide both a male and female referent because gender is a factor in the formation of friendships wherein children tend to be less accepting of opposite sex peers (Siperstein et al., 1988). To select the attitude referents, a pool of videotapes of children who stutter was reviewed. These videotapes were taken prior to treatment at the Institute for Stuttering Treatment and Research.

The following factors were considered in choosing the attitude referents: gender, age, stuttering severity (considering core and associated behaviors), vocal characteristics (pitch, loudness, and intonation), articulatory rate, content of conversation, personal appearance, absence of language and articulation deficits, and absence of stigmatizing nonverbal behaviors (facial expression, posture, and gestures). The nonstigmatizing criteria mitigated against selecting referents without misarticulations and matching referents on severity of stuttering.

A 9-year-old male and 8-year-old female were selected. The male had moderate stuttering characterized primarily by part word repetitions with associated head movements and broken eye contact. He stuttered on 16.5% of syllables spoken. He also had two slight articulatory distortions of /tʃ/

(as in chu<u>rch</u>) and /ʤ/ (as jud<u>ge</u>) and an inconsistent lateralized /s/ production. The stigmatizing nature of these articulatory distortions was probed in the pretesting procedure. The female had severe stuttering, characterized by audible prolongations and part-word repetitions with associated rapid jaw jerking, inversion and compression of lips on bilabial phonemes, pronounced breathing disruptions, and an almost constant downward head position and gaze. She stuttered on 43% of syllables spoken. Two, 2-minute VHS videotapes were prepared featuring 1 minute samples of each referent conversing with an interviewer. The order of the female and male referents was counterbalanced across the videotapes.

Pretesting

Pretesting was carried out to: (a) probe stigmatizing characteristics of the attitude referents other than stuttering, (b) determine the preferred Likert (1932) scale response descriptors, (c) validate respondents' understanding of the response format, and (d) evaluate administrative procedures.

Participants.   The 14 previously interviewed nonstuttering children participated in the pretesting phase that took place at the Institute for Stuttering Treatment and Research or in the homes of the children or primary investigator.

Materials.   A booklet was prepared that contained a section for collecting demographic data and information regarding contact or knowledge of a person who stutters, a training section, and a preliminary 32-item behavioral intent scale selected from the initial pool of 116 items.

Procedure.   Following a brief introduction, the videotape of the attitude referents was shown using VHS players and TV monitors available at each location at which pretesting was conducted. Immediately after viewing each attitude referent, children were asked what they thought about the child on the videotape and why. Demographic information was obtained, the training section was completed, instructions for completing the behavior intent scale were given, and the scale was completed. Each item was read aloud by the primary investigator to control for differing reading abilities. The order of presentation of the two response descriptor options was counterbalanced across the children to prevent order effects for preferred response option. The children were asked to choose their preferred set of response descriptors and their understanding of the response format was validated by determining the consistency between a response option chosen and a verbal explanation of why the choice was made. Each child was asked to provide a verbal elaboration of between four and seven items that utilized the preferred set of response descriptors. Items used for validation were randomly selected from both negatively and positively worded items.

Results. Comments made by the participants indicated that, other than stuttering, the children who stuttered looked like "normal kids." No comments were made about the male's mild articulatory distortions. Ten of the 14 children preferred the response descriptors with endpoints of *strongly disagree* and *strongly agree*. Verbal explanations of chosen responses were judged to be consistent 93% of the time. Only minor refinements to the administrative procedures were needed.

Phase II: Pilot Study

A pilot study was carried out to determine which of the 55 items had satisfactory item-total score correlations, thus rendering them potential items for a peer attitude scale.

Participants. The pilot scale was administered to 28 fifth-grade students aged 10 to 12 years, of which 15 were male and 13 were female. Eight students had contact with a person who stutters. Because this investigation did not include an educational component about stuttering, a classroom in which there were no children who stutter was selected to prevent possible embarrassment on the part of the child who stutters and any heightened sensitivity on the part of nonstuttering peers. Grade 5 was selected because it represented the median grade for which the attitude scale was being designed. Once the classroom had been selected, no additional selection criteria within the class were imposed. Participants were all students present in class on the day the scale was administered.

Materials. A booklet was prepared containing a section for demographic data, information regarding prior contact with someone who stutters, a training section (described in MacEachern, 1991), and the 55-item pilot scale. Items were initially arranged in random order. To disrupt response bias and minimize methodological artifacts, adjustments were made to ensure that: (a) not more than two positive or negative items and not more than two items from one subscale followed in succession, and (b) approximately equal numbers of positive and negative items and items belonging to each subscale were in each half of the pilot scale. The preferred 5-point Likert (1932) response scale with endpoints of *strongly disagree* and *strongly agree* was used.

Procedures. Administration of the pilot scale involved the following: (a) demographic data were obtained, (b) the training section was completed, (c) a videotape of the attitude referents was shown (the tape with the male first was chosen by chance), (d) information regarding previous contact with a person who stutters was obtained (the name of the person had to be provided as a way of validating responses), (e) instructions for completion of the pilot scale were given, and (f) the pilot scale was completed. Each item was read aloud by the primary investigator to control for differing reading abilities. After administration of the scale began, questions regarding interpretation of items were handled with a planned response that encouraged children to make their choice according to how they understood the statement. At the half-way point in the scale, children were told that they were half-way through and were reminded to make the choice that was best for them. A final debriefing was undertaken to discourage formation of a negative bias toward children who stutter, which may have been fostered inadvertently by the inclusion of negative items in the scale. Following Yuker's (1988) suggestions, children were cautioned against adopting negative items as statements of truth and fact. The purpose of including the negative items in the scale was discussed and the heterogeneity of children who stutter was stressed. Administration and debriefing were completed in 26 minutes.

Scoring.   Attitude items were scored using values ranging from *1* (*strongly disagree*) to 5 (*strongly agree*). Negative items were inversely coded. Higher scores reflected more positive attitudes. One response omission by one child was dealt with by computing the mean score on all completed items and selecting the response choice that was closest to the mean.

Results.   Item analysis was undertaken using Pearson product moment correlations of item scores with total scores. Item-total score correlations indicated the extent to which items discriminated among respondents in the same manner as the total score (Mueller, 1986). Correlation coefficients are shown in Table 8.1. Correlations ranged from a low of –.05 to a high of .87.

Mueller suggested that items having low or near zero correlations should be eliminated because they are not measuring the same construct as other items and do not contribute to the scale. Nunnally (1970) indicated that items having the highest item-total score correlations are the best items, because they have more variance relating to a common factor and thus will enhance scale reliability. According to Jackson (1988), items with item-total score correlations higher than .25 are potentially good items. As shown in Table 8.1, 53 of the 55 items had correlations greater than .25.

Twice the number of items desired in a final scale were selected for a revised scale, thus 40 items having the highest item-total score correlations were chosen. As shown in Table 8.1, pilot scale items having item-total score correlations of less than .50 were rejected. Although the item-total score correlation was the only criterion for item selection, satisfactory representation of positive and negative items, and each attitudinal component was obtained. The affective subscale was comprised of 14 items, of which 7 were positive and 7 were negative. The cognitive subscale had 10 items, of which 5 were positive and 5 were negative and the behavioral intent subscale had 16 items, of which 9 were positive and 7 were negative. Alpha coefficients (Cronbach, 1951) were .97 for the 40 items selected and .91, .87 and .95 for the affective, cognitive and behavioral intent subscales respectively. SPSS-X Statistical Package for the Social Sciences (SPSS Inc., 1988) was utilized for all statistical calculations in this study.

Phase III: Revised Scale

Testing of the revised scale was undertaken with a larger subject pool to: (a) determine which of the 40 items would be potential items for a final scale as determined by satisfactory item-total score correlations, (b) to evaluate internal consistency of items selected for a proposed final scale, and (c) investigate construct validity of the tripartite model of attitude to determine its utility in future development of the attitude scale.

Participants.   The revised scale was administered to 267 children, aged 8 to 13 years, enrolled in the fourth, fifth and sixth grades in four schools located in Edmonton, Alberta. Each gender (134 females and 133 males) and grade (88, 87, and 92 in grades 4, 5, and 6 respectively) were almost equally represented. Seventy-four students had contact with a person who stutters, whereas 193 did not. The size of the subject pool surpassed the minimum of five times the number of items (Nunnally, 1970) or 200 subjects. Again, classrooms without children who stutter were selected. Because there were no other selection criteria, all students present in class on the day that the scale was administered were included in the subject pool. Subjects represented a wide range of individual abilities typically found in regular classrooms in which children with normal and exceptional learning abilities are integrated. Although information regarding cognitive abilities or scholastic performance of the children was not solicited prior to selecting classrooms, it was learned immediately prior to, or after testing, that 11 children had learning difficulties. On visual inspection, it appeared that their responses were not distinct from those of their classmates, thus their completed attitude scales were included in all statistical computations.

Materials.   Preparation of the 40-item revised scale booklet followed procedures used in preparation of the pilot scale booklet.

Procedures.   Procedures described in administration of the pilot scale were followed, with the exception that the order of videotapes showing the attitude referents was counterbalanced across classrooms. Procedures described in scoring the pilot scale were followed for scoring the revised scale.

Results.   Pearson product moment correlations of item scores with total scores are shown in Table 8.1. Correlations ranged from .26 to .79. Using

Jackson's (1988) criterion of .25 for item selection, all items were potential items for a final scale.

Several options existed for construction of a final scale. One option was to utilize all 40 items. This was called the Peer Attitudes Toward Children who Stutter-40 item Scale (PATCS-40). A second option involved creation of two, 20-item alternate forms. These scales were called the PATCS-20 Form A and PATCS-20 Form B. Thus, subsequent analyses were made using the PATCS-40 and PATCS-20, Forms A and B.

PATCS-40.   Alpha coefficients (Cronbach, 1951) were .96 for the PATCS-40 and .92, .85 and .95 for the affective, cognitive, and behavioral intent subscales respectively. As an additional measure of construct validity, three way analyses of variance with independent variables being gender (2 levels), grade (3 levels), and contact (2 levels) were completed for the total scale and each subscale to determine the extent to which the total scale and each subscale differentiated between these groups of children. Descriptive statistics are shown in Table 8.2.

Although group means were consistently higher for females than males on the total scale and all subscales, significant main effects for gender were not found. Mean scores for females as compared to males were 3.80 and 3.62 on the total scale, 3.67 and 3.47 on the affective subscale, 3.83 and 3.74 on the cognitive subscale, and 3.90 and 3.69 on the behavioral intent subscale.

Significant main effects for grade, reported in Table 8.3, were found on the total scale and all subscales. Posthoc analyses using Newman-Keuls' multiple range test were carried out to determine which grade means differed significantly. Significant differences are reported in Table 8.4. In summary, mean scores for fifth and sixth graders were significantly higher than fourth graders on the total scale and all subscales.

Significant main effects for contact with a person who stutters are shown in Table 8.5. Again, significant differences in mean scores were found for the total scale and all subscales.

Significant first order and second order interactions also were found on the cognitive subscale only. The first order interaction among gender and grade is graphed in Fig. 8.1. As anticipated, fifth- and sixth-grade females had higher mean scores than their male counterparts, but unexpectedly fourth-grade females had lower mean scores than fourth-grade males. Significant posthoc comparisons of means, shown in Table 8.6, reveal that the group mean for fourth-grade females was significantly lower than group means for fourth-grade males and fifth- and sixth-grade males and females.

The second order interaction among gender, grade, and contact is graphed in Fig. 8.2. Interestingly, fourth-grade females who had contact with someone who stutters (FC-Y) had a lower mean score than fourth-grade males who had no contact with someone who stutters (MC-0), but the

TABLE 8.2
Descriptive Statistics of the Revised Scale Scores

Group (n)	Affective Subscale Mean (range)	SD	Cognitive Subscale Mean	SD	Behavioral Subscale Mean	SD	Total Revised Scale Mean	SD
F (133)	3.67 (1.71–5.00)	.63	3.83 (2.10–5.00)	.46	3.90 (1.44–5.00)	.66	3.80 (2.03–4.83)	.55
M (134)	3.47 (1.00–4.86)	.77	3.74 (2.00–4.90)	.55	3.69 (1.38–5.00)	.81	3.62 (1.40–4.90)	.70
C-0 (193)	3.48 (1.00–4.86)	.72	3.73 (2.00–4.80)	.51	3.69 (1.38–5.00)	.78	3.63 (1.40–4.75)	.65
C-Y (74)	3.80 (2.00–5.00)	.64	3.92 (2.60–5.00)	.51	4.06 (2.44–5.00)	.58	3.93 (2.53–4.90)	.54
G4 (88)	3.36 (1.57–4.86)	.82	3.57 (2.10–4.90)	.58	3.53 (1.38–4.94)	.87	3.48 (1.78–4.90)	.75
G5 (87)	3.74 (1.00–4.93)	.63	3.92 (2.00–5.00)	.48	3.96 (1.38–5.00)	.65	3.87 (1.40–4.80)	.55
G6 (92)	3.61 (1.64–5.00)	.62	3.85 (2.40–4.70)	.39	3.89 (1.75–5.00)	.63	3.78 (1.88–4.83)	.53
F4 (41)	3.42 (1.71–4.79)	.78	3.54 (2.10–4.40)	.51	3.60 (1.44–4.8)	.81	3.51 (2.03–4.70)	.68
F5 (44)	3.78 (2.57–4.93)	.50	3.97 (3.20–5.00)	.40	4.01 (2.25–5.00)	.54	3.92 (2.75–4.80)	.43
F6 (48)	3.78 (2.64–5.00)	.54	3.94 (3.30–4.70)	.35	4.07 (3.00–5.00)	.52	3.94 (3.13–4.83)	.44
M4 (47)	3.31 (1.57–4.86)	.86	3.60 (2.20–4.90)	.65	3.48 (1.38–4.94)	.93	3.45 (1.78–4.90)	.80
M5 (43)	3.71 (1.00–4.86)	.75	3.87 (2.00–4.60)	.54	3.91 (1.38–5.00)	.76	3.83 (1.40–4.78)	.66
M6 (44)	3.43 (1.64–4.71)	.65	3.76 (2.40–4.70)	.42	3.69 (1.75–4.75)	.68	3.62 (1.88–4.68)	.57
F4C-0 (30)	3.42 (1.71–4.79)	.84	3.60 (2.10–4.40)	.52	3.62 (1.44–4.81)	.87	3.54 (2.03–4.70)	.73
F4-C-Y (11)	3.41 (2.36–4.50)	.63	3.37 (2.60–4.10)	.48	3.48 (2.44–4.75)	.62	3.43 (2.55–4.50)	.56
F5C-0 (29)	3.67 (2.57–4.50)	.43	3.91 (3.50–4.50)	.26	3.88 (2.25–4.94)	.53	3.81 (2.75–4.43)	.36
F5C-Y (15)	4.00 (3.21–4.93)	.55	4.09 (3.20–5.00)	.58	4.25 (3.50–5.00)	.48	4.13 (3.33–4.80)	.48
F6C-0 (33)	3.66 (2.64–4.50)	.52	3.90 (3.30–4.70)	.37	3.93 (3.00–4.69)	.51	3.82 (3.13–4.63)	.43
F6C-Y (15)	4.04 (3.00–5.00)	.52	4.03 (3.50–4.50)	.31	4.40 (3.94–5.00)	.38	4.18 (3.58–4.83)	.36
M4C-0 (36)	3.17 (1.57–4.79)	.83	3.48 (2.20–4.80)	.64	3.32 (1.38–4.88)	.95	3.31 (1.78–4.75)	.80
M4C-Y (11)	3.75 (2.00–4.86)	.81	3.96 (2.90–4.90)	.54	3.99 (2.75–4.94)	.63	3.90 (2.53–4.90)	.65
M5C-0 (36)	3.72 (1.00–4.86)	.74	3.88 (2.00–4.60)	.55	3.88 (1.38–5.00)	.79	3.82 (1.40–4.75)	.67

TABLE 8.2 (*continued*)

| Group (n) | Affective Subscale | | | Cognitive Subscale | | Behavioral Subscale | | Total Revised Scale | |
	Mean (range)	SD	Mean	SD	Mean	SD	Mean	SD
M5C-Y (7)	3.65 (2.71–4.79)	.88	3.86 (3.20–4.50)	.55	4.05 (3.38–4.94)	.58	3.86 (3.13–4.78)	.65
M6C-0 (29)	3.25 (1.64–4.50)	.66	3.62 (2.40–4.30)	.41	3.53 (1.75–4.63)	.72	3.46 (1.88–4.48)	.58
M6C-Y (15)	3.76 (2.86–4.71)	.49	4.01 (3.70–4.70)	.32	4.00 (3.00–4.75)	.48	3.92 (3.38–4.68)	.39

Note. Groups are defined by gender, grade, and contact (e.g., F = female, M = male, G4 = grade 4, C-Y = children who had contact with a person who stutters, C-0 = children who did not have contact with a person who stutters, F4C-0 = females in Grade 4 who did not have contact with a person who stutters, and M6C-Y = males in Grade 6 who had contact with someone who stutters). Higher scores represent more positive attitudes.

TABLE 8.3
Significant ANOVA Differences Among Grades

| Scale | Mean | | | F(2,255) | p |
	Grade 4	Grade 5	Grade 6		
Affective	3.36	3.74	3.61	3.96	.020
Cognitive	3.57	3.92	3.85	9.26	.000
Behavioral Intent	3.53	3.96	3.89	6.92	.001
Total scale	3.48	3.87	3.78	6.97	.001

TABLE 8.4
Significant Differences in Posthoc Analyses of Grade Using
Newman Keuls' Multiple Range Test

Grades	Scale	Required Difference	Observed Difference (p = .05)
5 vs. 4	Affective	.29	.32
6 vs. 4	Affective	.22	.24
5 vs. 4	Cognitive	.20	.33
6 vs. 4	Cognitive	.16	.29
5 vs. 4	Behavioral Intent	.30	.42
6 vs. 4	Behavioral Intent	.23	.36
5 vs. 4	Total scale	.25	.36
6 vs. 4	Total scale	.20	.30

TABLE 8.5
Significant ANOVA Differences Between Children Who had Contact With Someone Who Stutters and Those Who Did Not

	Mean		F(1,255)	p
Scale	Contact	No contact		
Affective	3.80	3.48	9.32	.003
Cognitive	3.92	3.73	5.50	.020
Behavioral Intent	4.06	3.69	11.80	.001
Total scale	3.93	3.63	10.94	.001

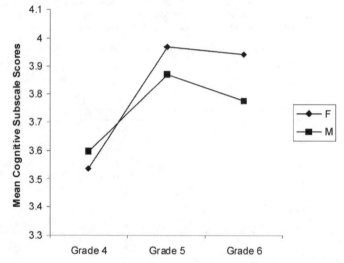

FIG. 8.1.   First order interaction of gender and grade on the cognitive subscale.

TABLE 8.6
Significant Differences in Posthoc Analyses of Gender and Grade Least Square Means in the First Order Interaction on the Cognitive Subscale Using Newman-Keuls' Multiple Range Test

Variable	Required Difference	Observed difference (p = .05)
F5 vs. F4	.33	.50
F6 vs. F4	.31	.48
M5 vs. F4	.34	.38
M6 vs. F4	.27	.34
M4 vs. F4	.23	.24

Note. Groups are defined by gender and grade (e.g., F5 = females in Grade 5 and M4 = males in Grade 4.

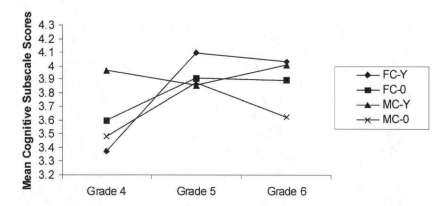

FIG. 8.2.   Second order interaction of gender, contact with a person who stutters, and grade on the cognitive scale. Note. FC-Y = females who had contact; FC-0 = females who did not have contact; MC-Y = males who had contact; and MC-0 = males who did not have contact.

difference between the means was not significant when subjected to post-hoc analyses. This finding may be sample specific. Significant posthoc comparisons are reported in Table 8.7. In summary, mean scores for fourth-grade females who had contact with someone who stutters and fourth-grade males who did not have contact were significantly lower than all fifth- and sixth-grade females, sixth-grade males who had contact with a person who stutters, and fifth-grade males who had no contact with a person who stutters. Thus, fourth-grade females with contact and fourth-grade males without contact had significantly less positive attitudes overall on the cognitive subscale.

To examine the extent to which the tripartite model should be used in further scale development, a principal components analysis, which attempts to explain as much variance in the data as possible (Kim & Mueller, 1978b), was used to obtain the initial factor solution. Three factors were extracted based on the hypothesis that three factors representing the tripartite model of attitude would emerge. Eigen values were 17.171 for Factor 1, 1.834 for Factor 2, and 1.445 for Factor 3. The variance accounted for by each factor was 42.9% for Factor 1, 4.6% for Factor 2, and 3.6% for Factor 3. The factor solution was then rotated using oblimin rotation, a method of oblique rotation which assumes that factors are correlated. If factors are uncorrelated, it is assumed that they represent distinctive underlying dimensions that make unique contributions to the attitude scale. Correlations of factor loadings, shown in Table 8.8, revealed low negative correlations between Factor 1 and Factors 2 and 3 and a low positive correlation between Factor 2 and Factor 3.

TABLE 8.7
Significant Differences in Post Hoc Analyses of Gender, Contact and Grade
Means in the Second Order Interaction on the Cognitive Subscale Using
Newman-Keuls' Multiple Range Test

Variable	Required Difference	Observed Difference ($p = .0.5$)
F5C-Y vs. F4C-Y	.62	.72
F4C-0	.48	.50
M4C-0	.48	.61
F6C-Y vs. F4C-Y	.61	.66
M4C-0	.47	.55
M6C-0	.47	.47
M6C-Y vs. F4C-Y	.60	.63
M4C-0	.46	.52
F5C-0 vs. F4C-Y	.52	.53
M4C-0	.35	.42
F6C-0 vs. F4C-Y	.49	.52
M4C-0	.33	.41
M5C-0 vs. F4C-Y	.47	.50
M4C-0	.31	.39

Note. Groups are defined by gender, grade, and contact (e.g., F5C-Y = females in Grade 5 who had contact with someone who stutters and M4C-0 = males in Grade 5 who did not have contact with someone who stutters).

TABLE 8.8
Matrix of correlations Among Factors after Oblimin Rotation ($p = .05$)

Factors	F1	F2	F3
F1	1	—	—
F2	−.36	1	—
F3	−.37	.33	1

To determine underlying dimensions, items were assigned to factors on which they loaded highest. Items that loaded within .05 on two factors were assigned to both factors (Rosenbaum et al., 1986) but were not considered in determining underlying dimensions because such items did not clearly represent one factor. High-loading items were considered to be those with loadings of ≥ .600. The hypothesis that factors would represent three distinct attitudinal components was tested by examining the items that loaded high on each factor. As shown in Table 8.1, affective and behavioral intent items loaded high on Factor 1, whereas affective and cognitive items loaded high on Factors 2 and 3.

PATCS-20 Form A and PATCS-20 Form B.   The second proposed option was to create two alternate forms that could be used in preintervention and postintervention measurement. Mueller (1986) suggested using an odd–even split procedure to create alternate forms wherein odd-numbered items are selected for one form and even-numbered items are selected for the other form. Revised scale items were rank ordered according to item-total score correlations and were grouped into positive and negative items. Working from the top downward on each group of positive and negative items, PATCS-20 Form A and PATCS-20 Form B were created. The procedure began with the first items in each group being assigned to Form A and the second items being assigned to Form B. It ended with the last two items in the positive group being assigned to Form B to achieve a 20-item scale. Items assigned to each scale are shown in Table 8.1. Alpha coefficients for Forms A and B were .93 and .92 respectively. Split half reliability for the alternate forms was .93.

DISCUSSION

The goal of Phase II was to determine which of the initial items should be retained for a field test version (Phase III, the revised scale) of the proposed attitude scale. Item analysis revealed that 53 items of the 55-item pilot scale were potentially good items for inclusion in the peer attitude scale. Forty items with the highest item-total score correlations were selected to form a revised scale, leaving 13 items that still may be considered as potential items in future scale development.

In Phase III, item analysis revealed that all 40 items were potential items for an attitude scale. Thus, it was proposed that a 40-item scale be considered, as well as two alternate form 20-item scales. Considering that an alpha greater than 0.70 is good (Jackson, 1988), the excellent measures of internal consistency achieved give good preliminary evidence of the reliability and validity of the PATCS-40 and the subscales. Results of the analyses of variance and posthoc analyses give further evidence of the construct validity of the PATCS-40 to the extent that predictions regarding the effects of contact and grade were observed. Children who had contact with a person who stutters had significantly more positive attitudes than those who did not, and attitudes tended to become more positive as grade levels increased, with fourth-grade children having significantly more negative attitudes than fifth- and sixth-grade children. Although there was no significant difference between fifth- and sixth-grades means, fifth-grade means were consistently higher than sixth-grade means. This finding does not follow a strict developmental trend in which attitudes become increasingly favorable from early childhood to late teens. It may be sample specific or it may reflect an unfavorability in attitudes of some sixth-grade children who are entering adolescence and are faced with unsettling changes that accompany pubescence and changing social interactions.

Construct validity of the PATCS-40 with respect to the hypothesized gender differences in attitude were not fully supported. Although female means were consistently higher than male means across the subscales and the total scale, the differences were not significant. Posthoc analysis of means arising from the first order interaction on the cognitive subscale only revealed that fourth-grade females had significantly more negative attitudes than their male counterparts. Although the difference was not significant in posthoc analysis of the second order interaction, fourth-grade females who had contact with someone who stutters had a lower mean score than all fourth-grade males. These findings may be responsible for the lack of predicted significant differences based on gender. It is possible that these findings are sample specific and will not bear out in future research.

Because experiment wise error rate was increased with four applications of ANOVA to data from the same subjects, probabilities of error exceeding .0125 (.05/4) must be viewed with caution. This applies to the significant findings of grade on the affective subscale, contact on the cognitive subscale, and the first and second order interactions on the cognitive subscale.

Construct validity of the tripartite model was supported to a limited degree by the high measures of internal consistency within the affective, cognitive, and behavioral intent subscales and the emergence of the significant first and second order interactions on the cognitive scale. The latter suggests that children responded differently to the cognitive subscale, however, factor analysis did not support the construct validity of the three component model of attitude. The aggregation of affective and behavioral intent items on Factor 1 and affective and cognitive items on Factors 2 and 3 suggests that a two-component model of attitude—affective-behavioral intent and affective-cognitive—may be more meaningful than the three dimensional model. These findings partially support those of Bagozzi and Burnkrant (1979) and Rosenbaum et al. (1986) to the extent that a two dimensional model may be more meaningful. However, unlike Bagozzi and Burnkrant and Rosenbaum et al., a clearly cognitive factor did not emerge in these results. These findings support Mueller's (1986) assertion that "affect for or against is a critical component of the attitude concept" (p. 2). It may be that, for this age group, verbal expressions of feelings about a psychological object are so intimately interwoven with expression of their beliefs or behavioral intentions that affective responses are not distinct from cognitive or behavioral intent responses when measured by verbal response indices. However, the lack of overlap between behavioral intent and cognitive items on the factors that emerged in this study and the emergence of the first and second order interactions on the cognitive subscale only provides minimal support for the distinctiveness of the cognitive component.

The substantive meaning of a factor is determined by examining the items that load high on the factor and deciding what such items have in common (Kim & Mueller, 1978a). Instead of representing distinct attitudinal components, factors represented content-defined dimensions. The highest loading items in Factor 1 were primarily positive and seemed to constitute a positive social distance construct in which general comfort in being with stuttering children is expressed. Factor 2 items were all negative and appeared to represent a verbal interaction dimension characterized by frustration. Factor 3 items were primarily negative and seemed to represent a social pressure factor relating to concern about what other peers or adults thought about children who stutter. These dimensions may be more meaningful and practically useful in future scale development and development of educational programs. The low correlations among factors suggest that, although there is overlap among the factors, they each make some distinct contributions to the revised scale.

LIMITATIONS AND FUTURE RESEARCH

This study represents the first stages in the development of an attitude scale. Limitations regarding the use of the proposed scales highlight the need for future investigations. These include the following: (a) cross validation of the PATCS-40 with a new subject pool and investigation of test/re-test reliability, concurrent validity, and predictive validity; (b) alternate form and test/re-test reliability of the PATCS-20, Forms A and B; (c) determination if a method factor exists that is specific to negative items; and (d) evaluation of the possible impact of socially desirable responding on scale scores.

The need to determine if a negative item method factor exists arises from the aggregation of primarily positive items on Factor 1 and negative items on Factors 2 and 3 in this study. These findings suggest that a positive construct (positive social distance) and two negative constructs (frustration associated with verbal interaction and social pressure related to a negative stereotype of stuttering children) constituted common underlying dimensions. It is possible that negative items contribute to a negative item factor that Marsh (1986) called a "method/halo bias ... specific to the negative items" (p. 37). Evidence presented by Benson and Hocevar (1985), Marsh (1986), and Rifkin, Wolf, Lewis, and Pantell (1988) indicated that the validity of children's rating scales may be reduced by including negative-item responses because children have difficulty responding appropriately to negatively worded items. It seems that the negative item bias gets weaker as age increases. However, Marsh (1986) found that it still existed for fifth-grade students. Although Rosenbaum et al. (1986) did not address the issue of a negative item method bias, inspection of their Factor 1 items revealed a preponderance of positive items, whereas Factor 2 items were primarily negative and Factor 3 items were all negative. Further research using confirmatory factor analysis is needed to determine whether negative items should be excluded from future revisions of the revised attitude scale.

Another possible threat to the validity of a scale of this type is the impact on scale scores of socially desirable responding (the tendency for respondents to make socially desirable responses at the expense of their true attitudes to achieve a better image of themselves). Mueller (1986) indicated that:

> The measurement problem occurs when this tendency is unequal among respondents. If some test takers gain many points, through socially desirable responding and others gain few or no points, then a large portion of variance (spread) in scale scores will be response-set variance rather than substantive (i.e. attitudinal) variance. (p. 74)

The effects of socially desirable responding were demonstrated by Hagler, Vargo, and Semple (1987) who found that university students' "faked" scores (condition in which subjects were asked to respond in a manner that reflected the most positive attitude possible) were significantly higher than "honest" scores on the Attitudes Toward Disabled Persons Scale (Yuker et al., 1970). Utilizing a scale such as the Social Desirability Scale for Children (Lunneborg & Lunneborg, 1964) and correlating summated scores with attitude scale scores in future research will inform the extent to which attitude scores are inflated by subjects' desire to present a better image.

The generalizability of findings regarding the degree of negativity or positivity of attitudes toward children who stutter is limited by the need for further reliability and validity investigations as discussed above. Mean attitude scores for Grades 4, 5, and 6 (3.48, 3.87, and 3.78 respectively) indicate that attitudes were moderately positive, however the range of scores within the groups indicate that there were students who had very negative attitudes (lows of 1.78, 1.40, and 1.88 for Grades 4, 5, and 6 respectively). These findings are preliminary, and they are also limited to the extent that they reflect attitudes toward children who stutter moderately and severely. Future research is needed using children who stutter mildly as attitude referents.

Definitive research is needed to evaluate the construct validity of the tripartite model of attitude in the measurement of children's attitudes. This study was not designed or intended to be a definitive study. Therefore, conclusions about the model's validity can not be reached. Breckler (1984) suggested that nonverbal measures, such as recordings of physiological responses of affect or overt behavior, should be used in addition to verbal report measures, because "one's cognitive system cannot be assumed to have complete access to emotional and behavioral experience" (p. 1193). Also, confirmatory factor analyses or covariance structure analyses, which test a model's goodness of fit to the data, should be used to validate the tripartite model rather than exploratory factor analysis. Factor analysis used in this study was essentially exploratory, being confirmatory only to the extent that the number of underlying common factors was hypothesized. Future scale development may involve the creation of factor subscales and further development of items to more comprehensively assess each dimension revealed in the factor analysis. Of particular interest is the social pressure factor associated with concern about what others think of children who stutter. The powerful impact of peer influence was revealed in the interviews of the children who do not stutter in the pre-testing procedures. The majority of these children were deeply and genuinely concerned with what their friends might think about children who stutter. They frequently indicated that their feelings and behaviors would be strongly influenced by their nonstuttering peers. Further research might indicate that the social pressure factor may be the most appropriate dimension to target and use as an outcome variable in intervention programs designed to improve peer attitudes.

CONCLUSION

The purpose of this investigation was to begin the development of a scale to measure peer attitudes toward children who stutter. Because satisfactory item-total score correlations were obtained for all 40 items of the revised scale, it was proposed that three scales, the PATCS-40 and the PATCS-20, Forms A and B, be developed further. Preliminary indications of reliability and validity of the PATCS-40 were demonstrated through satisfactory measures of internal consistency and construct validity in terms of the scale's ability to discriminate between groups of children on the basis of grade and contact. The lack of differences in gender may be sample specific. Cross validation with a larger population may be able to capture this type of discrimination better. Reliability and validity of the PATCS-20, Forms A and B, were demonstrated to the extent that satisfactory measures of internal consistency and split half reliability were obtained. Prior to recommending the use of either scale for measurement of attitudes toward children who stutter, further investigations of reliability and validity and threats to validity in terms of the effects of a negative item method bias and socially desirable responding are needed.

The validity of the tripartite model of attitude was evaluated to determine the extent to which it should guide further scale development. Factor analysis provided minimal support for a two-component model comprised of affective-cognitive and affective-behavioral intent dimensions. Instead of clearly representing attitudinal components, factors seemed to represent dimensions reflecting social distance (Factor 1), verbal interactions characterized by frustration (Factor 2), and a social pressure factor associated with concern about what others think about stuttering children (Factor 3). These factors may be used in guiding future development of subscales and possibly additional items. Directions for future research include the need to determine the discriminant validity of the tripartite model in measurement of children's attitudes.

The PATCS-40 appears to be a viable option for measuring peer attitudes toward stuttering children. Further investigation of the two forms of PATCS-20 is needed before viability can be ascertained. This was a promising first step in a series of investigations needed to develop a valid and reliable scale that can be used to (a) measure peer attitudes toward children who stutter, and (b) detect change as a result of educational interventions designed to improve the classroom environment of children who stutter.

REFERENCES

Ajzen, I. (1988). *Attitudes, personality, and behavior.* Milton Keynes, Buckinghamshire, UK: Open University Press.

Andrews, G., Craig, A., Feyer, A. M., Hoddinott, S., Howie, P., & Neilson, M. (1983). Stuttering: A review of research findings and theories circa 1982. *Journal of Speech and Hearing Disorders, 48,* 226–246.

Bagozzi, R. P., & Burnkrant, R. E. (1979). Attitude organization and the attitude-behavior relationship. *Journal of Personality and Social Psychology, 37*(6), 913–929.

Barbosa, L., Schiefer, A., & Chiari, B. (1995). How students of speech therapy perceive stuttering: A matter of prejudice. In C. W. Starkweather & H. F. M. Peters (Eds.), *Stuttering: Proceedings of the First World Congress on Fluency Disorders* (Vol. II, pp. 544–547). Nijmegen, The Netherlands: Nijmegen University Press.

Benson, J., & Hocevar, D. (1985, Fall). The impact of item phrasing on the validity of attitude scales for elementary school children. *Journal of Educational Measurement, 22*(3), 231–240.

Bloch, E. L., & Goodstein, L. D. (1971). Functional speech disorders and personality: A decade of research. *Journal of Speech and Hearing Disorders, 36,* 295–314.

Bloodstein, O. (1995). *A handbook on stuttering.* San Diego, CA: Singular Publishing Group.

Borhnstedt, G. (1970). Reliability and validity assessment in attitude measurement. In G. Summers (Ed.), *Attitude measurements,* (pp. 80–99). Chicago, IL: Rand McNally.

Breckler, S. J. (1984). Empirical validation of affect, behavior and cognition as distinct components of attitude. *Journal of Personality and Social Psychology, 47*(6), 1191–1205.

Carter, E. W., Hughes, C., Copeland, S. R., & Breen, C. (2001). Differences between high school students who do and do not volunteer to participate in a peer interaction program. *Journal of the Association of Persons With Severe Handicaps, 26,* 229–239.

Collins, C. R., & Blood, G. W. (1990). Acknowledgment and severity of stuttering as factors influencing nonstutterers' perceptions of stutterers. *Journal of Speech and Hearing Disorders, 55,* 75–81.

Cooper, E. B., & Cooper, C. S. (1985). Clinician attitudes toward stuttering: A decade of change (1973–1983). *Journal of Fluency Disorders, 10,* 19–33.

Cooper, E. B., & Cooper, C. S., (1996). Clinician attitudes towards stuttering: Two decades of change. *Journal of Fluency Disorders, 21,* 119–135.

Cooper, E. B., & Rustin, L. (1985). Clinician attitudes toward stuttering in the United States and Great Britain: A cross-cultural study. *Journal of Fluency Disorders, 10*, 1–17.

Craig, A., Hancock, K., Tran, Y., & Craig, M. (2000). Prevalence and stereotypes of stuttering in the community. In H. Bosshardt, J. S. Yaruss, & H. F. M. Peters (Eds.), *Fluency disorders: Theory, research, treatment and self-help: Proceedings of Third World Congress on Fluency Disorders in Nyborg, Denmark* (pp. 588–592). Nijmegen, The Netherlands: Nijmegen University Press.

Cronbach, L. J. (1951). Coefficient alpha in the internal structure of tests. *Psychometrika, 16*, 297–334.

Crowe, T. A., & Cooper, E. B. (1977). Parental attitudes toward and knowledge of stuttering. *Journal of Communication Disorders, 10*, 343–357.

Crowe, T. A., & Walton, J. H. (1981). Teacher attitudes toward stuttering. *Journal of Fluency Disorders, 6*, 163–174.

Crowe Hall, B. J. (1991). Attitudes of fourth and sixth graders toward peers with mild articulation disorders. *Language, Speech and Hearing Services in Schools, 22*, 334–340.

Dietrich, S., Jensen, K. H., & Williams, D. E., (2001). Effects of the label "stutterer" on student perceptions. *Journal of Fluency Disorders, 26*, 55–66.

Doody, I., Kalinowski, J., Armson, J., & Stuart, A. (1993). Stereotypes of stutterers and nonstutterers in three rural communities in Newfoundland. *Journal of Fluency Disorders, 18*, 363–373.

Dorsey, M., & Guenther, R. K. (2000). Attitudes of professors and students toward college students who stutter. *Journal of Fluency Disorders, 25*, 77–83.

Emerick, L. L. (1960). Extensional definition and attitude toward stuttering. *Journal of Speech and Hearing Research, 3*, 181–186.

Favazza, P. C., & Odom, S. L. (1996). Use of the acceptance scale to measure attitudes of kindergarten-age children. *Journal of Early Intervention, 20*, 232–249.

Favazza, P. C., & Odom, S. L. (1997). Promoting positive attitudes of kindergarten-age children toward people with disabilities. *Exceptional Children, 63*, 405–418.

Ferguson, J. M. (1998). High school students' attitudes toward inclusion of handicapped students in the regular education classroom. *The Educational Forum, 63*, 173–179.

Fowlie, G. M., & Cooper, E. B. (1978). Traits attributed to stuttering and non-stuttering children by their mothers. *Journal of Fluency Disorders, 3*, 233–246.

Freeby, N., & Madison, C. L. (1989). Children's perceptions of peers with articulation disorders. *Child Study Journal, 19*(21), 133–144.

Frewer, V. (1993). *Stammering: Educational implications and teacher awareness.* Unpublished doctoral dissertation, Gwent College of Higher Education, Gwent, Wales.

Fry, E. (1968). A readability formula that saves time. *Journal of Reading, 11*, 513–515, 575–578.

Gies-Zabrowski, J., & Silverman, F. H. (1985). *Documenting the impact of a mild dysarthria on peer perception. Language, Speech and Hearing Services in Schools, 17*, 143.

Girod, G. R. (1973). *Writing and assessing attitudinal objectives.* Columbus, OH: Merrill.

Grudner, T. M. (1978). Two formulas for determining the readability of subject consent forms. *American Psychologist, 33*, 773–775.

Hagler, P., Vargo, J., & Semple, J. (1987). The potential for faking on the Attitudes Toward Disabled Persons Scale. *Rehabilitation Counseling Bulletin, 31*, 72–76.

Ham, R. E. (1990). What is stuttering: Variations and stereotypes. *Journal of Fluency Disorders, 15*, 259–273.

Harter, S. (1982). The perceived competence scale for children. *Child Development, 53*, 87–97.

Horne, M. (1985). *Attitudes toward handicapped students: Professional, peer and parent reactions.* Hillsdale, NJ: Lawrence Erlbaum Associates.

Horsely, I. A., & Fitzgibbon, C. T. (1987). Stuttering children: Investigation of a stereotype. *British Journal of Disorders of Communication, 22*, 19–35.

Hulit, L. M., & Wirtz, L. (1994). The association of attitudes toward stuttering with selected variables. *Journal of Fluency Disorders, 19*, 247–267.

Hurst, M. I., & Cooper, E. B. (1983a). Employer attitudes toward stuttering. *Journal of Fluency Disorders, 8*, 1–12.

Hurst, M. A., & Cooper, E. B. (1983b). Vocational rehabilitation counselors' attitudes toward stuttering. *Journal of Fluency Disorders, 8*, 13–27.

Jaffe, J. (1966). Attitudes of adolescents toward the mentally retarded. *American Journal of Mental Deficiency, 70*, 907–912.

Jackson, W. (1988). *Research methods, rules for survey design and analysis.* Scarborough, ON: Prentice-Hall.

Johnson, D. W. (1981). Student-student interaction: The neglected variable in education. *Educational Researcher, 10*, 5–10.

Kalinowski, J., Armson, J., Stuart, A., & Lerman, J. W. (1993). Speech clinicians' and the general public's perceptions of self and stutterers. *Journal of Speech-Language Pathology and Audiology, 17*(2), 79–85.

Kalinowski, J. S., Lerman, J. W., & Watt, J. (1987). A preliminary examination of the perceptions of self and others in stutterers and nonstutterers. *Journal of Fluency Disorders, 12*, 317–331.

Katz, S., & Chamiel, M. (1989). Relationship between children's ages and parental attitudes and their attitudes toward a child with a physical disability. *International Journal of Rehabilitation Research, 12*, 190–192.

Kim, J., & Mueller, C. W. (1978a). *Introduction to factor analysis: What it is and how to do it.* Beverly Hills, CA: Sage.

Kim, J., & Mueller, C. W. (1978b). *Factor analysis: Statistical methods and practical issues.* Beverly Hills, CA: Sage.

Kishi, G. S., & Meyer, L. H. (1994). What children report and remember: A six-year follow-up of the effects of social contact between peers with and without severe disabilities. *Journal of the association for persons with severe handicaps, 19*, 277–288.

Klassen, T. R. (2000). The complexity of attitudes toward people who stutter. In H. Bosshardt, J. S. Yaruss, & H. F. M. Peters (Eds.), *Fluency disorders: Theory, research, treatment and self-help: Proceedings of Third World Congress on Fluency Disorders in Nyborg, Denmark* (pp. 605–609). Nijmegen, The Netherlands: Nijmegen University Press.

Klassen, T. (2001). Perceptions of people who stutter: Re-assessing the negative stereotype. *Perceptual and Motor Skills, 92*, 551–559.

Kothandapani, V. (1971). Validation of feeling, belief, and intention to act as three components of attitude and their contribution to prediction of contraceptive behavior. *Journal of Personality and Social Psychology, 19*, 321–333.

Krajewski, J., & Flaherty, T. (2000). Attitudes of high school students toward individuals with mental retardation. *Mental Retardation, 38*, 154–162.

Langevin, M. (2000). *Teasing and Bullying: Unacceptable Behaviour*. Edmonton, AB: Institute for Stuttering Treatment & Research.

Langevin, M., Bortnick, K., Hammer, T., & Wiebe, E. (1998). Teasing/Bullying experienced by children who stutter: Toward development of a questionnaire. *Contemporary Issues in Communication Science and Disorders, 25*, 12–24.

Lass, N. J., Ruscello, D. M., Pannbacker, M., Schmitt, J. F., & Everly-Myers, D. (1989). Speech-language pathologists' perceptions of child and adult female and male stutterers. *Journal of Fluency Disorders, 14*, 127–134.

Lass, N. J., Ruscello, D. M., Pannbacker, M., Schmitt, J. F., Kiser, A. M., Mussa, A. M., & Lockhart, P. (1994). School administrator's perceptions of people who stutter. *Language, Speech and Hearing Services in Schools, 25*, 90–93.

Lass, N. J., Ruscello, D. M., Schmitt, J. F., Pannbacker, M. D., Orlando, M. B., Dean, K. A., Ruziska, J. C., & Bradshaw, K. H. (1992). Teachers' perceptions of stutterers. *Language, Speech, and Hearing Services in Schools, 23*, 78–81.

Leahy, M. M. (1994). Attempting to ameliorate student therapists' negative stereotypes of the stutterer. *European Journal of Disorders of Communication, 29*, 39–49.

Likert, R. (1932). A technique for the measurement of attitudes. *Archives of Psychology, 140*, 44–53.

Lunneborg, P. W., & Lunneborg, C. E. (1964). The relationship of social desirability to other test-taking attitudes in children. *Journal of Clinical Psychology, 20*, 473–477.

MacEachern, M. (1991). Peer attitudes toward children who stutter. Unpublished master's thesis, University of Alberta, Edmonton, Alberta, Canada.

Madison, C. L., & Gerlitz, D. M. (1991). Children's perceptions of lisping and non-lisping female peers. *Child Study Journal, 21*, 277–284.

Manning, W. H. (1996). *Clinical decision making in the diagnosis and treatment of fluency disorders*. Albany, NY: Delmar Publishers.

Marge, D. K. (1966). The social status of speech-handicapped children. *Journal of Speech and Hearing Research, 9*, 165–177.

Marsh, H. W. (1986). Negative item bias in rating scales for preadolescent children: A cognitive-developmental phenomenon. *Developmental Psychology, 22*, 37–49.

McDonald, E. T., & Frick, J. V. (1954). Store clerks' reaction to stuttering. *Journal of Speech and Hearing Disorders, 19*, 306–311.

McGee, L., Kalinowski, J., & Stuart, A. (1996). Effect of a videotape documentary on high school students' perceptions of a high school male who stutters. *Journal of Speech-Language Pathology and Audiology, 20*, 240–246.

Most, T., Weisel, A., & Tur-Kaspa, H. (1999). Contact with students with hearing impairments and the evaluation of speech intelligibility and personal qualities. *The Journal of Special Education, 33*, 103–111.

Mueller, D. J. (1986). *Measuring social attitudes*. New York: Columbia University.

Naidoo, S., & Pillay, Y. G. (1990). Personal constructs of fluency: A study comparing stutterers and nonstutterers. *Psychological Reports, 66*, 375–378.

Nunnally, J. C. (1970). *Introduction to psychological measurement*. New York: McGraw-Hill.

Okasha, A., Bishry, Z., Kamel, M., & Hassan, A. H. (1974). Psychosocial study of stammering in Egyptian children. *British Journal of Psychiatry, 124*, 531–533.

Osgood, C. E., Suci, G. J., & Tannenbaum, P. H. (1957). *The measurement of meaning*. Urbana, IL: University of Illinois Press.

Ostrom, T. M. (1969). The relationship between the affective, behavioral, and cognitive components of attitude. *Journal of Experimental Social Psychology, 5*, 12–30.

Packman, A., & Onslow, M. (1999). The role of the environment in early stuttering. In K. L. Baker, L. Rustin, & F. Cook (Eds.), *Proceedings of the Fifth Oxford Dysfluency Conference* (pp. 20–25). Berkshire UK: Chappell Gardener.

Parish, T. S., & Taylor, J. C. (1978). The personal attribute inventory for children: A report on its validity and reliability as a self-concept scale. *Educational and Psychological Measurement, 38*, 565–569.

Patterson, J., & Pring, T. (1991). Listeners attitudes to stuttering speakers: No evidence for a gender difference. *Journal of Fluency Disorders, 16*, 201–205.

Perrin, E. H. (1954). The social position of the speech defective child. *Journal of Speech and Hearing Disorders, 19*, 250–254.

Ragsdale, J., & Ashby, J. (1982). Speech-language pathologists' connotations of stuttering. *Journal of Speech and Hearing Research, 25*, 75–80.

Ramig, P. R., & Bennett, E. M. (1995). Working with 7- to 12-year-old children who stutter: Ideas for Intervention in the Public Schools. *Language, Speech and Hearing, Services in Schools, 27*, 138–150.

Rifkin, L., Wolf, M. H., Lewis, C. C., & Pantell, R. H. (1988). Children's perceptions of physicians and medical care: Two measures. *Journal of Pediatric Psychology, 13*, 247–254.

Roberts, C. M., & Lindsell, J. S. (1997). Children's attitudes and behavioral intentions toward peers with disabilities. *International Journal of Disability, Development and Education, 44*, 133–145.

Rosenbaum, P. L., Armstrong, R. W., & King, S. M. (1986). Children's attitudes toward disabled peers: A self-report measure. *Journal of Pediatric Psychology, 11*, 517–530.

Rosenbaum, P. L., Armstrong, R. W., & King, S. M. (1988, Summer). Determinants of children's attitudes toward disability: A review of evidence. *Children's Health Care, 17*(1), 32–39.

Rosenberg, M. J., & Hovland, C. I. (1960). Cognitive, affective, and behavioral components of attitudes. In M. J. Rosenberg, C. I. Hovland, W. J. McGuire, R. P. Ableson, & J. W. Brehm (Eds.), *Attitude organization and change: An analysis of consistency among attitude components* (pp. 1–14). New Haven, CT: Yale University.

Ruscello, D. M., Lass, N. J., & Brown J. (1988). College students' perceptions of stutterers. *National Student Speech Language Hearing Association Journal, 16*(1), 115–120.

Ruscello, D. M., Lass, N. J., French, R. S., & Channel, M. D. (1989–1990). Speech-language pathology students' perceptions of stutterers. *National Student Speech Language Hearing Association Journal. 17*, 86–89.

Ruscello, D. M., Lass, N. J., Schmitt, J. F., & Pannbacker, M. D. (1994). Special educators' perceptions of stutterers. *Journal of Fluency Disorders, 19*, 125–132.

Ryan, K. M. (1981). Developmental differences in reactions to the physically disabled. *Human Development, 24*, 240–256.

St. Louis, K. O., & Lass, N. J. (1981). A survey of communicative disorders students' attitudes toward stuttering. *Journal of Fluency Disorders, 6,* 49–79.

St. Louis, K. O., Schiffbauer, J. D., Phillips, C. I., Sedlock, A. B., Hriblan, L. J., & Dayton, R. M. (2000). The public environment where attitudes develop: Stuttering versus mental illness and intelligence. Paper presented at the International Stuttering Awareness Day virtual conference. Retrieved March 21, 2001 from http://www.mankato.msus.edu/dept/comdis/ISAD3/papers/stlouis2.html

St. Louis, K., Yaruss, J. S., Lubker, B. B., Pill, J., Diggs, C. C., (2000). An international public opinion survey of stuttering: Pilot results. In H. Bosshardt, J. S. Yaruss, & H. F. M. Peters (Eds.), *Fluency disorders: Theory, research, treatment and self-help, Proceedings of Third World Congress on Fluency Disorders in Nyborg, Denmark* (pp. 581–587). Nijmegen, The Netherlands: Nijmegen University Press.

Selman, R. L. (1980). *The growth of interpersonal understanding: Developmental and clinical analyses.* New York: Academic.

Shapiro, D. A. (1999). *Stuttering Intervention.* Austin, TX: Pro-Ed.

Silverman, E. (1982). Speech-language clinicians' and university students' impressions of women and girls who stutter. *Journal of Fluency Disorders, 7,* 469–478.

Silverman, F. H. (1990). Are professors likely to report having "Beliefs" about the intelligence and competence of students who stutter? *Journal of Fluency Disorders, 15,* 319–321.

Silverman, F. H. (1996). Stuttering and other fluency disorders. Needham Heights, MA: Allyn & Bacon.

Silverman, F. H., & Marik, J. H. (1993). Teachers' perceptions of stutterers: A replication. *Language, Speech and Hearing Services in Schools, 24,* 108.

Silverman, F. H., & Paynter, K. K. (1990). Impact of stuttering on perception of occupational competence. *Journal of Fluency Disorders, 15,* 87–91.

Siperstein, G. N. (1980). Instruments for Measuring Children's Attitudes Toward the Handicapped. Unpublished manuscript, University of Massachusetts/Boston.

Siperstein, G. N., Bak, J. J., & Gottlieb, J. (1977). Effects of group discussion on children's attitudes toward handicapped peers. *The Journal of Educational Research, 70,* 131–134.

Siperstein, G. N., Bak, J. J., & O'Keefe, P. (1988). Relationship between children's attitudes toward and their social acceptance of mentally retarded peers. *American Journal on Mental Retardation, 93,* 24–27.

Snyder, G. J. (2001). Exploratory research in the measurement and modification of attitudes toward stuttering. *Journal of Fluency Disdorders, 26,* 149–160.

SPSS Inc. (1988). *SPSS-X User's Guide* (#rd ed.). Chicago: SPSS Inc.

Townsend, M. A. R., Wilton, K. M., & Vakilirad, T. (1993). Children's attitudes toward peers with intellectual disability. *Journal of Intellectual Disability Research, 37,* 405–411.

Triandis, H. (1971). *Attitude and attitude change.* New York: Wiley.

Turnbaugh, K. R., Guitar, B. E., & Hoffman, P. R. (1979). Speech clinician's attribution of personality traits as a function of stuttering severity. *Journal of Speech and Hearing Research, 22,* 37–45.

Turnbuagh, K., Guitar, B., & Hoffman, P. (1981). The attribution of personality traits: The stutterer and nonstutterer. *Journal of Speech and Hearing Research, 24,* 288–291.

Ventry, I., & Schiavetti, N. (1980). *Evaluating research in speech pathology and audiology.* Don Mills, ON: Addison-Wesley.

Voeltz, L. M. (1980). Children's attitudes toward handicapped peers. *American Journal of Mental Deficiency, 84*(5), 455–464.

Voeltz, L. M. (1982). Effects of structured interactions with severely handicapped peers on children's attitudes. *American Journal of Mental Deficiency, 86*(4), 380–390.

Welkowitz, J., Ewen, R. B., & Cohen, J. (1982). *Introductory statistics for the behavioral sciences.* Toronto, ON: Academic Press.

White, P. A., & Collins, S. R. C. (1984). Stereotype formation by inference: A possible explanation for the "stutterer" stereotype. *Journal of Speech and Hearing Research, 27*, 567–570.

Woods, C. L. (1974). Social position and speaking competence of stuttering and normally fluent boys. *Journal of Speech and Hearing Research, 17*, 740–747.

Woods, F. J., & Carrow, M. A. (1959). The choice-rejection status of speech-defective children. *Exceptional Children, 25*, 279–283.

Woods, C. L., & Williams, D. E. (1971). Speech clinicians' conceptions of boys and men who stutter. *Journal of Speech and Hearing Disorders, 36*, 225–234.

Woods, C. L., & Williams, D. E. (1976). Traits attributed to stuttering and normally fluent males. *Journal of Speech and Hearing Research, 19*, 267–278.

Yairi, E., & Williams, D. E. (1970). Speech clinicians' stereotypes of elementary-school boys who stutter. *Journal of Communication Disorders, 3*, 161–170.

Yaruss, J. S. (1997). Clinical implications of situational variability in preschool children who stutter. *Journal of Fluency Disorders, 22*, 176–203.

Yeakle, M. K., & Cooper, E. B. (1986). Teacher perceptions of stuttering. *Journal of Fluency Disorders, 11*, 345–359.

Yuker, H. E. (1988). *Attitudes toward persons with disabilities.* New York: Springer.

Yuker, H. E., Block, J. R., & Younng, J. H. (1970). *The measurement of attitudes toward disabled persons.* Albertson, NY: Human Resources Centre.

AUTHORS' NOTES

This chapter is based on a paper first presented at the 2002 University of Georgia State of the Art Conference on evidence-based treatment of stuttering. This study was conducted by the first author in partial fulfillment of the requirements for a master of science degree at the University of Alberta. The authors acknowledge the contributions of the late Dr. Einer Boberg, the late Dr. Helen Ilott, and Dr. Birendra Sinha for their assistance with this research as members of the thesis committee. The authors and the Institute for Stuttering Treatment and Research would like to acknowledge the Elks and Royal Purple Fund for Children for supporting the dissemination of the research reported in this paper.

Appendix A

INVESTIGATIONS EVALUATING ADULT ATTITUDES TOWARD PEOPLE WHO STUTTER

Attitudes toward people who stutter have been studied from the perspective of speech language pathologists and speech pathology students (Barbosa, Schiefer, & Chiari, 1995; Cooper & Cooper, 1985, 1996; Cooper & Rustin, 1985; Horsley & Fitzgibbon, 1987; Kalinowski, Armson, Stuart, & Lerman, 1993; Lass, Ruscello, Pannbacker, Schmitt, & Everly-Meyers, 1989; Leahy, 1994; Ragsdale & Ashby, 1982; Ruscello, Lass, French, Channel, 1989–1990; Silverman, 1982; St. Louis & Lass, 1981; Turnbaugh, Guitar, & Hoffman, 1979; Woods & Williams, 1971, 1976; Yairi & Williams, 1970), teachers, special educators, and administrators (Crowe & Cooper, 1977; Crowe & Walton, 1981; Emerick, 1960; Horsley & Fitzgibbon, 1987; Lass et al., 1994; Lass et al., 1992; Ruscello, Lass, Schmitt, & Pannbacker, 1994; Silverman & Marik, 1993; Woods & Williams, 1976; Yeakle & Cooper, 1986), university professors (Dorsey & Guenther, 2000; Silverman, F. H., 1990), parents (Crowe & Cooper, 1977; Fowlie & Cooper, 1978; Woods & Williams, 1976), college students (Collins & Blood, 1990; Dorsey & Guenther, 2000; Dietrich, Jensen & Williams, 2001; Ruscello, Lass, & Brown, 1988; Silverman, 1982; Silverman & Paynter, 1990; Turnbaugh, Guitar, & Hoffman, 1981; Woods & Williams, 1976; White & Collins, 1984), rehabilitation counselors and employers (Hurst & Cooper, 1983a, 1983b), store clerks (McDonald & Frick, 1954), the general public (Craig, Hancock, Tran, & Craig, 2000; Doody, Kalinowski, Armson & Stuart, 1993; Ham, 1990; Hulit & Wirtz, 1994; Kalinowski et al., 1993; Kalinowski, Lerman, & Watt, 1987; Patterson & Pring, 1991; St. Louis et al., 2000; St. Louis, Yaruss, Lubker, Pill, & Diggs, 2000), family, friends, colleagues, and teachers who know someone who stutters (Klassen, 2001), and people who stutter (Kalinowski, Lerman, & Watt, 1987; Naidoo & Pillay, 1990; Woods & Williams, 1976).

9

Quality of Life Measurement: Interdisciplinary Implications for Stuttering Measurement and Treatment

Bradley T. Crowe
Jason H. Davidow
Anne K. Bothe
The University of Georgia

The term *quality of life* has been defined in terms of material possessions (Alexander & Williams, 1981), general satisfaction with life (Abrams, 1973), and an individual's responses to an illness (Bowling, 1997), among other definitions. Even when the topic is narrowed to the construct often referred to as "health-related quality of life" (de Boer, Spruijt, Sprangers, & de Haes, 1998; Patrick & Erickson, 1988), it often seems as if every new publication begins with the same statement: There is no generally agreed upon definition of quality of life. As a rather predictable result, there is no single generally agreed upon way to measure quality of life. Despite the current popularity of the topic, there is not even a universal agreement as to the usefulness of attempts to measure quality of life.

The purpose of this chapter is to explore some of the issues of quality of life in light of current attempts to develop improved or standard measurement systems for stuttering. As this chapter makes clear, the measurement problems facing stuttering researchers and clinicians are not unique; they are simply variations on the problems faced by researchers and clinicians attempting to measure everything from acne to terminal cancer. By drawing on some of the solutions proposed and adopted in other areas, this chapter proposes several possible solutions for the questions of measuring stuttering, its effects, and the effects of its treatment.

DEFINING QUALITY OF LIFE

When the term first came into common use, just after World War II, *quality of life* was defined in terms of the financial and material goods a person had acquired, such as a car, a house, and a savings account (Alexander & Williams, 1981). During the 1960s, the definition shifted to a focus on personal freedom, enjoyment, and personal caring. More recently, quality of life has been defined in terms that focus on personal well being. Abrams (1973), for example, defined *quality of life* as the degree of satisfaction people feel in various aspects of life. Along the same lines, Andrews (1974) defined *quality of life* as the pleasure and satisfaction associated with human existence. Other authors have tried to explain what *satisfaction* might mean, or how it might be achieved; thus, Shin and Johnson (1978) defined *quality of life* as "the possession of resources necessary to fulfill individual needs, wants and desires, participation in activities enabling personal development and self-actualization and satisfactory comparison with others" (p. 475). The World Health Organization (WHO, 1995), similarly, defined quality of life as "individuals' perceptions of their position in life in the context of the culture and value systems in which they live and in relation to their goals, expectations, standards and concerns" (p. 1405). Interestingly, the WHO definition does not focus entirely on health: It also recognizes the interaction between psychological and social states, as well as recognizing the influence of environment on quality of life. Other definitions of quality of life focus primarily or even exclusively on some combination of general health, a specific health problem, the effects of health problems on functional abilities, and the effects of any attempts to treat health problems (Weinstein et al., 2001; Wilson & Cleary, 1995).

One distinction that is not always made in the literature needs to be introduced here: the difference between defining quality of life (i.e., defining the construct, or determining the elements of quality of life) and defining a *good* quality of life (i.e., determining what it is that would make a person report "My quality of life is good" or "My quality of life is poor"). The two are clearly related, of course; determining the features of a good quality of life presupposes some knowledge of the features of quality of life. Nevertheless, some of the apparent disagreement among definitions of quality of life can be resolved by distinguishing between two types of definitions. Some are clearly stated in positive terms or are attempting to define a good quality of life. Gotay, Korn, McCabe, Moore, and Cheson (1992), for example, defined *quality of life* as "a state of well-being which is a composite of two components: the ability to perform everyday activities ... and patient satisfaction with levels of functioning and the control of disease and/or treatment related symptoms" (p. 575). Most definitions, however, assume neither a positive nor a negative quality, attempting only to identify the relevant elements. In this tradition, Bowling (1997) combined several ideas to define quality of life as "a concept representing individual responses to the physical, mental, and social effects of illness on daily living which influence the extent to which personal satisfaction with life circumstances can be achieved" (p. 6). Bowling added that quality of life involves not only physical attributes, but also perceptions about health, satisfaction, and self-worth. Testa and Simonson (1996), even more broadly, defined *quality of life* by providing a statement about the theorized components of the construct: "the physical, psychological, and social domains of health, seen as distinct areas that are influenced by a person's experiences, beliefs, expectations, and perceptions" (p. 835). Such lists of components are probably the most common form of current definitions, with differences lying largely in the selected components; Kaplan, Anderson, and Ganiats (1993), to provide another example, discussed "mortality, dysfunction, symptoms/problems, relative importance, prognoses, and costs" (p. 69).

Although a review of the literature cannot identify a single, agreed upon, definition of quality of life, several points of agreement can be identified (Bullinger, 1993). First, essentially all workers in this area agree on the rather obvious point that quality of life is multidimensional (Bowling, 1995). Most current definitions include at least three components: the physical; the psychological, mental, cognitive, affective, or emotional; and the social or interpersonal. In fact, Fitzpatrick et al.'s (1992) review of various instruments used to measure health-related quality of life identified six dimensions that most of those instruments attempted to measure: physical function, emotional function, social function, role performance, pain, and other (e.g., fatigue, nausea) or disease-specific symptoms. Fitzpatrick et al. also emphasized the importance of keeping disparate dimensions separate in measurement, rather than collapsing to a single score or index, a point of some controversy (see de Boer et al., 1998; Kaplan et al., 1993) that is addressed in further detail in the following.

Essentially all authors also agree that quality of life is an inherently subjective or individually determined construct (Benner, 1985; Ziller, 1974). Bowling (1995), for example, surveyed 2,000 men and women, all at least 16 years of age, about things that they considered important in their lives or that contributed to their quality of life. Participants answered open-ended questions about what was important in their lives and then ranked their top five responses. Responses were analyzed by, among other variables, age, gender, marital status, health status, socioeconomic group, and education. Responses clearly demonstrated individual differences in beliefs about quality of life: 31% of respondents ranked relationship with family or relatives as the most important factor in determining quality of life, 23% identified their own health, 20% identified the health of someone else, and 10% nominated finances. Some of these differences could be explained by age: 37% of participants aged 25 to 45 identified family as the most important element, for example, as compared with only 21% of respondents aged 75 and older. Other differences could be explained, in part, by gender or other independent variables, but the data quickly become a complex list of different combinations of independent variables that affect quality of life for different subgroups of participants. Bowling's general conclusion, quite apparent from her data, was that the components believed to influence quality of life will be identified differently by essentially every respondent.

Similarly, Mozes, Maor, and Shmueli (1999) asked 2,040 adults in Israel to provide one global rating to a single question about their health-related quality of life over the past month. All participants also completed a questionnaire about socioeconomic status, a questionnaire about current disease or disorders, and a Hebrew translation of the "SF-36" (Ware & Sherbourne, 1992), which is a 36-item questionnaire widely used to measure health-related quality of life. Only 51% of the variance in global ratings could be accounted for by the other measures, clearly demonstrating that large portions of individuals' perceptions of quality of life are determined by elements that are not part of the standard definitions or assessments tools.

A related issue, also recognized in most of the current literature, is that both the elements that are seen as determining quality of life, and the perceived positive or negative quality of life at any given time, are dynamic constructs that are continually under development for individual persons (Allison et al., 1997). Both *bottom-up* and *top-down* theories (Deiner, 1984) have been proposed to explain this dynamism. According to a bottom-up theory, perceptions of quality of life are built from past experiences, or perceptions are built throughout a lifetime. This model predicts that individuals having more negative experiences throughout life should report poorer quality of life, whereas persons having more positive experiences will report better quality of life (Allison et al., 1997). Top-down theories, in contrast, suggest that quality of life is determined by the individual's general sense of well-being (Costa & McCrae, 1980) and is not determined by previous life experiences. This distinction has important implications for any attempts to change an individual's perceived quality of life. Bottom-up theories suggest that increasing positive experiences should improve perceived quality of life, but top-down theories suggest that even experiences described as objectively positive by other people might be interpreted as evidence of a poor quality of life by someone who begins with a poor perceived quality of life.

Finally, many discussions of perceived quality of life emphasize the influence of individual expectations (e.g., Testa & Simonson, 1996; WHO,

1995). The main premise of this argument is that people have different and constantly changing expectations about their lives, and that quality of life may be defined, in part, in terms of whether those expectations are being met (Carr, Gibson, & Robinson, 2001). Carr et al. showed that many expectations are related to age, gender, ethnicity, social or economic status, and other variables. Incorporating expectations into the definition of quality of life assists in explaining an apparent mismatch between objective life circumstances and perceived quality of life. A severe or terminal disease, for example, does not necessarily lead to a poor perceived quality of life (e.g., Evans, 1991; Fortune, Main, O'Sullivan, & Griffiths, 1997). The explanation, in terms of expectations, is that persons with permanent impairment or terminal disease who have come to accept the resulting disabilities or limitations may have an exceptionally good quality of life because of their low expectations of improvement. Individuals who have not accepted the fact that they have a permanent problem, on the other hand, may have a poor quality of life, explained in these terms as related to expectations that far outweigh what is objectively possible. Expectations are also theorized to be responsible for part of the dynamic nature of quality of life. As individuals realize or accept their limitations, their expectations can change, resulting in changes in their perception of quality of life (Carr et al., 2001).

Carr et al.'s (2001) discussion of how expectations are formed is essentially another example of bottom-up theorizing in quality of life. Carr et al. explained that expectations are developed through an individual's experiences and interactions with the environment, or that expectations may be formed by social, psychological, socioeconomic, demographic, and cultural factors of the individual. Therefore, for a person who has always been healthy, a serious illness may represent a drastic departure from all expectations and have devastating effects on quality of life. In contrast, an individual who is used to being sick may take even very serious illness in stride, so quality of life is not affected at all. The concept of expectations may also be applied to therapy outcomes. When a person who has attempted therapy several times before, only to fail each time, begins a new treatment regimen, quality of life may be negatively affected by the past experience of failure and the thought process of never being able to achieve a desired goal (Carr et al., 2001; Krueger et al., 2001). It is equally possible, however, for a history of failure to theoretically lead to improved quality of life, if expectations have been lowered by that history of failure.

In summary, the quality of life literature does not include a widely agreed upon definition of quality of life—a state of affairs that is all too familiar to those of us who work in stuttering. However, there is substantial agreement that quality of life is multidimensional, subjective, dynamic, and related to expectations about life events or even related to expectations about quality of life. It also becomes clear that some of the differences among definitions should be viewed as reflecting only artificial disagreements: A distinction should be made between definitions that are attempting to describe the construct known as *quality of life* and those few that are attempting to describe the construct one might call "a good quality of life."

The remaining sections of this chapter use these ideas to address the more complex questions of how, and why, quality of life can be or should be defined and measured for stuttering. One relatively widely used instrument for measuring health-related quality of life, the "Short Form 36" (SF-36; McHorney, Ware, Lu, & Sherbourne, 1994; McHorney, Ware, & Raczek, 1993; Ware & Sherbourne, 1992), is first reviewed, because several issues raised by the SF-36 have some important implications for current attempts to develop measures for stuttering. The discussion then turns to the quality of life for persons living with one of two disorders, psoriasis and laryngeal cancer, selected because they show many interesting parallels to stuttering. Many other examples could have been selected; cancer and cardiovascular disease, most notably, are both heavily represented in the quality of life literature. As discussed in the following sections, however, some intriguing similarities among psoriasis, laryngeal cancer, and stuttering make the first two well suited to the task at hand: attempting to determine how, and why, we might choose to develop and use measures of quality of life as part of research and treatment for stuttering.

MEASURING HEALTH-RELATED QUALITY OF LIFE: THE SF-36

The Medical Outcomes Study 36-Item Short-Form Health Survey (McHorney et al., 1993, 1994; Ware & Sherbourne, 1992), known as the "SF-36," is a 36-item questionnaire created by adapting items from longer and more complex measures (Davies & Ware, 1981; Donald & Ware, 1984; Stewart & Ware, 1992; Stewart, Ware, Brook, & Davies-Avery, 1978; Veit & Ware, 1983). The SF-36 was intended to be a brief but comprehensive measure of general health that could be used in clinical and research settings to determine whether and how health is interfering with respondents' lives. The developers of the SF-36 did not describe the instrument as a quality of life measure, but it has become as close to a standard measure of health-related quality of life as can be found in the quality of life literature. The SF-36 has been translated into several languages and validated against interview data, clinical data, biological or physiological data, and other questionnaires for many subject groups around the world (e.g., Mozes et al., 1999; Shadbolt, McCallum, & Singh, 1997).

The SF-36 includes questions:

> measuring eight health concepts: (1) physical functioning; (2) role limitations because of physical health problems; (3) bodily pain; (4) social functioning; (5) general mental health (psychological distress and psychological well-being);

(6) role limitations because of emotional problems; (7) vitality (energy/fatigue); and (8) general health perceptions. (Ware & Sherbourne, 1992, p. 474)

All questions focus on how respondents' health has affected their activities over the past month and how respondents have felt physically and emotionally over the past month. Responses are given as *yes/no* or using Likert-type scales. One of the most interesting features of the SF-36 is that all questions were created from previously available instruments that measured the same concepts. The similarity to familiar instruments might explain, in part, the SF-36's relatively rapid acceptance and relatively widespread usage (Shadbolt et al., 1997). Its relative popularity might also be explained, in part, by the fact that the instrument is relatively short, easy to complete, easy to score, and yet relatively comprehensive with respect to many of the dimensions of quality of life.

The SF-36 clearly is not a psychometrically ideal instrument, as might be expected from the problems in defining the construct it is attempting to measure, but it has had what Shadbolt et al. (1997) described as exemplary psychometric rigor associated with its development (see also Brazier, Harper, & Jones, 1992). Correlations from tests of convergent validity with other measures range from low to high; the mental health subscale, for example, correlates fairly well with tests purporting to measure psychological well-being or mental health ($r = .52 - .95$) (see Bowling, 1997). Ware et al. (1993) found test–retest correlation coefficients of .43 to .90 for the subsections of the SF-36, and other researchers have since reported a similar range (e.g., Shadbolt et al., 1997). One problem with interpreting these data, however, is that the lower test-retest coefficients are often associated with a change in health status. Shadbolt et al., for example, reported correlations of .4 to .5 and significant differences (by paired-samples *t*-tests) for administrations of the SF-36 3 weeks before hospitalization for vascular surgeries and at hospitalization. The silver lining in the low reliability coefficients, then, is the suggestion that SF-36 scores are responsive to changes in health status.

MEASURING DISEASE-SPECIFIC QUALITY OF LIFE: PSORIASIS AND LARYNGECTOMY

Disease-specific measures, in contrast to the SF-36 and other general measures, are designed and intended for use with persons who have a single disorder. The relative advantages and disadvantages of general versus disease-specific measures have been rather heatedly debated, but the most common view is that both are useful for different reasons and in different situations (Read, 1993). General measures such as the SF-36 allow comparisons across patient populations and allow the detection of effects across multiple physiological or functional domains within individual patients, but they cannot provide detailed information about the particular effects of a given disease or its treatment as well as a good disease-specific instrument can. Disease-specific instruments, in contrast, are more likely to identify significant changes or differences associated with a given disease, but they are also more likely to miss important systemic changes. In addition, disease-specific instruments, by definition, cannot be used to compare quality of life across diseases or conditions. Because of these differences, many studies use both a general measure, often the SF-36, and a disease-specific measure. The following studies exemplify this trend for two disorders selected for their perhaps unexpected parallels to stuttering: psoriasis and laryngeal cancer.

Quality of Life in Psoriasis

Psoriasis is a skin condition that affects more than 5.5 million persons in the United States, occurring equally in men and women. Physical signs of this fairly common disease include reddish, scaly skin, primarily located on the elbows, knees, scalp, and trunk. The parallels between stuttering and psoriasis are striking, beginning with their etiologies: neither disorder is well understood, although both are currently believed to probably be genetic disorders influenced by some environmental factors. Psoriasis is generally viewed as a chronic disease, at least in adults, and many authors discuss the possibility of psychological, cognitive, affective, or interpersonal aspects in addition to the physical skin lesions. Mild psoriasis is treated with topically applied creams or lotions that can control the maculopapules and the symptoms of dryness and itching, and more severe psoriasis may be treated with phototherapy or systemic treatment. As is often the case with stuttering, these treatments must be actively continued if their benefits are to continue. Another similarity, then, is that treatment goals are often discussed in terms of controlling or living with the disease instead of curing or eliminating it.

In contrast to stuttering, however, several disease-specific quality of life instruments have been developed for psoriasis. One of the most common is the Psoriasis Disability Index (PDI; Finlay & Kelly, 1987). The PDI is a self-rating instrument designed to measure the impact of psoriasis on different life situations within 1 month before the initiation of treatment and 1 month after termination of treatment. Originally consisting of 28 questions about daily activities, work or school, and treatment, the PDI was narrowed to 10 questions after pilot work with 54 psoriasis patients identified highly correlated, redundant, ambiguous, or irrelevant items. A more current version of the PDI (Finlay, Khan, Luscombe, & Salek, 1990) added the category of personal relationships (5 questions), to make a total of 15 questions. All questions are answered using a 7-point scale (1 = *not at all*, 7 = *very much*). The scoring is summative, so the high score on the original version was 70 and the high score on the updated version is 105.

Psychometric quality of the PDI has been investigated by several research groups, using detailed literature reviews, discussions with participants, and pilot administrations. Internal reliability for the 10-item version is only moderate ($r = .32 - .40$) (Finlay & Kelley, 1987), but this result is to be expected given the efforts to develop a scale with little or no redundancy across items. Finlay and Kelley's attempts at establishing construct validity have also resulted in low (.29) correlations with severity of psoriasis (defined as percent of skin surface affected). This result is not good evidence of construct validity, but it does show that PDI scores are not necessarily related to disease severity. The 15-item version was revalidated (Finlay et al., 1990) by administering it to only 32 persons with psoriasis, and by comparing the PDI to similar scales. Finlay and Kelly also determined that the PDI was responsive to changes across time by comparing mean scores for pretreatment (mean = 34.1, SD = 11.1) and post treatment (mean = 22.3, SD = 10.9) assessments, but this assessment included only hospitalized psoriasis patients.

Finlay and Coles (1995) reported a relatively comprehensive assessment of the influence of severe psoriasis that used the PDI and that exemplifies some of the methodological issues and the common results in this area. Survey respondents included 369 men and women (mean age 46.8 years; male to female ratio approximately 50:50), out of 745 who were originally contacted by 149 participating dermatologists. Eighty percent of respondents had been admitted to the hospital as a result of their psoriasis, an average of three times each. Respondents completed a four-part questionnaire: six questions to describe background and present information about their psoriasis; the 15-item version of the PDI (Finlay et al., 1990); questions that compared psoriasis with asthma, diabetes, and bronchitis; and a final section that asked questions about treatment regarding expenses, outcomes, and time. The final section included such questions as "How much time would you be prepared to spend on treating the skin each day if there was a daily treatment which kept your skin completely normal for that day?" and "How much would you be prepared to pay for a cure?" This measurement system is a clear example of purely disease-specific assessment; all questions were explicitly tied to the respondents' psoriasis.

More than 50% of respondents in Finlay and Coles' (1995) study indicated that psoriasis interfered "a lot" or "very much" with their lives, as measured by the PDI questions associated with clothes, sports, baths, and home messiness. Fewer than 30% of respondents, however, indicated many problems associated with friends, career, smoking, and alcohol. From the third section of their questionnaire, Finlay and Coles reported that psoriasis patients thought it would be better to suffer from asthma, diabetes, or bronchitis than to have psoriasis; this finding was reversed, however, for those respondents who by chance were actually afflicted with one of these other comparative diseases. Part four of the questionnaire revealed that 98.9% of respondents would rather have a cure than receive money; 78% indicated they would pay 1,000 pounds ($2,000) or more for a cure, and 38% indicated they would pay 10,000 pounds ($20,000). The mean time that participants reported they would spend per day to cure their disease for that day was 1 hour, with 49% of respondents indicating they would spend 2 to 3 hours per day. Overall, Finlay and Coles concluded that severe psoriasis may affect all aspects of life, a conclusion that was not entirely supported by their data, although it is clear that some aspects of life were affected for many respondents.

Finlay and Coles also emphasized the importance of quality of life measures in making clinical decisions (Patrick & Erickson, 1993). They suggested that if an individual's quality of life is known, then therapeutic judgments can be made about preferred or recommended treatments to meet that patient's particular needs. Although such a notion seems obvious enough in one sense, it also introduces a series of problems that become apparent throughout the entire quality of life literature. It is not clear, for example, that different psoriasis treatments are available to match different quality of life needs, an issue that raises empirical questions as well as clinical ones. Although dermatologists might reasonably suggest aggressive systemic therapy over topical approaches for patients who report serious quality of life issues with respect to their psoriasis, there has been little effort to validate the need for a quality of life scale to gather that information (which, physicians argue, can be gathered in the briefest of clinical interviews or from the physical exam) or to validate any potential improvement in dermatological outcomes or in quality of life outcomes associated with treatment choices based on quality of life issues.

Gupta and Gupta's (1995a) study exemplifies another trend in the quality of life literature. Gupta and Gupta studied 110 men and 105 women with varying degrees of psoriasis. The participants were separated into age brackets of 18 to 29 years, 30 to 45 years, 46 to 65 years, and over 65 years. Participants completed two disease-specific self-report measures: a series of 10-point scales (1 = *not at all*, 10 = *very markedly*) to rate the severity of their psoriasis, and a checklist similar to the PDI that required *yes* or *no* answers to statements about experiences within the last month pertaining to their psoriasis. The severity measures included "overall redness of skin rash, overall scaling or shedding of skin, overall thickness of psoriasis plaques, and overall severity of psoriasis." The checklist contained questions pertaining to different aspects of life, reflecting Gupta and Gupta's own working definition of quality of life: appearance and socialization, occupation and finances, symptoms and treatment, and so forth.

Gupta and Gupta's (1995a) results identified no significant differences in severity of psoriasis across age or gender groups. Gender differences on the quality of life measure were significant only for occupational functioning, with men reporting feeling more concerned than women about taking time off work for treatment and reporting more fear of losing their jobs. Interpreting this result is difficult, however, because it was not reported how many of the men and how many of the women had jobs or provided the sole or primary income for their families. Significant differences between age groups were identified for the quality of life measure with older persons (45 and above) reporting better quality of life than the younger patients (under 45). Specifically, younger persons reported more socialization problems, more appearance problems, and more occupation and finance problems than older respondents.

Gupta and Gupta (1995a) concluded that chronological age plays a critical role in the impact of psoriasis on quality of life by speculating that younger people may be trying to make more social connections and thus are more affected by a disorder that they see as limiting them socially. This conclusion raises several additional issues that also recur throughout the quality of life literature. First, results can be explained in terms of individuals' expectations about their lives; as such, they appear to present some support for Carr et al.'s (2001) assertion of the importance of expectations to perceived quality of life. It quickly becomes apparent, however, that a confirming evidence fallacy may be in force here: The proposition that quality of life is determined by whether or not an individual's expectations are or are not met has not yet been tested in the obvious, easily designed, but ethically very questionable experiment. Second, much of the disease-specific quality of life research has been conducted without the appropriate control groups or the appropriate reference to normative data. Counterexamples exist in several large projects that have attempted to measure well-being or quality of life for entire populations (e.g., McEwan, 1993; Mishra & Schofield, 1998) and in several studies that have compared obtained data to available norms. On the whole, however, measurement systems for disease-specific quality of life work from the assumption that the disease is, in fact, relevant to whatever findings are obtained. Gupta and Gupta, for example, found that a group of people younger than 45 were more concerned about social activities, their own physical appearance, occupational issues, and financial instability than older respondents, and they concluded that psoriasis has more of an effect on younger people than on older people with respect to these variables. Their data can not support such a conclusion, however, because psoriasis was common to both groups, and enough of the questions are general enough (e.g., "feeling self-conscious among strangers") that it seems possible for age to be the functional variable in the obtained quality of life differences. It seems quite possible, in other words, that Gupta and Gupta's results simply confirmed that young people are concerned about social activities, their own physical appearance, their jobs, and their finances.

A later study, also by Gupta and Gupta (1998), is affected by some of the same issues. In this study, Gupta and Gupta sought to assess the ability of skin diseases (acne, alopecia areata, atopic dermatitis, and psoriasis) to cause depression and suicidal thoughts. Retrospective analyses of data they had collected for several previous studies identified 72 respondents with acne, 45 with alopecia areata, 146 with atopic dermatitis, and 217 with psoriasis. The groups were subdivided into a more severe inpatient group ($n = 138$) and a less severe outpatient group ($n = 79$). Severity of the disease varied within all groups of respondents, including the two psoriasis groups.

Questions about depression and suicidal tendencies were asked of all 480 participants using the Carroll Rating Scale for Depression (CRSD; Carroll, Feinburg, Smouse, Rawson, & Greden, 1981). The CRSD is a self-rated scale to screen for possible depression, developed by adapting the Hamilton Rating Scale (HRS; Hamilton, 1969) from a clinician-rating format to a self-reporting format. The CRSD comprises 52 statements for which the patient must circle either *yes* or *no*, each scored on a simple 0 or 1 system for a possible total score of 52. Scores of 10 or higher are interpreted as suggesting the need for further evaluation because of possible depression, based on results from one sample of 199 adults described as reflecting the general population.

Gupta and Gupta's (1998) results showed that the acne group and the inpatients with psoriasis had statistically significantly higher mean CRSD scores (13.4, SD = 8.0, and 11.12, SD = 6.8, respectively) than the other groups (outpatient psoriasis mean 8.6, SD 6.5; alopecia areata mean 7.5, SD 7.3; atopic dermatitis mean 7.6, SD 6.2). Individual item analyses presented without inferential statistics showed that between 8.3% and 10% of all groups except the respondents with atopic dermatitis often wished they were dead; 10.3% of the psoriasis inpatient group felt that life was not worth living, as compared with 1.4%, 2.2%, 3.4%, and 5.1% in the acne, alopecia, atopic dermatitis, and outpatient psoriasis groups, respectively.

Gupta and Gupta (1998) interpreted the results by suggesting that acne and psoriasis may increase the chance of depression, and they discussed the effects of these disorders on body image and life development, particularly for the adolescent respondents with acne. It is important to note, however, that these data were based on a questionably validated instrument, showed very large standard deviations for all groups, and showed substantial group overlap. It is also important to recognize that depression is common for adolescents in general, so the finding of slightly increased depression in the acne group is not surprising, given that the mean age of participants was only 23.7 years (SD = 6.8) [other groups were much older: 44.7 (11.6) for alopecia, 42.0 (15.6) for atopic dermatitis, and 47.8 (16.2) for the combined psoriasis groups]. Gupta and Gupta's overall conclusions were that depression may be associated with some dermatological diseases, but their data provided only minimal support for the specific causal relation that this conclusion implies.

As a final example, Fortune, Main, O'Sullivan, and Griffiths (1997) used a multidimensional approach to examine the effects of psoriasis on quality of life, physical health, and mental health. This study used both general health and disease-specific scales: the SF-36 and the PDI, both discussed previously, and the Psoriasis Life Stress Inventory (PLSI; Gupta & Gupta, 1995b). Participants included 77 women and 73 men, aged 18 to 79 years, all of whom were patients in a psoriasis specialty clinic. Severity of psoriasis was determined from a variety of clinical indicators and summarized using a point system that ranged from 0 (*no psoriasis*) to 72 (*very severe psoriasis*). Self-reports of severity were also gathered for each patient based on a 10-point scale (0 = *no psoriasis* and 10 = *very severe psoriasis*). Patients were also asked what treatments were being received, in an attempt to determine whether different aspects of quality of life were affected by different treatments. Questions about family history of psoriasis, alcohol consumption, age of psoriasis onset, and employment history were also asked during the clinical assessment.

Results included a replication of Gupta and Gupta's (1995a) finding of no differences between males and females on quality of life. Fortune et al. (1997) also reported that the clinical severity and location of the psoriasis were not correlated with quality of life, although location of the psoriasis was correlated with physical and mental health scores. Respondents who reported higher psoriasis-related stress also scored significantly lower on the mental health subsection of the SF-36 than participants who reported low stress according to the PLSI, suggesting that the SF-36 can also identify psoriasis-related mental health problems. It should be noted, in addition, that 116 participants were classified as displaying "high stress" by the PLSI and only 34 were classified as displaying low stress.

In summary, several conclusions may be drawn from these and other sources (e.g. Salek, 1993) about measuring quality of life in psoriasis. First, and most basically, both general health measures and disease-specific measures do appear to identify measurable effects of psoriasis on life activities and functions for at least 30% to 50% of patients (Finlay & Coles, 1995; Fortune et al., 1997; Gupta & Gupta, 1995a). Equally importantly, it appears that the psoriasis literature is making progress toward what Patrick and Erickson (1996) described as three distinctly different goals or applications of quality of life assessments: to describe the differences (if any) between affected and nonaffected persons, to allow the prediction of future outcomes, and to measure change over time.

Quality of Life in Laryngeal Cancer

Quality of life measures are also being used in voice disorders generally, and for laryngeal cancer in particular, to address many of the goals or scientific foci discussed by Patrick and Erickson (1996). This use is an example of the relatively widespread use of quality of life measures in cancer treatment and research: Bardelli and Saracci (1978) reported that between 1956 and 1976 less than 5% of the clinical studies published in six major cancer journals addressed any aspect of quality of life, but since at least the early 1980s (Selby, 1993) quality of life has become an increasingly important issue in mainstream cancer research and treatment. Ringash and Bezjak (2001) recently described an explosion of interest in quality of life among researchers concerned with head and neck cancer in particular. Many of these studies, as discussed in the following, have used both general quality of life measures and cancer-specific measures, and they have not only addressed the question of developing measures for cancer-related quality of life but have also used quality of life measures for several reasons. The focus here is on cancers of the head and neck, and largely on laryngeal cancer, because of our original hypothesis that the effects of laryngeal cancer on communication would provide a parallel to the effects of stuttering. As seen in the following, however, quality of life research has provided evidence to contradict our initial assumption, thus actually providing evidence of another parallel with stuttering.

Morton (1997), to begin with, examined quality of life and cost-effectiveness of treatments for 46 patients with laryngeal cancer. Morton used only general quality of life scales, without cancer-specific measures: a general health questionnaire, a global (single-item) life satisfaction question, and a 10-item life satisfaction instrument. All questionnaires were completed at the time of diagnosis and again at 3, 12, and 24 months postdiagnosis. No differences in life satisfaction could be attributed to age, sex, or tumor stage at the time of diagnosis, suggesting that disease severity does not always take an active role in the determination of quality of life (Evans, 1991; Testa & Simonson,1996). Other important findings included a negative correlation between pain and life satisfaction at the 12- and 24-month assessments, which the authors explained in terms of a decrease in quality of life that can be attributed to the treatment for laryngeal cancer. Laryngectomy, in particular, was associated with increased difficulty with verbal communication at the 3- and 12-month measures, but this difficulty was not enough to create any differences in quality of life between those treated by laryngectomy and those treated by radiation therapy. As Morton (1997) discussed, this negative result may have been due to the small number of participants in the study, the particular aspects of life assessed on the questionnaire, or the preoperative counseling received by the laryngectomy patients. Nevertheless, he concluded that even though there is an impact on speech and communication for laryngectomy patients, the surgery and its effects are not different from radiation therapy with respect to effects on quality of life. Indeed, Morton concluded, overall, that laryngectomy is not a "disastrous event" (p. 249) for quality of life.

Armstrong et al. (2001) focused on laryngectomy patients only, during presurgery and at 1, 3, and 6 months postsurgery, and reported similar results. Of 40 initial subjects, only 20 participated at every stage of the study, completing one general and two laryngeal-cancer-specific questionnaires about general health, psychosocial and communication status, and eating status. Questionnaires included the SF-36, discussed earlier; the Royal Prince Albert Hospital Profiles Patient Questionnaire (RPAH; Armstrong et al., 2001), which was developed through collaboration of researchers, professionals, and laryngectomees to measure background information, treatment details, length of hospital stay, and questions related to risk factors of laryngeal cancer; and an Outcomes Measures Questionnaire, used postsurgery only to assess communication, swallowing, psychosocial status, emotional support, prosthesis management, stoma care, smoking, body image, medical complications, and readmission to the hospital.

Armstrong et al. (2001) reported that speech was affected up to 6 months after surgery for many patients and that 63% of participants reported continuing problems with oral communication at 6 months postsurgery. Only 8%, however, reported that they felt limited in communication. Swallowing difficulties were reported by 75% of respondents at the 6-month assessment, with 42% reporting swallowing trouble that limited their willingness or ability to eat in public and 21% reporting pain associated with swallowing. The general health of these participants was lower than that of matched individuals without cancer as judged by physical, emotional, and social scores on the SF-36, and some improvement in general health was shown between the initial measure and the 3-month follow-up. Overall, Armstrong et al. concluded that the low SF-36 scores reflected a poor quality of life among participants in this study as compared to individuals without a major illness. The findings that only 8% of participants felt limited in their communication abilities, but 42% were not willing to eat in public, replicated Morton's (1997) earlier finding and suggests that the most important quality of life concerns for laryngectomy patients might not be in communication after all, but might be associated with the social importance of eating.

Hammerlid, Silander, Hornestam, and Sullivan's (2001) study of 232 patients with head and neck cancer replicated this finding in addition to providing other information. Hammerlid et al. used three instruments: a quality of life scale designed for cancer, a quality of life scale designed specifically for head and neck cancer, and the Hospital Anxiety and Depression Scale (HADS; Zigmond & Snaith, 1983). Results were assessed separately for the 133 patients who completed the 3-year longitudinal investigation and for the 80 who died during those 3 years. In general, quality of life scores for those patients who completed the study were lowest at 3 months or 1 year postdiagnosis, recovering by 1 year or 3 years postdiagnosis. As Hammerlid et al. were careful to address, however, these relatively positive conclusions about the recovery of quality of life must be substantially qualified by the fact that the patients who did not complete the later assessments had died of their cancer. Hammerlid et al. also found that scores from the head-and-neck cancer specific questionnaire varied more across the four administration times than did scores from the general cancer questionnaire, and that subgroups of patients with different tumor locations and with different ultimate outcomes (3-year survival or not) showed larger differences on the head-and-neck questionnaire than on the general cancer questionnaire. Thus, their results, that specialized disease-specific instruments may be more responsive to change and more sensitive to subgroup differences than general disease instruments, and certainly more sensitive and responsive than general quality of health scales, confirmed some of the advantages of disease-specific measures discussed previously (Read, 1993).

A study reported by de Graeff et al. (1999) provides a final example of the contribution of quality of life measures. de Graeff et al. studied 65 patients with laryngeal cancer who were treated with radiotherapy rather than surgery. Assessment instruments included the European Organization for Research and Treatment of Cancer Core Questionnaire, the Organization's Head and Neck Cancer Module, and a depression scale. All were administered before treatment and then 6 and 12 months after treatment. Six-month measures showed a significant decrease in most quality of life variables, as compared with pretreatment measures, that again appeared to represent the effects of the radiation therapy. One important exception must be noted, however: Speech was actually significantly improved at the 6-month measure, even during the time that most other indices were very negative. Again, quality of life research has provided evidence to contradict our original assumptions that laryngeal cancer, laryngectomy, or the side effects of radiation therapy to the larynx would have significant negative effects on speech and speech-related quality of life.

MEASURING QUALITY OF LIFE: APPLICATIONS TO STUTTERING

Given the many issues discussed earlier, it is obvious that several questions will need to be answered before quality of life measurements can be meaningfully developed and used as part of stuttering measurement. The first question is an obvious one: Why should quality of life be measured? The standard answer is that quality of life measurements can assist with clinical decision-making, but, as alluded to above with respect to the psoriasis literature, this answer is more complex than it first appears. Patrick and Erickson (1996), for example, identified at least four different meanings of *clinical decision making*: assessing and monitoring an untreated individual patient, while making decisions about diagnoses, severity, or the need for treatment; selecting a treatment for an individual patient; monitoring the effects of a treatment for an individual patient, while making decisions about progress or the need to change or discontinue treatment; and developing a shared view of the usual or potential progress of a disease to shape research agendas, political agendas, and the information and recommendations that are provided to individual patients. In addition, the simple fact that an assessment possibility exists does not mean that it can necessarily make any contribution to any of these levels of clinical decision-making. For stuttering, certainly, future research might profitably address the question of which, if any, clinical decision-making activities can be improved by the use of quality of life measures.

Second, if the decision is made to measure quality of life in stuttering, then stuttering researchers must determine whether a stuttering-specific quality of life measure needs to be developed or whether the SF-36 or a similar general instrument would be a better choice. It seems clear from the literature reviewed above that disease-specific measures and general measures provide different information, and that only disease-specific measures can provide the detailed information that may be desired in some situations (Read, 1993). Kaplan et al. (1993), in their discussion of this point, used an example of a questionnaire item about whether finger dexterity is adequate to open a bag of potato chips. For the vast majority of respondents, with the vast majority of diseases and disorders, such an item would be seen as trivial if not burdensome, completely unrelated to the reasons they sought professional assistance. General quality of life measures clearly should not address such levels of detail for all aspects of life and functioning. For patients recovering from hand burns, however, or patients with severe arthritis, such details as opening a bag of potato chips can be directly relevant to their functional abilities and to their perceived quality of life and must be assessed. The trade-off, as previously mentioned, is that disease-specific measures do not allow the comparisons across disorders that might be desirable in some situations. If the decision is made to develop and use a stuttering-specific quality of life instrument, therefore, the challenge will be to identify those stuttering-related issues that are directly relevant to functional abilities and to daily life for enough persons who stutter that the entire instrument is not viewed by clients and professionals alike as trivial if not burdensome.

A related question involves how a new instrument designed to measure stuttering-specific quality of life could complement the plethora of stuttering assessment instruments already in existence. Until very recently (Blood & Conture, 1998; Yaruss, 2001), stuttering researchers have not used the term *quality of life*, but an interest in assessing aspects of life that could be affected by speech problems goes back for decades. Measures such as Williams, Darley, and Spriestersbach's (1978) original *Stutterer's Self-Ratings of Reactions to Speech Situations*, Andrews and Cutler's (1974) S24 scale, Erickson's (1969) original S-scale, the Stuttering Problem Profile (Silverman, 1980), and more recent emotion and attitude scales (e.g.,

Crowe, Di Lollo, & Crowe, 2000) are all based on the speaker's feelings, thoughts, attitudes, and experiences regarding speaking situations. The assumptions driving these instruments appear to have had much in common with the ideas being more explicitly expressed in the quality of life literature, including, for example, the bottom-up explanation (Carr et al., 2001) that successful or unsuccessful completion of various speaking situations throughout life would contribute to happiness or quality of life.

Several major problems for stuttering treatment and research, however, are perfectly parallel to the issues previously discussed and exemplified. First, neither top-down nor bottom-up theories of quality of life have been strongly supported. As applied to stuttering, there is no more reason to accept the bottom-up assumption that increased success in speech will necessarily lead to happiness on the job, in social activities, and so forth, than there is to accept the top-down assumption that people who feel good about their general quality of life will necessarily feel good about their speech related activities. Second, as illustrated by the psoriasis literature, quality of life research for stuttering, when it is completed, might show that the disorder is relevant to quality of life for only a minority of persons with the disorder (Finlay & Coles, 1995) or that factors other than the disorder are more important to quality of life (Gupta & Gupta, 1995a). Similarly, and as perfectly illustrated by our experience with the laryngeal cancer literature, the assumption that stuttering will affect general communication and therefore affect all communication-related aspects of life might be shown, when good quality of life research is completed, to be incorrect. In fact, one overriding impression to be gained from the literature on disease-specific quality of life, including the small sample reviewed earlier, is that the authors and instruments appear to adopt a "disorder-centric" view that assumes, probably incorrectly, that the client's disorder is the overriding determiner of quality of life. In other words, many of the definitions of quality of life, and measurements used to determine quality of life, place a rather large, if not complete, emphasis on issues related to the disease itself. This problem is somewhat reduced for general health measures such as the SF-36, but even then, the assumption is that health status does have an impact on quality of life, with the instrument intended merely to quantify that impact. As stuttering researchers and clinicians begin to consider quality of life measurements, we need to be aware of this potentially unsupported assumption and allow the possibility that a quality of life instrument might show that stuttering is largely irrelevant to overall quality of life for many persons who stutter.

Next, if the decision is made to develop a stuttering-specific measure of quality of life, decisions must be made about the design of that instrument and about its specific intended uses. Patrick and Erickson (1996) identified three distinctly different goals or applications of quality of life assessments: to differentiate between affected and nonaffected persons; to allow the prediction of future outcomes or the prediction of results from another test that would have been too intrusive or too costly to administer; and measuring change over time. We would subdivide their first, or add a fourth: Differentiating between affected and nonaffected persons might mean using a quality of life scale to identify those persons with a disorder who need help with quality of life, and it might also mean using a quality of life scale to differentiate between two different subtypes, two different disorders, or the presence or absence of a disorder. All the common psychometric and methodological issues that must be solved in designing and validating any new instrument must also be solved, for individual items and for the instrument as a whole (and speech-language pathology, on the whole, does not have a good record of developing psycho-metrically trustworthy instruments; e.g., McCauley & Swisher, 1984). It is also worth noting in this context, however, that several issues commonly raised as complicating the analysis of quality of life data are essentially red herrings that can relatively easily be dealt with (Bullinger, 1993): the "subjectivity" of quality of life data, for example, is relevant to instrument development and interpretation but does not have to affect data analysis. Similarly, Bullinger explained that the multifactorial data obtained from profiles or test batteries are not "too complex" to analyze statistically, as some have claimed; such relatively straightforward procedures as the a priori definition of orthogonal comparisons, the use of multivariate anal-yses of variance, and the use of such rules as Bonferroni corrections can solve most of the problems.

How, then, might an appropriate instrument for measuring quality of life in persons who stutter be identified or developed? The Special Interest Division for Fluency Disorders of the American Speech-Language-Hearing Association tried a decision-by-committee method at a 1999 conference, with 5-point scales imposed for all questions, that has predictably stalled into apparent failure. Yaruss (2001) also provided preliminary information about his attempts to construct three related instruments about speakers' reactions to stuttering, functional communication and stuttering, and qual-ity of life in stuttering (QOL-S). Those instruments appear to have been combined into the current *Overall Assessment of the Speaker's Experience of Stuttering* (*OASES*; Yaruss & Quesal, 2002), which was circulated at a con-ference in an unpublished form labeled "draft September 2002" (Yaruss & Quesal, 2002, n.p.). This scale is still in initial stages of development, and it is yet to be demonstrated that the QOL-S or the complete OASES will be able to address many of the complexities, previously discussed, that are in-herent in developing or using quality of life measurements (Guyatt, Bom-bardier, & Tugwell, 1986; Patrick & Erickson, 1993). In particular, it is important to note that the initial development of the QOL-S and the OASES was described with reference only to self-selected members of a stuttering self-help organization and self-selected audience members; it may be that neither the intent nor the design of these scales will make them useful for assessing quality of life in a less selective group of persons who stutter.

If we are not yet prepared to accept previous efforts in this domain, then, what recommendations might we make? First and foremost, it appears to us that the bias discussed earlier with respect to quality of life measures, that overall quality of life is necessarily affected by a single disorder or other single part of an individual's life, must be carefully considered. Simply put, and as the psoriasis literature demonstrated, stuttering might not be relevant to quality of life for every person who happens to stutter. Even those who seek assistance with their speech may consider their lives to be progressing well, with stuttering not affecting any aspects of life except for their speech. Empirically, attempts to describe stuttering-related quality of life may be severely compromised if the truth is bimodal (some not at all affected, some severely affected) and the resulting answer is a mean that describes no one. There are no answers here; these are clearly empirical questions that might be solved by good descriptive research with a good quality of life measure.

Second, any instrument that will be used for either research or clinical work must somehow solve the problem of the subjective and dynamic nature of quality of life. One possible solution, depending on the purpose of the assessment and the requirements of the data, would be to ask simple open-ended questions, as Farquhar (1995) and Bowling (1995) have done. A question such as "How is your quality of life?" can elicit respondent-specific information that may be arguably the best indicator of quality of life for any single person. Conceivably, as a clinical practice, such a question could also be viewed as a screening tool, with more comprehensive assessment completed only for those whose screening data suggest a possible need. Alternatively, instruments do exist that are essentially organized ways to gather open-ended information. The *Schedule for the Evaluation of Individual Quality of Life* (Brown, O'Boyle, McGee, & McDonald, (1997), for example, asks respondents to nominate five domains that they consider important to their quality of life; these domains are then ranked and described using judgment analysis or weighted. Several problems with such an approach are obvious, of course: Answers may or may not reflect disorder-specific information, recency effects might affect a client's answers, and important information might simply be forgotten or missed.

The alternative is to identify or develop an interview or questionnaire protocol, similar to the many available disease-specific instruments. Prepared instruments have the advantage and the disadvantage of being more focused than open-ended questions on specific issues; this property ensures some consistency in administration but may result in a failure to capture the subjectivity or the dynamism of quality of life. In addition, development of an instrument that can provide reliable, valid, and worthwhile information is a long and complex process; McEwen (1993) claimed that it reasonably takes no less than 10 years for a quality of life measure. Several authors have described the multiple stages that must each be thoughtfully accomplished; Guyatt et al.'s (1986) circular 10-step model requires five steps of conceptual work before any items are first developed and then five steps of item testing, the result of which is not a completed instrument but more conceptual work and more item testing. Among the more important questions for stuttering raised by models such as Guyatt et al.'s are the specification of the intended population for measurement (e.g., adults seeking treatment for stuttering vs. all persons who stutter); the specification of the intended application, purposes, and goals of the instrument, and of how it will complement existing measurements; and the identification of relevant items for that population and for those applications, purposes, and goals, as judged by a truly representative cross section of professionals, members of that population, other persons who stutter, and other affected persons. Appropriate data analysis methods must also be developed and validated, keeping in mind all the standard data analysis issues and some issues specific to quality of life measurement (e.g., the difference between causal indicator items and effect indicator items; Fayers, Hand, Bjordal, & Groenvold, 1997). Although the task is daunting, several examples of solid, thorough instrument development are also readily available from other disciplines and could serve as models for stuttering (e.g., Kirkley, Griffin, McLintock, & Ng, 1998).

In conclusion, we find ourselves returning to the common notion that assessing and treating any disorder can be conceptualized in two ways: with a focus on the disorder or with a focus on the person as a whole who has that disorder. Despite some pronouncements to the contrary, neither focus is necessarily better than the other; they simply serve different purposes and are appropriate in different situations or for different reasons. Quality of life measures, carefully developed and thoughtfully used, can assist in describing the characteristics or the course of the person with a given disorder, and can provide information about the general tendencies for a group of persons with a disorder. Such measures are not equivalent to, and cannot replace, measures of the basic physiology or physical behaviors associated with a given disorder. Nevertheless, it appears to us, on balance, that the effort of developing a good stuttering-specific quality of life measurement might be well spent, because the thoughtful use of such a measure might have at least one important purpose for stuttering: It could provide some data to support or refute the common but as yet empirically unsupported notion that stuttering has widespread effects on the entire life of all persons who stutter.

REFERENCES

Abrams, M. A. (1973). Subjective social indications. *Social Trends, 4*, 35.

Alexander, J. L., & Willems, E. P. (1981). Quality of life: Some measurement requirements. *Archives of Physiotherapy Medical Rehabilitation, 62*, 261.

Allison, P. J., Locker, D., & Feine, J. S. (1997). Quality of life: A dynamic construct. *Social Science and Medicine, 45*, 221–230.

Andrews, F. M. (1974). Social indicators of perceived life quality. *Social Indicators Research, 1*, 279.

Andrews, G., & Cutler, J. (1974). Stuttering therapy: The relation between changes in symptom level and attitudes. *Journal of Speech and Hearing Disorders, 39*, 312–319.

Armstrong, E., Isman, K., Dooley, P., Brine, D., Riley, N., Dentice, R., King, S., & Khanbhai, F. (2001). An investigation into the quality of life of individuals after laryngectomy. *Head and Neck, 23*, 16–24.

Bardelli, D., & Saracci, R. (1978). Measuring the quality of life in cancer clinical trials. Methods and impact of controlled therapeutic trials in cancer. *IUCC Technical Report Series, 36*, 75–97.

Benner, P. (1985). Quality of life: A phenomenological perspective on explanation, prediction, and understanding in nursing science. *Advances in Nursing Science, Special Issue: Quality of Life, 8*, 1–14.

Blood, G. W., & Conture, E. G. (1998). Outcomes measurement issues in fluency disorders. In C. M. Frattali (Ed.), *Measuring outcomes in speech-language pathology* (pp. 387–405). New York: Thieme.

Bowling, A. (1995). What things are important in people's lives? A survey of the public's judgments to inform scales of health related quality of life. *Social Science and Medicine, 41*, 1447–1462.

Bowling, A. (1997). *Measuring health: A review of quality of life measurement scales* (2nd ed.). Buckingham, PA: Open University Press.

Brazier, J. E., Harper, R., Jones, N. (1992). Validating the SF-36 Health Survey questionnaire: A new outcome measure for primary care. *British Medical Journal, 305*, 160–164.

Browne, J. P., O'Boyle, C. A., McGee, H. M., & McDonald, N. J. (1997). Development of a direct weighting procedure for quality of life domains. *Quality of Life Research, 6*, 301–307.

Bullinger, M. (1993). Indices versus profiles—advantages and disadvantages. In S. R. Walker, & R. M. Rosser (Eds.), *Quality of life assessment: Key issues in the 1990s* (pp. 209–220). Boston: Kluwer Academic Publishers.

Carr, A. J., Gibson, B., & Robinson, P. G. (2001). Measuring quality of life: Is the quality of life determined by expectations or experience? *British Medical Journal, 322*, 1240–1243.

Carroll, B. J., Feinberg, M., Smouse, P. E., Rawson, S. G., & Greden, J. F. (1981). The Carroll Rating Scale for Depression: I. Development, reliability, and validation. *British Journal of Psychiatry, 138*, 194–200.

Costa, P. T., & McCrae, R. R. (1980). Influence of extra-version and neuroticism on subjective well-being: Happy and unhappy people. *Journal of Personality and Social Psychology, 38*, 668–678.

Crowe, T. A., Di Lollo, A., & Crowe, B. T. (2000). *Crowe's Protocols: A Comprehensive Guide to Stuttering Assessment*. The Psychological Corporation.

Davies, A. R., & Ware, J. E. (1981). *Measuring Health Perceptions in the Health Insurance Experiment*. Santa Monica, CA: The RAND Corporation.

de Boer, A., Spruijt, R., Sprangers, M., & de Haes, J. (1998). Disease-specific quality of life: Is it one construct? *Quality of Life Research, 7*, 135–142.

de Graeff, A., de Leeuw, R., Ros, W., Hordijk, G. J., Battermann, J., Blijham, G., & Winnubst, J. (1999). A prospective study on quality of life laryngeal cancer patients treated with radiotherapy. *Head and Neck, 21,* 291–296.

Diener, E. (1984). Subjective well-being. *Psychological Bulletin, 95,* 542–575.

Donald, C. A., & Ware, J. E. (1984). The measurement of social support. In J. R. Greenley (Ed.), *Research in Community and Mental Health* (p. 325). Greenwich, CT: JAI Press.

Erickson, R. L. (1969). Assessing communicative attitudes among stutterers. *Journal of Speech and Hearing Research, 12,* 711–724.

Evans, R. W. (1991). Quality of life. *The Lancet, 338,* 636.

Farquhar, M. (1995). Elderly people's definitions of quality of life. *Social Science and Medicine, 41,* 1439–1446.

Fayers, P. M., Hand, D. J., Bjordal, K., & Groenvold, M. (1997). Causal indicators in quality of life research. *Quality of Life Research, 6,* 393–406.

Finlay, A. Y., & Coles, E. C. (1995). The effect of severe psoriasis on the quality of life of 369 patients. *British Journal of Dermatology, 132,* 236–244.

Finlay, A. Y., & Kelly, S. E. (1987). Psoriasis: An Index of Disability. *Clinical and Experimental Dermatology, 12,* 8–11.

Finlay, A. Y., Khan, G. K., Luscombe, D. K., & Salek, M. S. (1990). Validation of Sickness Impact Profile and Psoriasis Disability Index in psoriasis. *British Journal of Dermatology, 123,* 751–756.

Fitzpatrick, R., Fletcher, A., Gore, S., Jones, D., Spiegelhalter, D., & Cox, D. (1992). Quality of life measures in health care. I: Applications and issues in assessment. *British Medical Journal, 305,* 1074–1078.

Fortune, D. G., Main, C. J., O'Sullivan, T. M., & Griffiths, C. E. M. (1997). Quality of life in patients with psoriasis: The contribution of clinical variables and psoriasis-specific stress. *British Journal of Dermatology, 137,* 755–760.

Gotay, C. C., Korn, E. L., McCabe, M. S., Moore, T. D., & Cheson, B. D. (1992). Quality of life assessment in cancer treatment protocols: Research issues in protocol development. *Journal of the National Cancer Institute, 84,* 575–579.

Gupta, M. A., & Gupta, A. K. (1995a). Age and gender differences in the impact of psoriasis on quality of life. *International Journal of Dermatology, 34,* 700–703.

Gupta, M. A., & Gupta, A. K. (1995b). The Psoriasis Life Stress Inventory: a preliminary index of psoriasis-related stress. *Acta Dermato-Venereologica, 75,* 240–243.

Gupta, M. A., & Gupta, A. K. (1998). Depression and suicidal ideation in dermatology patients with acne, alopecia areata, atopic dermatitis and psoriasis. *British Journal of Dermatology, 139,* 846–850.

Guyatt, G. H., Bombarbier, C., & Tugwell, P. X. (1986). Measuring disease-specific quality of life in clinical trials. *Canadian Medical Association Journal, 134,* 889–895.

Hamilton, M. (1969). Standardized assessment and recording of depressive symptoms. *Psychiatry, Neurology, and Neurosurgery, 72,* 201–205.

Hammerlid, E., Silander, E., Hornestam, L., & Sullivan, M. (2001). Health-related quality of life three years after diagnosis of head and neck cancer—A longitudinal study. *Head and Neck, 23,* 113–125.

Kaplan, R. M., Anderson, J. P., & Ganiats, T. G. (1993). The Quality of Well-being Scale: Rationale for a single quality of life index. In S. R. Walker & R. M. Rosser (Eds.), *Quality of life assessment: Key issues in the 1990s* (pp. 65–94). Boston: Kluwer Academic Publishers.

Kirkley, A., Griffin, S., McLintock, H., & Ng, L. (1998). The development and evaluation of a disease-specific quality of life measurement tool for shoulder instability:

The Western Ontario Shoulder Instability Index (WOSI). *The American Journal of Sports Medicine, 26*, 764–772.

Krueger, G., Koo, J., Lebwohl, M., Menter, A., Stern, R. S., & Rolstad, T. (2001). The impact of psoriasis on quality of life: Results of a 1988 National Psoriasis Foundation patient-membership survey. *Archives of Dermatology, 137*, 280–284.

McCauley, R. J., & Swisher, L. (1984). Psychometric review of language and articulation tests for preschool children. *Journal of Speech and Hearing Disorders, 49*, 34–42.

McEwan, J. (1993). The Nottingham Health Profile. In S. R. Walker & R. M. Rosser (Eds.), *Quality of life assessment: Key issues in the 1990s* (pp. 111–130). Boston: Kluwer Academic Publishers.

McHorney, C. A., Ware, J. E., Lu, J. F. R., & Sherbourne, C. D. (1994). The MOS 36-item Short Form Health Survey (SF-36): III. Tests of data quality, scaling assumptions and reliability across diverse patient groups. *Medical Care, 32*, 40–66.

McHorney, C. A., Ware, J. E., & Raczek, A. E. (1993). The MOS 36-item Short Form Health Survey (SF-36): II. Psychometric and clinical tests of validity in measuring physical and mental health constructs. *Medical Care, 31*, 247–263.

Mishra, G., & Schofield, M. J. (1998). Norms for the physical and mental health component summary scores of the SF-36 for middle-aged and older Australian women. *Quality of Life Research, 7*, 215–220.

Morton, R. P. (1997). Laryngeal cancer: Quality of life and cost-effectiveness. *Head and Neck, 19*, 243–250.

Mozes, B., Maor, Y., & Shmueli, A. (1999). Do we know what global ratings of health quality of life measure? *Quality of Life Research, 8*, 269–273.

O'Boyle, C. A., McGee, H., & Hickey, A. (1989). Reliability and validity of judgment analysis as a method for assessing quality of life. *British Journal of Clinical Pharmacology, 339*, 1088–1091.

Patrick, D. L., & Erickson, P. (1988). What constitutes quality of life? Concepts and dimensions. *Clinical Nutrition, 7*, 53–63.

Patrick, D. L., & Erickson, P. (1993). Assessing health-related quality of life for clinical decision making. In S. R. Walker & R. M. Rosser (Eds.), *Quality of life assessment: Key issues in the 1990s* (pp. 11–64). Boston: Kluwer Academic Publishers.

Patrick, D. L., & Erickson, P. (1996). *Health status and health policy: Allocating resources to health care.* New York: Oxford University Press.

Read, J. L. (1993). The new era of quality of life assessment. In S. R. Walker, & R. M. Rosser (Eds.), *Quality of life assessment: Key issues in the 1990s* (pp. 3–10). Boston: Kluwer Academic Publishers.

Ringash, J., & Bezjak, A. (2001). A structured review of quality of life instruments for head and neck cancer patients. *Head and Neck, 23*, 201–213.

Salek, M. S. (1993). Measuring the quality of life of patients with skin disease. In S. R. Walker & R. M. Rosser (Eds.), *Quality of life assessment: Key issues in the 1990s* (pp. 355–370). Boston: Kluwer Academic Publishers.

Selby, P. (1993). Measuring the quality of life of patients with cancer. In S. R. Walker & R. M. Rosser (Eds.), *Quality of life assessment: Key issues in the 1990s* (pp. 235–268). Boston: Kluwer Academic Publishers.

Shadbolt, B., McCallum, J., & Singh, M. (1997). Health outcomes by self-report: Validity of the SF-36 among Australian hospital patients. *Quality of Life Research, 6,* 343–352.

Shin, D. C., & Johnson, D. M. (1978). Avowed happiness as an overall assessment of quality of life. *Social Indicators Research, 5,* 475–492.

Silverman, F. H. (1980). The stuttering problem profile: A task that assists both client and clinician in defining therapy goals. *Journal of Speech and Hearing Disorders, 45,* 119–123.

Stewart, A. L., & Ware, J. E. (Eds.). (1992). *Measuring Functioning and Well-being: The Medical Outcomes Study Approach.* Duke University Press.

Stewart, A. L., Ware, J. E., Brook, R. H., & Davies-Avery, A. (1978). *Conceptualization and measurement of health for adults in the health insurance study, volume II, physical health in terms of functioning.* Santa Monica, CA: The RAND Corporation.

Sullivan, M. D., Kempen, G., Sonderson, E. V., & Ormel, J. (2000). Models of health-related quality of life in a population of community-dwelling Dutch elderly. *Quality of Life Research, 9,* 801–810.

Testa, M. A., & Simonson, D. C. (1996). Assessment of quality of life outcomes. *New England Journal of Medicine, 334,* 835–841.

Veit, C. T., & Ware, J. E. (1983). The structure of psychological distress and well-being in general populations. *Journal of Consulting Clinical Psychology, 51,* 730.

Ware, J. E., & Sherbourne, C. D. (1992). The MOS 36-item Short-form Health Survey (SF-36): I. Conceptual framework and item selection. *Medical Care, 30,* 473–483.

Ware, J. E., Snow, K. K., Kosinski, M., & Gandek, B. (1993). *SF-36 Health Survey: Manual and Interpretation Guide.* Boston, MA: The Health Institute, New England Medical Center.

Weinstein, G. S., El-Sawy, M. M., Ruiz, C., Dooley, P., Chalian, A., El-Sayed, M. M., & Goldberg, A. (2001). Laryngeal preservation with supracricoid partial laryngectomy results in improved quality of life when compared with total laryngectomy. *Laryngoscope, 111,* 191–199.

The WHO Group (1995). The World Health Organization quality of life assessment (WHOQOL): Position paper from the World Health Organization. *Social Science and Medicine, 41,* 1403–1409.

Williams, D. E., Darley, F. L., & Spriesterbach, D. C. (1978). *Diagnostic methods in speech pathology.* New York: Harper & Row.

Wilson, I. B., & Cleary, P. D. (1995). Linking clinical variables with health-related quality of life: a conceptual model of patient outcomes. *Journal of the American Medical Association, 273,* 59–65.

Yaruss, J. S. (2001). Evaluating treatment outcomes for adults who stutter. *Journal of Communication Disorders, 34,* 163–182.

Yaruss, J. S., & Quesal, R. W. (2002, November). Overall assessment of the speaker's experience of stuttering (OASES). Paper presented at the Annual Convention of the American Speech-Language-Hearing Association, Atlanta, GA, November 2002.

Zigmond, A. S., & Snaith, R. P. (1983). The Hospital Anxiety and Depression Scale. *Acta Psychiatry Scandinavia, 67,* 361–370.

Ziller, R. C. (1974). Self-other orientations and quality of life. *Social Indicators Research, 1,* 301–327.

AUTHORS' NOTES

This chapter is based on a paper first presented at the 2002 University of Georgia State of the Art Conference on evidence-based treatment of stuttering. Our thanks to Robin Bramlett for her assistance in final preparation of this chapter, and to Duska Franic for discussions about quality of life research.

IV

STUTTERING TREATMENT RESEARCH: EVALUATING THE AVAILABLE EVIDENCE

10

"Gradual Increase in Length and Complexity of Utterance" and "Extended Length of Utterance" Treatment Programs for Stuttering: Assessing the Implications of Strong but Limited Evidence

Jason H. Davidow
Bradley T. Crowe
Anne K. Bothe
The University of Georgia

The *Gradual Increase in Length and Complexity of Utterance* (GILCU) (Ryan, 1974, 2001) and *Extended Length of Utterance* (ELU; Costello, 1983; Ingham, 1999) stuttering treatments evolved several decades ago as combinations of at least two treatment elements. The first was the growing evidence that operant conditioning principles, or response-contingent stimulation (RCS) procedures, could effectively increase fluent speech and reduce stuttering. Investigations that employed RCS to reduce adults' stuttering began in the 1950s (see Ingham, 1984) and, as the lingering effects of Johnson's diagnosogenic theory were gradually overcome, these procedures were also shown to be effective in reducing stuttering in older children (Martin & Berndt, 1970; Rickard & Mundy, 1965; Ryan, 1971) and finally in very young children (Martin, Kuhl, & Haroldson, 1972). At the same time, procedures were developing to reinforce increasingly longer (e.g., from words to phrases to sentences) and more difficult (e.g., assuming that conversation is more difficult than short monologues) speaking tasks (Rickard & Mundy, 1965; Ryan, 1971), or to reinforce specific time periods of fluent speech (Leach, 1969). The combination of these two ideas evolved into the GILCU (Ryan, 1974) and then the ELU (Costello, 1983) programs, which provide response contingencies for stuttered and fluent speech within progressively longer or more difficult speaking tasks.

GILCU and ELU were one of the four treatment types identified in a recent review (Cordes, 1998) as having published posttreatment maintenance data showing less than 1% syllables stuttered (%SS). Cordes's review also identified response contingent approaches as another apparently efficacious treatment, again based on published maintenance data. The fact that these two approaches were identified as efficacious in isolation and can also be identified within larger treatment packages (that use, for example, fluency-skills training and feedback to modify stutters in a framework that begins with words and progresses to phrases and sentences) also led Cordes to suggest that these two approaches might be so powerful that the functional variable in some combined treatment packages might actually be the response contingencies or the control of utterance length.

The strength of these conclusions was limited, however, by the fact that Cordes's (1998) review included only four investigations of GILCU and ELU procedures; it also excluded several investigations that had tested modifications of ELU and GILCU procedures. Thus, as part of a larger effort to identify the functional components of stuttering treatment and recovery, the present chapter was written to extend the findings of the 1998 review by providing a more complete evaluation of the available literature about GILCU and ELU procedures. The purpose of this chapter is four-fold: (1) to summarize the speech data reported following establishment, transfer, and maintenance phases of these treatments; (2) to evaluate the methodologies of these investigations; (3) to determine the effectiveness of these treatments for clients of different ages; and (4) to compare the effectiveness of these procedures to that of other treatment programs reported within the same investigations.

IDENTIFICATION OF REPORTS AND SUMMARY TABLES

Experimental investigations involving GILCU, ELU, and GILCU-like or ELU-like procedures (hereafter, "modifications") were identified via a computer literature search, review of available printed sources, and personal contacts. Care was taken to identify articles that used the GILCU or ELU procedural framework without incorporating direct manipulation of the participant's speech pattern. [Shine's (1980, 1984) treatment program, for example, controls length and complexity of utterance but also incorporates fluency procedures such as whispering and prolonged speech characteristics. Programs such as these were not included in this review.] In addition, investigations for this review were limited to those that involved increasing utterance length, with increases in syntactic complexity assumed to co-occur. Treatments involving systematic desensitization (Brutten & Shoemaker, 1967; Wolpe, 1958) that require increasingly difficult tasks but do not control utterance length were excluded.

Each report was reviewed by the first author, who summarized the speech performance data to produce Table 10.1. This table is intended to allow visual inspection of summarized speech performance data, including information about the inclusion and exclusion of important aspects of treatment. The first column in Table 10.1 lists identifying information for each study. Columns 2 through 5 then summarize the available information about four dependent variables measured at up to five points during each study. Dependent variables include stuttering frequency [as stuttered words per minute (SW/M) or as percent of syllables stuttered (%SS)], speech naturalness (SN; measured on a 9-point scale where 1 = *most natural* and 9 = *least natural*; Martin, Haroldson, & Triden, 1984), and speech rate (SR, measured as words or syllables spoken per minute). The dependent variables and the five stages of treatment used for Table 10.1 were selected because they are viewed as essential to the description of stuttering treatment outcome (Ingham & Riley, 1998). Footnotes in Table 10.1 label the situation in which the dependent variables were measured, and the lengths of follow-up checks are also noted. Empty cells in Table 10.1 reflect either the omission of that treatment phase in the reported studies or no measurement taken after that phase, usually the former.

Effort was taken to include in Table 10.1 data from only those participants who had completed the entire relevant phase; thus, if a participant had only completed a portion of a given phase, those data were not included in Table 10.1 if it was possible to remove them (e.g., Mowrer, 1975). In some situations, however, the original publications provided only group data or did not require participants to complete a phase, so it was impossible to determine which subjects had or had not completed certain phases. Also, in some instances (e.g. Ryan & Ryan, 1983) data in Table 10.1 are from the last assessment during a phase, allowing the inclusion of more beyond-clinic measures than would otherwise have been possible. The present authors' decisions in these respects are explained in further detail in the following.

One important dilemma in compiling Table 10.1 involved the particular measures to use, because studies varied in providing within-clinic data or beyond-clinic data and in the use of reading, monologue, or conversational contexts. The choice was made to err on the side of creating a stringent review, or to include the measure or measures that most resembled the natu-

TABLE 10.1
Mean Speech Performance Data for Literature Reviewed*

Study	Pretherapy SW/M	% SS	N	SR	Postestablishment SW/M	% SS	N	SR	Posttransfer SW/M	% SS	N	SR	Postmaintenance SW/M	% SS	N	SR	Follow-up SW/M	% SS	N	SR
Rickard & Mundy (1965)[1]: One 9 year (yr.) old (Data is for number of repetition errors)	128				17.5				0								16			
Rustin, Ryan, & Ryan (1987)[2]: 90 participants (part.) (6–45 yrs. old)	10.4			97.9 WS/M	0.2			116.3 WS/M												
Ryan & Ryan (1995): 9 part.: mean age = 12.2	6.2^3			106.05^3 WS/M	1.75^3			117.35^3 WS/M												
6 part.: mean age = 11.5					0.9^3			114.4^3 WS/M	0.9^3			132.9^3 WS/M								
3 part.													0.65^3							
6 part.: mean age = 11.5	5.9^2			125.2^2 WS/M													0.6^4			
Ryan & Ryan (1983)[5]: 4 part.: mean age = 11.3	5.35			153.95 WS/M	1.5			160.25 WS/M												

Study	%SS	%SS	rate	%SS	rate	%SS	rate	%SS	rate	%SS	rate
3 part.	6.15	1.7	152.50 WS/M	0.6	156.15 WS/M	1.05	147.5 WS/M	1.0	146.85 WS/M		136.5 WS/M
Ryan (1981): 8 part.: mean age = 12.5	6.9[12]		125.63[12] WS/M					0.55[6]			
Ryan (1974)[c]: 9 part.: mean age = 14.7	11.2[12a]	0.29[12a]									
5 part.: mean age = 7.8	5.78[13]							0.2[14b]			
Mallard & Westbrook (1988)[12]:											
12 part.[e]: mean age = 7.5		11.75		7.17				4.75			
Costello (1980)[12]: one 11 yr. old		20.0	125 SPM	1.2	132 SPM						
Riley & Ingham (2000)[11]:											
6 part.: mean age = 5.9		5.89		2.16							
Druce et al. (1997)[7]:											
15 part.: mean age = 7 yrs., 4 months		9.31 4.87	92.3 SPM			1.75[d] 2.27	112.7 SPM	2.48 2.54	107.1 SPM	3.83 2.67	140.3 SPM
Mowrer (1975)[8]: 3 part. (ages = 8, 8, 27 yrs.)	11.13	1.6									
one 14 yr. old	8			0.9							

(continued on next page)

TABLE 10.1 (continued)

Study	Pretherapy SW/M	% SS	N	SR	Postestablishment SW/M	% SS	N	SR	Posttransfer SW/M	% SS	N	SR	Postmaintenance SW/M	% SS	N	SR	Follow-up SW/M	% SS	N	SR
3 part. (ages = 10, 31, 23 yrs.)	6.83												0.23							
Johnson et al. (1978)[6]: one 6 yr. old	17.4				4.4												3.7			
Ryan (1971): one 6 yr. old (part. # 2)	14[12]				0.2[9]								0.3[10]							

[1]Reading in clinic with clinician (or experimenter, researcher, etc.); [2]reading, monologue, and conversation with clinician; [3]averaged data from home and school conversations; [4]recorded conversations gathered by clinicians; [5]averaged data from home and school samples of talking; [6]conversation collected by clinicians (setting unclear); [7]conversation with stranger and conversation with family member in clinic room; [8]stuttering interview (different variations) with clinician; [9]presumably data from therapy activities; [10]monologue and conversation with clinician (most likely); [11]averaged data from multiple within- and beyond-clinic conversations over several points in time; [12]conversation with clinician; [13]mainly from reading monologue and conversation, but not all participants had data for all three tasks; [14]presumably reading, monologue and conversation with clinician for four participants and a tape recording for one participant; [a]one participant's data are from monologue; [b]only 2 participants performed at least transfer or maintenance; [c]four of the original nine subjects were run on variations of GILCU establishment program but were included here because they were run by Ryan or his lab; [d]data are categorized as posttransfer because activities that were clearly considered to be transfer were completed before the first data point after the establishment program; [e]The number of participants in the published study is greater than 12, however, some received a therapy program during the previous year so were excluded here in order to increase the value of the GILCU program without previous treatment being a confounding variable. *Footnote numbers listed with a study's identifying information in Column 1 indicate that all measures reported are from the assessment task listed. Follow-up measurements were taken at the following times: Rickard and Mundy (1965), 6 months after transfer; Ryan and Ryan (1995), average of 15.2 months after last maintenance step; Ryan and Ryan (1983), 9 months after maintenance; Ryan (1981), average of 12.5 months after last maintenance step; Ryan and Ryan (1974), 4 participants 8 months after completion of their individual program and one participant 21 months after; Mallard and Westbrook (1988), about 4 months after program; Druce et al. (1997), 18 months after maintenance; Johnson et al. (1978), 1 month after establishment.

ral environment. Thus, if stuttering data were provided from (a) reading in the clinic, (b) reading and monologue at school, and (c) conversation at school, the third of these would be presented in Table 10.1; if conversation in school and conversation at home were used, these numbers were averaged for the purposes of Table 10.1. When the available data did not fit the categories selected for this review, the present authors placed them in the best possible category; many such decisions and their implications are discussed below or in notes to the table. Due to subject attrition in the original studies, participant numbers may vary across the phases of the same study (e.g. Ryan & Ryan, 1995). Additionally, if discrepancies existed in a report (e.g., conflicting or different numbers in a table versus in text), and if the present authors could not make a reasonable determination, those data were not used in this table.

The methodology of each experimental investigation assessed for this review was also evaluated, based on a model of treatment efficacy evaluation discussed by Ingham and Cordes (1999), and summarized in Table 10.2. Methodological criteria, noted with an X in Table 10.2 if they were judged by the present authors to exist, include the following:

1. Data from any evaluation (reading, monologue, conversation, etc.) of speech performance (stuttering, speech rate, or speech naturalness) within the clinic before treatment;
2. Stuttering data collected during therapy (either described or published) or an evaluation completed between treatment phases;
3. Speech performance data provided from at least 3 months after the end of the relevant phase of treatment;
4. Same as Category 1 but requiring beyond-clinic data;
5. Speech performance data collected beyond the clinic during the program;
6. Same as Category 3 but requiring beyond-clinic data;
7. Any stuttering-judgment reliability data provided from at least one judge who had not worked directly with the client;
8. Same as Category 7 but for speech rate; and
9. Same as Category 7 but for speech naturalness.

The data summarized in Tables 10.1 and 10.2 are further addressed and discussed in the following sections. As this chapter shows, it appears that both the ELU and GILCU programs can successfully reduce or eliminate stuttering in children, adolescents, and adults; the evidence to support them is quite strong in several ways. A surprising lack of high-quality experimental investigations about these treatments must also be acknowledged, however, and the amount of speech performance data in the natural environment (e.g., home and school settings) is also quite limited. The implications of these complexities are also addressed below.

TABLE 10.2

Evaluation of The Methodological Quality of Treatments Reviewed, Per Ingham and Cordes's (1999) Criteria (see text)

Study	(1) Evaluation of Speech Performance Before Treatment Within Clinic	(2) Evaluation of Speech Performance During Treatment Within Clinic	(3) Evaluation of Speech Performance for a Clinically Meaningful Period After Treatment Within Clinic	(4) Evaluation of Speech Performance Before Treatment Beyond Clinic	(5) Evaluation of Speech Performance During Treatment Beyond Clinic	(6) Evaluation of Speech Performance for a Clinically Meaningful Period After Treatment Beyond Clinic	(7) Reliable and Independent Measure of Stuttering	(8) Reliable and Independent Measure of Speech Rate	(9) Reliable and Independent Measure of Speech Quality
Rickard & Mundy (1965)	X	X	X				X		
Ryan & Ryan (1995)	X	X	X	X	X	X	X	X	
Ryan & Ryan (1983)	X	X	X	X	X	X	X	X	
Rustin, Ryan, & Ryan (1987)	X	X	X						
Mallard & Westbrook (1988)	X	X					X		
Costello (1980)	X	X	X				X		
Druce et al. (1997)	X	X					X		
Mowrer (1975)	X	X	X						
Johnson et al. (1978)	X	X							
Ryan (1971): Participant 2	X	X					X		
Riley & Ingham (2000)	X	X	X	X	X				

LITERATURE REVIEW

The Beginning: Rickard and Mundy (1965)

Rickard and Mundy's (1965) article is especially noteworthy because of its importance to the development of the GILCU program and because it reveals some of the problems that continue to influence this literature. One 9-year-old male who stuttered completed a series of gradually longer and more difficult speaking tasks. He was socially reinforced ("great," "nice job," etc.) for speech that was fluent or more fluent than his baseline speech, and, in the later stages of the program, he earned points that could be exchanged for prizes. Stuttering was measured by "repetition errors per task unit" (p. 269; e.g., "c-c-cat" contains two repetition errors for the task unit of "cat"). The tasks included, in order, reading two-word phrases from cue cards, reading sentences, reading paragraphs, conversation with the experimenter (telling stories and normal conversation) and conversation with the parents. Reinforcement consisted of social praise and various extrinsic rewards for phrases, sentences, paragraphs, and 5-minute periods of conversation that involved fewer repetitions than baseline (this system was used when repetition rates were not approaching zero) or no repetitions.

The child worked through the stages, advancing to the next stage when repetition errors reached near zero levels (zero stuttering was reached at each level, but criterion for progression is unclear). Measures of repetition errors were also collected before, during (after 35 sessions of phrase reading, sentences paragraphs, and storytelling), and after treatment (after the conversation stage with the experimenter and parents, which consisted of 21 30-minute conversation sessions) while the child read paragraphs (173 total words). As can be seen in Table 10.1, repetition errors dropped from 128 before treatment to 17.5 after 35 sessions (preconversation) to 0 after the transfer portion. These results are intriguing, but it is important to note that the child's parents reported that he still stuttered, especially during stressful conversation. Also, during a 6-month follow-up the child produced 16 repetition errors on the first word of a paragraph, and stuttering and repetition errors had returned in the natural environment.

Many of the methodological details that may have contributed to the poor maintenance of fluency shown in Rickard and Mundy's (1965) investigation continue to be seen in some subsequent treatment investigations, as is discussed in further detail later. These include pass criteria within and between steps that allow some stuttering, unclear criteria for progression between steps, no data from the natural environment, questionable definitions of stuttering, and no maintenance program.

The GILCU Program

General Description and Initial Issues. Some aspects of the following general description were altered for individual studies, but Ryan's (1974) GILCU program generally begins with an establishment phase, the key element of which is that the client responds with increasingly longer utterances in three different speaking conditions. The program begins with reading single words fluently, progresses up to six words, then progresses to four sentences, and ends with 5 minutes of fluent reading. The same steps are then completed for monologue and conversation, and transfer and maintenance phases are also completed. All conditions are recommended, but it is possible to perform the program without using all conditions (Ryan, 1974, 2001), especially for clients who can not read. If a client fails a step consistently, a branch step is introduced until the client is ready to return to the program. Social praise (and tokens, in some applications) is provided contingent on fluent speech, and "stop, speak fluently" is used contingent upon stuttering. The transfer phase addresses the goal of fluent utterances in multiple speaking conditions and situations, and with multiple people; verbal reinforcement and punishment are used in the transfer phase. The maintenance program consists of reading, monologue, and conversation measurements (less than 0.5 stuttered words per minute; SW/M, is required to pass each step), along with reports of the client's speech from the client and from persons in his/her environment, which are gradually faded.

Progression through the establishment, transfer, and maintenance phases requires the client to produce no more than 0.5 SW/M during 5 minutes of reading, 5 minutes of monologue, and 5 minutes of conversation in a "Criterion Test" before progressing to the next phase of the program. If any one of these three situations is failed, the client repeats the steps of the program congruent with the failure (e.g., repeats the reading steps if more than 0.5 SW/M was produced on the reading portion of the criterion test). Criterion tests are given before establishment, after establishment, and after transfer. Clients, parents, or spouses are also taught to identify stutters so that home practice can be conducted.

One critical element of the GILCU literature is the stuttering measurement system used. A stutter was usually defined as whole-word repetitions, part-word repetitions, prolongations, and struggle behaviors (stutter with struggle, normal disfluency with struggle, or secondary behavior before producing a word), but this may vary depending on the client's speech. Interjections, revisions, incomplete phrases, pauses, and phrase repetitions are seen as normal disfluencies in the GILCU program, with a few exceptions (e.g., if these occur at a high rate or are near stuttered words). Ryan (2001) provided preliminary normative data for both stutters and normal disfluencies from small groups of speakers, showing that a group of normally fluent 3- to 5-year-old males produced a mean of 2.2 SW/M; a group of 6- to 8-year-old males produced a mean of 1.4 SW/M; and a group of 9- to 12-year-old males produced a mean of 0.8 SW/M. Therefore, presumably, any SW/M score at or below these numbers for the respective age group can be seen as normally fluent. Another table from Ryan (2001), however, shows that only very few of the stutters from fluent speakers in these age groups contain struggle. In fact, the data reveal that the number of stutters labeled struggle per 100 words for the 3- to 5-year-olds and 9- to 12-year-olds was zero.

These data result in two concerns about GILCU reports. First, the authors may have overidentified normal disfluencies as stutters, if all whole-word repetitions, part-word repetitions, and prolongations were necessarily labeled as *stutters*. Such a pattern would result in higher reports of stuttering or less positive treatment outcome numbers, potentially hiding the beneficial effects of the treatment. Second, according to Ryan's (2001) Table 6, 2.0 SW/M is below the mean for fluent 3- to 5-year-olds. However, according to Table 5 in Ryan (2001), none of the normal 3 to 5 year olds produced any stutters classified as struggle. Therefore, a child who produces 2.0 struggles per minute may be far from normal, although 2.0 per minute of the other three types of stuttered words in this measurement system may be perfectly normal. In other words, it appears that data about stutter type would be necessary to the appropriate interpretation of data presented using this measurement system because normal speakers produce whole-word repetitions, part-word repetitions, and prolongations that could inappropriately be labeled as *stutters* if struggle is not explicitly identified. Regardless of this issue, however, some of the GILCU posttreatment SW/M numbers presented later are very low, reflecting excellent treatment outcomes even if all the stuttered words did indeed include struggle.

Review of Available Reports. Nine publications were identified that included data relevant to the effectiveness of the GILCU program. Four were peer-reviewed experimental reports (Mallard & Westbrook, 1988; Rustin, Ryan, & Ryan, 1987; Ryan & Ryan, 1983, 1995); five were not (Ryan, 1971, 1974, 1979, 1981, 2001). There are several complications, as discussed later, but the general conclusion to be drawn from these reports is that the GILCU program appears to be very effective in reducing stuttering frequency.

Explanation of the Ryan (1974) data is warranted. Four of these subjects completed variations of the GILCU program but are included in Table 10.1 because Ryan or a clinician directly under his supervision was responsible for their treatment. Fluency was maintained in the five participants who completed follow-up checks, but only one participant completed transfer and maintenance activities (this participant was also Participant 5 from Ryan, 1971) and one other completed maintenance activities. The latter two subjects reached zero SW/M at follow-up checks 21 months (this participant's data are from a telephone conversation) and 8 months after the program ended, respectively.

As Ryan (1971) stated, the success of Participant 5 may have been due to the concurrent clinic, home, and school establishment programs. Stokes and Osnes (1989) discussed the importance of generalization activities from the beginning of a treatment program, and perhaps future programs will involve these types of activities. Because of the home and school programs, however, it is difficult to determine the actual value of the within-clinic program for these subjects. Stuttered words per minute were also low for Participant 2 in Ryan's study, who performed a modification of GILCU, after a maintenance program that included home practice and practice with the school clinician. Another complexity in interpreting these data, however, is that this participant received a similar type of therapy during the previous school year; the value of the second program in itself remains unclear. However, the other reports included here reveal the success of the within-clinic establishment program.

The three highest stuttering frequency numbers in Table 10.1 involving the GILCU program come from studies by Ryan and Ryan (1983, 1995) and Mallard and Westbrook (1988). The data from the two former studies are from home and school speech, not within-clinic samples. Within-clinic reading, monologue and conversation samples revealed rates of 0.4 SW/M and 127.9 words spoken per minute (WS/M; Ryan & Ryan, 1995), and 0.3 SW/M and 133.7 WS/M (Ryan & Ryan, 1983), after the establishment phase. Therefore, generalized stuttering rates were not as low as within-clinic rates, but generalization did occur. The goal of the Mallard and Westbrook study was to find the amount of success that could be obtained in a year of school in a public school setting. It is unclear how far the clients progressed in the program because all posttest data were taken at a similar time for all participants (the data were placed in the Establishment portion of Table 10.1). Therefore, the value of their program is difficult to analyze.

From the literature gathered here, three aspects of the GILCU program need to be addressed. First, there were only two peer-reviewed experimental reports (Ryan & Ryan, 1983, 1995), plus one participant in Ryan (1971; who performed a modification of GILCU) who completed a GILCU program (establishment, transfer, and maintenance), in which GILCU subjects could be directly identified. These two studies defied the trend in this literature by reporting beyond-clinic data; nevertheless, given the very small number of subjects involved, it is difficult to claim that the long-term real-world effectiveness of the GILCU approach has been established in the experimental literature. This situation is unfortunate, primarily because the data that do exist are very positive; there is every indication that GILCU may be a powerful treatment technique that should be more widely investigated.

Second is the issue of counting stuttered words. Ryan and Ryan (1995) noted that clinicians undercounted stuttering instances during therapy, with their agreement with the project supervisors being low during posttreatment measurements when instances of stuttering were low. In fact, the majority of the GILCU clients reported by Ryan and Ryan had to repeat steps, and the authors hypothesize this result to be a consequence of the undercounting of stuttered words during therapy by the clinicians and accurate counts by the experimenter and clinician during criterion tests. Similarly, because progression through the program requires less than 0.5 SW/M on the criterion tests, one or two missed instances of stuttering in each minute can be substantial. Regarding this issue, Ryan (1985) stated, "There has been some improvement, since our more recent data indicate less recycles, but this will probably continue to be a problem" (p. 162). Training clinicians to be as accurate as possible in identifying stuttering would appear to be important to the success of GILCU and similar programs (Cordes & Ingham, 1999), as discussed in further detail in the following.

Lastly, the studies reported by Ryan and his colleagues (Ryan & Ryan, 1995) are marked by subject attrition, with some participants moving or failing to complete parts of the program in time to be included with the reported results. Their discussion of reasons for attrition is exemplary and a necessary part of proper experimental protocol, but the resulting differences in group sizes do complicate interpretation of data from transfer and maintenance phases.

Overall, and despite these methodological questions, the available data about the GILCU program suggest that it can be effective. Ryan (1979) reported on 15 children (4–8 years old) performing the GILCU program who reduced SW/M from 11.8 before treatment to 0.2 after maintenance. Ryan (2001) included data from many of the GILCU investigations (some already reviewed here) and reports postestablishment rates of 0.4 SW/M or lower for all data sets except one (2.5 SW/M postestablishment), presumably on the criterion test. The exception was a study of the GILCU program in Hong Kong (Ryan, 2001) in which a set number of hours was used for treatment, so many if not all of the clients may have not completed the program as written.

Ryan (2001) also presented preliminary data from preschool children, a population that has been absent from the GILCU literature, who completed a revised GILCU program. Ryan reported that all six children "demonstrated less than 3.0 SW/M and normal speaking rates on the [fluency interview] after treatment" (p. 208). Further data from the preschool study appear to be in preparation. In addition, some of the data reported by Ryan were from administering GILCU in the schools, suggesting that this program may be effectively used in the schools (Bothe, 2002).

Ryan (2001) also compiled transfer and maintenance data for GILCU, but some of these data were combined with data from other programs for publication so, from this piece of literature, the reader is unable to determine the success of GILCU clients in particular. In addition, when discussing the DAF and GILCU programs, Ryan (1984) stated that "the data—based on over 500 clients—indicate that the average child entered the program at 7 percent stuttering, that is, 93 percent fluency, and left the program at less than 1 percent stuttering—99 percent fluency—or demonstrated normal-sounding speech fluency" (p. 103). However, due to the nature of this summary report, and the combination of data from different establishment programs, the 1984 and 2001 reports did not contribute much additional evidence to the exact long-term effectiveness of the GILCU program.

In conclusion, it appears that the GILCU program, if run completely, is effective in establishing fluency; the follow-up data in Table 10.1 reveal that stuttering rates hover around 0.5 to 0.8 SW/M. Additionally, the data provided for speaking rates during maintenance and at follow-up checks are either well within or just slightly below those of conversational rates for young adults (Walker, 1988). It also appears that reduced stuttering can be achieved in various manners. Some of the GILCU data include the use of cancellations, simultaneous home and school programs, and varying tasks within the framework of gradually increasing length of utterance. However, the influence on fluency of these different variables cannot be determined (Ingham, 1984). Finally, only three of the GILCU reports (only two of which are experimental) included in this review presented beyond-clinic data, although it is also reasonable to note that some of the projects were apparently not intended to be complete treatment outcome evaluation studies; that is, criticisms of their methodology as treatment outcome evaluation studies are to some extent unwarranted. Given the very positive results that are available, however, it would seem to be of some importance and of great value for additional long-term and beyond-clinic data to be collected and presented about the GILCU treatments.

ELU Program

The ELU (Costello, 1983; Ingham, 1999) establishment phase is quite similar to GILCU, beginning with the production of monosyllabic words and progressing to six-syllable utterances, various monologue lengths culminating in 5-minute monologues, and finally various lengths of conversation culminating in 5 minutes of conversation. Progression between steps is reliant on consecutive fluent responses, usually ten at each step. Positive reinforcers (social and token) are provided for each fluent response (token reinforcers are faded near the completion of establishment), and a punisher ("stop") is provided for each moment of stuttering until the final stages when feedback for stuttering is given following the timed conversation. Failure to complete a step in a certain number of trials calls for the inclusion of a branch step. When the branch step is completed, the client continues with the regular program. No set transfer program is included, and Ingham (1999) stated that children under 9 years old usually generalize their fluency, but variables such as self-management, parent training for home practice, peer or sibling participation in treatment, and treatment in various settings are used to enhance transfer.

Four reports (two experimental) regarding the effectiveness of the ELU treatment program were obtained for this review. Costello (1980) presented a case study of an 11-year-old boy who completed part of the ELU program. Costello's report did not incorporate conversation into the program, an aspect of the most recent description of the program (Ingham, 1999). As shown in Table 10.1, Costello reported substantial reductions in %SS and an increase in SPM during a 5-minute conversation taken within the clinic. These data are from conversation, revealing transfer from the program; monologues rates improved from 12.0%SS and 110 SPM to 0.7%SS and 138 SPM. Average length of disfluency decreased during monologue but not during conversation. Costello also reported that recordings from home revealed that fluency transferred to that setting near the completion of therapy, but no transfer or maintenance data were provided.

Riley and Ingham (2000) presented the results of 24 hours of ELU treatment for six children who stutter (mean age = 5.9) in their study of acoustic duration changes after Speech Motor Training (SMT) and ELU. As can be seen in Table 10.1, the ELU program was successful in reducing %SS after treatment, with one participant finishing the 24 sessions under 1%SS. Median percent differential for %SS from before therapy to after therapy was 63.5. Table 10.3 reveals that the two youngest children had the lowest posttherapy %SS scores, but the 3.8 year old had the fifth lowest percentage difference between measurement periods, a finding that could reflect his low pretherapy measure. It should be noted that all participants completed exactly 24 sessions due to the need to keep the treatment time consistent for both types of treatment, so it is likely that many of the children had not finished the program at the point when these measures were completed [especially given that the Costello (1980) participant took 33 hours to complete an ELU program without conversation steps]. In addition, posttherapy data were collected from within- and beyond-clinic conversations during an 8-week period, so it is difficult to determine the rate of stuttering immediately after treatment. It should also be noted that the Riley and Ingham (2000) and Costello (1980) articles were not intended to be treatment outcome studies; criticisms raised here are unfounded, in a sense, given the intent of the studies.

Long-term data were also obtained from one participant performing the ELU program as part of an experimental investigation (Riley & Ingham, 1997). Exact numbers are not provided for inclusion into the tables of this review, but the authors report that stuttering was reduced to less than 2%SS after transfer (parental reinforcement of fluent utterances and some punishment) and the participant was "essentially free of stuttering" (p. 42) at the final maintenance check 2 years following therapy. Interestingly, stuttering continued to decrease for this child during an

TABLE 10.3
Single-Subject Data From Studies Reviewed*

Study	Pretherapy				Postestablishment				Posttransfer, Postmaintenance, or Follow-Up			
	SW/M	% SS	N	SR	SW/M	% SS	N	SR	SW/M	% SS	N	SR
Ryan (1981)[a]:												
7 yr. old	10.2								1.0			
8 yr. old	5.5								0.6			
9 yr. old	8.4								1.2			
9 yr. old	6.9								0.2			
12 yr. old	4.0								0.4			
13 yr. old	8.2								0.4			
16 yr. old	5.2								0.4			
16 yr. old	6.8								0.2			
Ryan (1974)[1a]:												
7 yr. old	5.1				0.1				0			
7 yr. old	14.6				0				0.5			
8 yr. old	2.4				0				0.2			
8 yr. old	11.0				0							
8 yr. old	9.6				0.5				0.3			
9 yr. old	15.0				0				0			
16 yr. old	10.5				0							
35 yr. old	12.7				0.5							
Mallard & Westbrook (1988)[2a]:												
6 yr. old		9				5				3		
6 yr. old		20				6				6		
6 yr. old		16				2				1		
7 yr. old		4				9				2		
7 yr. old		13				5				4		
7 yr. old		13				6				4		
8 yr. old		11				4				2		
8 yr. old		11				4				2		
8 yr. old		13				11				15		
9 yr. old		9				17				8		
9 yr. old		14				15				7		
9 yr. old		8				2				3		
Mowrer (1975)[3]:												
8 yr. old	2				0.5							
8 yr. old	8.4				0.3							
10 yr. old	10.3								0.0[b]			
14 yr. old	8								0.9[c]			
23 yr. old	7.0								0.4[b]			

Study	Pretherapy				Postestablishment				Posttransfer, Postmaintenance, or Follow-Up			
	SW/M	% SS	N	SR	SW/M	% SS	N	SR	SW/M	% SS	N	SR
27 yr. old	23				4							
31 yr. old	3.2								0.3[b]			
Riley & Ingham (2000)												
3.8 yrs.		2.6				1.2						
4.3 yrs.		2.74				0.48						
5.3 yrs.		11.34				3.24						
6.3 yrs.		5.36				1.68						
7.5 yrs.		10.14				4.28						
8.4 yrs.		3.14				2.10						
GILCU study in Hong Kong: From Ryan (2001)												
4 yr. old	9.1			189.6	11.7			259.0				
5 yr. old	6.9			169.0	1.1			74.6				
6 yr. old	18.6			185.0	4.1			182.0				
8 yr. old	12.5			142.4	4.0			173.7				
25 yr. old	0.9			225.3	0.3			213.1				
28 yr. old	1.7			192.0	0.6			197.0				
30 yr. old	6.5			288.4	1.1			319.0				
30 yr. old	5.9			191.0	2.4			183.7				
30 yr. old	6.5			198.7	0.7			172.3				
34 yr. old	1.4			176.6	0.8			193.0				
45 yr. old	2.1			255.0	0.2			253.1				

*The reader is referred to Table 10.1 for data-collection conditions; [1]Some participants performed variations of the GILCU program; [2]Because only grades were given for the participants in Mallard & Westbrook (1988), these grades were converted to ages: Kindergarten = 5 yrs.; first grade = 6 yrs.; second grade = 7 yrs.; third grade = 8 yrs.; fourth grade = 9 yrs.; fifth grade = 10 yrs; [3]Only participants who did not drop out in the middle of a phase (i.e., those whose data were taken after the completion of an entire phase) are included here; [4]Speech rate data from Hong Kong study is in syllables per minute; [a]Data for this study in the "Posttransfer, Postmaintenance, or Follow-Up" column is after a follow-up period; [b]Postmaintenance data; [c]Posttransfer data.

8-week withdrawal period after treatment and before transfer, suggesting that treatment to a final 0%SS criterion in all environments may not be necessary (cf. Gierut, 1998); as the authors state, however, this issue also suggests that the treatment may not have been entirely responsible for the reduction in stuttering.

Data from one case report (Onslow, 1996) and four participants from the previously mentioned Riley and Ingham (1997) were also found. However, all five of these children completed or performed part of another treatment program prior to their ELU participation, so the exact effects of the ELU portion remain unclear. The child from Onslow (1996), who completed the entire ELU establishment program, produced less than 0.5%SS at follow-up during conversations with a clinician and during two beyond-clinic recordings. The four participants reported by Riley and Ingham (1997), who each completed only 24 hours of ELU treatment, produced the following results: mean 1.3%SS at last maintenance step; mean 1.2%SS at last maintenance step; a severe child reduced %SS to 30; and one child reduced stuttering below 2%SS up to 36 weeks after treatment, but the authors report an increase of stuttering after this measurement but not a return to baseline levels. These data were from within- and beyond-clinic conditions.

In conclusion, the limited data that are available are consistent in suggesting that the ELU program appears effective in reducing fluency. It is unclear, however, how many of the reported children actually completed the entire ELU establishment program, as it has been most recently outlined (Ingham, 1999), due to the exclusion of conversation (Costello, 1980) and the use of a predetermined number of therapy hours (Riley & Ingham, 1997, 2000). It is possible that the case report by Onslow (1996) is the only one in which the client finished the entire Establishment phase. This client had successful outcomes, including reductions in %SS in both within- and beyond-clinic samples, suggesting that reductions in fluency had transferred. Ingham (1999) also indicated that the ELU program has been successful for children in her clinic and experimentation, and complete transfer, maintenance, follow-up, speech naturalness, and speech rate data have been collected on a number of ELU participants that will likely be reported in the near future (Riley & Ingham, 1997).

Modifications

One of the more interesting features of the GILCU and ELU approaches, despite the limited data available for them, is that they have clearly been adapted and adopted into clinical practice. Johnson, Coleman, and Rasmussen (1978), Druce, Debney, and Byrt (1997), and Mowrer (1975), for example, used variations on the GILCU or ELU approach (see Appendix A), with varying success (see Table 10.1). As later discussed, these studies include several methodological weaknesses, but they do serve several important purposes.

The data from Johnson et al. (1978) and Mowrer (1975), to begin with, are difficult to interpret because their evaluation procedures used Ryan's (1979) stuttering interview, a comprehensive assessment strategy which involves singing and several speaking situations. Ryan provided data to show that overall SW/M tended to be lower in the fluency interview than in natural settings, especially after transfer. Therefore, the fluency interview data may not be representative of real-world fluency.

In addition, these studies are influenced by such factors as an absence of reliability data, a short 1-month follow-up, and punishment of only certain disfluencies. Mowrer (1975), for example, defined *stuttering* as "any part or whole word repetition, any pause or hesitation lasting approximately two seconds or more and occurring before or during the utterance of word, any prolongation of consonant or vowel sounds" (p. 29). This definition excludes many acts of stuttering (e.g. blocks less than approximately 2 seconds and phrase repetitions), so accurate feedback to the children about their stuttering may not have occurred; similarly, accurate data about all stuttering may not have been gathered. Druce et al. (1997) defined *stuttering* only as "bumpy talking," with no further clarification. In addition, the pass criterion is not clear, and it is also not clear whether each child actually completed the whole program. Druce et al. stated that "success at each step was equated with fluent speech containing no bumps" (p. 172), but there is no mention of how much speech or how many trials needed to be judged fluent for the client to progress (cf. Rickard & Mundy, 1965). Druce et al. also required the children to practice at home, so variations in practice time could be a confounding variable; it is also unclear what exactly the home practice encompassed. Finally, the goal of Druce et al.'s study was to examine the effectiveness of an intensive one-week program, so the poor outcomes reported might simply reflect that ELU and GILCU type procedures need more than 1 week to be effective.

As shown in Table 10.1, the results from these three investigations of modified procedures are quite poor. Only one study reported mean stuttering rates of less than 1 SW/M or 1%SS after establishment and transfer, and the number of subjects with that score is low. In addition, only one reported less than 1 SW/M or 1%SS after maintenance or during follow-up. There was also only one investigation that reported speech rate and speech naturalness data (Druce et al., 1997), which are extremely important to the evaluation of a treatment to instate normal-sounding speech. Table 10.2 reveals that only one investigation (Druce et al., 1997) met at least four of the quality criteria used for this review. Intriguing, as well, is the observation that Mowrer's (1975) study appeared to be the one with the most structure, the most concrete explanation of procedures, and also the best results.

Treatment Methodology

As can be seen from Table 10.2 and as previously discussed, the investigations reviewed here lack many of the elements specified by Ingham and Cordes's (1999) treatment efficacy evaluation model. Druce et al. (1997), for example, were the only authors to include naturalness ratings, and beyond-clinic data tended not to be presented. Again, it should be noted that many of these investigations were not designed to examine real-world effectiveness; nevertheless, only four experimental investigations (Ryan, 1971; Riley &

Ingham, 2000; Ryan & Ryan, 1983, 1995) with a limited number of subjects provide real-world data, the necessary target of stuttering treatments.

Because the Ryan and Ryan (1983, 1995) investigations met most of the methodology criteria in Table 10.2, they were further evaluated against Ingham and Riley's (1998) "Guidelines for Documentation of Treatment Efficacy for Young Children Who Stutter" to determine if they meet the most recent standards for treatment outcome evaluation for data-based investigations. These studies met most of the guidelines, with three possible exceptions. First, speech naturalness ratings were not provided. Second, the program might not have been administered properly throughout the study, as judged by the present authors from Ryan's discussion about clinicians often undercounting stuttering. In addition, relatively small numbers of participants completed these studies, three and six respectively, making subject mortality problematic.

Effectiveness By Age

Another goal of the present review was to examine the importance of age to the effectiveness of GILCU, ELU, and modifications of these programs. Comparisons are limited by the data provided in the individual reports, but, as can be seen in Table 10.3, no clear pattern emerged from analyses of stuttering frequency following establishment or during follow-up. It appears that these programs may be effective for clients of many ages; Rustin, Ryan, and Ryan (1987), in particular, showed that groups of 6 to 12 year olds, 13 to 19 year olds, and 29 to 45 year olds reduced SW/M from 10.0 to 0.2, 9.5 to 0.3, and 10.0 to 0.3, respectively, after the establishment phase of the GILCU program. Even more intriguing is Ryan's (1981) report that teenagers maintained low rates of stuttering as well as, and sometimes better than, the school-age children. In discussing the DAF and GILCU programs, Ryan (1984) suggested that children fared better than adults, but percentages of decrease in stuttering (as calculated by the authors of this review) and the provided SW/M scores do not vary consistently by age. Indeed, for the very few speakers represented here, the older teens and adults have results comparable to the children.

Comparisons Among Treatments

Finally, one of the more interesting features of the aforementioned studies is that several of them had included other treatment programs for comparison. Thus, data were extracted from those reports in which the present authors could determine that the different treatment programs were performed at similar times and by similarly trained clinicians, with comparisons limited to within-study assessments because of substantial methodological differences across studies. As shown in Table 10.4, the one comparison of ELU to another treatment showed that children who received ELU outperformed children who received Riley and Riley's (1995, 1999) Speech Motor Therapy. Similarly, comparisons of the GILCU program with other approaches showed that the GILCU procedure was comparable if not better in establishing fluency (see Table 10.4), with the largest differences occurring for within-clinic assessments of WS/M (Rustin et al., 1987; Ryan & Ryan, 1983, 1995). Generalization of treatment gains was also better for the GILCU program than for the DAF program, and Ryan and Ryan (1995) also reported descriptively (but not significantly) better follow-up data for GILCU (mean 0.6 SW/M) than for DAF (mean SW/M = 1.1).

Another interesting aspect of treatment that has been measured during the GILCU studies is time to complete establishment. Ryan and Ryan (1983) reported that the average time for completion of the GILCU establishment program (9.6 hours) was greater than DAF (6.0 hours) but less than Programmed Traditional (17.9 hours) and Pause (14.4 hours). However, the number of subjects was small during this investigation and subsequent investigations revealed similar therapy hours to complete DAF and GILCU programs (Rustin et al., 1987; Ryan & Ryan, 1995).

CONCLUSIONS AND CLINICAL IMPLICATIONS

In general, the extent and the quality of the experimental literature reviewed here must be described as rather limited. Given those caveats, however, the results reported for GILCU, ELU, and to a lesser extent, Mowrer's (1975) modification are quite good, with the GILCU literature in particular reporting stuttering rates around 1.0 SW/M at the end of treatment using a measurement system that might be including normal disfluencies within those counts. Very limited data are available about the ELU program, but the data that are available suggest that it can be effective. In addition, the similarities between the two programs suggest that there is, to a certain extent, little to be gained by separating them; reports of success with the GILCU program, in other words, provide some evidence in support of the ELU program.

Among the many issues that deserve some discussion are the beyond-clinic data used for this review, the duration of the treatment programs, the age of the clients, some methodological details about administering these programs and the functional elements of these treatments, and a contribution that clinicians might be able to make to all of these questions. First, it bears repeating that this review was based on the most stringent test of treatment success, where those data were provided in the original reports: maintenance of nonstuttered speech in beyond-clinic settings. This is the most relevant test, in many senses, but any unfavorable comparison of the data summarized here with positive reports of in-clinic success from other procedures would be inappropriate. Similarly, and as also discussed

TABLE 10.4

Mean Speech Performance Data Comparing Types of Treatments[a]

Study	Pretherapy				Postestablishment				Posttransfer, Postmaintenance, or Follow-Up			
	SW/M	%SS	N	SR[1]	SW/M	%SS	N	SR	SW/M	%SS	N	SR
Ryan & Ryan (1995)[2]												
DAF: 11 participants (part.), mean age = 11.4 years	6.95			110.2	4.3			124.6				
GILCU: 9 part., mean age = 12.2	6.2			106.05	1.75			117.35				
DAF: 5 part., mean age = 11.2					3.5			129.85	1.2[e]			126.1[e]
GILCU: 6 part., mean age = 11.5					0.9			114.4	0.9[e]			132.9[e]
DAF: 4 part.									0.85[c]			
GILCU: 3 part.									0.65[c]			
DAF: 5 part., mean age = 11.2									1.1[d]			
GILCU: 6 part., mean age = 11.5									0.6[d]			
Rustin, Ryan, & Ryan (1987)[3]												
DAF: 17 part., mean age = 17.1	13.8			86.1	0.2			87.8				
GILCU: 48 part., mean age = 9.7	10.0			91.1	0.2			108.4				
DAF: 22 part., mean age = 14.7	9.5			104.2	0.3			124.9				
GILCU: 20 part., mean age = 29.6	10.0			107.7	0.3			125.9				

Ryan & Ryan (1983)[3b]						
Programmed						
Traditional	6.9	126.3	0.7		144.4	
DAF	6.4	119.0	0.1		39.4	
Pause	7.6	115.7	0.7		119.2	
GILCU	5.9	128.7	0.3		133.7	
Mallard & Westbrook (1988)[4]						
Van Riper approach: 17 part., mean age = 7.4	12.88			11.05		
GILCU: 12 part., mean age = 7.4	11.75			7.17		6.76[d]
Riley & Ingham (2000)[5]						
SMT: 6 part., mean age = 6.3	8.54			6.6		
ELU: 6 part., mean age = 5.9	5.89			2.16		4.75[d]

[1]All speech rate data are in WS/M; [2]Data from Ryan and Ryan (1995) are from speech samples taken from home and at school (numbers were added and divided by two), except for follow-up data, which are from recorded conversations taken by the clinicians at an average of 14.1 months after completion of maintenance; [3]Data from Rustin, Ryan, and Ryan (1987) and Ryan and Ryan (1983) are from reading, monologue, and conversation within the clinic; [4]Mallard and Westbrook (1988) data are from conversations with the clinician in a therapy room. Follow-up data are about 4 months after establishment; [5]Data from Riley and Ingham (2000) are from within- and beyond-clinic conversations; [a]Studies that could not be compared because of factors such as wide differences in the number of participants were not included in this table; [b]All groups contained four participants. Mean ages in years were 11.5 for Programmed Traditional, 12.0 for Delayed Auditory Feedback, 11.8 for Pause, and 11.3 for GILCU; [c]Postmaintenance data; [d]Follow-up data; [e]Posttransfer data.

throughout this chapter, many of the participants in these studies had not completed the entire treatment programs when the final data were collected for these reports, for several reasons. It is impressive, therefore, that they had done as well as they had done; the literature about GILCU and ELU procedures might be even more impressive when results are available from larger numbers of participants who have completed the full length of the programs. As also discussed, the limited data that are available seem to suggest that GILCU and ELU procedures might be equally effective for clients of essentially all ages. This possibility deserves further exploration because it may be in direct conflict with suggestions that these are programs for children.

One of the more complex remaining issues involves specific details about the programs and the related issues of determining what the functional elements might be in these programs and in other programs that also control utterance length. It would be interesting, for example, to assess a GILCU program that required 0.0 SW/M at each criterion test and each maintenance step; it is possible that a stricter criterion could result in better fluency or better maintenance (Ingham, 1984). Similarly, the studies reviewed here do support Cordes's (1998) earlier suggestion that controlling utterance length may be a functional part of treatment programs that consist of, for example, learning prolonged speech skills by starting with words or phrases. Whether control of utterance length alone is sufficient as a treatment, however, has not yet been firmly established by this literature, especially given that both GILCU and ELU also include punishers for stuttering and reinforcers for fluent speech; such response-contingent procedures have been shown to control stuttering frequency in the absence of overt control over or changes in utterance length (e.g., Bonelli, Dixon, Ratner, & Onslow, 2000; Martin et al., 1972). In addition, control of utterance length clearly is not necessary for the reduction of stuttering; effective fluency-shaping treatments, for example, do not necessarily begin with short utterances (e.g., Ingham et al., 2001). The remaining need, then, is to determine the relative contributions of fluency-shaping skills, utterance length, and reinforcing or punishing feedback about fluent or stuttered speech, respectively, to successful stuttering treatment programs. Even more important, perhaps, is the need to determine how any two of these elements might interact to be significantly more effective than could be predicted from their isolated effects.

In conclusion, the strong but limited results of the relatively few available studies about GILCU and ELU procedures suggest that future experimentation could be extremely valuable, not only to determine the effectiveness of these particular programs but also as part of determining the relative and interactive contributions of several treatment elements. It is also intriguing to note that the sources reporting the best results appear to be the ones that described the treatment procedures most clearly and incorporated the best speech performance data measurements. There are not enough of these reports, however, to serve as the basis for a final conclusion, a problem that clinicians who do not see themselves as researchers might actually be in the best position to solve: One of the greatest needs with respect to these programs appears to be large-scale clinical application, with careful documentation that can then be reported in the literature.

REFERENCES

Bonelli, P., Dixon, M., Ratner, N. B., & Onslow, M. (2000). Child and parent speech and language following the Lidcombe Programme of early stuttering intervention. *Clinical Linguistics and Phonetics, 14,* 427–446.

Bothe, A. K. (2002). Speech modification approaches to stuttering treatment in schools. *Seminars in Speech and Language, 23,* 181–186.

Brutten, G., & Shoemaker, D. (1967). *The modification of stuttering.* Englewood Cliffs, NJ: Prentice-Hall.

Cordes, A. K. (1998). Current status of the stuttering treatment literature. In A. K. Cordes & R. J. Ingham (Eds.), *Treatment efficacy for stuttering: A search for empirical bases* (pp. 117–144). San Diego, CA: Singular.

Cordes, A. K., & Ingham, R. J. (1999). Effects of time-interval judgment training on real-time measurement of stuttering. *Journal of Speech, Language, and Hearing Research, 42,* 862–869.

Costello, J. M. (1980). Operant conditioning and the treatment of stuttering. *Seminars in Speech, Language and Hearing, 1,* 311–325.

Costello, J. M. (1983). Current behavioral treatments for children. In D. Prins & R. J. Ingham (Eds.), *Treatment of stuttering in early childhood: Methods and issues* (pp. 69–112). San Diego, CA: College-Hill.

Costello, J. M. (1984). Treatment of the young chronic stutterer: Managing fluency. In R. F. Curlee & W. H. Perkins (Eds.), *Nature and treatment of stuttering: New Directions* (pp. 375–395). San Diego, CA: College-Hill Press, Inc.

Druce, T., Debney, S., & Byrt, T. (1997). Evaluation of an intensive treatment program for stuttering in young children. *Journal of Fluency Disorders, 22,* 169–186.

Gierut, J. A. (1998). Treatment efficacy: Functional phonological disorders in children. *Journal of Speech, Language, and Hearing Research, 41,* S85–S100.

Ingham, J. C. (1999). Behavioral treatment of young children who stutter: An extended length of utterance method. In R. F. Curlee (Ed.), *Stuttering and related disorders of fluency* (2nd ed., pp. 80–109). New York: Thieme.

Ingham, J. C., & Riley, G. (1998). Guidelines for documentation of treatment efficacy for young children who stutter. *Journal of Speech, Language, and Hearing Research, 41,* 753–770.

Ingham, R. J. (1984). *Stuttering and behavior therapy.* San Diego, CA: College-Hill Press.

Ingham, R. J., & Cordes, A. K. (1999). On watching a discipline shoot itself in the foot: Some observations on current trends in stuttering treatment. In N. B. Ratner & E. C. Haley (Eds.), *Stuttering research and practice: Bridging the gap* (pp. 211–230). Mahwah, NJ: Lawrence Erlbaum Associates.

Ingham, R. J., Kilgo, M., Ingham, J. C., Moglia, R., Belknap, H., & Sanchez, T. (2001). Evaluation of a stuttering treatment based on reduction of short phonation intervals. *Journal of Speech, Language, and Hearing Research, 44*, 841–852.

Johnson, G. F., Coleman, K., & Rasmussen, K. (1978). Multidays: Multidimensional approach for the young stutterer. *Language, Speech, and Hearing Services in Schools, 9*, 129–132.

Leach, E. (1969). Stuttering: Clinical application of response-contingent procedures. In B. Gray & G. England (Eds.), *Stuttering and the conditioning therapies* (pp. 115–127). Monterey, CA: Monterey Institute for Speech and Hearing.

Mallard, A. R., & Westbrook, J. B. (1988). Variables affecting stuttering therapy in school settings. *Language, Speech, and Hearing Services in Schools, 19*, 362–370.

Martin, R. R., & Berndt, L. A. (1970). The effects of time-out on stuttering in a 12 year old boy. *Exceptional Children, 36*, 303–304.

Martin, R. R., Haroldson, S. K., & Triden, K. A. (1984). Stuttering and speech naturalness. *Journal of Speech and Hearing Disorders, 49*, 53–58.

Martin, R. R., Kuhl, P., & Haroldson, S. (1972). An experimental treatment with two preschool stuttering children. *Journal of Speech and Hearing Research, 15*, 743–751.

Mowrer, D. (1975). An instructional program to increase fluent speech of stutterers. *Journal of Fluency Disorders, 1*, 25–35.

Onslow, M. (1996). *Behavioral management of stuttering.* San Diego, CA: Singular.

Rickard, H. C., & Mundy, M. B. (1965). Direct manipulation of stuttering behavior. An experimental-clinical approach. In L. P. Ullman & L. Krasner (Eds.), *Case studies in behavior modification* (pp. 268–277). New York: Holt, Rinehart & Winston.

Riley, G., & Ingham, J. C. (1997). *Stuttering treatment project final project.* Report to National Institute of Deafness and Other Communication Disorders. Bethesda, MD.

Riley, G. D., & Ingham, J. C. (2000). Acoustic duration changes associated with two types of treatment for children who stutter. *Journal of Speech, Language, and Hearing Research, 43*, 965–978.

Riley, J., & Riley, G. (1995). Speech motor improvement program for children who stutter. In C. W. Starkweather & H. F. M. Peters (Eds.), *Stuttering: Proceedings of the first world congress on fluency disorders* (pp. 269–272). New York: Elsevier.

Riley, J., & Riley, G. (1999). Speech motor training. In M. Onslow & A. Packman (Eds.), *The handbook of early stuttering intervention* (pp. 139–158). San Diego, CA: Singular.

Rustin, L., Ryan, B. P., & Ryan, B. V. (1987). Use of the Monterey programmed stuttering therapy in Great Britain. *British Journal of Disorders of Communication, 22*, 151–162.

Ryan, B. P. (1971). Operant procedures applied to stuttering therapy for children. *Journal of Speech and Hearing Disorders, 36*, 264–280.

Ryan, B. P. (1974). *Programmed therapy for stuttering in children and adults.* Springfield, IL: Charles C. Thomas.

Ryan, B. P. (1979). Stuttering therapy in a framework of operant conditioning and programmed learning. In H. H. Gregory (Ed.), *Controversies about stuttering therapy* (pp. 129–173). Baltimore, MD: University Park Press.

Ryan, B. P. (1981). Maintenance programs in progress—II. In E. Boberg (Ed.), *Maintenance of fluency: Proceedings of the Banff conference* (pp. 113–146). New York: Elsevier.

Ryan, B. P. (1984). Treatment of stuttering in school children. In W. H. Perkins (Ed.), *Current therapy of communication disorders: Stuttering disorders* (pp. 95–105). New York: Thieme-Stratton Inc.

Ryan, B. (1985). Training the professional. *Seminars in Speech and Language, 6,* 145–168.

Ryan, B. P. (2001). *Programmed therapy for stuttering in children and adults: Second edition.* Springfield, IL: Charles C. Thomas.

Ryan, B. P., & Ryan, B. V. (1983). Programmed stuttering therapy for children: Comparison of four establishment programs. *Journal of Fluency Disorders, 8,* 291–321.

Ryan, B. P., & Ryan, B. V. (1995). Programmed stuttering treatment for children: Comparison of two establishment programs through transfer, maintenance, and follow-up. *Journal of Speech and Hearing Research, 38,* 61–75.

Shine, R. E. (1980). Direct management of the beginning stutterer. *Seminars in Speech, Language and Hearing, 1,* 339–350.

Shine, R. E. (1984). Direct management of the beginning stutterer. In W. Perkins (Ed.), *Current therapy of communication disorders: Stuttering disorders* (pp. 57–75). New York: Thieme-Stratton.

Stokes, T. F., & Osnes, P. G. (1989). An operant pursuit of generalization. *Behavior Therapy, 20,* 337–355.

Walker, V. G. (1988). Durational characteristics of young adults during speaking and reading tasks. *Folia Phoniatrica, 40,* 12–20.

Wolpe, J. (1958). *Psychotherapy by reciprocal inhibition.* Palo Alto, CA: Stanford University Press.

Appendix A

Mowrer (1975) administered a treatment program to 20 persons who stutter (mean age = 22.1 years; range = 8–43 years). The establishment portion began with the participant uttering monosyllabic words that he felt he could speak fluently following a tone every 5 seconds, and terminated with 5 minutes of conversation. In general, responses were longer with each step; the tone was used in some steps to signal the participant to respond. The intermediate steps consisted of responses such as two word phrases, three word phrases, four word phrases, and so forth; sentences, answering questions, and telling stories. "Good" was uttered by the clinician following fluent responses and "stop" following a stutter. Criteria for advancement to subsequent steps in the establishment phase were 95% fluency and in most steps 100 or more WS/M. Branch steps were used if the criterion was not met in a certain amount of time. The transfer phase for children included similar tasks, performed at school and with students taking on some of their own clinical responsibility. Children also completed a home transfer program involving the reinforcement of a series of fluent sentences and punishment when disfluency occurred. Adult transfer programs involved various beyond-clinic tasks accompanied by the clinician. The maintenance phase consisted of 2 monthly conversations in the clinic and weekly phone calls to the clients. A test with various speaking conditions was given by a clinician before and upon completion of therapy (seemingly when each participant completed the program); number of disfluent words was counted. Not all participants completed all three phases (establishment, transfer, maintenance) or even all steps in the phases, which is the reason for the unusual arrangement in the present Table 10.2.

Johnson, Coleman, and Rasmussen (1978) completed a 21-session (1 hour each), 3-week treatment structured around the GILCU procedure with a 6-year-old male who stuttered. Their program consisted of producing single vowels to eight-word sentences, including tasks such as imitation, labeling pictures, producing a phrase, and answering questions. The criterion to pass each step was 90% fluency on 20 consecutive responses. Branch steps were included if the child had difficulty on a certain step. Activities allowed for spontaneous speech acts that were verbally rewarded when the preceding program was finished. In addition, the child had to repeat, after the clinician, disfluent words followed by the phrase containing the word during the spontaneous speech acts. Physical reinforcers were also used in the program for the completion of activities but not individual responses. Throughout the program, a prolonged type of speech was modeled by the clinicians. The child's mother was taught some of the same activities to use for transfer of fluent speech to the home environment, which appeared to be used during the time period of the establishment program. Stuttering interviews (Ryan, 1974) were completed before, immediately after, and 1 month after treatment.

Druce, Debney, and Byrt (1997) performed an intensive therapy program with 15 children (mean age = 7;4; age range = 6;9–8;1) who had been stuttering for at least a year and were assessed as having language abilities similar to a child not more than 1 year younger. Six children were bilingual. The children were treated in 5 consecutive days for 6.5 hours each day in groups with one clinician for every client. The program began with the children identifying stutters followed by the establishment program. The establishment portion began with repeating words, picture naming, and producing monosyllabic words, which was followed by these same steps for bisyllabic words, multisyllabic words, and increasingly longer phrases. Repeating sentences, using a carrier phrase to complete sentences, sentences, retelling stories, monologues, questioning, and conversation followed. Reinforcement, which was intermittent and decreasing in frequency throughout, was provided via social praise, games, and stickers. The clinician also modeled a speaking rate of 120 to 150 syllables per minute, but the child was not told to imitate it. The children also spent time in groups speaking to each other. On the fourth day several different transfer tasks such as talking to strangers and telephone calls were performed and reinforced monetarily. Home practice was also recommended throughout the program. Tokens were gained for fluency beginning on the third day and removed for "bumpy talking" beginning on the fourth during therapy and group socializing time. The maintenance program (3 months) involved less frequent clinical contacts involving certain aspects of the establishment and transfer phases along with the parents providing rewards for fluent speech in the home. Two minutes of speech with just a member of the child's family and with just a stranger were used to collect data.

AUTHORS' NOTES

This chapter is based on a paper first presented at the 2002 University of Georgia State of the Art Conference on evidence-based treatment of stuttering. It is dedicated to Bruce Ryan and Janis Costello Ingham, who could not attend the conference but whose decades of careful work we believed deserved to be represented at a conference about the evidence-based treatment of stuttering. We hope that our analysis has done justice not only to their publications but also to their exemplary spirit and style as evidence-based scientists and practitioners.

11

Long-Term Follow Up of Speech Outcomes for a Prolonged-Speech Treatment for Stuttering: The Effects of Paradox on Stuttering Treatment Research

Mark Onslow
Sue O'Brian
Ann Packman
Isabelle Rousseau
The University of Sydney

PARADOXES AND STUTTERING TREATMENT

The Oxford English Dictionary defines *paradox* as "a statement or proposition which on the face of it seems self-contradictory, absurd, or at variance with common sense, though, on investigation or when explained, it may prove to be well founded." It has not been widely recognized as such, but Johnson's (1942) theory about the cause and development of stuttering was a paradox: namely, that stuttering is caused by its diagnosis. Of course, it was eventually recognized to be untrue, but for around 40 years everyone thought that Johnson's paradox was true, and during that period speech-language pathologists tried to come to grips with clinical management of stuttering while under the shadow of this paradox, which caused many problems. Clinically, for example, it was considered unwise to directly treat children who were stuttering because it was thought that such treatment would make them worse. Instead, the trick was to convince the parents that the children were not stuttering at all. As Bloodstein (1986) wrote, this was virtually impossible, when the children obviously were stuttering and their parents knew it.

For researchers, it was also difficult to develop treatments for stuttering children when the most powerful yet paradoxical theory ever in our field dictated that it was unethical professional behavior to draw attention to a child's stuttering. In the mid-1990s we, as developers of the Lidcombe Program (for an overview, see Onslow, 2003), had to endure criticism that, although the data showed that the children in our clinical trials were not stuttering, somehow, and completely unbeknown to us, the treatment was harmful to them (Cook & Rustin, 1997). We were strongly encouraged by some speech-language therapists in the United Kingdom to produce data showing that the Lidcombe Program caused no psychological harm to children. In a real sense, then, a recent publication of ours can be directly attributed to the effects of Johnson's theory: We showed that children do not become anxious or withdrawn after the Lidcombe Program, and that their emotional relationships with their mothers do not deteriorate (Woods, Shearsby, Onslow, & Burnham, 2002).

This is presented by way of background because the topic of the present chapter concerns paradox in scientific and clinical reasoning. If paradoxes find their way into our science, they are likely to filter down to our clinical practices with unwanted effects. In the case of the Johnson (1942) paradox, the effects were not only strange but quite spectacular: Speech-language pathologists all through the Western world spent several decades avoiding directly drawing attention to a serious speech disorder in children. This chapter submits that the effects of another paradox—this one related to long-term effects of treatments—are on the verge of also becoming spectacular.

A NEW PARADOX

The development of Prolonged-Speech is now a well-known part of the history of our profession (for an overview, see Ingham, 1984). Goldiamond's (1965) initial report on the promise of Prolonged-Speech to control stuttering resulted in the proliferation of variants of the method around the world during the 1970s.[1] Today, most behavioral treatments for adults who stutter incorpo-

---

[1] Ingham also documented the considerable controversy that surrounded the development of Prolonged-Speech treatments for the control of stuttering. It seems the development of treatments in this field is never straightforward.

rate some variation of Prolonged-Speech, and Prolonged-Speech procedures are generally recognized to be reasonably effective with many clients.

So now, what is the rest of the picture that we, as a group of stuttering treatment researchers, might want to know? Among other things, one of the issues we are now interested in addressing is how long we can control stuttering with Prolonged-Speech or other procedures: Surely we should strive to find the treatments with the longest effects. If all else is equal, and one treatment is capable of achieving near-zero stuttering rates for 3 years and another is capable of doing the same for 5 or 10 years, then the latter is superior.

That being said, the past years have seen many clinical trials published in our journals with posttreatment periods of 12 to 24 months (for a review, see Onslow, Costa, Andrews, Harrison, & Packman, 1996). At this stage of the evolution of our discipline, such pretest/posttest data sets are all we have to rely on when considering treatment effectiveness. Yet, as previously noted, what is really needed are long-term outcome data. Preliminary results for Ingham et al.'s (2001) Modification of Phonation Interval procedure most recently showed near-zero stuttering rates after a year or so. That is a favorable result, of course, but there have been many similar results in recent years (e.g., Boberg & Kully, 1994; Craig et al., 1996; Onslow et al., 1996; O'Brian, Onslow, Cream, & Packman, 2003). All these different methods—Modification of Phonation Intervals, Prolonged-Speech, Electromyographic feedback—can result in near-zero stuttering rates for some speakers at 1 or 2 years posttreatment. The problem is how to choose between them. Surely, one factor in the choice is which of those treatments is most effective for the longest period. Longer is better, obviously. Now that the research literature has made it clear that stuttering can be at near-zero rates 1 or 2 years posttreatment under overt recording conditions, we need to go beyond this and press on to obtain long-term evidence of effectiveness. There are many things today that are controversial in stuttering treatment, but the need for long-term outcome data surely is not one of them.

This situation makes it important for us to be alert to another somewhat paradoxical situation that looks as if it has the potential to hold us up in our work for a few more decades. Just when we got over "diagnosogenesis," and we know that paradox not to be true, now we might have another paradox that stands in our way of knowing the really long-term effects of our treatments. This paradox may be worse because, unlike Johnson's (1942), it may, in fact, be true.

The origins of the Johnson (1942) paradox were unremarkable enough; he was doing some reading on general semantics while convalescing after an illness (see Bloodstein, 1986). The origins of the new paradox to which we refer are also unremarkable, contained in a throw-away line back in 1981. In a book chapter with a truly Inghamesque title—something to do with ecstasy and agony—which appeared in the proceedings of a conference, Ingham (1981) wrote that "the number of nontreatment variables,

which may be significant sources of variance in outcome data, increase ex-
ponentially (and uncontrollably) as the posttreatment interval increases"
(p. 180).

Indeed, there are any number of things that might influence how well
clients maintain the effects of their treatment: They may go to self-help
groups, or they may have generally supportive life experiences such as
finding a new partner or a religion, and so on. In effect, what Ingham (1981)
meant is that the longer the period after treatment, the less confident we can
be that on-going low levels of stuttering are due solely to that treatment.

A good point, and quite true of course. However Ingham's (1981) point
was never taken up in the literature, so he said it again in his 1984 text: "the
fact that a subject has improved or not improved speech performance at follow-up may have very little to do with the treatment" (Ingham, 1984, p.
462). And in Ingham and Costello (1985), we have "the longer the interval
between cessation of treatment and follow up evaluation, the more likely it
is that this interval will be filled with variables of far more relevance to current performance than the original treatment" (p. 216). He has probably
also said it again since, but the point is clear. There is little experimental
control in a scenario that includes a treatment and a very long
posttreatment period. In other words, if an adult is stuttering severely immediately before treatment and is stuttering very mildly, or not at all, directly after treatment, then it is likely that the treatment was responsible for
that reduction in stuttering, particularly if there are baseline data showing
that stuttering was stable in the months preceding the treatment. However,
if the person is still stuttering at a very low level, or not stuttering at all, 5 or
10 years after treatment, it is not possible to know if this is still due entirely
to the treatment, or whether other intervening variables may be contributing to the treatment effects or assisting the individual to maintain the treatment effects. As alluded to earlier, these variables may be unique to the
individual: finding love, a new career, and so on.

As mentioned earlier, evidence that their previous clients' stuttering is
still under control many years after treatments is sorely needed by clinicians who are committed to evidence-based practice. But there is a paradox
here: The ever decreasing scientific control after treatment, which Ingham
referred to (Ingham, 1981, 1984; Ingham & Costello, 1985), means that
long-term treatment outcome studies are unlikely to be accepted for publication in our scientific journals. In short, clinicians need evidence of treatment outcomes in the long-term, but such evidence is unlikely to be
published—a paradox indeed.

AN EMPIRICAL INVESTIGATION OF THE PARADOX

This paradox could be clinically disastrous, and the grave importance of
the matter spurred us to put it to an empirical test. The place to test it, we

reasoned, was with the gatekeepers of our clinical science, those who regulate the publication of our scientific treatment outcome data: journal editors and their editorial consultants. If they are reticent to publish very long-term treatment outcome data, then the paradox will really have disastrous effects. None of us will have access to the critical evidence that could support the selection of a particular treatment from among others, if that evidence is systematically excluded from our professional journals.

Our hypothesis was that stuttering treatment outcome studies with long posttreatment periods are rejected more often than those with short posttreatment periods. Our method was a case controlled study, with one report having a posttreatment interval of 1 year and the second, with the same cohort of subjects, having a posttreatment interval of 9 to 12 years. We chose this posttreatment interval to test the hypothesis as stringently as possible: Lincoln and Onslow (1997) and Hancock et al. (1998) published data up to 6 years posttreatment, so we took it even further. The dependent variable was the number of journal rejections of a submitted treatment outcome manuscript, and a secondary dependent variable was the number of derogatory remarks from editorial consultants and editors during the review process.

Our first report in our case controlled study was of 12 clients before and after our intensive, residential Prolonged-Speech treatment (Ingham, 1987). We measured their speech rate, stuttering rate (percent syllables stuttered, or %SS), and speech naturalness, three times prior to treatment and many times over a 1-year posttreatment period. Each beyond-clinic assessment involved talking to a family member, talking to a friend, and talking on the telephone, and each within-clinic measure involved talking to a clinician, talking to a stranger, and talking on the telephone. The tape recordings of the subjects were randomized and presented blind to a clinician who was independent of the study, who made measures of %SS online.[2] These measures were collected with acceptable reliability.

Figure 11.1 shows the within- and beyond-clinic pretreatment data for each subject, averaged over the three assessment situations and over the three assessment occasions. Also in Fig. 11.1 are the within- and beyond-clinic 1-year posttreatment data for each subject, averaged over the three assessment situations. Figure 11.1 shows that subjects were between 0 and 1%SS at the posttreatment assessments, with the exception of Subject MR, whose pretreatment stuttering was extremely severe and who averaged slightly more.

In addition to the 1-year posttreatment assessment, we set ourselves the somewhat onerous task of following up these 12 subjects 9 to 12 years after they received their treatment. We managed to make contact with all 12 of them, all of whom agreed to participate. We asked them to provide three be-

---

[2]Measures of speech naturalness and syllables per minute were also collected, but we have not presented these details in the present context.

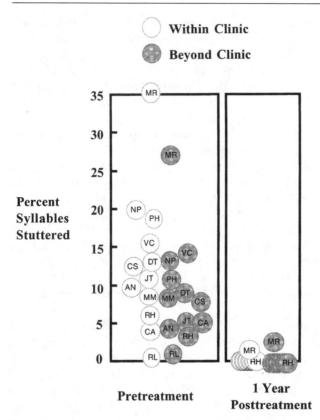

FIG. 11.1. Pretreatment and 1-year posttreatment percent syllables stuttered (%SS) measures, for participants in the case control studies.

yond-clinic tape recordings, each of 10 minutes duration, while (a) conversing with a family member, (b) conversing with a friend, and (c) talking on the telephone. We also asked them to come to the clinic so we could make audiotape recordings for 10 minutes while (a) speaking with an investigator and (b) speaking on the phone. Four of the subjects (MR, PH, VZ, CS) did not comply with all the requirements for the study: One declined to be tape recorded, one failed to produce beyond-clinic recordings, and two produced beyond-clinic recordings but did not come into the clinic. Hence, we were left with eight subjects from the original 12 for whom we had a full set of within- and beyond-clinic data. The age of the subjects at this stage ranged from 22 to 51 years. Two of the subjects were women. These eight cases constitute our case controlled report in our study. Four subjects were 9 years posttreatment, two were 10 years posttreatment, one was 11 years posttreatment, and one was 12 years posttreatment. We randomized their tape recordings and presented them blind to the same speech pathologist who had made online measures of %SS for the pretreatment and 1-year posttreatment recordings.

The results are presented in Fig. 11.2, along with the pretreatment and 1-year posttreatment data that we collected years before. Again, the data are presented individually for each subject as means of within- and beyond-clinic scores. Figure 11.2 shows that subjects' stuttering rates were still near zero, under these assessment conditions, at 9 to 12 years posttreatment. One exception was Subject NP's mean within-clinic recording, which was greater than 1%SS.

In short, then, there was considerable stuttering in the subjects pretreatment, little stuttering 1 year posttreatment, and little stuttering at 9 to 12 years posttreatment. Our research method was to submit these data sepa-

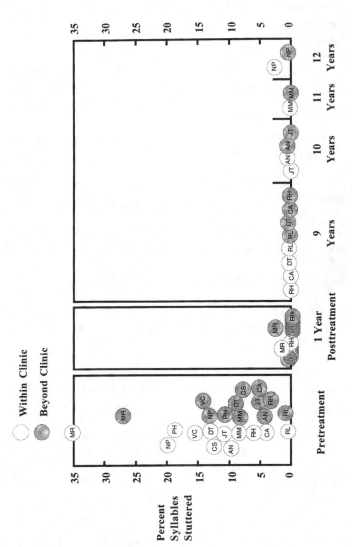

FIG. 11.2.   Pretreatment and long-term posttreatment %SS data for participants.

rately to journals for publication, one reporting 1-year outcome and one reporting 9- to 12-year outcome.

The results of our study are summarized in Table 11.1. For the 1-year post-treatment report, there were no journal rejections, and the report was duly published in the *Journal of Speech and Hearing Research* (Onslow et al., 1996). The 9- to 12-year report was rejected by the *Journal of Speech, Language and Hearing Research*, the *Journal of Fluency Disorders*, the *International Journal of Language and Communication Disorders*, the *Journal of Communication Disorders*, and *Folia Phoniatrica*. For the dependent variable "number of derogatory remarks from editorial consultants and editors," the 1-year posttreatment report attracted two derogatory comments, but the 9- to 12-year posttreatment report elicited 97 derogatory comments.

So, on the face of it, the raw data clearly support our hypothesis. It appears that the paradox is true, and stuttering treatment outcome studies with long posttreatment periods are rejected more often than those with short posttreatment periods. Some of the derogatory comments attracted by the 9- to 12-year posttreatment report were along the lines predicted by Ingham (1981). For example,

"The most important issue, it seems to me, is just what interpretation can be confidently placed on these findings"

Another comment:

"The findings really amount to a set of observations—much like a case report—rather than a controlled study."

Another:

"The lack of a control or comparative group (over the 9–12 years) means that changes observed cannot be assumed to be the result of the therapy in question."

Another remark, from an editor, was the following:

While it certainly is recognized that subject attrition is an inherent fact of longitudinal studies like this one, I agree with Dr. X that for this study it seri-

TABLE 11.1
Numbers of Journals Rejecting the Two Reports,
and Number of Derogatory Remarks
From Editorial Consultants and Editors (see text)

Paper	Journal Rejections	Derogatory Remarks from Editorial Consultants and Editors	Journals Rejecting
1-year posttreatment report	0	2	–
9- to 12-years posttreatment report	5	97	JSLHR, JFD, IJLCD, JCD, FP

ously questions the validity of any statement regarding the effectiveness or long-term effects of the Prolonged-Speech program. I'm not sure how this problem can be alleviated in the current study, other than (maybe) by attempting to contact all original 32 clients and collecting a variety of data, including detailed questionnaire, self-recorded speech samples, telephone call recordings, etc.

Interestingly, the editors clearly recognized the need for the data:

"While I, as well as the two reviewers, agree that ... data generated from longitudinal studies, which follow clients for more than a year, are desperately needed in our field, the nature of the data in the study reported on in your manuscript, and the manner in which these data were collected, creates too many unknowns for the results to be interpretable."

And another comment:

"This manuscript has attempted to determine if prolonged speech controls long-term treatment gains. This was an ambitious and worthwhile question but one that, in my opinion, the study's method could not adequately answer."

And another:

"I am certainly sympathetic to the need for this type of information, but at best they can only be considered speculative contributions to the understanding of the causes of therapy gains."

Overall, the obvious conclusion here is that Ingham (1981) was right. The longer after treatment we measure stuttering reductions with objective data, the less our scientific community is prepared to attribute those reductions solely to the treatment. And here is the rub: Although they express the view that long term-treatment data are desperately needed, our journal editors are not prepared to publish them. A paradox indeed. As much as clinicians need such data about long-term outcome, they cannot have them.

It seems, then, that after all this time we are finally over Johnson's (1942) paradox but we have found another to replace it. Unlike Johnson's paradox, this one is true and, unfortunately, it has wide-reaching implications for our pursuit of evidence-based practice. In light of Ingham's (1981) contribution to this paradox, we have decided to name it after him. In the physical sciences, researchers may have comets or elements named after them. But in our soft science of speech-language pathology, Roger Ingham will have to settle with having a paradox named after him: Ingham's Paradox.

CONCLUSIONS AND CLINICAL IMPLICATIONS

We waited 40 or 50 years to get over Johnson's (1942) paradox, but let's not wait that long before publishing long-term data on our subjects. Let's do something proactive about Ingham's Paradox right now. We certainly need to, because presently we know of many treatments that may prove to be efficacious in the long-term. If one of these treatments now in existence—or one that is yet to be thought of—is an ultimate treatment break-through that is capable of controlling the problem behaviors of stuttering for 10 years or for a lifetime, then, according to Ingham's paradox, we just won't ever know. Maybe Ingham et al.'s (2001) Modification of Phonation Intervals device is the breakthrough we have all dreamed about. Maybe it is better, in terms of achieving near-zero stuttering rates for a lifetime, than anything, ever. But he will be stung by his own paradox, and Ingham's research group will not be able to publish long-term outcome data to establish that information.

Theoretically, a solution to this problem is simple: Conduct a random-ized controlled trial, spanning a long period of 10 years, during the course of which a number of our treatments are compared for their effectiveness. Such a megastudy would surely offset the concerns of our journal editors because the rogue variables that might influence treatment outcome would be randomly distributed across the treatment arms and hence would not be the troubling confound that they were found to be in interpreting long-term data presented for a single treatment.

However, it is difficult to accept this as the solution to our problem. In the first instance, obviously, such a time consuming and expensive study would need to be quite definitive and would require considerable power— proba-bly 95%—to ensure that a failure to find any differences between treatments would be convincing (Jones, Gebski, Onslow, & Packman, 2002). Subject numbers in that case would need to be huge, especially considering the sub-ject attrition rate that might be expected over 10 years. Equally intimidating would be the demographic problems encountered with such a large cohort study, with unbalanced posttreatment intervening variables across treat-ment arms. Also, such a trial would likely be beset with ethical problems in the event that several treatments were shown to be inferior at, say, the 5-year posttreatment mark. Taking for granted that a 10-year no-treatment control arm is out of the question, it seems clear that there is only one realistic method available to us to establish information about long-term treatment effectiveness. That method is for groups of researchers who are involved with one particular treatment to publish studies of the very long-term out-come of their clients. At least that is ethically, methodologically, and practi-cally possible. But if Ingham's Paradox has struck, then such data will not be published.

Perhaps this is not a serious issue with adults who stutter. But Ingham's Para-dox is particularly worrying in the case of treatment for preschool children who stutter because that is where we will really want to know about long-term out-come. Currently we have objective stuttering rate data on 42 children who fig-ured in our preliminary studies (Onslow, 2003). It is quite alarming to think that stuttering measures for these children 15 years after treatment will not be con-strued as interpretable, and so not publishable. In the bigger picture, we are heading to an era when treatments other than the Lidcombe Program will be put to the test. But, with Ingham's Paradox upon us, we will never be in a position to judge the long-term outcomes of such treatments and so to come to truly informed decisions about which treatment to choose.

What is the solution? First of all, we must accept the situation that prompted the development of the paradox and its looming impact. So, let us accept that, 10 years after treatment, the link between the treatment and a measure of stuttering rate is weakened. And naturally, we are going to have subject attrition during a 10-year period. And we can not have a control group for 10 years, and we can not foresee a randomized controlled trial with a 10-year postrandomization period.

Given all that, for what it is worth, we can see only one way out here: We could lighten up a bit. This chapter, like others in this text, is based on the proceedings of a conference. One evening at the conference venue we were having a drink with a heart transplant surgeon, who led us to the "lighten up" scenario. As we got to chatting, it occurred to us that his problem was far greater than ours. One of us asked him whether his transplant patients lived to a ripe old age, and he said, "They do, of course." "But," we said to him, "what if all your patients have stopped eating cholesterol and have begun to exercise after their surgery, and these variables have contributed to their longevity? Surely that weakens the confidence you have in the specific effects of your transplant procedure." He replied, "Well, sure it does, but it's still a lot better than having all my patients drop dead 2 weeks after surgery."

Perhaps we should not throw out the baby with the bathwater, so to speak. If someone is not dead 20 years after a heart transplant, surely that does say something about the operation. We can not be too sure what, but it must say something. If one of our clients is not stuttering after 20 years, perhaps that does say something about our treatment. For our heart transplant surgeon, and for all of us with an interest in the effects of health interventions after long periods, there is a sea of variables that are rampant and beyond control. Perhaps we should lighten up and not let that bend us completely out of shape. Surely we can live with the fact that self-help groups, changed speaking situations, new religions, other therapies—all sorts of things—will be interposed between treatment and long-term measurements of outcome. Surely we could just ask our subjects whether they had further therapy, and whether they think any other factors may have influenced the treatment effects. Indeed, we did that in our 9 to 12 year posttreatment study. Only one of the eight subjects reported having further treatment and only one reported attending a self-help group.[3] Although such evidence consists of self-reports, it is the best we can do under the circumstances.

There are other ways, too, of examining long-term data for treatment effects. For example, some speech naturalness data that we gathered on our 9- to 12-year posttreatment subjects confirm that, in some measure, our data do reflect very long-term effects of treatment. A 15-second interval

---

[3]All eight subjects indicated in response to our questionnaire that they would do the treatment again.

from the recordings of each within-clinic conversational speech sample was dubbed on to a listening tape, along with one 15-second sample of conversational speech of each of 28 other speakers. Of these 28 samples, eight were from control subjects, matched for age and gender to the experimental subjects. For the purposes of this study the control subjects were recorded conversing with an acquaintance under quiet conditions. The remaining speech samples were from 20 other clients who had participated in the same Prolonged-Speech program. These recordings had been used in the Packman, Onslow, and van Doorn (1994) study and were of clients at various stages of learning Prolonged-Speech. The additional 28 samples were used to investigate whether the speech of the experimental subjects was discernible from control speakers and speakers using a pronounced version of Prolonged-Speech.

The stimulus tape was played to 16 unsophisticated adult listeners for whom English was a first language. The listeners were instructed to rate the naturalness of each sample with a 9-point naturalness scale using the procedures developed by Martin, Haroldson, and Triden (1984). The listeners had an intraclass correlation score of 0.81 with a narrow 99% confidence interval, so they were acceptably reliable.

Figure 11.3 shows the results of this analysis. Clearly, the subjects were not using an exaggerated speech pattern as occurs during the typical instatement stages of a Prolonged-Speech treatment. However, in our view, a striking aspect of this analysis is how similar the results are to the speech naturalness of other subjects shortly after treatment with Prolonged-Speech (e.g., O'Brian, Onslow, Cream, & Packman, 2003). The experimental subjects generally did well in terms of speech naturalness, as compared to controls. There is some overlap of scores, but they are nonetheless scored generally higher than controls. Further, there was a strong positive correlation in our 12 subjects between speech naturalness scores and pretreatment stuttering rate (Rho = 0.72). This finding suggests that, even 9 to 12 years after treatment, subjects whose stuttering was more severe before treatment tended to use a more unnatural version of the Prolonged-Speech pattern than the subjects whose stuttering was less severe before treatment; presumably in order to achieve the same low level of stuttering. It appears then, that although we have indeed lost tight experimental control over variables that might have influenced treatment outcomes, there is some evidence that these subjects were still doing something that they learned 9 to 12 years previously to control their stuttering. They were apparently using Prolonged-Speech to trade off natural sounding speech in the interests of not stuttering. This claim is bolstered by the fact that only one of the subjects reported seeking a second treatment, and only one reported attending a self-help group, where speech patterns are typically practiced.

In short, the lighten-up approach to long-term outcome is one that will cost us our cherished tight control over independent and dependent variables (in this case treatment and stuttering rate, respectively). But we believe this is far

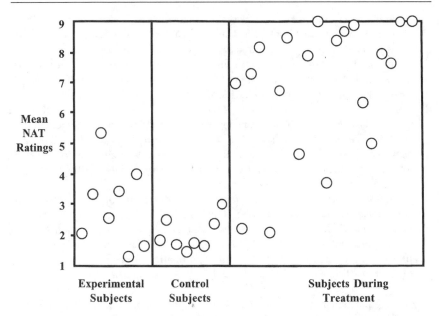

FIG. 11.3. Mean long-term speech naturalness (NAT) ratings for the participants from Figs. 11.1 and 11.2, compared with ratings for control participants and clients undergoing prolonged speech treatment.

better than not having any long-term objective speech data at all. Perhaps in this lighten-up scenario all we can hope to do is to re-establish contact with treated subjects after 10-plus years and measure their stuttering rate objectively, and to look at those data with appropriate caution. And of course there is no reason to forget that there are all sorts of measures that can supplement our objective measure of stuttering rate. There are other ways of measuring outcome, as discussed in other chapters in this volume and elsewhere: quality of life, self report, and qualitative methods such as phenomenology. This lighten-up approach may be a little disturbing to our control-conscious editors. However, arguably, it would be more disturbing in our field if clinicians were never to have scientific guidance in knowing the long-term effects of their treatments.

REFERENCES

Bloodstein, O. (1986). Semantics and beliefs. In G. H. Shames & H. Rubin (Eds.), *Stuttering then and now* (pp. 130–139). Columbus: Charles E. Merrill.

Boberg, E., & Kully, D. (1994). Long-term results of an intensive treatment program for adults and adolescents who stutter. *Journal of Speech and Hearing Research, 37,* 1050–1059.

Cook, F., & Rustin, L. (1997). Commentary on the Lidcombe Programme of early stuttering intervention. *European Journal of Communication Disorders, 32,* 250–258.

Craig, A., Hancock, K., Chang, E., McCready, C., Shepley, A., McCaul, A., Costello, D., Harding, S., Kehren, R., Masel, C., & Reilly, K. (1996). A controlled clinical trial for stuttering in persons aged 9 to 14 years. *Journal of Speech and Hearing Research, 39*, 808–826.

Goldiamond, I. (1965). Stuttering and fluency as manipulatable operant response classes. In L. Krasner & L. P. Ullman (Eds.), *Research in behavior modification* (pp. 106–156). New York: Holt, Rinehart & Winston.

Hancock, K., Craig, A., McCready, C., McCaul, A., Costello, D., Campbell, K., & Gilmore, G. (1998). Two- to six-year controlled-trial stuttering outcomes for children and adolescents. *Journal of Speech, Language, and Hearing Research, 41*, 1242–1252.

Ingham, R. J. (1981). Evaluation and maintenance in stuttering treatment: A search for ecstasy with nothing but agony. In E. Boberg (Ed.), *Maintenance of fluency* (pp. 179–218). New York: Elsevier.

Ingham, R. J. (1984). *Stuttering and behavior therapy: Current status and experimental foundations.* San Diego, CA: College-Hill Press.

Ingham, R. J. (1987). *Residential prolonged speech stuttering therapy manual.* Santa Barbara, CA: Department of Speech and Hearing Sciences, University of California.

Ingham, R. J., & Costello, J. M. (1985). Stuttering treatment outcome evaluation. In J. M. Costello (Ed.). *Speech disorders in adults* (pp. 189–223). San Diego, CA: College-Hill Press.

Ingham, R. J., Kilgo, M., Ingham, J. C., Moglia, R., Belknap, H., & Sanchez, T. (2001). Evaluation of a stuttering treatment based on reduction of short phonation intervals. *Journal of Speech Language and Hearing Research 44*, 1229–1244.

Johnson, W. (1942). A study of the onset and development of stuttering. *Journal of Speech and Hearing Disorders, 7*, 251–257.

Jones, M., Gebski, V., Onslow, M., & Packman, A. (2002). Statistical power in stuttering research: a tutorial. *Journal of Speech, Language, and Hearing Research, 45*, 243–255.

Lincoln, M., & Onslow, M. (1997). Long-term outcome of an early intervention for stuttering. *American Journal of Speech-Language Pathology, 6*, 51–58.

Martin, R. R., Haroldson, S. K., & Triden, K. A. (1984). Stuttering and speech naturalness. *Journal of Speech and Hearing Disorders, 49*, 53–58.

O'Brian, S., Onslow, M., Cream, A., & Packman, A. (2003). The Camperdown Program: Outcomes of a new prolonged-speech treatment model. *Journal of Speech, Language, and Hearing Research., 46*, 933–946.

Onslow, A. (2003). Overview of the Lidcombe Program. In M. Onslow, A. Packman, & E. Harrison (Eds.), *The Lidcombe Program of Early Stuttering Intervention: A clinician's guide* (pp. 3–20). Austin, TX: Pro-Ed.

Onslow, M., Costa, L., Andrews, C., Harrison, E., & Packman, A. (1996). Speech outcomes of a prolonged-speech treatment for stuttering. *Journal of Speech and Hearing Research, 39*, 734 749.

Packman, A., Onslow, M., & van Doorn, J. (1994). Prolonged speech and the modification of stuttering: perceptual, acoustic, and electroglottographic data. *Journal of Speech and Hearing Research, 37*, 724–737.

Woods, S., Shearsby, J., Onslow, M., & Burnham, D. (2002). The psychological impact of the Lidcombe Program of early stuttering intervention: Eight case studies. *International Journal of Language and Communication Disorders, 37*, 31–40.

12

Measuring the Outcomes of Behavioral Stuttering Treatments Across Situations: What Are Our Data Telling Us?

Ann Packman
Mark Onslow
Sue O'Brian
Anna Huber
The University of Sydney

An important source of evidence for evaluating treatments in speech-language pathology is data relating to outcome and efficacy (Worrall & Bennett, 2001). Ingham and Cordes' (1997) 3-factor model for stuttering treatment outcome evaluation states that it is necessary to establish that (a) treatment results in clinically significant changes in speech production, (b) the speech changes generalize across situations, and (c) the speech changes are maintained over time. Of course, it is not easy to establish all that in the course of stuttering treatment research. As stated by Ingham and Cordes:

> The three-factor model is logically sound, but applying it in treatment research, much less in routine clinical settings, is enormously demanding. Multiple (and nonreactive) recordings of the subject's speech must be obtained across different speaking situations for months or years. (p. 423)

Indeed, measuring treatment outcomes over months or years is time consuming and tedious, not only for the researchers but also—more importantly—for the subjects of that research.

It is the second of the factors in the Ingham and Cordes 3-factor model that is the topic of this chapter, namely the generalization of treatment effects across situations. The investigation here is confined to outcomes related to speech performance.

Of course it has been known for decades that the effects of behavioral treatments do not necessarily generalize to nontreated situations (for an early demonstration of this, see Ingham & Packman, 1977), and many writers in addition to Ingham and Cordes (1997) have highlighted the need to assess treatments outcomes beyond the clinic (see Hillis & McHugh, 1998). For example, Bloodstein has stated that "Improvements must be shown to carry over to speaking situations outside the clinical setting" (1987, p. 401; 1995, p. 440), and Ingham and Riley (1998) stated that "speech samples reflecting outcome should be obtained from nontreatment conditions" (p. 754) and that "at least some of the speech samples should be obtained from the natural environment" (p. 754). These guidelines for documentation of treatment efficacy put forward by Ingham and Riley have the added dimension that outcome measures—regardless of whether they are made within or beyond the clinic—should be made from speech samples that are not associated with treatment.

IN WHAT SITUATIONS DO WE MEASURE
SPEECH OUTCOMES?

Ingham (1990) stressed the need to identify "'pivotal' situations; that is, situations which act as 'barometers' for all or most speech performance" (p. 92). However, it seems that we have not progressed very far in identifying such "pivotal" situations, if in fact there are such situations. Despite the fact that a number of recent treatment studies have measured stuttering outcomes outside the clinic, there seems little consistency in the making of those measures. Table 12.1 presents 11 treatment reports that have appeared in the stuttering literature since 1990 that have gathered objective stuttering outcome measures outside the clinic. The subjects in these studies range from preschool to adult. All measures were made from audiotape recordings. The majority of the studies measured stuttering both inside and outside the clinic, while some measured stuttering outside the clinic only.

Four studies that measured stuttering beyond the clinic only (Bray & Kehle, 1996, 1998; Onslow, Andrews, & Lincoln, 1994; Onslow, Costa, Andrews, Harrison, & Packman, 1996) are of interest because the treatments in these studies were conducted, in effect, outside the clinic. Thus, the issue of transfer and generalization of treatment effects from within the clinic to beyond the clinic does not apply. The two Onslow et al. studies are both out-

TABLE 12.1

Stuttering Treatment Outcome Studies Since 1990 That Have Included Beyond-Clinic Stuttering Outcome Measures

Study	Subjects	Situations in Which Outcome was Measured
Onslow, Costa, & Rue (1990)	Preschool-age children	Within-clinic: conversing with clinician Beyond-clinic: conversing at home, conversing at home in various situations (covert), conversing in the home of a family member or family friend
Boberg & Kully (1994)	Adults & adolescents	Within-clinic: speaking on the telephone to local businesses Beyond-clinic: Talking on the telephone during an unexpected call from a research assistant
Onslow, Andrews, & Lincoln (1994)	Preschool-age children	Beyond-clinic: conversing with family members at home, conversing with family members at home (covert), conversing with non-family members in the home of a family member or friend
Ryan & Ryan (1995)	School-age children	Within-clinic: 14 speaking tasks Beyond-clinic: conversing with family members at home, conversing with a teacher and another student at school
Onslow, Costa, Andrews, Harrison, & Packman (1996)	Adults	Within-clinic: conversing with a clinician, speaking on the telephone, speaking to a stranger Beyond-clinic: conversing with a friend, conversing with a family member, talking on on the telephone
Lincoln, Onslow, Lewis, & Wilson (1996)	School-age children	Beyond-clinic: conversing with a family member at home, conversing with a friend, talking on the telephone
Craig, et al. (1996) Hancock et al. (1998)	School-age children and adolescents	Within-clinic: conversing with the clinician, talking on the telephone to a family member or friend Beyond-clinic: conversing with a family member or friend at home
Bray & Kehle (1996, 1998)	School-age children and adolescents	Beyond-clinic: Conversations on topics of interest to the children in a variety of school and social settings
Harrison, Onslow, Andrews, Packman, & Webber (1998)	Adults	Within-clinic: conversing with a clinician, conversing with a stranger, talking on the telephone (before treatment only) Beyond-clinic: conversing with family, conversing with friends, talking on the telephone
Ingham et al. (2001)	Adults	Within-clinic: reading aloud, speaking in monologue on self-selected topic, speaking on the telephone

come studies of the Lidcombe Program. This is an operant treatment for young children who stutter in which parents deliver the treatment (verbal contingencies) in everyday situations (see Onslow, Packman, & Harrison, 2003). Because the treatment occurs in the situations where the problem behavior (stuttering) occurs, the idea of ensuring that treatment effects generalize to beyond the clinic is irrelevant. However, because treatment occurs beyond the clinic it is particularly important to ensure that outcome measures of this treatment are gathered from speech samples that are free of parental verbal contingencies.

The other two studies that measured stuttering beyond the clinic only are not so straightforward. Both the Bray and Kehle (1996, 1998) studies incorporated self-modeling. Self-modeling refers to the improvements in behavior that occur when people observe themselves performing the desired behavior. In these two studies, the subjects watched video recordings of themselves speaking but with stuttering edited out. These were school-based studies and the subjects were withdrawn from class for a short period twice a week to watch the videos. There was no direct work on the subjects' speech and subjects did not practice speaking at all in the room in which they watched the videos. Again, then, the issue of generalization is irrelevant for this particular treatment. The issue of obtaining stuttering outcome measures from treatment-free samples is also irrelevant in the Bray and Kehle studies.

As mentioned, there is little consistency across the studies in the selection of situations in which outcome measures are made, particularly beyond the clinic. This inconsistency arises from two factors, the type of situations selected and the number of situations selected.

Type of Situations

Here, attention is drawn to the fact here that when we talk about speaking situations it is not only the location in which speech samples are recorded that is of interest (home, away from home, etc.) but also the modality (face to face, on the phone, conversation, monologue, etc.), the conversation partner (family member, stranger, research assistant, etc.), and whether the interaction is self-initiated or experimenter initiated. The purpose of the communicative exchange (requesting information, relating an incident, chatting, etc.) is rarely stipulated. Given all these considerations, it is probably more accurate to speak of communicative contexts rather than speaking situations. Of course, one of the reasons for this lack of consistency is that we simply do not know, in general, which situations are representative, or important, or more or less difficult, in the everyday lives of our subjects. Further, individuals are likely to differ in the way they rank the difficulty of various communicative contexts. For example, one person may report that speaking on the telephone is always difficult, whereas another person may report that speaking on the telephone is only difficult in the workplace, and then only when dealing with complaints from customers. However, it would seem that more consistency across studies would be desirable, as it would make comparisons of the evidence base of various treatments more valid.

One possible approach to this problem is to have subjects select their own speaking contexts, as occurred in the Ingham et al. (2001) study. In that study, subjects chose three situations in which outcome would be measured and were instructed that one of these should be problematic. Self-selection has social validity because the contexts are relevant to, and representative of, each person's daily communicative experiences. Further, it increases the likelihood that the contexts sampled cover a range of difficulty, at least as judged by the individual. Allowing subjects to select individual communicative contexts—particularly when one of those contexts is to be problematic—dispenses with experimenters' preconceived ideas about what situations or contexts are easy and difficult for people who stutter.

The downside to self-selection is that contexts will not be the same for all subjects. Although this may not be problematic for single-subject studies, this is not the case for group studies where subject data are combined. This should not be a problem in repeated-measures outcome studies, however, as long as situations remain the same for each subject before and after treatment.

Of course, self-selection is not an option for young children. However, it is quite feasible for parents to nominate contexts in which to make outcome recordings of their own children, provided they include one in which they judge their child's stuttering to be most severe.

Number of Situations

There is variation across studies in the number of communicative contexts in which outcome is measured. For example, Boberg and Kully (1994) measured outcome on telephone calls only, whereas Onslow et al. (1996) gathered measures from three within-clinic situations and three beyond-clinic situations.

This raises the issue of whether more is better. Do the six situations of the Onslow et al. (1996) study provide a more valid picture of outcome than the telephone calls in the Boberg and Kully (1994) study? The answer is not known. Certainly, the extensiveness of Onslow et al.'s outcome measures has appeal. Not only do they cover a variety of speaking situations, but they also provide large samples (in terms of number of words) on which to evaluate outcome. However, there is a down side to this rigorous recording protocol: In our experience, it contributes to lack of subject compliance. We have found that many subjects are simply not prepared to continue to record themselves for the purposes of outcome evaluation over many months or years. For example, only 18 of the original 32 subjects complied with the demands of the Onslow et al. (1996) study.

This issue of compliance is particularly problematic in countries that are large in area but small in population, like Australia and Canada. Indeed, Boberg and Kully (1994) noted this in their study—which was conducted in Canada—giving this as the reason for having telephone calls as the modality for their outcome measures. In fact, Boberg and Kully argued that their use of the telephone-based speech measures may be "one of the most stringent measures of outcome" (p. 1052). A disadvantage of the procedure is that it cannot be used with young children. However, one obvious advantage is that it reduces the potential for subject attrition because stuttering measures can be obtained without the requirement that subjects return to the clinic. Further, the procedure has the advantage of removing subject bias in selection of the recording situation because the experimenter can telephone at unexpected times. With modern telephone and recording technology, this assessment method has become feasible. One of us was recently involved in a project that involved scrutiny of the speech of stuttering subjects recorded while on the telephone, and formed the impression that online measurement of stuttering rate might be accomplished from a telephone recording with the same reliability that is possible from a standard, conversational recording. Whether this is the case is unknown and calls for empirical investigation. Likewise, the representativeness of stuttering measures obtained from telephone calls alone is unknown.

ARE WITHIN-CLINIC OUTCOME MEASURES RELEVANT?

It is well known that stuttering varies across communicative contexts, both within and beyond the clinic. However, it is not clear if that variability is still apparent after treatment. Published studies suggest that this may in fact be the case. In other words, as stuttering decreases after treatment, so variability across situations apparently decreases. This is certainly the case in the data presented in the Onslow et al. (1994, 1996) studies. This can be seen where individual data are presented for the children for whom treatment was most effective. This is also apparent in a single case that was presented in detail by Ingham and Riley (1998). Ingham and Riley gathered percent syllables stuttered (%SS) data over 2 years and 9 months for a child (S.T.) who received treatment for stuttering. Measures were gathered in three within-clinic situations and three beyond-clinic situations for 6 months before treatment and for 80 weeks after treatment. Although there is considerable variation in %SS across situations before treatment, that is not the case after treatment. It is also of interest that there appeared to be no consistent difference between within-clinic and beyond-clinic %SS scores either before or after treatment. Interestingly, in the same report there was also no apparently consistent difference between within- and beyond-clinic %SS in the child who did not receive treatment (M.B.). The individual data in the Ingham et al. (2001) study also indicate that there were no clear differences between within- and beyond-clinic measures for adults, either before or after treatment.

If there is no difference between within- and beyond-clinic differences, it could be argued that there is little value in measuring treatment outcomes inside the clinic at all. To investigate the relation between the two locations—within and beyond the clinic—we inspected %SS measures that we had gathered for previously published prolonged-speech outcome studies (Harrison, Onslow, Andrews, Packman, & Webber, 1998; Onslow et al., 1994). The reliability of these measures has been established and was reported in those studies. Comprehensive before- and after-treatment data were available for 24 subjects. For these subjects, %SS measures had been made within and beyond the clinic at least once before treatment and at least once after treatment. The %SS score for each subject on each occasion was an amalgam of measures made in three different situations. The before-treatment data and the after-treatment data were collapsed, and the means are shown in Fig. 12.1. The data were analyzed using a repeated measures analysis of variance. Means were compared using a post-hoc least significant difference at the 5% level. The data were log transformed to correct for heterogeneity of variance.

The interaction between occasions (before and after treatment) and situations (within the clinic and beyond the clinic) is highly significant ($p <$

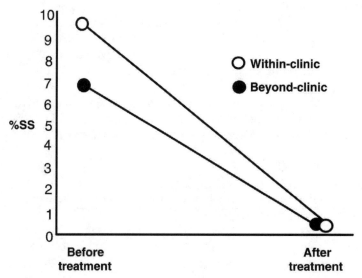

FIG. 12.1.   Mean %SS scores for 24 subjects, within and beyond the clinic, before and after treatment.

0.001). This means that the difference between the %SS scores within and beyond the clinic is different on the before-treatment and after-treatment occasions. Comparisons of the means at each occasion show that the difference in %SS after treatment is not significant ($p > 0.05$), whereas the before-treatment means are significantly different ($p < 0.05$). Also the after-treatment %SS scores are significantly lower than the before-treatment %SS scores ($p < 0.001$). The retransformed means and confidence intervals are shown in Table 12.2.

These findings came as a surprise to us, particularly the finding that before treatment stuttering rates were significantly higher inside the clinic. We had thought on the basis of previous studies (see aforementioned) that there would be no significant differences between these two locations. And if there was a difference, we thought that it would be in the other direction.

We are left to ponder, then, on the clinical significance of this finding. Why would subjects stutter more in the clinic than in everyday situations? Could it be that they were more anxious in the clinic? Or could it be that they chose to make their beyond-clinic recordings at times and in surroundings that were conducive to lower rates of stuttering than would normally occur?

The possibilities raised here lead us to question the degree of confidence we can place in the story that these situational data are telling us. One of the major problems with the protocol that we—and others—use relates to the last of the questions posed. The fact that the generation of speech samples within the clinic are investigator-initiated, whereas the generation of speech samples outside the clinic are subject initiated, could be a major source of variance. This has prompted us to consider the merits of another of Boberg and Kully's (1994) situations, namely an unexpected telephone call from an unfamiliar person who is, nonetheless, associated with the study. Boberg and Kully used this procedure only after treatment, and so treatment-related change cannot be estimated. However, it would be quite feasible to incorporate an unsolicited telephone call into an outcome protocol before treatment as well.

The findings also led us to question the need to report within-clinic measures at all, at least for the purposes of measuring outcome. The clinic bears no relation to a person's everyday speaking contexts, and the clinic itself is

TABLE 12.2
Retransformed Means for %SS Scores for 24 Subjects, Within the Clinic (WC) and Beyond the Clinic (BC), Before and After Treatment

		Mean %SS	95% Confidence Interval
Before treatment	WC	6.01	(5.30–6.81)
	BC	8.21	(7.32–9.20)
After treatment	WC	0.32	(0.25–0.40)
	BC	0.26	(0.21–0.31)

of course bristling with discriminative stimuli, including the clinician. This is not to say that there is no need for within-clinic measures: Naturally, it is desirable to show that control of stuttering was due to the treatment, and not to some other factor. That can be done in a number of ways, however, and not necessarily with traditional outcome sampling procedures.

HOW REPRESENTATIVE ARE OUR AFTER-TREATMENT STUTTERING MEASURES?

We are somewhat skeptical of the very low after-treatment %SS measures shown in Fig. 12.1. Although they may truly represent the outcomes of highly effective treatments, we must not forget the reactivity involved in af-ter-treatment assessments. Tape recorders alone can act as discriminative stimuli, even outside the clinic, given their widespread use in treatment programs. What confidence can we have, then, in our after-treatment data?

To gain some insights here, we looked at a subset of 8 of the 24 subjects in the aforementioned study. These were the 8 subjects in the 9- to 12-year outcome study that is reported in detail in (chap. 11 this volume). We se-lected these subjects for further study here because we had gathered self-reports to supplement our objective speech measures. In short, the sub-jects were contacted 9 to 12 years after participating in a prolonged-speech treatment and they agreed to furnish us with, among other things, three 10-minute beyond-clinic recordings in which they were talking with a family member, talking with a friend, and talking at home on the tele-phone. Only one of the eight subjects received another treatment after the original one as reported by Onslow et al. (1996), and that was some years previously.

Reliable %SS measures were obtained for these 24 beyond-clinic speech samples (eight subjects, three samples each). Of the 24 samples, 11 were en-tirely free of stuttering, and the remaining 13 samples all yielded stuttering rates below 1%SS. The objective stuttering measures indicated, then, that they were not stuttering, or stuttering at negligible rates, even 9 to 12 years after treatment.

However, the self-reports of these subjects are at odds with this picture. To illustrate this, the subjects' responses to four items on a self-report inventory are reported. First, when asked to rate their current stuttering status on a 7-pont scale, in which 1 = *no stuttering* and 7 = *significant stuttering*, no sub-jects rated themselves as not stuttering (see Fig. 12.2a). One interpretation of this is that the zero or near-zero %SS scores obtained from the recordings are not representative. Second, when asked whether their current speech was *better than, the same as,* or *worse than* at the end of treatment, three of the eight subjects rated their speech as the same or worse (see Fig. 12.2b). Again, this indicates that these subjects may have been stuttering to a considerable ex-tent when the long-term follow up was conducted that suggested zero or near-zero %SS. Finally, when asked how long the effects of treatment lasted, only four of the eight subjects reported that effects lasted more than 5 years (see Fig. 12.2c), and 2 subjects reported that treatment effects lasted less than 3 months. Again, these reports are at odds with the objective speech data.

Taken together, these self-reports cast considerable doubt on the outcome story told by the %SS measures for these subjects at long-term follow up. Of course, it is not possible to establish the validity, or truth, of self-reports. Nonetheless, we are of the opinion that they do provide another perspective on the outcome story. What is clear is that we simply cannot capture all possible communicative contexts in the sampling methods we use for the purposes of measuring stuttering objectively. At least self-reports such as those used in our investigation provide some sort of global indicator, albeit a subjective one, of stuttering status.[1]

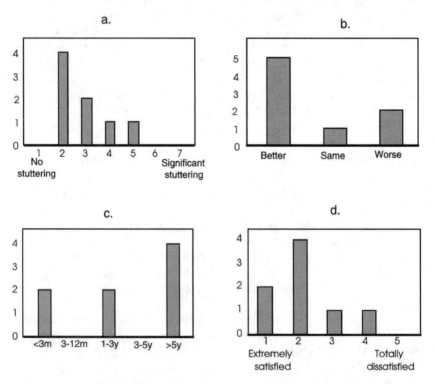

FIG. 12.2.   Results for eight subjects on four self-report items: (a) Rate your current stuttering status; (b) Rate your current speech compared to immediately following treatment; (c) How long did the treatments effects last?; and (d) How satisfied are you with your speech now?

---

[1]Self-reporting is not the same as self-measurement (Ingham & Cordes, 1997). Self reports involve global judgments about feelings, behaviors, or situations, rather than the measurement of events.

However, the discrepancy between situation-based objective measures and global self-reports observed in these subjects may not be a serious cause for alarm. When asked to rate how satisfied they were with their current speech on a 5-point scale, six of the eight subjects could be considered to have reported that they were very satisfied (see Fig. 12.2d). Perhaps one interpretation that can be placed on these findings is that some, or even many, people who have participated in behavioral treatments are satisfied with the treatment if they can control their stuttering when they want to. These eight subjects spoke without stuttering under assessment conditions, and it may be the case that they can speak without stuttering in other situations as well, when they want or need to. However, we are speculating here, as we did not ask the right questions this time. Being able to control stuttering when required seems to be a perfectly acceptable outcome of treatment. It all depends, it would seem, on what it is about their stuttering that a person complains about when they first request treatment (Baer, 1988, 1990), and what he or she wants to achieve with treatment. For example, does a person seek treatment in order to be stutter-free at all times, or simply to be stutter-free when speaking to customers on the telephone at work? We do not know the complaints of our eight subjects because, again, we did not ask—or perhaps did not record the answers to—the relevant question. Our experience of working with many people who stutter over many years, however, suggests that people may be very satisfied being able to control their stuttering on demand. We know of at least two professional people who tell us that they can be stutter-free all day, if their work requires it, but that they are comfortable to stutter freely when they return to the comfort of their own home.

DISCUSSION

We have raised a number of issues in relation to the situations, or communicative contexts, in which we make objective stuttering outcome measures. A review of studies published in the past 12 years that have included beyond-clinic outcome measures indicates that there is little consistency in the selection of location, modality, or communication partner across speaking situations, or in the number of contexts tapped. We have suggested that although a variety of contexts increases the size of the speech samples on which outcome measures are made and so increases face validity, such a protocol may also be regarded by subjects as onerous, and therefore constitutes a threat to subject compliance. The onerous nature of making those numerous tape recordings, in various contexts, over a clinically meaningful period, may be one reason for the problems we have encountered with subject compliance (Onslow et al., 1996). Indeed, it may be one of the prime reasons why journal editors are apprehensive about publishing long-term follow-up data, as reported in chapter 11 (this volume). There just may be too few subjects prepared to comply with such demands on them for so long.

There is one issue that has not been addressed so far and that is the fact that the beyond-clinic stuttering measures reported in the studies reviewed are typically based on audio recordings, rather than video recordings. Exceptions to this are the Bray and Kehle (1996, 1998) studies. It is concerning that without video recordings we can never be certain that our outcome measures are detecting inaudible stuttering behaviors. Stutters that consist of fixed postures without audible airflow and superfluous nonverbal stuttering behaviors (see Packman & Onslow, 1998) will not be detectable on audio recordings if they occur without the presence of audible stuttering behaviors. This is particularly problematic in young children because, in our experience, silences occur more frequently in the audio recordings of children than they do in the audio recording of adolescents and adults. Visual cues can contribute to the judgment of whether a child at these times is stuttering or is simply formulating language.

At present, it remains to be demonstrated empirically that any additional information about stuttering outside the clinic obtained from video recordings is clinically significant. Videorecording oneself while communicating in naturalistic contexts is logistically difficult, not to mention intrusive. Further, it is likely to be expensive because not all subjects will have access to videorecording equipment. If it were to be shown that clinically significant information were to be obtained from such procedures, then we would need to choose between the logistical difficulties of obtaining such information during the course of our outcome studies, or simply living without it.

On reflection, the following are suggestions to improve the validity of our situational outcome measures:

- Establish the person's pretreatment complaints in regards to their stuttering, and consider these when determining the contexts in which outcomes will be measured;
- Have the subject select some or all of the contexts;
- For adolescents and adults, include at least one investigator-initiated context, such as an unsolicited telephone call;
- Have fewer rather than more contexts, for the sake of subject compliance;
- Measure outcome beyond the clinic only; and
- Include supplementary self-reports or parent reports

Again, the contribution—if any—of these suggestions to the validity of our evaluation of treatment outcomes is an empirical question. This seems to be fertile ground for future research.

REFERENCES

Baer, D. (1988). If you know why you're changing a behavior, you'll know when you've changed it enough. *Behavioral Assessment, 10*, 219–223.

Baer, D. (1990). The critical issue in treatment efficacy is knowing why treatment was applied: A student's response to Roger Ingham. In L. B. Olswang, C. K. Thompson, S. Warren, & N. J. Minghetti (Eds.), *Treatment efficacy research in communication disorders* (pp. 31–39). Rockville, MD: American Speech-Language-Hearing Foundation.

Bloodstein, O. (1987). *A handbook on stuttering* (4th ed.). Chicago: National Easter Seal Society.

Bloodstein, O. (1995). *A handbook on stuttering* (5th ed.). San Diego, CA: Singular Publishing Group.

Boberg, E., & Kully, D. (1994). Long-term results of an intensive treatment program for adults and adolescents who stutter. *Journal of Speech and Hearing Research, 37*, 1050–1059.

Bray, M. A., & Kehle, T. J. (1996). Self-modeling as an intervention for stuttering. *School Psychological Review, 25*, 358–369.

Bray, M. A., & Kehle, T. J. (1998). Self-modeling as an intervention for stuttering. *School Psychological Review, 27*, 587–598.

Craig, A., Hancock, K., Chang, E., McCready, C., Shepley, A., McCaul, A., Costello, D., Harding, S., Kehren, R., Masel, C., & Reilley, K. (1996). A controlled clinical trial for stuttering in persons aged 9-14 years. *Journal of Speech and Hearing Research, 39*, 808–826.

Harrison, E., Onslow, M., Andrews, C., Packman, A., & Webber, M. (1998). Control of stuttering with prolonged speech: Development of a one-day instatement program. In A. Cordes & R. J. Ingham (Eds.), *Treatment efficacy in stuttering* (pp. 191–212). San Diego, CA: Singular Publishing.

Hancock, K., Craig, A., McCready, C., McCaul, A., Costello, D., Campbell, K., & Gilmore, G. (1998). Two- to six-year controlled-trial stuttering outcomes for children and adolescents. *Journal of Speech, Language and Hearing Research, 41*, 1242–1252.

Hillis,. J. W., & McHugh, J. (1998). Theoretical and pragmatic considerations for extraclinical generalization. In A. Cordes & R. J. Ingham (Eds.), *Treatment efficacy in stuttering* (pp. 243–292). San Diego, CA: Singular Publishing.

Ingham, J. C., & Riley, G. (1998). Guidelines for documentation of treatment efficacy for young children who stutter. *Journal of Speech, Language and Hearing Research, 41*, 753–770.

Ingham, R. J. (1990). Research on stuttering treatment for adults and adolescents: A perspective on how to overcome a malaise. In J. A. Cooper (Ed.), *Research needs in stuttering: Roadblocks and future directions* (pp. 91–94). Rockville, MD: American Speech-Language-Hearing Association.

Ingham, R. J., & Cordes, A. (1997). Self-measurement and evaluating stuttering treatment efficacy. In R. F. Curlee & G. M. Siegel (Eds.), *Nature and treatment of stuttering: New directions* (2nd ed., pp. 413–437). Boston: Allyn & Bacon.

Ingham, R. J., Kilgo, M., Ingham, J. C., Moglia, R., Belknap, H., & Sanchez, T. (2001). Evaluation of a stuttering treatment based on reduction of short phonation intervals. *Journal of Speech, Language and Hearing Research, 44*, 1229–1244.

Ingham, R. J., & Packman, A. (1977). Treatment and generalization effects in an experimental treatment for a stutterer using contingency management and speech rate control. *Journal of Speech and Hearing Disorders, XLII,* 394–407.

Lincoln, M., Onslow, M., Lewis, C., & Wilson, L. (1996). A clinical trial of an operant treatment for school-age children who stutter. *American Journal of Speech-Language Pathology, 5,* 73–85.

Onslow, M., Andrews, C., & Lincoln, M. (1994). A control/experimental trial of an operant treatment for early stuttering. *Journal of Speech and Hearing Research, 37,* 1244–1259.

Onslow, M., Costa, L., Andrews, C., Harrison, E., & Packman, A. (1996). Speech outcomes of a prolonged-speech treatment for stuttering. *Journal of Speech and Hearing Research, 39,* 734–749.

Onslow, M., Costa, L., & Rue, S. (1990). Direct early intervention with stuttering: Some preliminary data. *Journal of Speech and Hearing Disorders, 55,* 405–416.

Onslow, M., Packman, A., & Harrison, E. (Eds.). (2003). *The Lidcombe Program of early stuttering intervention: Clinician's guide.* Austin, TX: Pro-Ed.

Packman, A., & Onslow, M. (1998). The behavioral data language of stuttering. In A. Cordes & R. J. Ingham (Eds.), *Treatment efficacy in stuttering* (pp. 27–50). San Diego, CA: Singular Publishing.

Ryan, B. P., & Ryan, B. V. K. (1995). Programmed stuttering treatment for children: Comparison of two establishment programs through transfer, maintenance, and follow-up. *Journal of Speech and Hearing Research, 38,* 61–75.

Worrall, L. E., & Bennett, S. (2001). Evidence-based practice: Barriers and facilitators for speech-language pathologists. *Journal of Medical Speech-Language Pathology, 9,* xi–xvi.

AUTHORS' NOTE

This chapter is based on a paper first presented at the 2002 University of Georgia State of the Art Conference on evidence-based treatment of stuttering.

V

CONCLUSION

13

Evidence-Based, Outcomes-Focused Decisions About Stuttering Treatment: Clinical Recommendations in Context

Anne K. Bothe
The University of Georgia

The chapters in this volume touched on some of the many questions and problems currently facing clinicians and researchers interested in stuttering treatment. This chapter summarizes some of the clinical recommendations provided by the chapter authors and then suggests a larger context within which the many remaining questions might be addressed.

SUMMARY OF CLINICAL RECOMMENDATIONS

To begin with, several of the chapters in this volume address the nature of stuttering, or our theories of stuttering, and the influence of that information on treatment. Webster (chap. 2, this volume), for example, reviewed his and others' neuropsychological research and suggested that successful stuttering treatment should incorporate two factors. First, treatment should require the speaker to pay attention to deliberate speech motor movements, to overcome the deficits in kinesthetically controlled movement that appear to characterize persons who stutter. Second, treatment should work to reduce avoidance, withdrawal, and apprehension, because these changes may reduce right-hemisphere activations that Webster posits as interfering with speech production. Ingham (chap. 3, this volume), in his related review of neuroimaging studies in stuttering, also provides two clinical suggestions, one that is similar to Webster's and one that may be in conflict. First, Ingham suggests that the neural areas functionally related to stuttering are auditory and motor areas; thus, he suggests that neuro-imaging research might support auditory and speech motor production ap-proaches to treatment. In particular, Ingham suggests heightened self-monitoring of speech production, a recommendation based directly on the apparent role of temporal lobe deactivations in stuttering that may be quite similar to Webster's call for attention to deliberate speech-motor move-ments. The differences between Ingham's and Webster's conclusions lie in the role they ascribe to affective and cognitive variables, including avoid-ance, withdrawal, and apprehension; Ingham discounts them, based on his interpretation of neuroimaging findings.

Packman, Onslow, and Attanasio (chap. 4, this volume) also address the implications for treatment of a theoretical explanation of stuttering, in their case Starkweather's (1987) demands and capacities model (DCM). In con-trast to the complex neurological issues recognized by both Ingham and Webster, Packman et al.'s conclusions are straightforward: Not only is there no evidence to support the clinical usefulness of recommendations based on the demands and capacities model, there is actually substantial evi-dence that contradicts the clinical usefulness of recommendations based on the DCM. In particular, as Packman et al. make clear, there is empirical evi-dence to contradict claims that reducing the number of questions asked of children who stutter (Wilkenfeld & Curlee, 1997) or reducing the syntactic complexity of language directed toward children who stutter (Miles & Ratner, 2001; Ratner & Silverman, 2000) will be useful in reducing chil-dren's stuttering. As Packman et al. also emphasize, direct treatments do appear to be able to reduce children's stuttering, despite the DCM's claims that increasing the demand for fluency should make stuttering worse (see also Ingham & Cordes, 1999).

Shenker (chap. 5, this volume) and Nippold (chap. 6, this volume) also address timely issues that combine questions about the nature and theory of stuttering with questions about its treatment. Shenker discusses stutter-ing treatment in the context of bilingual or multilingual families; Nippold discusses stuttering treatment in the context of coexisting phonological dis-orders. The two topics are surprisingly similar, both reducing to questions about whether other speech or language variables should influence the de-cisions made in stuttering treatment, and Shenker and Nippold reach simi-lar conclusions. First, as Packman et al. (chap. 4, this volume) conclude, theories that posit an influence of larger speech or language issues on children's stuttering have not been well supported. Second, and as a result, there is little reason to allow such variables as multilingualism or phonological disorders to influence decisions about stuttering treatment, in most cases. Shenker's case study of a child who made little progress until direct intervention was introduced provides an excellent example not only of the power of direct intervention but also of the advantages of evidence-based, outcomes-focused stuttering treatment.

Finn (chap. 7, this volume) also raises issues related to how the nature of stuttering might influence its treatment. Finn's discussion of self-mediated recovery in adults is consistent with the larger possibility that stuttering is a self-limiting disorder that often does not need professional intervention (or, in another form of the argument, does not need universal early intervention) because its primary natural course is toward recovery. For young children, this area continues to be the focus of heated debate (see, e.g., Curlee & Yairi, 1997, 1998; Ingham & Cordes, 1998; Packman & Onslow, 1998), for stuttering as well as for several other speech and language disorders (e.g., Bothe, 2002; Nippold & Schwarz, 2002). Finn complicates the matter considerably by emphasizing that it is not only children but also adolescents and adults who report recovering from stuttering by self-directed means. The implications of this argument for clinicians are not easily identified; certainly the extreme view that stuttering treatment is not necessary, because all persons who stutter will recover on their own, cannot be supported. It does seem reasonable to highlight one element of Finn's chapter, however: the possibility that self-mediated practice with self-designed tasks intended to achieve self-identified goals may be necessary to the success of any stuttering treatment program. It is apparent that some adults report having successfully completed all of these things with no outside assistance; others might need some assistance but nevertheless benefit from a treatment program that is as close to being self-managed as possible. One implication of Finn's chapter, therefore, is that clinicians might do well to give clients most of the responsibility for, and most of the control over, such variables as goals, schedules, measurements, activities, passage to the next phase of treatment, and even definitions of success (see, e.g., Ingham, 1982; Ingham & Cordes, 1997; Ingham et al., 2001; Stokes & Osnes, 1989).

The chapters in Part III (Langevin & Hagler, chap. 8, this volume; Crowe, Davidow, & Bothe, chap. 9, this volume) address a second important issue facing stuttering treatment: our measurement tools and specifically the relations among our measurement tools, our goals, our procedures, the evidence that our procedures are achieving our goals, and our beliefs about the nature of stuttering and of stuttering treatment. Langevin and Hagler raise two interesting points. First, it is simultaneously necessary, possible, and difficult to measure the effects of such diffuse goals as improving the attitude of a schoolroom full of children. The psychometric detail that Langevin and Hagler provide, and their careful efforts to develop and validate their attitude measure, are unusual in the stuttering literature but should not be; the decisions made in any discipline are only as good as the supporting data, which are only as good as the measurement tools. Even more intriguing, however, is Langevin and Hagler's second conclusion, that the results obtained from their newly developed scale did not reflect the constructs of affect, behavior, and cognition that they had designed the scale to measure. The implications here are interesting, for many reasons; if further research confirms their original result, it may be that the development of a measurement tool, and assessment of the resulting data, will force an evidence-based re-evaluation of this tradition-based division and structure for stuttering treatment. Such a possibility clearly links Langevin and Hagler's chapter and conclusions to Crowe et al.'s (chap. 9, this volume) ensuing discussion of measuring quality of life in stuttering. As Crowe et al. also discuss for other disorders, it may be that the future development of a quality of life scale for stuttering will force an evidence-based re-evaluation of current views about quality of life in stuttering. Overall, both of these chapters imply a challenge to researchers and clinicians alike: As a discipline and as a profession, we must develop and use validated measures of the constructs we believe exist and of the constructs we attempt to change.

The three chapters in Part IV address a different issue: the amount and the quality of published evidence that is available to serve as a basis for clinical decision making in stuttering. Together, these three chapters exemplify two of the criticisms often raised about evidence-based practice (EBP; see Bothe, chap. 1, this volume; Trinder, 2000): EBP requires published research that does not always exist, and research evidence does not necessarily apply to real-world practice. Davidow, Crowe, and Bothe (chap. 10, this volume), first of all, provide a comprehensive review of research about treatment programs based on systematic increases in utterance length. As they note, the limited published and unpublished research that does exist supports the conclusion that these programs can effectively reduce or eliminate stuttering. Nevertheless, further comprehensive evaluations of the ELU and GILCU programs are clearly needed, given what must be described as a paucity of long-term, beyond-clinic data.

Onslow, O'Brian, Packman, and Rousseau (chap. 11, this volume) address similar issues with their discussion of the inherent conflict between experimental control and long-term assessment of treatment results. For GILCU and ELU, the evidence is limited to relatively few clients; for prolonged-speech programs, the evidence is limited to time periods of only a few years or limited to outcomes that cannot be definitively linked solely to specific treatments. Packman, Onslow, O'Brian, and Huber (chap. 12, this volume), finally, raise very similar issues in their discussion of within- and beyond-clinic speech samples. As they conclude, even beyond-clinic data that are intended to measure the generalization of treatment effects may not be pure tests of generalization to nontreatment conditions. In summary, these three final chapters all address complex questions related to the design, conduct, interpretation, distribution, and application of high-quality treatment research. All are important questions that have been addressed in multiple previous forums well beyond stuttering (e.g., Hayes, Barlow, & Nelson-Gray, 1999; Kendall & Butcher, 1982; Olswang, Thompson, Warren, & Minghetti, 1990); all deserve further thought.

Overall, the chapters in this volume might be reduced to the following few conclusions. First, the evidence suggests that children's stuttering treatment can safely be designed without undue concern for such other speech or linguistic variables as coexisting disorders or multilingual environments (see chaps. 5 and 6). Second, stuttering treatment can eliminate or at least significantly reduce children's stuttering, if that treatment provides direct feedback about their stuttered and nonstuttered speech (see chaps. 1, 4, 5, and 6). This feedback might effectively be provided using reduced utterance length in initial treatment stages, especially for children with more severe stuttering (Onslow, Andrews, & Lincoln, 1994), although the relative contributions of corrective feedback, reinforcement, and systematic increases in utterance length have not been definitively identified (see chap. 10). Stuttering treatment for adults should be self-managed as far as possible, incorporating self-monitoring of deliberate motoric activities (see chaps. 2, 3, and 7) and possibly including activities designed to address avoidance or withdrawal (but compare chaps. 2 and 3). Continuing needs in stuttering measurement extend to such larger issues as measuring attitudes (chap. 8) and quality of life (chap. 9). These and other larger variables still need to be carefully defined, assessed, and shared within treatment research designs, and within professional and discipline-wide activities including treatment, research, and publishing (see chaps. 11 and 12). Finally, such activities should be consciously crafted not only to address stuttering-specific variables but also to link stuttering treatment and research to the many issues that stuttering research and treatment share with many other attempts to study or achieve behavioral or cognitive change in clinical or research settings.

AN EVIDENCE-BASED, OUTCOMES-FOCUSED
CONTEXT FOR DECISION MAKING
IN STUTTERING TREATMENT

Obviously, such lists of oversimplified conclusions are incomplete and unsatisfying; no one book can answer all the questions facing stuttering treatment. In an effort to move beyond the static conclusions provided, toward a dynamic framework that might help with some of the many as yet unsolved issues, this final section suggests an evidence-based, outcomes-focused context for considering future treatment and research questions in stuttering. This context draws on the strengths of three different organizational and heuristic frameworks: the fundamentals of evidence-based practice (see, e.g., Bothe, chap. 1, this volume; Law, 2002; Sackett, Richardson, Rosenberg, & Haynes, 1997), a multidimensional treatment outcome evaluation framework such as that provided by Kendall and Norton-Ford (1982), and the notion of immediate, instrumental, and ultimate treatment outcomes (Rosen & Proctor, 1981).

First, in the terms used in the EBP literature, the most important decisions to be made by clinicians are those based on clinical questions that include at least two and up to four elements: a specific client and a specific desired outcome, probably a specific treatment, and possibly a specific alternative treatment (see, e.g., Dawes, 1999). Thus, regardless of the importance of a sound, generalizable knowledge base, the question from an EBP point of view is not necessarily whether preschool children who stutter should receive direct early intervention, for example, to select a common point of disagreement. The question is not even whether certain treatments should be designated as "empirically supported" in an abstract sense (see Chambless & Hollon, 1998; Kazdin, 1996) that is separated from the needs of a particular client–clinician pair. Instead, from the EBP point of view, the more important and more relevant question is simply whether the 4-year-old girl in my office this morning, who has been stuttering moderately for 6 months, whose uncle stutters severely, should receive *Treatment* X or *Treatment* Y in order to reach her parents' goal of achieving *Outcome* Z.

Kendall and Norton-Ford's (1992) ideas can then be incorporated, as a framework for identifying the outcomes that might be of interest. From this point of view, all assessment and treatment decisions (including the decision not to assess or not to intervene) may be evaluated in terms of their effectiveness (does the selected activity result in the achievement of the desired goal?), any other effects they may create (what other outcomes, either positive or negative, appear to be associated with the selected activity?), and their efficiency (does the selected activity maximize effectiveness, minimize suffering, and minimize the expenditure of emotional, financial, and other resources, as compared with other possible activities?). To continue with the example raised previously, the combination of an EBP approach and this treatment outcome evaluation model emphasizes that for clinicians the question is not necessarily "Should preschool children receive early direct treatment for their stuttering?," which may be better suited to academic arguments (Curlee & Yairi, 1997, 1998; Ingham & Cordes, 1998; Packman & Onslow, 1998) than to actual clinical practice. Instead, the question might be as narrow as "Will providing this specific child with this specific treatment probably maximize effectiveness, maximize positive other effects, minimize negative other effects, and maximize efficiency, with respect to this specific desired outcome?," which is the question that is central to clinical practice.

Thirdly, the proposed evidence-based, outcomes-focused context for stuttering treatment and treatment research also recognizes a distinction among what Rosen and Proctor (1981) described as intermediate, instrumental, and ultimate outcomes. Intermediate outcomes are those session-to-session clinical achievements that are not ends in themselves but that are recognized as necessary steps toward a desired end; in practice, intermediate outcomes may focus on the treatment process itself and are often phrased as short-term goals. Instrumental outcomes are those treatment-induced changes that are instrumental to, or are themselves the cause of, further changes without treatment; the classic example in speech-language pathology is the evidence that articulation or phonology treatment need not continue until children have achieved 100% success at each of several intermediate levels (see Gierut, 1998). Ultimate outcomes, in contrast, are the final desired states or objectives of treatment, the achievement of which renders that treatment "successful." Ultimate outcomes can be broadly defined, to address the different problems that are described as, for example, impairment, disability, and handicap, and to address clinical, functional, social, emotional, vocational, financial, and other possible outcomes of a treatment. Thus, ultimate outcomes are often measured in terms of social validity or the client's or family's subjective judgments of whether their desired status with respect to communication, broadly defined, has been achieved. In practice, the ultimate outcome is usually specified as a long-term goal, but many long term goals do not capture the broad spirit that is embodied in the notion of an ideal "ultimate outcome."

How, then, can this proposed combination of abstractions and frameworks assist with the discussions, disagreements, and decisions that characterize stuttering and stuttering treatment? Three issues seem worthy of a final comment. First, one of the many problems that continue to complicate stuttering treatment is that many questions about the nature and treatment of stuttering have not yet been answered. Discussions during the conference at which these chapters were originally presented recognized this problem, and even took it a step further: Regardless of whether final or complete empirical evidence is yet available, clients and clinicians must and do make decisions now. In fact, the complexity facing researchers, clinicians, persons who stutter, parents of children who stutter, and many others, is that the true context for our decisions is not a theoretical decision-making framework, but a real-world environment characterized by questions and unknowns. Some critics argue that EBP can not be an option until all desired evidence is available (see Trinder, 2000). It is incumbent on both clinicians and researchers, however, to make use of such syntheses of information as is provided in these chapters and in other sources, to make the best possible evidence-based decisions using all the information that is available, to recognize where our evidence base is lacking, and then to do what can be done to develop the missing knowledge.

Second, the real context within which stuttering treatment decisions are made is actually often a small room containing a clinician, a worried parent, and a preschooler who has unquestionably been stuttering for some number of months or even years. Alternatively, the room might contain a clinician and a slightly diffident teen who would rather not stutter but who is not entirely comfortable seeking help, or even a clinician and a cautiously hopeful adult who has decided to try stuttering treatment again. In these and most other clinical situations, the theoretical and academic arguments discussed here become much less relevant, and the practicalities of clinical decision-making take precedence. Given this context, many authors writing about stuttering treatment seem to agree that restricting oneself or one's clients to only one approach may be artificially limiting, recommending combined or eclectic treatments as an alternative. This approach seems reasonable at first, but it raises a problem similar to the problem Bloodstein (1995) raised for the multiplicity of theories about stuttering: If none is correct, what argument could possibly be made to support the notion that all are correct? The answer, for the individual client in my clinic this morning as well as for our discipline as a whole, cannot come from accepting all common or proposed treatments as reasonable. It might come, however, from an evidence-based focus on effective and efficient treatments that are known to result in well-defined intermediate, instrumental, and ultimate goals. Individual client–clinician pairs need to identify their desired outcomes and then use evidence-based treatments that have been shown to result in those outcomes; our discipline as a whole needs to focus on developing the information base necessary to make such evidence-based, outcomes-focused treatment possible.

Thus, thirdly and finally, evidence-based clinicians and researchers suggest using treatment approaches that have been well-supported in the literature and that seem to the client and the clinician in question to be a reasonable way of effectively and efficiently approaching their mutually agreed upon goals. Evidence-based thinkers, in addition, share with scientist practitioners and other empirically based clinicians and researchers the assumption that data must be gathered during treatment, used as the basis for decisions in that treatment, and then publicized to become the source of improved future treatments (see Hayes et al., 1999). Stuttering treatment and stuttering treatment research can only move forward, for individual clients and as a professional discipline, with a commitment to increasing the quantity and the quality of the evidence that selected approaches can effectively and efficiently reach a series of well-defined intermediate, instrumental, and ultimate goals and outcomes.

REFERENCES

Bloodstein, O. (1995). *A handbook on stuttering* (5th ed.). San Diego, CA: Singular.

Bothe, A. K. (2002). Thoughts on recovery: A response to Nippold and Schwarz. *Advances in Speech-Language Pathology, 4*, 55–58.

Chambless, D. L., & Hollon, S. D. (1998). Defining empirically supported therapies. *Journal of Consulting and Clinical Psychology, 66*, 7–18.

Curlee, R. F., & Yairi, E. (1997). Early intervention with early childhood stuttering: A critical examination of the data. *American Journal of Speech-Language Pathology, 6*(2), 8–18.

Curlee, R. F., & Yairi, E. (1998). Treatment of early childhood stuttering: Advances and research needs. *American Journal of Speech-Language Pathology, 7*(3), 20–26.

Dawes, M. (1999). Formulating a question. In M. Dawes, P. Davies, A. Gray, J. Mant, K. Seers, & R. Snowball, *Evidence-based practice: A primer for health care professionals* (pp. 9–13). London: Churchill Livingstone.

Gierut, J. (1998). Treatment efficacy: Functional phonological disorders in children. *Journal of Speech, Language, and Hearing Research, 41*, S85–S100.

Hayes, S. C., Barlow, D. H., & Nelson-Gray, R. O. (1999). *The scientist practitioner: Research and accountability in the age of managed care* (2nd ed.). Boston: Allyn & Bacon.

Ingham, R. J. (1982). The effects of self-evaluation training on maintenance and generalization during stuttering treatment. *Journal of Speech and Hearing Disorders, 47*, 271–280.

Ingham, R. J., & Cordes, A. K. (1997). Self-measurement and evaluating stuttering treatment efficacy. In R. F. Curlee & G. M. Siegel (Eds.), *Nature and treatment of stuttering: New directions* (2nd ed., pp. 413–437). Boston: Allyn & Bacon.

Ingham, R. J., & Cordes, A. K. (1998). Treatment decisions for young children who stutter: Further concerns and complexities. *American Journal of Speech-Language Pathology, 7*(3), 10–19.

Ingham, R. J., & Cordes, A. K. (1999). On watching a discipline shoot itself in the foot: Some observations on current trends in stuttering treatment research. In N. B. Ratner & E. C. Healey (Eds.), *Stuttering research and practice: Bridging the gap* (pp. 211–230). Mahwah, NJ: Lawrence Erlbaum Associates.

Ingham, R. J., Kilgo, M., Ingham, J. C., Moglia, R., Belknap, H., & Sanchez, T. (2001). Evaluation of a stuttering treatment based on reduction of short phonation intervals. *Journal of Speech, Language, and Hearing Research, 44*, 841–852.

Kazdin, A. E. (1996). Validated treatments: Multiple perspectives and issues—Introduction to the series. *Clinical Psychology: Science and Practice, 3*, 216–217.

Kendall, P. C., & Butcher, J. N. (Eds.). (1982). *Handbook of research methods in clinical psychology*. New York: Wiley.

Kendall, P. C., & Norton-Ford, J. D. (1982). Therapy outcome research methods. In P. C. Kendall & J. N. Butcher (Eds.), *Handbook of research methods in clinical psychology* (pp. 429–460). New York: Wiley.

Law, M. (Ed.). (2002). *Evidence-based rehabilitation: A guide to practice*. Thorofare, NJ: Slack Inc.

Miles, S., & Ratner, N. B. (2001). Parental language input to children at stuttering onset. *Journal of Speech, Language, and Hearing Research, 44*, 1116–1130.

Nippold, M. A., & Schwarz, I. E. (2002). Do children recover from specific language impairment? *Advances in Speech-Language Pathology, 4*, 41–49.

Onslow, M., Andrews, C., & Lincoln, M. (1994). A control/experimental trial of an operant treatment for early stuttering. *Journal of Speech and Hearing Research, 37*, 1244–1259.

Olswang, L. B., Thompson, C. K., Warren, S. F., & Minghetti, N. J. (1990). *Treatment efficacy research in communication sciences and disorders*. Rockville, MD: American Speech-Language-Hearing Foundation.

Packman, A., & Onslow, M. (1998). What is the take-home message from Curlee and Yairi? *American Journal of Speech-Language Pathology, 7*(3), 5–9.

Ratner, N. B., & Silverman, S. (2000). Parental perceptions of children's communicative development at stuttering onset. *Journal of Speech, Language, and Hearing Research, 43*, 1252–1263.

Rosen, A., & Proctor, E. (1981). Distinctions between treatment outcomes and their implications for treatment evaluation. *Journal of Consulting and Clinical Psychology, 49*, 418–425.

Sackett, D. L., Richardson, W. S., Rosenberg, W. M. C., & Haynes, R. B. (1997). *Evidence based medicine: How to practice and teach EBM*. New York: Churchill Livingstone.

Starkweather, C. W. (1987). *Fluency and stuttering*. Englewood Cliffs, NJ: Prentice-Hall.

Stokes, T. F., & Osnes, P. G. (1989). An operant pursuit of generalization. *Behavior Therapy, 20*, 337–355.

Trinder, L. (2000). A critical appraisal of evidence-based practice. In L. Trinder & S. Reynolds (Eds.), *Evidence-based practice: A critical appraisal* (pp. 212–243). Oxford: Blackwell Science.

Wilkenfeld, J. R., & Curlee, R. F. (1997). The relative effects of questions and comments on children's stuttering. *American Journal of Speech-Language Pathology, 6*, 79–89.

Author Index

Subject Index

A

Academic achievement, 140
Apprehension, 22, 262
Assessment decisions, *see* Evidence-based practice
Attitudinal change, *see* Attitudes
Attitudes, 123–125, 130, 132–133, 264–265
Avoidance reduction, 132

B

Behavioral tradition, 9
Beyond-clinic measurement, 246–251, 264
Bimanual motor performance, 18–19
 sequence reproduction
  performance, 18–19
  interference effects, 19–23
 sequential finger tapping, 18–19
  interference effects, 19–23
Bilingualism, 81–94
 advising parents, 86, 93
 assessment, 86
 consecutive, 83
 definitions, 82–83
 early, 83, 86, 89–90
 and reducing languages of input,
  86, 89, 91
 second language, 83
 and Specific Language Impairment,
  86, 93
 spontaneous, 83
 third-language, 83

C

Carroll Rating Scale for Depression, 184
Clinical recommendations, 261
Code-mixing, 87, 89–90, 93
Communicative contexts, 248–250, 255
 self-selection of, 249, 256
Concomitant disorders, 97–111
 frequency of, 102–103
 treatment, 105–110, 262–263
  guidelines, 110–111
Co-occurring disorders, *see*
  Concomitant disorders

D

Demands and capacities model, *see*
  Models, demands and
  capacities

E

Early childhood stuttering, 117
Educational interventions, 164
Evidence, *see* evidence-based practice
Evidence-based practice, xi–xiii, 17, 70,
  75–76, 82, 99, 262, 265–268
 controversies, 6–8
 definitions of, 3–6
 and health care, 3–4
 steps in, 5–6
 and stuttering treatment, 8–10
Evidence-based medicine, *see*
  Evidence-based practice